Object-Oriented Information Systems:

Planning and Implementation

Object-Oriented Information Systems:

Planning and Implementation

David A. Taylor, PhD

John Wiley & Sons, Inc.

New York • Chichester • Brisbane • Toronto • Singapore

Taylor, David. 1943-
   Object-oriented information systems: planning and implementation
/David Taylor
      p. cm.
   Includes bibliographical references and index.
   ISBN 0-471-54363-2 (cloth). — ISBN 0-471-54364-0 (paper)
   1. Management information systems. 2. Object-oriented data bases.
3. System design. I. Title.
T58.6.T39 1992   91-38263
658.4′038—dc20

Printed in the United States of America

10 9 8 7 6 5 4 3 2 1

Printed and bound by Malloy Lithographing, Inc.

Dedication

This book is dedicated to my wife, Nina, for her love, patience, and sage advice; and to my brother Bill for his abiding friendship and wise counsel.

About the Author

David Taylor is the principal of Taylor Consulting in San Mateo, California. His goal is to help Fortune 500 companies understand the benefits of object technology and make the transition to this technology in a graceful, cost-effective manner. In addition to his technical and management articles, Dr. Taylor speaks at numerous industry conferences and co-chaired the program committee for Object Management Group's Object World '91 conference. He is also the author of two previous books: *Mind* (Simon & Schuster, 1982) and *Object-Oriented Technology: A Manager's Guide* (Addison-Wesley, 1991).

Prior to becoming a consultant, Dr. Taylor was division manager for the Business Applications Group at Servio Corporation, makers of the Gem-Stone object DBMS. In that capacity, he managed the development of Facets, an object-oriented, fourth-generation application generator, and the CRP CIMulator, an interactive graphical system for planning the use of manufacturing capacity. He also conducted a productivity assessment project for EDS, demonstrating a 14:1 productivity benefit through the use of object technology.

Before entering business in 1983, Dr. Taylor was a professor of psychology at the University of Rochester in New York, where he pioneered computer-based techniques for studying mental events. He was one of the founders of cognitive science, which combines psychology, computer science, and other disciplines into a unified study of human and machine intelligence.

Dr. Taylor received his PhD in cognitive psychology from the University of California at Irvine in 1971. His ongoing education has focused on corporate management issues and advanced manufacturing methods. He is APICS certified in just-in-time (JIT) manufacturing and capacity resource management. In his off hours, he may be found simulating evolution on a computer, composing electronic music, or diving the North Wall off Grand Cayman Island.

Contents

Foreword

When David asked me to write a foreword for his new book, my first thought was, What could I say of any resounding nature that David hasn't already said? But perhaps that's the essential point; we are finally experiencing some consensus on software development. Getting general agreement on software technology has been the "dark side" of computing for too many years. Now, at last, the software Hydra is dying. Object technology is making the dream of standard, reusable software components a commercial reality.

Object technology offers a more natural approach to building business systems because software objects correspond directly to real-world objects in a company. Simply put, an object-oriented software system mirrors a business the same way a blueprint mirrors a building. This direct correspondence makes it almost as easy to understand and modify a software system as it is to work with a blueprint.

Better still, the software objects that model a company can be used in many different applications. This reuse of existing work accounts for the remarkable productivity gains being realized with object technology. It also makes it possible to assemble objects from many different vendors, just as manufactured goods are assembled from standard parts. If we all persevere and adhere to standards for object components, the days in which every software program is created from scratch will soon be behind us.

Dr. Taylor's eloquent description of what object technology is and how to apply it will be a cornerstone of reference for years to come. As David points out, companies that make the transition to this technology first will have a tremendous competitive advantage over those who wait. It's like sitting at the water's edge at low tide hoping you won't get wet. You can either jump in now, run the other way, or just sit there until the tide surrounds you. This book will teach you how to swim. Read it, then come on in — the water's fine!

Christopher Stone
President, Object Management Group

Preface

After 20 years of patient refinement, object technology has wound its way out of the research labs, survived the exploratory phase, made it past the early adopters, and burst into the mainstream of business application development. Here are a few examples of the companies that are adopting the technology:

Major companies are adopting object technology

- **IBM** has adopted an object-oriented language as its primary development vehicle for Presentation Manager applications.

- **EDS** has developed several applications using object-oriented languages and databases for such clients as General Motors, and more projects are in the works.

- **Texaco** is rebuilding a major portion of its information systems using object technology.

- **General Dynamics, Martin Marietta, Boeing,** and other defense contractors are using object technology to help build the next-generation space shuttle.

- **Texas Instruments** and the **Department of Defense** are using object technology to build a state-of-the-art manufacturing facility for fabricating integrated circuits.

- **NCR** is using object technology at every level of COOPERATION, its ground-breaking enterprise integration product.

The results of a recent study by International Data Corporation (*Survey on Object Technology*, 1991) confirm the increasing acceptance of object technology. Forty-five percent of the Fortune 500 companies sampled are now working with object technology in some capacity, and 60 percent of these companies are building real, deployable applications. More important, they are developing applications not just for esoteric scientific and engineering applications, but for mainstream business use. In fact, in 57 percent of the companies making the move to objects, the MIS department is the primary advocate for adopting object technology.

Survey results indicate widespread adoption

Why is object technology suddenly taking off in corporate America? The answer is simple: The technology has a proven record of delivering dramatic improvements in software productivity and quality. In fact, it is arguably the only technology available today that can produce the robust, flexible, and cost-effective information systems that modern organizations must have to remain competitive.

Object technology is succeeding because it works

Most books on object technology are narrowly focused

Despite it's increasing popularity, it's hard for business people to gain an adequate understanding of object technology. Most books on the subject focus on specific aspects, such as object-oriented design or programming in Smalltalk, and they tend to provide much technical detail. Even after reading four of five of these books, it's hard to assemble all the diverse perspectives into a larger picture.

This book is a comprehensive guide

This book is intended to give managers the overview they need by providing a comprehensive guide to object technology and its applications to corporate information systems. It is written for CEOs, CIOs, MIS directors, project managers, and anyone else who needs to understand how objects can contribute to software solutions in business. Although the book provides adequate detail on the technical aspects of object technology, it is meant to be readable by all levels of management, including those who are not directly involved with the technical aspects of systems development.

The book is constructed in layers

To meet the varying needs of its diverse audience, the book consists of three distinct layers, as shown below:

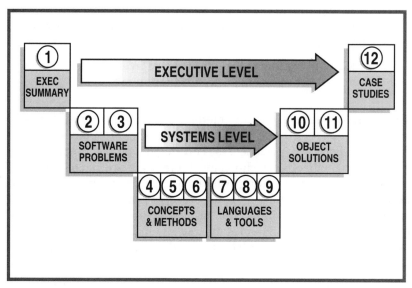

Architecture of the Book

This layered architecture allows the book to be read on three different levels:

It can be read on three levels

- The **Executive Level**, consisting of the first and last chapters, offers a succinct management briefing together with a set of real-world case studies to show how other companies are using the technology.

- The **Systems Level** builds on the executive briefing by reviewing the problems of developing robust, flexible information systems (Chapters 2 and 3), then showing how object technology can solve these problems (Chapters 10 and 11).

- The **Technology Level** (Chapters 4 through 9) provides a more detailed description of the concepts, methodologies, languages, and tools of object technology. Anyone who will be working directly with the technology should read these chapters.

Above all, this book is meant to be a pragmatic guide to planning and implementing successful systems. Many issues and distinctions are still being hotly debated in the academic community. That's all to the good because it keeps the technology growing to meet future needs. But most of these academic concerns will be ignored here in favor of a practical, hands-on approach. This book is not meant to provoke discussion and further research. It is a call to action.

This book is a pragmatic guide

Acknowledgments

Some of the themes of this book began to crystallize in a course I developed for the Object Management Group (OMG) in fall 1990. I thank the OMG for its contributions to the ideas expressed in the book and for its continuing assistance as I have moved into the role of consultant and educator. I am an ardent supporter of the OMG, and I hope that this book contributes to the cause of standards in the object arena.

Thanks to the OMG

I express my appreciation to Servio Corporation for the opportunity to learn from its many talented people during the five years I spent with the company. I also appreciate Servio's permission to reuse many graphic images and explanatory devices I developed while employed there.

To Servio Corporation

I am indebted to the many people who reviewed the first draft of this book and gave me constructive feedback on how to make it better. Thanks to Tom Atwood of Object Designs, Steve Burbeck of Knowledge Systems, Chuck Durrett of EDS, Bob Haugen of Pansophic Systems, Rob Howell of Ford Motor Company, Robert Johnson of CIMdata, Tom Jordan of the Executive Information Group, Mary Loomis of Versant Object Technology, Dan Shafer of Strategy Consulting, Chris Stone of OMG, and King Walling of EDS.

To the reviewers of the book

I owe a special thanks to Mike DeSanti, who not only reviewed the entire book but helped me so extensively with Chapters 7, 8, and 9 that he is virtually a co-author of this section. Mike has been my friend and partner since we first worked together at Servio, and I still find myself learning something new from him every time we talk about object technology.

To Mike DeSanti

The illustrations for the book were done by Dan Schumaker of Contrast Graphics in Walnut Creek, California. Dan does the graphics for all my presentations, books, and articles, and I couldn't ask for a more talented partner for expressing complex ideas in visual form.

And to Dan Schumaker

I am also indebted to the companies who contributed to the final chapter of this book by providing candid accounts of their experiences with object technology. Thanks — and apologies — are also due to the numerous other companies that provided case studies I wasn't able to include.

Thanks also to those who supplied case studies...

in engineering...

The information on the Falcon Framework product came from Rick Samco, John Schwartz, and other members of Mentor Graphics. The story of the QDES "Quick and Dirty Editor" was provided by Sandy Ressler of the U.S. Department of Commerce. HP's "faceless instrument" project was described to me by Tom Kraemer of Hewlett-Packard.

manufacturing...

The account of building the Maintenance Management System for EDS is based on firsthand experience and additional information from OMG. The Semiconductor CIM project at TI was described to me by Jack Mahaffey at Texas Instruments. Dale Goebel of Sequent Computer Systems provided the account of his object-oriented diagnostics system.

geographical information systems...

Harvey Alcabes of Apple Computer led me to Mike Wirth of Petroleum Information, who provided a compelling description of their experience in developing the Sorcerer's Apprentice product. The description of the automated cartography system at NOAA is based both on firsthand experience and a subsequent account provided by Dave Pendleton. Don Willis of Command System Inc. demonstrated his command-and-control software to me and related his experiences in developing it.

financial systems...

Barbara Noparstak of Digitalk provided the descriptions of both the Wyatt Portfolio Management System and the Midland Bank trading system. The information on the development of H&Q's Phoenix Broker System was provided by Harvey Alcabes of Apple Computer.

management systems...

The Brooklyn Union Gas story was provided by John Davis of Andersen Consulting. James Joaquin of Apple Computer gave me the description of how his team built Apple's desktop decision-support system. The development of Guiness Peat's aircraft configuration project was described to me by Jeffrey Sutherland of Object Databases.

...and enterprise models

Ken Auer of Knowledge Systems Corp. worked with Larry Marran of HP to put together the information on Hewlett-Packard's Process Modeling System. The description of the Business Animator was provided by John Davis of Andersen Consulting. Steve Forgey of Digital Equipment Corporation provided me with a compelling account of DEC's enterprise modeling system and its educational impact.

Object-Oriented Information Systems:

Planning and Implementation

1

Executive Summary

A NEW APPROACH TO SOFTWARE CONSTRUCTION

Object-oriented technology is a new approach to software construction that shows considerable promise for solving some of the classic problems of software development. The core concept behind object technology is that all software should be constructed out of standard, reusable components wherever possible.

Object technology is based on software reuse

There are three key mechanisms underlying object technology:

There are three key mechanisms

1. **Objects** are software packages that contain related data and procedures. In most cases, objects correspond to real-world business objects, such as products, machines, divisions, and people.

2. **Messages** are the means by which objects communicate. In essence, objects request services from one another, working together to carry out essential business operations.

3. **Classes** are templates for defining kinds of objects. For example, all purchase-order objects would be described by a single *purchase_order* class. Classes are usually defined as special cases of each other, organizing information about business objects in a natural, intuitive manner.

BUILDING SOFTWARE LIKE HARDWARE

The goal is to duplicate the success of hardware

The basic idea behind object technology is to build software the way we build hardware. Rather than handcrafting every program from scratch, software is assembled out of standard object components. For example, an employee object would capture all the information about an individual employee together with all the standard interactions employees can have with other components of the company.

Computers are constructed in layers

As with hardware, object-oriented software is constructed in discrete layers. In the case of hardware, there are typically three layers: Computers are built up out of printed circuit boards and other standard devices such as disk drives and power supplies. Printed circuit boards, in turn, are built up out of integrated circuits and other standard electronic components.

Object software also has layers

Object-oriented software also tends to have three layers, although it may have more or less. The bottom layer consists of objects, which are often referred to as "software ICs" to emphasize their role as standard, reusable components. The middle layer, if present, is a collection of working models of the organization that can be used by many applications. The top layer consists of applications that solve specific business problems.

THE BENEFITS AND COSTS OF OBJECT TECHNOLOGY

There are three key benefits

The essential benefits of object technology are:

1. By reusing existing objects wherever possible, object technology **allows software to be developed in a fraction of the time and cost** of conventional methods.

2. Given that new software is largely constructed from existing, proven components, object technology typically **yields higher-quality systems** that have fewer bugs and offer better solutions to the business problems they address.

3. Because individual objects can be modified without affecting other objects, object-oriented software is generally **easier to modify and maintain** than conventional software. This reduces maintenance costs and allows software systems to grow and evolve in response to changing circumstances.

These benefits aren't free. Some of the costs of adopting object technology include:

There are significant costs

1. **Investing in new computing platforms and development software** to support this new approach to development.

2. **Training development personnel** in new tools and techniques.

3. **Educating management** in a new way of thinking about software systems.

4. **Developing reusable software components** for future development efforts.

OBJECT-ORIENTED INFORMATION SYSTEMS

Object technology offers significant benefits in the construction of individual programs, but the real power of this technology is that it enables a new generation of corporate information systems. For the first time, information systems can model the actual elements and real-time behavior of an organization. Because object systems are easily modified, this corporate model can rapidly adjust to changing business conditions and strategies.

Objects build better information systems

In short, companies that adopt object technology on a broad scale will no longer be frozen in place by rigid, obsolete information systems. They will be able to adapt to changing markets, react to new opportunities, and adjust their operations to better meet their customers' needs. Instead of being obstacles to change, their information systems will become enablers of change.

Object technology facilitates change

2

Competing in a Changing World

We live and work in an age of continuous change. In fact, about the only thing we can be certain of today is that things will continue to change at an ever-increasing rate.

Change is the only constant

Nowhere is this constant change felt more keenly than in the world of corporate management. Unlike individuals, corporations have only a limited capacity to detect change, modify their behavior to meet new conditions, and learn from collective experience. An economic, political, or technological development that is merely disruptive to an individual may prove devastating to a large organization simply because the organization can't absorb the change and react to it.

Corporations are strongly affected by change

In this chapter, we take a brief look at some of the changes that are affecting businesses today, then consider how the process of corporate management must evolve to better cope with these changes. Given this background, we consider the problem of how corporate information systems will have to evolve to meet the demands of the 1990s.

This chapter examines changes and their effects

MEETING THE CHALLENGES OF THE NINETIES

There are so many different kinds of change facing modern organizations that it's difficult even to catalog them, much less cope with them. However, there are four basic types of change that are particularly problematic for modern organizations:

There are many different kinds of change

1. **Globalization**—Where companies were once regional or at most national, large organizations now operate on a global scale.

2. **Decentralization**—The classic hierarchical organizational structure with centralized control is rapidly giving way to more decentralized, network-based management systems.

3. **Customization**—Where companies once offered a limited range of products or services, competition is now forcing them to develop increasingly customized offerings to meet the needs of specialized markets.

4. **Acceleration**—Even companies that have coped reasonably well with change in the past are now confronted with an accelerating rate of change that threatens to overload their adaptive mechanisms.

Change can shatter an organization

I think of these as four wedges of change. As the illustration implies, any one of these wedges can split a company apart. The impact of two or more could literally shatter an organization.

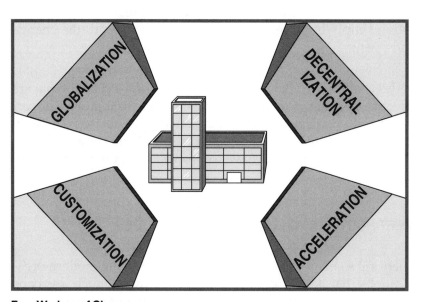

Four Wedges of Change

1. Globalization

Consider the pressures that globalization exerts on an organization. Clearly, there are significant benefits to operating globally, including massive economies of scale and the ability to move operations into the nations where they are most profitable. But these benefits carry some major costs with them.

Globalization has its costs

Global operations require bridging multiple economies, taking advantage of the strengths of each and avoiding their weaknesses wherever possible. Of course, global companies must also deal with multiple monetary systems, and they must be capable of moving assets and liabilities among countries to take advantage of shifting exchange and interest rates.

Global companies bridge multiple economies

Moreover, the constantly changing regulatory constraints of all the various countries must be taken into account. In addition, communication among the various divisions of the company is complicated by physical distance, language differences, and incompatible technologies. And these are just a few of the problems that global operations present.

They must also overcome other barriers

2. Decentralization

Decentralization also creates problems for corporate management. The reasons for the move toward decentralized operations include the following:

Decentralization has a variety of causes

- The sheer **scale** of today's megacorporation makes it difficult or impossible to manage operations effectively from a central location.

- The globalization of organizations creates **communication barriers** among their divisions that make centralized control difficult.

- The **diversification** of large corporations makes it difficult for a central group of executives to understand all the different businesses and run them effectively.

- **Mergers and acquisitions** have led to organizations that are no more than loose federations. Attempts to force acquired companies into a single corporate mold often destroy the value of these acquisitions.

Decentralization creates new problems

Decentralization can help deal with these problems, but it often creates problems of its own. These may include loss of corporate focus, breakdowns in standards, and decreased coordination among the various units. One of the major challenges facing corporations today is figuring out how to give more autonomy to their individual business units without compromising the integrity of the organization as a whole.

3. Customization

Mature markets differentiate

As markets mature, they tend to differentiate. New players carve out increasingly specialized niches, and existing vendors are forced to match these specialized offerings or give up portions of their established market on a piecemeal basis.

Products are becoming highly personalized

The natural end point of this trend, as many management experts have pointed out, is the generation of fully customized products precisely geared to individual buyers (Davis, *Future Perfect*: Addison-Wesley, 1987). In manufacturing, this goal is supported by the advent of flexible manufacturing systems (FMS), which allow a single assembly line to create a nearly infinite variety of products in lots as small as a single unit. In the financial sector, many companies are breaking down fixed packages and creating custom combinations of financial services for individual customers.

Custom products complicate management

Unfortunately, creating and maintaining individual products for each customer can escalate the complexity of business operations to a potentially devastating level. Coping with this increased complexity is one of the major challenges facing modern organizations.

4. Acceleration

As disruptive as these changes may be, they aren't the most serious problem. Not only is the business environment changing radically, the rate of change itself is changing—it's coming faster all the time. As Tom Peters puts it, the accelerating rate of change has thrust modern businesses into a world of chaos (Peters, *Thriving on Chaos*: Knopf, 1987).

The pace of change is also changing

Part of this acceleration is due to external factors: Society, technology, politics, and culture are evolving at an ever-increasing rate, and there's nothing we can do to slow them down. Corporations must adapt to survive, and the adaptation process itself must constantly accelerate.

Much acceleration is externally caused

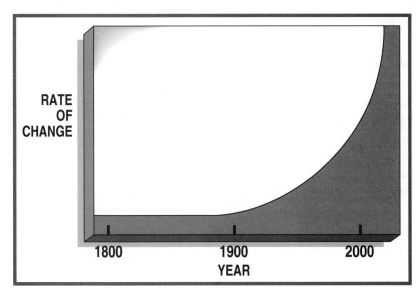

Acceleration of External Changes

The other major source of acceleration comes from competitive pressures. To paraphrase Stanley Davis, customers have a natural desire for instant gratification, and companies that can meet peoples' needs the fastest usually get their business (Davis, *Future Perfect*: Addison-Wesley, 1987). The natural consequence of this competition is that goods must be produced and delivered faster all the time.

Acceleration is also caused by competition

Acceleration Due to Shorter Lead Times

NEW REQUIREMENTS FOR INFORMATION SYSTEMS

Information systems must undergo major changes

All these changes in the business environment have profound implications for how we build and use corporate information systems. Although many improvements have been made in information management over the past two decades, information systems are lagging far behind the increasing demands of modern business conditions. If, as Peters argues, we must learn to thrive on chaos, our information systems will have to deal with constantly changing conditions.

New information systems will have to satisfy countless requirements in order to meet the demands of competition in the 1990s. However, four requirements will play a crucial role: The new information systems must be more capable of handling complexity, more flexible in their structure, more responsive to changing needs, and higher in quality than contemporary systems.

There are four major requirements

1. Complexity

To provide better support for the increasingly varied kinds of data corporations must deal with, information systems will need to handle a wider range of data types than names, dates, and dollar amounts. They must also store and process free-form text, outlines, pictures, diagrams, voice, and even video sequences. The move toward multimedia documents, which combine text with spreadsheets, charts, photographs, and voice annotations, is a clear example of this need.

Multimedia information is important

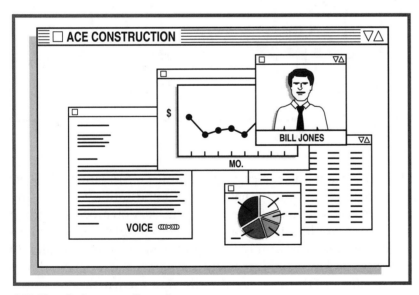

A Multimedia Customer Record

We also need complex representations

The next generation of information systems will also need to support much more complex representations for the organization, products, customers, and operations of a company. We must be able to build complex structures out of our new multimedia data types and have these structures represented as new, elementary data types that can be manipulated as unitary entities. For example, we should be able to create any number of multimedia customer records as basic data types and combine these into higher-level structures.

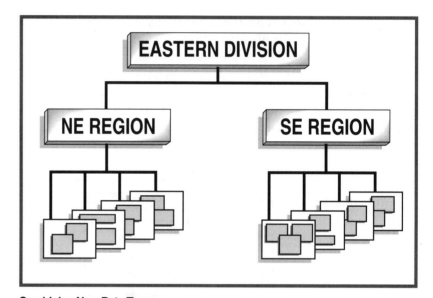

Combining New Data Types

This complexity must be handled naturally

Most important, this increasingly complex information will have to be managed in a way that is natural and intuitive to the end user. We need to eliminate the tedious translation process required to go from simple database tables to such complex entities as customers, products, assembly lines, and business units. We should be able to look into our information systems and see these things represented just the way we naturally view them in the real world.

2. Flexibility

Today's information systems are highly flexible when it comes to changing data. For example, changing a customer address is quick, and the change is readily absorbed by the rest of the system. But changing the *structure* of the data is far more difficult. Database administrators (DBAs) must intervene to alter database structures, and programs that access those structures must be modified to adjust to the new structures. These are slow and cumbersome processes with today's technologies.

It's hard to change the structure of information

As a result of these limitations, most organizations are locked into their existing information structures. Even if they are willing and able to change the way they do business to meet new requirements, they are unable to make these changes because they can't afford the time and expense required to modify their information systems.

This limits a companys ability to change

To meet the requirement for increased flexibility, we have to go beyond information systems that require fixed structures. We need systems that are capable of evolving naturally over time, absorbing change just as fast as the organization can embrace it. Wherever possible, managers should be able to modify these structures directly, without having to convince a DBA to make the required changes.

We need a better way of handling structure

A further aspect of flexibility is the ability to handle special cases. Contemporary database management systems (DBMSs) require that all information fit into fixed forms called *records*, and all entries of a given type must match the template of the record exactly.

Existing systems don't handle special cases well

Information doesn't always take the same form

This arrangement is satisfactory as long as all the information is highly consistent in nature. But the real world is rarely this orderly. Some customers live in countries that require four address lines or special mailing codes. Certain products are just like other products but have additional features that must be described. Field service records may vary according to the type of problem and its resolution. To handle this variation in structure, we need information systems that are designed to handle special cases

Example: Special cases of customers

For example, to handle the increased requirements for customization, we need to differentiate among things that are true of all customers, customers of a particular age or income bracket, customers in particular brackets that live in different geographical regions, and so on, right down to the level of individual customers. To do this efficiently, we need systems that can handle special cases without repeating the information that is common to all the more general cases.

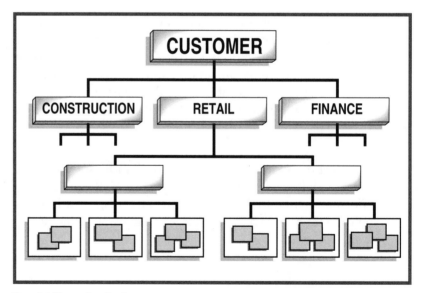

Special Cases for Customers

3. Responsiveness

There is a classic tradeoff in database design between speed and flexibility. In an organization that survives by its ability to make swift use of up-to-date information, choosing a database often represents selecting the lesser of two evils. Ideally, the next generation of information systems should be able to *combine* speed and flexibility rather than trading one for the other.

Databases must offer speed as well as flexibility

With contemporary information systems, managers must use a special language (such as SQL) if they want to access their data directly. For the most part, these languages are complex and hard to learn, and it often takes repeated, time-consuming queries to discover the desired information. To be truly responsive, the next generation of information systems should allow managers to view their data directly, in the form they naturally understand it. Ideally, they should be able to do so visually, navigating smoothly through large amounts of information to find the answers they are looking for.

Managers should have direct and easy access

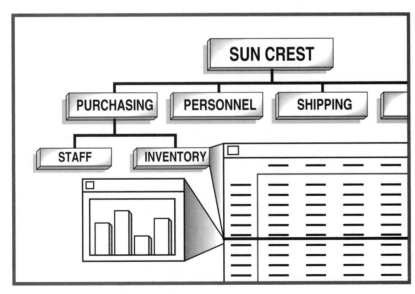

Browsing a Database Graphically

New applications must be developed faster

The responsiveness of contemporary information systems is also limited by the ability to generate new applications quickly. Most information management organizations are so overbooked that getting even the simplest program constructed typically takes eighteen months to two years. This *application backlog*, as it is known, greatly restricts the ability to alter the corporate process. It does no good for management to respond to external events quickly if their information systems can't change along with the company.

4. Quality

Defects in software are considered a fact of life

The prevalence of defects in contemporary information systems is one of the most serious problems with conventional software development. Yet all of us, as consumers of this critical technology, have been conditioned to accept defects as a fact of life. Consider the disclaimer that appears on virtually all shrink-wrapped software. Simply by opening the package, we waive any right to expect the software to work correctly, perform as described, or refrain from causing damage to our existing information.

The problem is worse with corporate software

The problem is even more serious with software developed within organizations because the user base is much smaller. If a PC-based spreadsheet is shipped with a serious bug, tens of thousands of users will quickly flush out the problem and demand that it be fixed. By contrast, custom software may be used by only a handful of individuals. Major defects can go undetected for years, doing silent damage to a company's operations.

Quality also means fitness to purpose

Defined more generally, quality is not simply the absence of defects—it's a reflection of how well a system fulfills its intended purpose. Fitness to purpose means that a system represents a good solution to the business problem it was designed to address. Even a totally bug-free program is useless if it doesn't meet this criterion.

A third aspect of quality is the ease with which end users can do their work using a system. Increased usability shortens learning time, reduces errors, and enhances productivity. All of these benefits are vital to successful software systems.

Usability is another aspect of quality

All three factors—absence of defects, fitness to purpose and usability—are critical aspects of quality. The next generation of information systems will need to take a broad view of quality in order to produce systems that are truly better than their predecessors.

A broader definition of quality is called for

Competition Among the Requirements

In sum, to meet the current and emerging needs of large organizations, information systems will need to handle more complex information, be more flexible, be more responsive, and be higher in overall quality than our current systems. These are all demanding requirements in themselves. But what makes them particularly hard to meet is the fact that they are in competition with each other.

These four requirements compete with each other

In the past, satisfying one requirement has meant making a tradeoff against another requirement. For example, more complex systems are typically less reliable and usable than simple systems because they are harder to build and debug. Similarly, flexibility is at odds with responsiveness because systems with many alternative responses typically function more slowly as they sort their way through the internal choices.

This has led to difficult tradeoffs

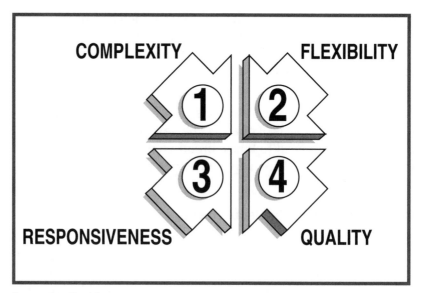

Competing Requirements

We have to satisfy all four at once

So the real challenge for the next generation of information systems is far more than the sum of these parts. It is to meet all four requirements at the same time, without trading any of them off for the others.

3

The Evolution of Information Systems

If we are to meet the requirements for complexity, flexibility, responsiveness, and quality set forth in the preceding chapter, we must do much more than figure out how to program faster. We need to rethink the way we deal with information, including its acquisition, storage, retrieval, and application.

We need to rethink our view of information

There is a hidden assumption underlying the way we currently handle corporate information: that the structure and use of information are relatively static. We expect that the data in our information systems will change, often quite rapidly. Customers will change their addresses, new orders will be entered, inventory will be turned over, and so on. But what we don't build into our systems is the ability to continuously redefine the way we view our customers, process orders, or calculate inventory turnover ratios.

Structure and usage are often viewed as static

If we are to thrive in an increasingly volatile business environment, we will need information systems that are dynamic not just at the level of content but at the level of structure and process as well. Mechanisms for making information systems more dynamic are evolving, but the pace of that evolution is glacial in comparison to the accelerating needs of modern businesses.

All aspects of information systems must be dynamic

MANAGING INFORMATION EFFECTIVELY
Storing Data in Flat Files

The basic problem of information management is not one of storage. Virtually any kind of information can be stored in a computer file and retrieved. In fact, storing data in a so-called "flat file" is often the best approach for information that doesn't need to be shared among users.

The problem doesn't lie in storing data

The problems have to do with sharing

Unfortunately, flat files are not very efficient for sharing information across multiple users. Without some mechanisms for structuring information, controlling simultaneous access, and maintaining security, flat files can easily lead to inconsistent results or corrupted data.

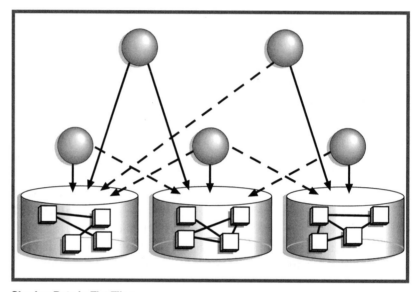

Sharing Data in Flat Files

Sharing Data in a Database

Database managers solve these problems

The solution to these problems is the database management system (DBMS), which is a program that structures information in files and regulates access to that information. It solves the problems mentioned above by adding:

- **Security**—A DBMS requires passwords, performs automatic backups, and provides other services that secure data against theft and loss.

- **Concurrency control**—A DBMS controls simultaneous access to data so that potential conflicts are avoided and the data is always maintained in a consistent state.

- **Structure**—A DBMS provides mechanisms for representing the structure of data in addition to the raw data itself.

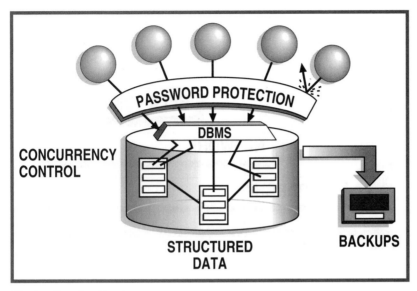

Sharing Data in a Database

DBMSs also provide other useful services, such as checking to make sure the data are internally consistent and making periodic backups to ensure against loss.

DBMSs also pro-vide other services

The Evolution of Database Structure

Of all the problems that DBMSs address, the most challenging has been developing a mechanism for representing structure. In fact, the evolution of databases over the past 30 years consists primarily of developing new generations of technology to better represent the structure of information.

The most challeng-ing problem is structure

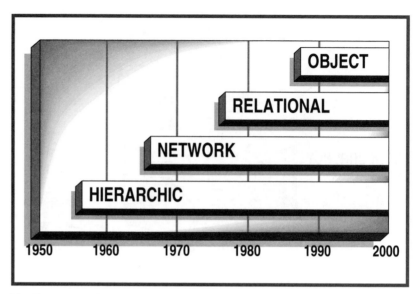

The Evolution of DBMS Structure

Hierarchic and Network Databases

*The earliest struc-
ture is hierarchical*

One of the earliest kinds of DBMS, the *hierarchic DBMS*, stores data
as a hierarchy. For example, a department entry can refer directly
to its employees, and each employee entry, in turn, can refer to
such basic data as name, title, department, and date of hire.

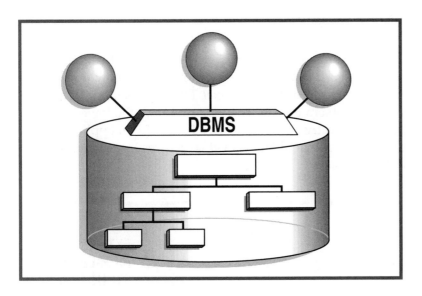

The Hierarchic DBMS

Although the hierarchic model is very general, it isn't sufficient to capture all possible information structures. Sometimes information doesn't follow a neat, hierarchical pattern. *Network DBMSs* solve this problem by allowing all possible connections among data entries, permitting any possible structure to be represented.

The network DBMS allows richer structures

Hierarchic and network DBMSs make data understandable to the people who use them because they are able to reflect the natural structure of real-world information. Because the structure is designed right into the database, access to the data is generally very fast.

Both offer built-in structure and fast access

Unfortunately, network and hierarchic DBMSs allow the data to take on only a single structure, and it's hard to access the data in any way that doesn't fit the built-in structure. Doing so is very slow and takes a lot of programming.

But they allow only a single structure

Moreover, it's hard to change the structure in these databases once it's set. The database has to be shut down and rebuilt, and any programs that depended on the data structure have to be modified to use the new structure. And the entire changeover has to be accomplished simultaneously or serious errors will result.

This structure is hard to change

Relational Databases

Relational databases are more flexible

The frustrations created by the rigidity of network and hierarchic DBMSs led to the development of an entirely new approach to storing information, the *relational DBMS*. Relational databases solve the problem of rigidity by storing only the lowest-level associations directly in the database. They rely on application programs to reconstruct higher-level structures by reconnecting the low-level pieces.

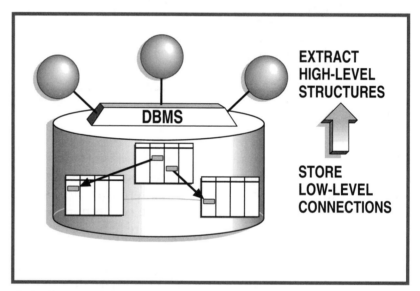

The Relational DBMS

But they may be less efficient

Relational databases are more flexible than their predecessors because they allow different programs to extract different high-level structures. They also allow new kinds of information to be added without shutting down the database. But this approach tends to slow down access for complex structures due to the time required for the reconstruction process. It also makes application software more complex because each program has to contain the code to perform this reconstruction.

Some companies believe that these are worthwhile tradeoffs and have converted their information systems to relational databases. Others disagree, and they refuse to give up the speed and structure of their hierarchic or network databases. Although relational databases are the best-selling form of database technology today, they still represent a small minority of the installed base.

Many companies have avoided moving to relational

The Database Dilemma

This is where we stand with traditional DBMS technology. Companies can have a rigid system that captures complex structures and provides fast and easy access, or they can have a more flexible system that allows multiple views but is slower and harder to access.

Companies are left with two alternatives

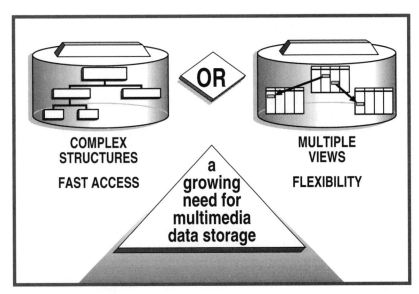

The Database Dilemma

The problem of multi-media remains

Further complicating matters is the fact that none of the traditional approaches to data management is very flexible regarding the kinds of information that can be stored. Modern business calls for the storage of charts, diagrams, blueprints, maps, voice annotations, and many other forms of multimedia information that simply don't fit well in traditional DBMSs. We need data management systems to support these varied kinds of information.

BUILDING BETTER SOFTWARE

Things are worse on the application side

If things are difficult on the storage side, they are much more problematic on the processing side. The problem of developing timely, robust applications is so serious that the term "software crisis" is now a standard component of the corporate vocabulary.

The Seemingly Incurable Software Crisis

The software crisis needs no introduction

So many books and articles have been written about the software crisis that most managers dealing with software development are tired of hearing about it, much less trying to cope with it. The symptoms are familiar to all: 18-month backlogs, late deliveries, blown budgets, and applications that are bug-ridden, don't perform as promised, and—more often than not—are obsolete by the time they are delivered.

Accelerating business trends make the crisis worse

As bleak as this picture may seem, things are going to get worse before they get better. When businesses tended to be regional, centralized, and relatively stable, these problems were frustrating but bearable. But all these conditions have changed. Given the demanding new requirements for complexity, flexibility, responsiveness, and quality, the current problems with software development represent a recipe for disaster on a grand scale.

A Problem of Scale

We've learned a great deal about the software problem during the many years we have lived with it. Perhaps the most important lesson is that the problem stems from the increasing size of the systems we are building. As Fred Brooks learned from his experience developing the operating system for the IBM 360 back in 1965, the resources required to build a software system go up *exponentially* with the number of lines of code, not linearly (Brooks, *The Mythical Man Month*: Addison-Wesley, 1972). The additional, non-linear part is due to the coordination that has to take place to make all the different efforts mesh.

The problem is one of scale

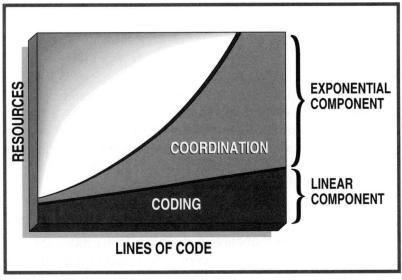

A Problem of Scale

The Evolution of Modularity

We have also figured out the key to solving the problem of scale: to break complex systems down into a collection of independent modules. Ideally, these modules should have a consistent, well-defined interface, and they should have minimal interactions with each other in order to be as independent as possible.

The solution is modularity

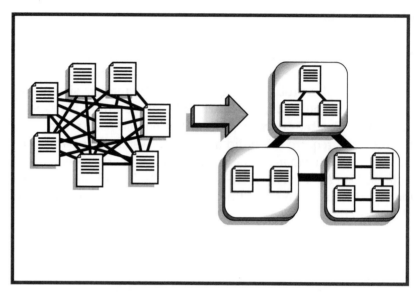

The Key is Modularity

This permits a divide-and-conquer strategy

Given such modules, it's possible to build large systems using a divide-and-conquer strategy. Each module performs a distinct task, so it can be programmed by a different individual or team. Moreover, the same module can be used in more than one location in a program, providing added flexibility in the way programs are constructed.

The function is the most common module

In most programming languages, the basic modular unit is the *function*, a dedicated sequence of computer instructions that carries out a specific task. The accepted technique for structuring programs is *functional decomposition*, in which a program is broken down into the basic functions it must provide to achieve its intended purpose. Each function is then broken down into smaller functions, and so on, until a level is reached where the functions are very small and simple to program.

Example: A loan-approval program

For example, the process of approving a loan would be broken down into a series of steps having to do with assessing credit history, current liabilities, and so on. Where appropriate, these steps would be broken down further, although only the first three levels are shown in the illustration.

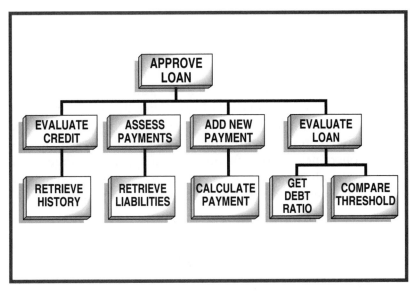

A Structured Program

Although functions make reasonably good modules, the most modern practice is to combine collections of related functions when defining a module. Such languages as Modula-2 and Ada reflect this trend, as do all object-oriented languages.

Modules can also contain groups of functions

INTEGRATING INFORMATION AND PROCEDURES

Traditionally, the two problems discussed previously—managing information and writing programs—have been addressed by different groups of people using different tools and techniques. However, these two problems are not independent. A look at some of their interactions suggests that the historical tendency to treat them separately may have led to some of the difficulties of building complex systems.

Information and procedures aren't independent

Storing Data Within Programs

Data may be shared by all procedures

Procedures and data come together within every program. In the early days, programmers simply placed data in a common area where all the various functions of a program could access it. For programs with only a handful of functions, this was a fine solution. But for programs with hundreds or even thousands of functions, shared data was an invitation to disaster because it violated the independence of the functions. Even a minor change in the structure or value of a data element to suit the needs of one function could have unpredictable effects on the other functions.

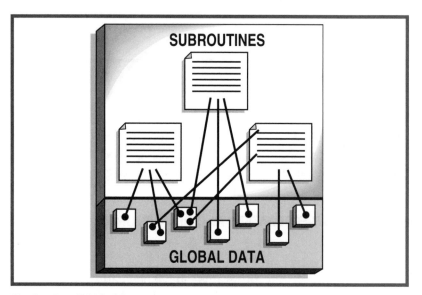

Sharing Data Within a Program

Data must be packaged with procedures

The more modern practice is to modularize data right along with the procedures that operate on it. That way, changing the structure or value of any one data element affects only the module that contains it. Other modules are unaffected by this change because they don't even know about the existence of the data.

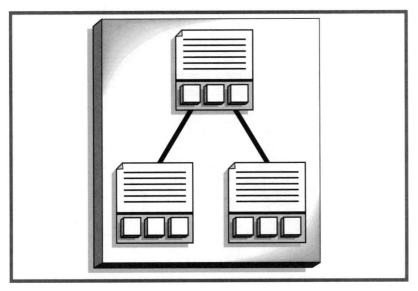

Packaging Data Within Procedures

The common term for this technique is *encapsulation*. The idea behind the term is that related data and procedures are packaged together in the same module or "capsule," and other modules are not allowed to penetrate the "invisible shield" formed by that capsule. In fact, well-designed modules actually "hide" information about their internals from other modules. The use of *information hiding*, as this technique is called, is one of the keys to successful modularization.

This is called encapsulation

Storing Data in Databases

Controlling the relationship between data and procedures *within* programs is relatively easy. New problems arise when data and procedures interact *across* programs.

Sharing data across programs is harder

Handling these interactions is, of course, the reason for the development of database management systems. DBMSs mediate among the programs that access their data, preventing conflicts among users, ensuring that the data is consistent at all times, and performing other vital services.

DBMSs mediate this sharing

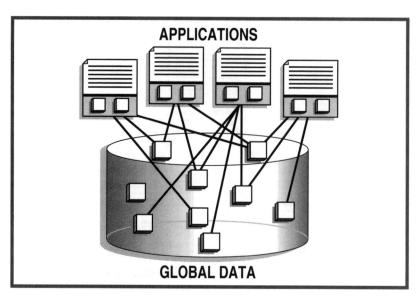

Programs Accessing a Database

This can lead to complications

Unfortunately, the use of shared data in a database takes us right back to the problem of global data. In effect, every program that uses the database depends on its internal structure, and any change to the database can require updates to all these programs. For example, if you change a database to handle nine-digit zip codes, every program that accesses zip codes must be modified, recompiled, and redeployed. And all these changes must be made at the same time to avoid inaccurate results and loss of data.

We need information hiding on a larger scale

There is a clear moral to this example. To be fully effective, information hiding must work on a larger scale. It has to work across programs and databases, not just within programs. The solution to this problem is now beginning to emerge within database technology.

Embedding Procedures in Databases

The solution is to put procedures in the database

The solution to this problem is the same as with individual programs: to package related data and procedures together. In fact, many modern DBMSs are able to store procedures right in the database along with the data they manage.

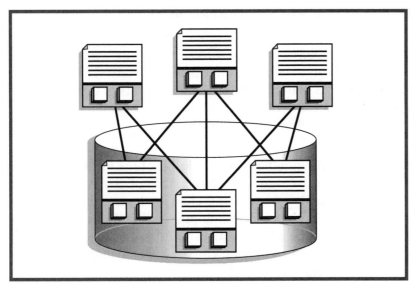

Procedures in the Database

Putting procedures in the database offers two major benefits:

1. **It eliminates redundant code.** Instead of placing a copy of a procedure that accesses a data element in every program that deals with that data, the procedure is stored only once, right in the database.

2. **It makes an information system more flexible.** Changing a procedure for data access requires changing it in one place only. All the programs automatically switch over to the same procedure. All the rebuilding, retesting, and redistribution of programs is eliminated.

If we look at this idea closely, we see that it's simply another example of encapsulation at work: The data structures are hidden behind the embedded procedures, so they are free to change without causing major disruption. This practice can greatly simplify the construction of large-scale information systems, and many information managers consider it the wave of the future.

This has two important benefits

This is encapsulation at work again

INTRODUCING THE OBJECT APPROACH

Object technology offers new solutions

The advent of object-oriented software offers new solutions to the classic problems of building large-scale software systems. The remainder of this book is devoted to describing the object-oriented approach and explaining how to use it to meet the needs of the next generation of information systems.

A simple analogy explains the basic concepts

Before plunging into the inner workings of the technology, however, I'd like to introduce the basic concepts by way of a brief analogy. This analogy may be sufficient for those who simply want to understand how object technology is different from previous approaches. On the other hand, it should provide a basic conceptual framework for those who choose to delve into the technical level in Chapters 4 through 9.

Complex Systems in Nature

Nature builds extremely complex systems

When it comes to building complex systems, nature has no peer. In fact, nature builds systems that are not only very complex but also highly flexible, very responsive to changes in the environment, and quite robust in quality—to the point of being self-repairing in most cases.

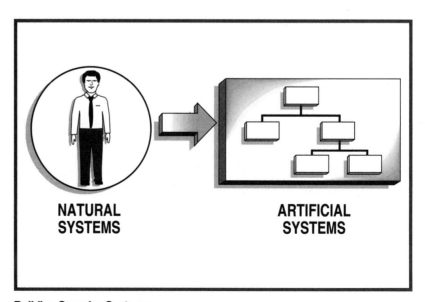

NATURAL SYSTEMS   **ARTIFICIAL SYSTEMS**

Building Complex Systems

In short, living systems satisfy all the requirements for the next generation of information systems. If we could duplicate even a small fraction of nature's success in this regard, our information systems would be much more sophisticated than the ones we rely on today. Is it possible for us to duplicate this success by imitating some of the mechanisms of living systems?

We may be able to mimic nature's approach

Let's take a brief look at how nature builds complex systems and see what we can learn from that. Without looking very deeply, we can observe three basic principles that underlie all living systems, each of which plays a key role in nature's success with complex systems.

We can observe three key principles in living systems

1. Living Building Blocks

The first key is that all of life is constructed around a single building block—the cell. If you think about that for a moment, it's a remarkable observation. All of the infinite variety of life is built out of one kind of stuff!

All life is constructed out of cells

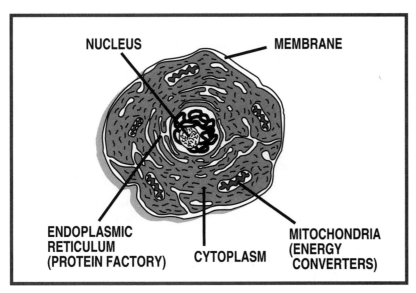

Nature's Building Blocks

*Cells encapsulate
data and procedures*

If we look inside the structure of a cell, ignoring all the variation and complexity, we can make a couple of interesting observations.

1. **The cell is enclosed by a membrane** that controls access to its internals. In effect, the membrane *encapsulates* the cell, protecting its inner workings from outside intrusion.

2. **The cell contains mechanisms for handling both information and behavior.** Most of the information is contained in the nucleus at the center of the cell. The behavior, such as protein synthesis and energy conversion, is carried out in the outer body of the cell.

2. Interactions Between Cells

*Cells interact
through messages*

The second key principle we can observe in nature is that cells interact through a message-based interface. That is, when one cell wants to affect the behavior of other cells, it sends to those cells a chemical signal that triggers the desired response. The membranes of other cells filter incoming messages, accepting only the ones that are meant for them, and then respond internally based on their coded behaviors.

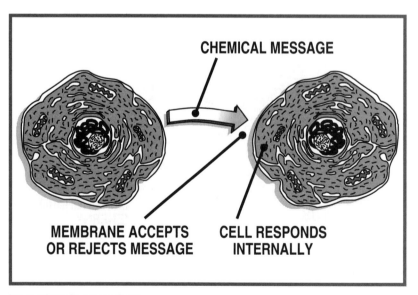

CHEMICAL MESSAGE

**MEMBRANE ACCEPTS
OR REJECTS MESSAGE**

**CELL RESPONDS
INTERNALLY**

Interactions Between Cells

In short, cells do not interact by interfering with each others' DNA. They mind their own business and issue polite requests to other cells rather than trying to control the internal operations of those cells directly. This arrangement offers two different kinds of protection:

Messages offer important benefits

1. First, it **protects the internals of each cell** from intrusion by other cells. Each living cell is more complex than the most sophisticated information system ever built. Protecting the internals of a cell from outside interference is vital to the integrity of the cell.

2. More important, it **protects other cells from having to know about the internals of this cell**. Imagine how complicated the body would be if every different kind of cell contained working descriptions of every other kind of cell!

This second kind of protection is a living example of information hiding. In effect, the cell is functioning as a good module in a complex system by protecting the rest of the system from having to deal with its internal complexities.

The second protection is a form of information hiding

3. Specialization of Cells

The final key principle from living systems is that the basic building blocks come in a wide variety of specialized forms, and these various forms fall into a neat hierarchical organization in which each form shares the characteristics of all the types above it in the hierarchy.

Cells take on specialized forms

Specialization of Cells

Example: Striate muscle cells

For example, striate muscle cells are able to expand or contract along one of their axes, a characteristic they share with all other muscle cells. They also are able to manufacture proteins, a quality they share with all the cells in the body.

Three Keys to Object Technology

These principles underlie all of life

Of course, there's a bit more to living systems than this, but these three mechanisms do seem to provide a solid framework for understanding how nature builds such an infinite variety of complex living systems.

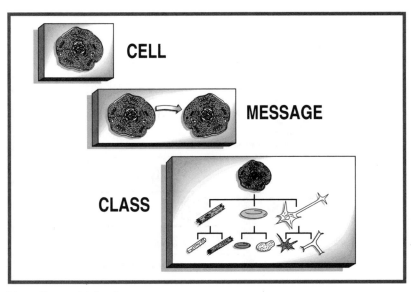

Three Keys to Living Systems

These three mechanisms are also the key to understanding object technology. The basic building blocks are called objects rather than cells. Otherwise, the mapping is quite direct. Object technology consists of:

These are the mechanisms of object technology

- **Objects**—All software systems are built out of a single kind of element, the object, which combines data and processes to perform a specialized role in a system.

- **Messages**—Objects interact through a message-based interface that allows them to cooperate without having to understand or interfere with each others' internal processes.

- **Classes**—Objects come in a wide variety of different types, depending on their function, and these types fall into a neat hierarchical organization of increasing specialization.

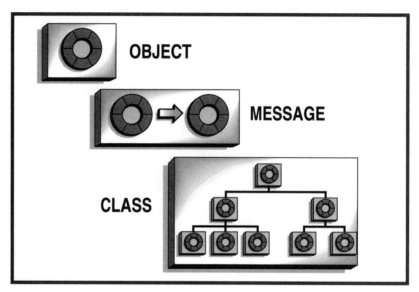

Three Keys to Object Technology

Building software with objects

Everything we discuss in the remaining chapters builds on these mechanisms. If you remember these three mechanisms, you have the essential ingredients for understanding the benefits of this seemingly new yet highly refined approach to building complex systems. Briefly put, object technology leads to better software because it reflects basic principles that proved their worth long before the invention of software.

4
—

Three Keys to Object Technology

In this chapter, we take a closer look at each of the three basic mechanisms of object technology and see how it is actually realized in software. Throughout the chapter, I describe object technology in its purest form. In later chapters, we consider variations on these basic concepts that distinguish the many different implementations of object technology.

This chapter describes objects, methods, and classes

OBJECTS — NATURAL BUILDING BLOCKS
Inside Objects

Here is a graphic representation of an object. Again, the object is the basis for all software, and it encapsulates related data and functions into a self-contained package.

Objects are the basis for all software

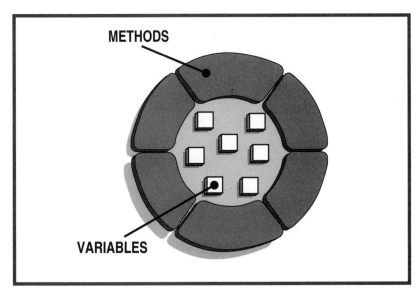

Inside Objects

Procedures are called methods

In the case of object technology, functions have a special name: they are usually called *methods*. The name change is not significant. The only real difference between a classic function and an object method is the fact that a method is embedded within an object rather than operating as a freestanding entity.

Data is kept in variables

In keeping with normal programming practice, the data elements within an object are referred to as *variables* because their values can vary over time. For example, an object might contain a variable called *balance_due*, and its value at a particular moment might be $3,400.

Objects protect their variables

I've drawn the methods as a kind of shell that surrounds the data to reflect the fact that objects are accessed only through their methods. Just as cells don't interfere with each others' DNA, objects don't interfere with each others' data.

A Typical Object

An object is a self-contained universe

Here is an example of a typical object, one that happens to represent a customer. Think of this object as a tiny, self-contained universe. Everything known about a customer is captured in its variables, and all the interactions with a customer are expressed in its methods.

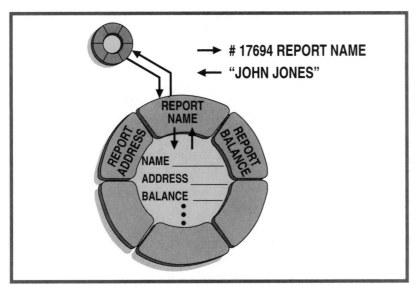

A Customer Object

This customer object illustrates how methods protect their variables. If a customer object is asked to report its outstanding balance, the method for doing that looks up the information it needs and returns the answer. It's no one else's business what variable the balance is kept in, or whether it's a floating-point number, a binary-coded decimal, or in some other form.

Only methods access variables

Here is where the benefits of information hiding come in. If you decide to change the way you store balances, no other part of the system is affected by the change. This means you don't have to modify, retest, and redeploy every program or subroutine that accesses the balance information. As long as the response of the method is unchanged, nothing outside the object is affected in any way.

This is information hiding at work

You can even elimi-nate variables

In fact, you can significantly alter the way an object works without affecting anything outside of an object. For example, suppose you have a problem with customer balances getting out of date and decide that it would be more effective to calculate them on the fly. In a traditional system, you would have to convert every program that dealt with customer balances to compute these balances rather than look them up. In an object-oriented system, you would simply delete the *balance* variable and modify the *report_balance* method to calculate the balance rather than look it up.

Building Objects Out of Objects

Objects can contain other objects

If objects could contain only simple variables such as names and numbers, they would have rather limited usefulness. What makes objects powerful is that they can contain other objects as well. Objects that contain other objects are known as *composite objects*.

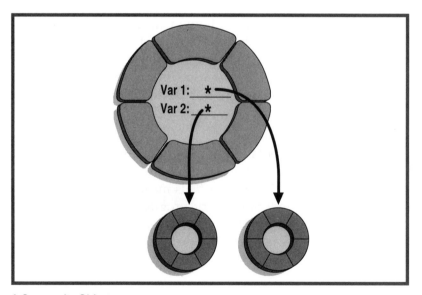

A Composite Object

They actually point to contained objects

In most systems, composite objects don't literally "contain" other objects. Rather, they contain variables that *refer* to other objects. For convenience, the reference actually stored in the variable is called an *object identifier*, or *object ID* for short.

This may sound like a technical detail, but it offers two important advantages:

Object IDs
increase flexibility

1. The **"contained" objects can change in size** and composition without affecting the composite object that "contains" them. That makes maintaining complex systems of nested objects far simpler than it would otherwise be.

2. The **"contained" objects are free to participate in any number of composite objects** rather than being locked into a single composite object. This becomes vital for capturing real-world information.

An Example of Composite Objects

The next illustration shows two objects that represent purchase orders. Their variables contain information about customers, products purchased, and other data. But rather than enter all that information directly into the purchase-order objects, we simply store references to these component objects in the form of object IDs.

Purchase orders
refer to customers

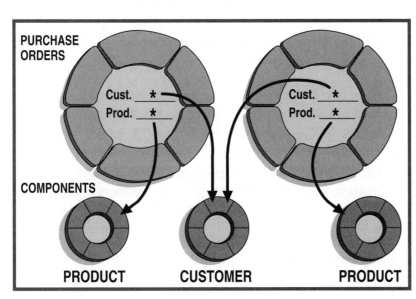

Two Purchase Order Objects

Each product is free to change

Because the purchase order contains only a reference to a product object—not the product object itself—the product object is free to change in any way without affecting the purchase-order object. For example, we could give the product an expanded description, which would increase its size, without affecting the size of the purchase order object.

Each customer can be in many POs

Also, a single customer object can participate in any number of purchase orders. That's the other advantage of building up composite objects by reference rather than by actual, physical containment.

The Power of Object Identifiers

Every object has a unique ID

Object identifiers are invisible helpers—you never have to deal with them directly, but they simplify your life in many ways. Basically, object IDs are arbitrary numerical values assigned by whatever language, database, or other object-oriented system you may be using. You never have to be concerned about these identifiers—they are automatically assigned and maintained by the system, and the system ensures that they are unique.

Object IDs have important advantages

Object identifiers have important advantages for building information systems. In a nutshell:

- **They are efficient,** in that they require minimal storage within the composite object. They are typically much smaller than human-readable names, foreign keys, or other content-based references.

- **They are fast.** Object IDs point to an actual address or to a location within a table that gives the address of the referenced object, which means that objects can be located quickly regardless of whether they are currently stored in local memory, a remote hard disk, or on some device in a networked system.

- **They are independent of content**, in that they don't depend on the data contained in the object in any way. You can change every single variable in a customer object, including the customer's name, address, and tax ID number, and the system will still access the correct customer object.

Object IDs not only simplify the construction of complex information systems, they also reflect our experience of the real world. A real-world object is, in fact, a unique entity, even though it may appear to be the same as some other object in all the characteristics we choose to record. For example, two different machines may be identical in every respect, but they are still different machines.

Object IDs reflect natural identity

In most systems, we would have to assign identifying numbers to the two machines and store those numbers to keep track of them. No such extra work is required in an object-oriented system.

They avoid the need for assigning identifiers

Modules on Multiple Levels

The objects contained in composite objects can themselves be composite objects, and this nesting can go to any depth. This means you can build structures of any complexity by plugging objects together. This is important because we usually need more than one level of modularization to avoid chaos in large-scale systems.

Objects can be nested to any degree

Here again, we can take a lesson from nature's notebook. Consider how natural systems handle the problem of high-level structures. A living organism is not an undifferentiated mass of cells. Rather, cells are "organized" into functional units called *organs*, such as the heart and the brain. Organs, in turn, are grouped into *systems*, such as the circulatory system and the nervous system. Finally, these systems are tied together to form the *organism* as a whole.

Nature uses this technique extensively

LEVEL	EXAMPLE
organism	cheetah
system	circulatory
organ	heart
cell	blood cell

Nature Modularizes on Multiple Levels

Each level is understandable

The four-level modularization of organisms is very convenient for life scientists because it brings a clear order to what might otherwise be a chaotic collection of cellular interactions. Particularly valuable is that fact that we can understand each level without immediate recourse to the other levels. For example, we can understand the functioning of the body as the interaction of its systems without getting caught up in the details of the organs that comprise those systems or the cells that make up the organs.

Individual systems are also understandable

Similarly, we can understand any given module in isolation because most have a clear function that is relatively separable from the other modules. The heart, for example, is a pump, and we can understand how this pump works without worrying about what kind of fluid it pumps or how its individual muscle cells contract to create the pumping action.

Levels facilitate independent changes

Although we can only guess at the origins of this kind of structuring, the most likely reason that living systems evolved this kind of multilevel modularity is that modularization facilitates the process of evolution itself. The more independent organs and systems are, the more easily each of them can evolve into improved forms without disrupting the operation of other organs and systems.

That's precisely why we should follow the same approach in building software. In fact, we can extend this logic to any number of levels, although four or five is usually enough for the kinds of systems most organizations need.

We should use multiple levels in software

MESSAGES — ACTIVATING OBJECTS
Interacting Through Messages

A message is simply a request from one object to another object asking the second object to carry out one of its methods. By convention, the object sending the request is called the *sender* and the object receiving the request is known as the *receiver*.

Messages request services of other objects

Structurally, a message consists of three parts: the identity of the receiver, the method the receiver is being asked to carry out, and any special information the receiver may need to perform the requested method.

A message has three parts

This last information is sent in the form of *parameters*, which can be either specific data values or the identifiers of other objects that the method will operate on. Parameters are strictly optional and typically vary in number from zero to four or five.

Parameters are optional

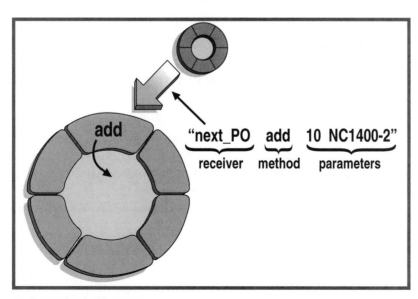

An Example of a Message

Example: Add a line item

In the example shown in the illustration:

- **The receiver** is *next_PO*.

- **The method** is *add*, which requests the purchase order to add another line item to itself.

- **The parameters** are *10* and *NC1400-2*, which tell the PO to add ten copies of the inventory item known as NC1400-2.

The receiver responds to a message

The actual sequence of events is that the sender sends its message; the receiver executes the appropriate method, consuming the parameters; then the receiver returns some kind of response to the sender to acknowledge the message and return any information it may have requested.

The Benefits of Messages

Messages confer the same benefits as in nature

Using messages to carry out interactions between objects offers the same benefits it provides in nature—namely, it protects the internals of objects from outside intrusion, and it protects all the other objects from having to contain information about the structure of any one object.

Objects don't access each others' internals

Here is an example of the first kind of protection. In the pure form of object technology described here, no other object can dive directly into a purchase-order object and alter its internal variables. Only the object's own methods can manipulate these variables, which makes it reasonably easy to verify that all variables are accessed correctly.

Objects don't under- stand each others internals

We can also see the other kind of protection at work in this example. None of the other objects in a system needs to worry about how purchase orders are structured or processed. All they have to do is know what messages they can respond to.

This encapsulation of data and procedures within an object makes the object much easier to modify. In this case, we could change the internal structure of a purchase-order object completely and modify the way its methods worked to accommodate the new structure. As long as the messages it responds to don't change, nothing else in the system is affected by these changes.

This makes modification easier

The Power of Polymorphism

Here is another benefit of using messages. Because objects are defined independently of one another, the same name can be used for different methods in different objects.

The same name can be used for many methods

For example, consider the message "add." Sent to a purchase order, it might mean add a new line item. Sent to an account object, it could be an instruction to increase the current balance. Sent to a department object, it might mean add a new employee.

"Add" can mean many things

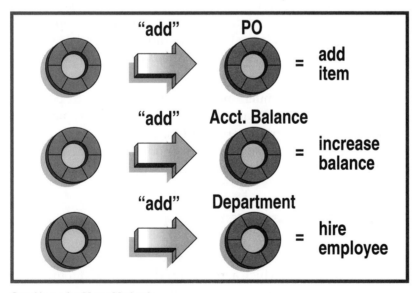

One Name for Many Methods

Different versions usually require separate names

These are very different kinds of operations, and in traditional programming they would all require unique names. For example, they might be called:

> *add_line_item*
> *add_to_balance*
> *add_new_employee*

Method names can be used many ways

With object-oriented programming, each object only knows about its own definition of the "add" procedure, so there's never any questions about which one to carry out. All of these operations can be called "add" with no danger of confusion.

This reduces the number of names

Using the same name for different operations in different circumstances is called *polymorphism*, which is a Greek term meaning "many forms." In retrospect, polymorphism may seem like an obvious idea because we use this principle all the time in everyday language. But for software systems, it's a genuine breakthrough. It greatly reduces the number of names programmers have to deal with, allowing context to determine which meaning is appropriate at any given moment. In systems with thousands or tens of thousands of functions, this can be a major advantage.

It also simplifies complex systems

There is, however, a much more important benefit to polymorphism than reducing the name space. Polymorphism actually simplifies the way programs are written, allows them to execute faster, and makes them much easier to modify. All of these benefits result from reducing the role of the case statement.

The Demise of the Case Statement

Case statements control what a program does

Most modern languages have multi-way "branching" or *case statements* that determine which action should be carried out in a given situation. They typically do this by comparing the value of a variable against a number of alternative special cases until they find the one that matches.

For example, suppose you have a portfolio of financial instruments, and you want to compute your current net worth. To do this, you would write a simple program that looked at each instrument in turn, determined its current value, and added that value to a running total. However, the method for calculating the current value might well be different for each kind of instrument. To address this complication, your program would need a case statement to make sure that the correct subroutine was called, as shown in the illustration.

Example: Evaluating a portfolio

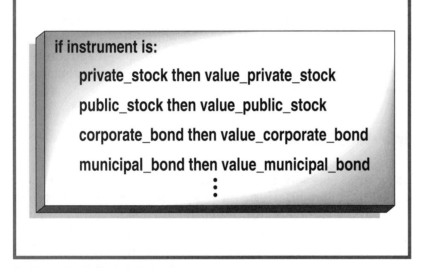

if instrument is:

    private_stock then value_private_stock

    public_stock then value_public_stock

    corporate_bond then value_corporate_bond

    municipal_bond then value_municipal_bond

An Example of a Case Statement

Case statements are generally accepted as a fact of life in software development, so little attention is paid to the problems they create. They do, however, have some serious drawbacks:

Case statements create problems

- Case statements are **tedious to write** and they comprise a fair amount of the total bulk of many applications.

- Case statements are **slow to execute** because the computer has to perform a number of comparisons to decide which branch to take.

- Identical case statements **have to be duplicated** throughout a program or system. For example, the code in the financial illustration would have to be included in every program or subroutine that needed to value a financial instrument.

- With case statements, **all options are "hard-coded"** into the program. If you want to add a new option or delete an old one, you have to go back and modify the case statement everywhere it appears in the system.

The most serious problem is rigidity

The last problem is by far the most serious. A large system may have thousands or even tens of thousands of case statements, all of which lock important decisions into the structure of many programs. Changing any one of these decisions—for example, deciding to add a new kind of finanical instrument—may require reworking multiple programs, with the attendant problems of retesting and redeployment.

Extensibility Through Messages

Messages offer a simple solution

Using messages solves this problem in an elegant way. Each different kind of financial instrument knows how to compute its own value, and the method for doing this is called "value" in every kind of instrument. No matter what type of instrument the current one happens to be, the correct method automatically gets called. There can never be any confusion about which method to use.

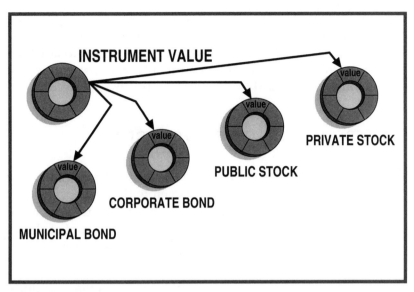

The Message Solution

In effect, polymorphism eliminates the need for most case statements. All the code required to select the appropriate routine for valuing financial instruments, for example, is reduced to a single instruction: *instrument value*. This direct calling of methods solves all of the problems associated with the case statement it replaces:

This eliminates most case statements

- It is **trivial to write** and takes up very little code space in the program.

- It **executes very quickly** because the computer doesn't have to perform a sequence of comparisons to decide which action to carry out. In this example, the program jumps directly to the method *value* in the object pointed to by *instrument*.

- It **makes programs smaller** and easier to maintain because duplicate case statements are eliminated.

- It **makes programs more modifiable** because special cases can be added just by defining new objects.

Modifiability is the biggest benefit

This last benefit is the most powerful because it solves the most difficult problem. With object technology, you don't need to code all the options directly into a program. If you want to add new options, such as new financial instruments, you just define new objects for them and add those objects to the program.

CLASSES — BRINGING ORDER TO OBJECTS

Objects and messages bring much to software

If objects and messages were all there were to object technology, it would be a powerful technology even without the concept of classes. In fact, there are programming languages that make extensive use of objects and messages but have no concept of classes at all. Ada is the most notable example of such a language.

But classes really make a difference

However, the concept of classes greatly increases the usefulness of object technology. Classes augment the efficiency and power of objects and messages in a number of important ways.

Templates for Objects

A class is a template for similar objects

A class is simply a template for a particular type of object. If you have many objects of the same type, you only have to define the general characteristics of that type once, in the class, rather than in every object.

Example: PO objects all belong to a class

For example, a real purchasing system would deal with not one but many thousands of purchase orders. It would be hopelessly inefficient to duplicate the code for all the methods and the definitions of all the variables in every single purchase-order object.

Classes eliminate this duplication

This is where classes come into play. Classes define the aspects of objects that are the same for all the actual realizations or *instances* of that class. For example, a class called *purchase_order* would define the methods and variables associated with all purchase orders. The individual instances of this class, the actual purchase-order objects, would contain only the values of the variables for each particular purchase order.

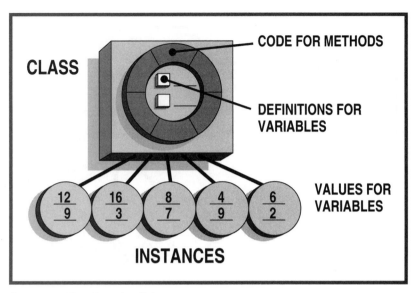

Classes as Templates for Objects

In short, an object is an instance of a class. As such, it is a combination of the shared characteristics contained in the class and the unique characteristics contained in the instance. Given this definition, it is perfectly appropriate to say that an object has methods, even though the methods are actually contained in the class to which the object belongs.

An object is an instance of a class

A Comparison with Data Tables

Those familiar with database systems can think of classes and instances as being like tables and records, respectively. Like a class, a table defines the names and data types of the information it will contain. Like an instance, a record in that table gives the specific values for a particular entry. The main difference, at the conceptual level, is that classes contain methods in addition to data definitions.

Instances are like records in a table

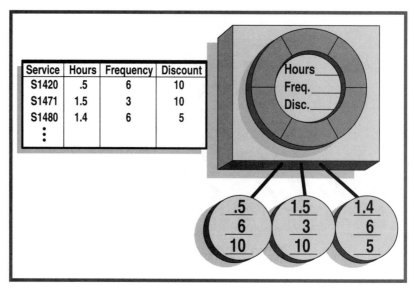

Instances as Records

When Classes Act Like Instances

Classes can contain class variables

Not all variables are contained in instances. There are certain cases where all instances of a class refer to the same value rather than maintaining a unique value of their own. In such cases, it is more efficient to store the value directly in the class rather than duplicating it in every instance. Such a variable is called a *class variable* to distinguish it from the more common type of variable, which is formally known as an *instance variable*.

Example: Maintaining a count of purchase orders

For example, suppose you wanted to keep a count of all the outstanding purchase orders. Since there would be only one count for all purchase-orders, it wouldn't make much sense to duplicate the count in every instance of the purchase order class. Instead, a single copy of the count would be placed in the class definition itself, using a class variable to contain it.

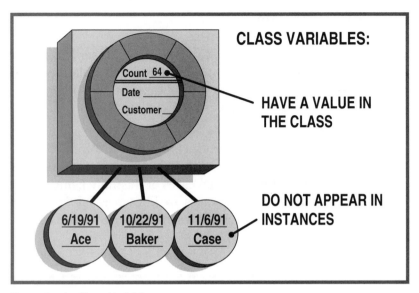

CLASS VARIABLES:

HAVE A VALUE IN THE CLASS

DO NOT APPEAR IN INSTANCES

Example of a Class Variable

Similarly, classes can contain methods that are executed by the class itself and not by its instances. In keeping with the terminology for variables, such methods are called *class methods* to distinguish them from the usual kind of methods, which are formally known as *instance methods*.

Classes can also contain class methods

Here's an example of a method that is typically carried out by a class rather than one of its instances. When you want to create a new instance of a class, you call a method in the class itself to carry out the construction process. Such a method is usually called a *constructor*. To see why constructors are defined as class methods, consider the problem of creating the first instance of any given class. There would be no existing instances to receive the construct message!

Example: Constructors

Similarly, the methods for destroying objects and reclaiming the memory they occupied are also carried out by classes. Such methods are typically called *destructors*. Again, it is best to have the class carry out the destruction of instances because it avoids the problem of having an object continue to function long enough to destroy itself even as it was in the process of tearing itself apart.

Destructors are also defined as class methods

Specialization of Classes

Classes are defined as special cases of each other

Many different kinds of classes can be defined to serve different purposes. The various classes are not defined in isolation, however. Rather, they are defined as special cases of each other, forming what's known as a *class hierarchy*.

Example: Classes of products

For example, the collection of products a company offers could all be defined as specialized versions of more general products, all of which could be considered special cases of the more general class *product*. Formally, these special cases are known as *subclasses*. The classes of which they are special cases, in turn, are known as their *superclasses*.

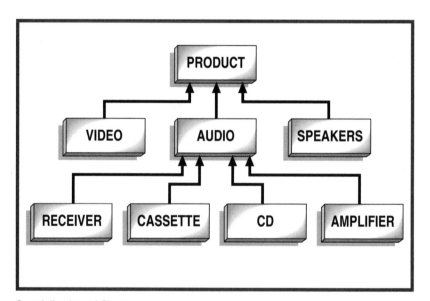

Specialization of Classes

Inheritance allows classes to share properties

The advantage of defining classes in a hierarchy is that, through a mechanism called *inheritance*, special cases share all the characteristics of their more general cases. For example, a *CD player* would inherit all the methods and variables of an *audio component*, which in turn would inherit all the methods and variables of a *product*.

Eliminating Redundancy Through Inheritance

This is a very efficient arrangement because each method or variable is only defined once, at the most general level it applies. For example, methods for handling serial numbers would be coded in the *product* class because they would apply equally to all kinds of products, whereas methods for dealing with wattage would apply to all audio products, and methods for number of disks would be coded down in the *CD player* class.

Example: CD players inherit many properties

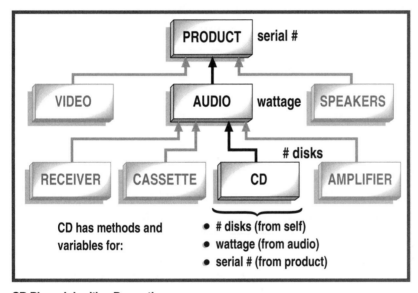

CD Player Inheriting Properties

The CD, then, would have methods for dealing with all three of these variables, but only the ones for the number of disks would actually be coded in the CD class.

Only one of these properties is coded in the CD class

Inheritance in Action

Of course, this could complicate the execution of a program, as any given object might have to do a little searching to find the definition of a particular method or variable. Here's an example of how this search process might work.

This does complicate the execution of a program

Example: A CD reporting its serial number

Suppose an instance of a CD player gets a message requesting it to report its serial number. The instance would first check its own class, *CD*, to see if it contained a method by that name. It doesn't, so a search would ensue up the hierarchy until it hit the *product* level. Here it would find the method for reporting the serial number and the definition of the variable that contains the serial number. The method would then execute, using the definitions found in the *product* class and taking the actual value for the serial number from the instance that received the method.

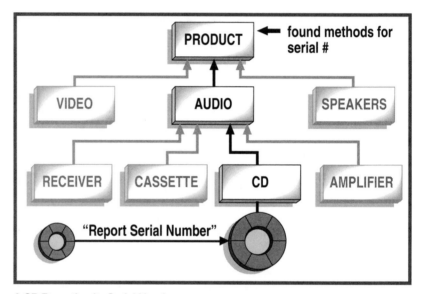

A CD Reporting Its Serial Number

Actual performance is usually optimized

Now, all this searching could extract a significant performance penalty, but most object languages and databases have taken care of that problem. Through a process called *folding*, they inform each class of all its inherited methods so the system doesn't actually have to search to find them. The system behaves as though it were performing a search up the hierarchy without paying the performance penalty of actually conducting a search at execution time.

Broadcasting Changes

Using class hierarchies also makes object software easier to modify. Suppose you sell more audio electronics than you ever imagined, and you start to run out of serial numbers. Somehow, you have to expand the number of digits in your serial numbers and change the access methods to handle this change.

Hierarchies make software easier to modify

Given the way inheritance works, you only have to make this change in a single class—the *product* class. Since all the different kinds of products inherit their serial-number methods from this class, they are all "changed" immediately, with no further programming required. They simply use the new methods automatically they next time they search up the hierarchy to the *product* class.

Example: Changing serial numbers

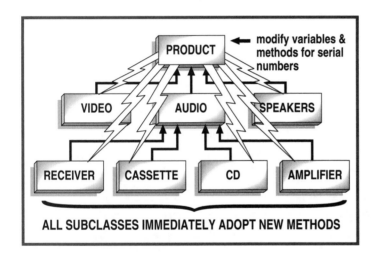

"Broadcasting" a Change in Serial Numbers

Handling Exceptions

Now imagine that out of a catalog of 3,000 products we needed to handle serial numbers differently in just one category. For example, suppose that we decide we need a different numbering system for audio receivers.

Hierarchies can also handle exceptions

This can be done without duplication

One solution would be to move the methods for handling serial numbers down to the level of the lowest-level categories. But that would mean duplicating these methods in all the low-level categories, which would be highly inefficient and hard to maintain.

Just redefine a method at a lower level

Fortunately, there's a simpler solution—redefine the method in the class that needs to have the exception and leave the other classes alone. The way instances search for their methods guarantees that exceptions will always be favored over general rules.

This technique is know as overriding

For example, when a receiver is asked for its serial number, it will find a routine for handling that method in its own class, so it will search no further. All other products will still search all the way up to the *product* class before finding a definition, so they will continue to use the general rule. In effect, the special case "overrides" the general case.

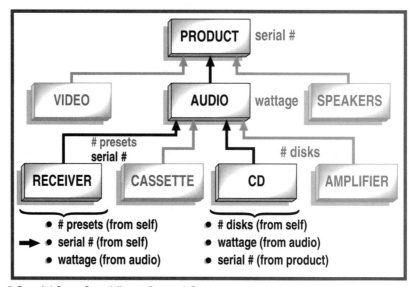

A Special Case Overriding a General Case

Multiple Inheritance

So far, we have considered only the special case in which inheritance follows a strict hierarchical structure. According to this model, each class has, at most, a single superclass. This kind of inheritance is called *single inheritance*.

We have considered only single inheritance

A more general approach to inheritance is to allow a class to inherit methods and variable definitions from any number of superclasses. With *multiple inheritance*, the class "hierarchy" is no longer a simple hierarchy but a network of overlapping inheritance structures.

The alternative is multiple inheritance

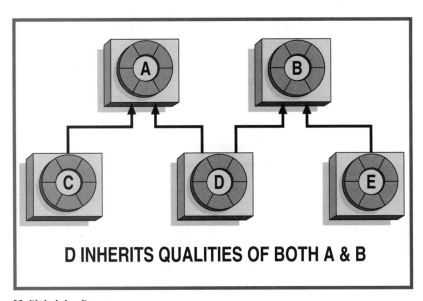

D INHERITS QUALITIES OF BOTH A & B

Multiple Inheritance

Suppose, for example, that you have an existing class hierarchy of customers with several levels of specialization. Everything works fine until you start getting customers in foreign countries. At this point you realize that you have defined all your customer classes with seven-digit phone numbers, two-letter state codes, and nine-digit zip codes. Worse yet, all your methods and variables assume a single currency and have no provision for monetary conversions and exchange rates.

Example: Foreign and domestic customers

Changing the customer class is a poor solution

How do you fix this problem? One solution is to revise your existing definition of the high-level *customer* class to generalize it and all its special cases so that they work for customers all over the world. Unfortunately, that solution means giving up the simple data structures for domestic customers and adding extra complexity and storage space to the great majority of your customers who don't require it.

Multiple inheritance works better

Multiple inheritance offers a more efficient way to solve this problem. You create two high-level classes, *domestic company* and *foreign company*, and put all the country-specific variables and methods in those classes. Then you have any given customer inherit both from its superclass in your existing hierarchy and also from one of these two new classes, as shown in the following figure. If you need special cases of *foreign company* to handle conflicting procedures or data structures, you can always add subclasses to this class and inherit from these instead.

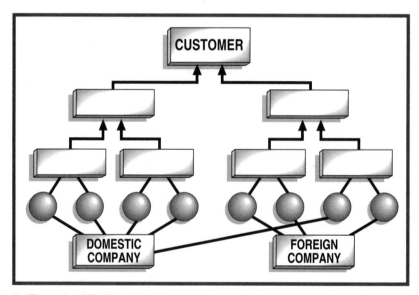

An Example of Multiple Inheritance

Multiple inheritance is not universal

Not all object languages and databases support multiple inheritance. This is not an oversight on the part of some vendors—the inclusion of this feature is generally regarded as a matter of principle and is currently a hotly debated issue.

Those who favor multiple inheritance argue that it's required to model reality, in that real-world objects typically belong to multiple classes. For example, a person can be a boss, a mother, a wife, a student, and a musician, all of which would involve the inheritance of different qualities. They also argue that it's always better to support the most general case; if single inheritance suffices, then you don't have to get involved with multiple inheritance. But it's better to have it on tap when you *do* need it.

Some people think it's essential

Those who oppose multiple inheritance counter that it introduces a level of complexity that is very hard to manage safely and consistently. For example, objects may inherit conflicting definitions of the same method from two different superclasses—how do they know which one to use? They also maintain that most applications of multiple inheritance—such as the woman who is a boss, mother, musician, etc.—are better handled as *roles*, although the support for roles is limited in contemporary systems.

Others are strongly opposed

My own view on multiple inheritance is cautiously favorable. It's better to have the option of using it, but it should only be used when no simpler solution is available. And when you *do* use it, keep the class structure as close to a hierarchy as possible or you can wind up with an inscrutable model of reality that hinders rather than helps your designs.

If you use it, do so with caution

The Naturalness of Class Hierarchies

Classes are the true genius of object technology. Not only do they provide efficient mechanisms for eliminating redundancy and capturing relationships among different kinds of objects, they also reflect the way we naturally think about the real world.

Class hierarchies reflect natural understanding

Two of the most fundamental learning processes are *generalization* and *discrimination*. In generalization, we discover and remember the characteristics that things have in common. In discrimination, we learn the characteristics that make similar things different. These are very basic processes. Virtually all animals that are capable of learning exhibit them.

We code information through two basic mechanisms

Each of these is reflected in class hierarchies

These basic mechanisms of understanding are naturally reflected in the class hierarchies of object languages. Generalization is expressed as placement of properties higher up in the hierarchy, and specialization is expressed as placement lower in the hierarchy. As with natural learning, specialization at one level may be generalization at another level—it's really just a matter of discovering the most general level at which each property applies.

This naturalness is a potent advantage

This naturalness of expression is important because it means that we can readily translate our real-world knowledge into object-oriented information systems. We can store, exchange, and manipulate information in a manner that leverages the knowledge skills we have built up throughout our lifetimes rather than having to learn new and arbitrary techniques for handling computer-based information. This naturalness is a significant advantage of object technology.

5

Methodologies for Object Development

In this chapter, we examine how the three basic mechanisms of object technology are applied in the actual construction of information systems. We do so in two ways. First, we consider object technology as a way of improving the execution of the traditional software development life cycle. Then we look at the limitations of that approach and examine an emerging methodology that offers greater potential for leveraging the benefits of object technology.

This chapter reviews methodologies

ENHANCING TRADITIONAL METHODOLOGIES
The Software Development Life Cycle

The traditional software development life cycle is often called the "waterfall" method because it assumes that the development effort flows through a series of stages. The actual breakdown of stages varies from one authority to the next, but the most common stages are *requirements analysis, system design, implementation, testing,* and *maintenance.*

The "waterfall" model has a series of stages

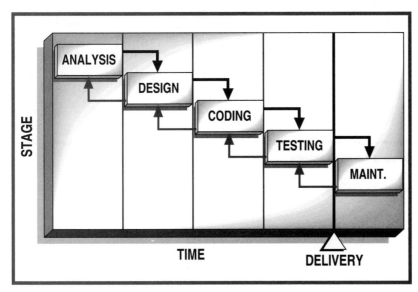

The Software Development Life Cycle

The stages are mostly sequential

The intent of the methodology is that each stage in the sequence should be triggered when the preceding one is completed, with explicit sign-offs at the conclusion of each stage to make sure that the project is on track. However, the methodology does allow for feedback from each stage to the preceding stage for the sake of flexibility. For example, any defects found in the testing phase are fed back to the programmers so they can fix the problems.

Object technology facilitates transitions

Object technology can enhance the traditional life cycle in two major ways. First, it can reduce the barriers between stages by providing a common set of constructs for use at every stage. At present, very different terms and descriptions are used at each stage of development, including verbal descriptions and entity-relationship models for requirements analysis, functional decomposition diagrams for system design, and language-specific program code for implementation.

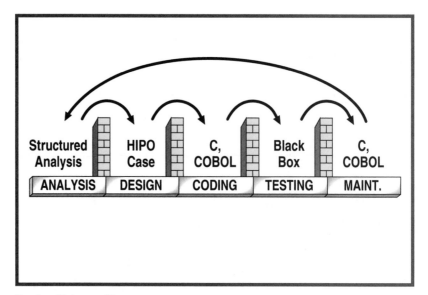

Barriers Between Stages

Object technology provides a common language that helps reduce the barriers between the stages. The real-world objects discussed in the requirements analysis are translated directly into system objects in the design phase, which are implemented as software objects in the programming phase, and so on. This approach allows much more direct mapping from a functioning program back to the original requirements, making a system easier to maintain and modify.

Object technology provides a common language

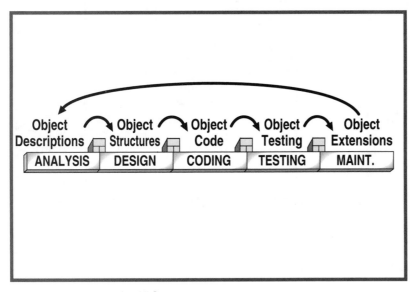

A Common Language for All Stages

Object techniques can improve each stage

The second way object technology helps the traditional development life cycle is by providing specific tools to assist each stage. The tools for the implementation stage are, of course, well established. This is the heart of object programming. The tools for the other stages are still in development, but they are far enough along to assist to the process.

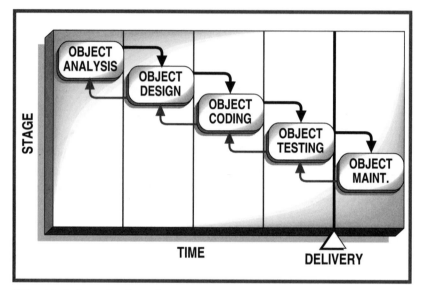

Object Techniques for Every Stage

Object-Oriented Analysis

Object-oriented analysis builds a model

Object-based requirements analysis essentially consists of looking at all the potential objects in a system and capturing their characteristics and relationships in a formal notation. In essence, it consists of building an abstract model of what a solution to the business problem would look like, keeping a close correspondence between the abstract objects and their real-world counterparts.

There is, as yet, no standard notation for building this abstract representation. Peter Coad and Ed Yourdon (*Object-Oriented Analysis*: Yourdon Press, 1991) have developed a notation based on their previous experience with entity-relationship diagramming. Their approach is consistent with the basic goal of modeling the physical structure of the real world closely, but it's too soon to tell whether their particular notation will catch on.

There is no standard notation yet

Object-Oriented Design

Once the requirements for a system are well understood, the actual structure of the system can be designed. Traditionally, this is a very distinct step from analysis, but object technology brings these stages so close together that they often blur.

Design is similar to analysis

Again, there is no standard notation for expressing object-based designs, but there are several candidates:

Again, there is no standard notation

- Sally Shlaer and Steve Mellor (*Object-Oriented Systems Analysis*: Prentice Hall, 1988) provide a straightforward extension of entity-relationship modeling to accommodate object constructs.

- Grady Booch (*Object-Oriented Design with Applications*: Benjamin/Cummings, 1991) proposes a notation based on his experience in building large systems in Ada, but some find the complexity of his notation a bit daunting.

- Rebecca Wirfs-Brock, Brian Wilkerson, and Lauren Wiener (*Designing Object-Oriented Software*: Prentice Hall, 1990) offer a refreshingly simple notation for object-oriented design together with a new technique called responsibility-driven design.

- James Rumbaugh et al. describe an approach that places a strong emphasis on modeling (Rumbaugh, Blaha, Premerlani, Eddy, and Lorensen, *Object-Oriented Modeling and Design*: Prentice Hall, 1991).

Object-Oriented Programming

The programming stage is the most affected

The implementation phase of software development is, of course, the one that is most radically transformed by object technology. Part of the difference comes from the technology itself—the use of objects, messages, and classes instead of functions.

The biggest change is reuse

A more important difference in the programming process, however, stems from the extensive reuse of existing code. This allows object-based programs to be developed largely by assembling existing classes of objects in new ways. It also speeds up the programming process considerably because assembling existing objects is much faster than writing software from scratch.

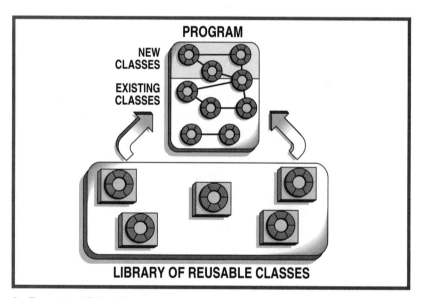

An Example of Object Reuse

Object-Oriented Testing

Object testing is not yet well developed

To my knowledge, there haven't been any formal techniques developed for object-oriented testing, but the use of objects is having considerable impact on this stage as well. I won't be surprised if the next spate of object-oriented books is devoted to the subject of object-based quality control.

The main effect of object technology on software testing is that it tends to improve the quality of the software because new programs consist mostly of existing, proven objects that have already demonstrated themselves to be reliable in previous applications.

Quality is improved because of reuse

Another important benefit is that the good modularity of object software makes it easier to isolate the cause of software malfunctions. The fact that program objects correspond very closely to real-world objects also helps the detection and isolation of defects. If there is something wrong with the way invoices are being totalled, the problem almost certainly lies in the definition of the invoice class.

Good modularity helps isolate defects

Object-Oriented Maintenance

As with object-oriented testing, there are no published works as yet that focus on this stage of development. However, it is generally established that object technology facilitates program maintenance in at least three important ways:

Maintenance is facilitated three ways

1. It can reduce the amount of maintenance because the initial quality of software is higher due to the extensive reuse of proven components.

2. The close mapping between software objects and real-world objects can make it easier for someone other than the original programmer to understand and maintain the system.

3. The natural extensibility of object software usually facilitates the addition of features at a later date.

This last benefit is particularly important because the vast majority of what is called "software maintenance" actually consists of modifications and extensions of the original functionality. The examples of commercial applications described in Chapter 12 illustrate this improved extensibility in action.

Extensibility is especially important

LIMITATIONS OF THE TRADITIONAL APPROACH
Problems with the Waterfall Model

The waterfall method is limited

Object technology can certainly extend the life of the traditional development methodology, but there are limits to what it can do. Fundamental limitations are designed into this methodology that even the most dedicated use of objects cannot overcome.

The waterfall isn't flowing

The traditional development life cycle has been in use for so many years that its shortcomings are readily apparent. Here are some of the problems that have been observed:

- It **rarely delivers the solutions that managers want**. Managers don't really know what they want until they see it, at which point it's impossible to make significant modifications without going back to the beginning of the process.

- It requires specialized personnel for analysis, design, programming, testing, and maintenance. This means that all significant **development must be centralized**, a requirement that is difficult to enforce in today's distributed computing environment.

- It's **very difficult to execute as described**. Studies show that the stages rarely begin on schedule and almost never terminate when they're supposed to. Often as not, new requirements are being established even as parts of a program are undergoing final testing.

- It **takes too long**, requiring months or years to develop an application. The majority of applications are obsolete by the time they are delivered.

Compressing Development Time

Objects can alleviate some of these problems, but they can't really solve them. Consider the problem of speed. Suppose for the sake of argument that object technology was so good that it cut programming time to zero — just think up the design and the software is done. Unfortunately, implementation typically takes up no more than about 20 percent of the software development life cycle, so the miracle of instantaneous coding would shave only 20 percent off the total development time.

Objects can't solve all these problems

Let's push the argument further. Imagine that object technology not only eliminates all programming time but also shaves a third off of all the other stages by lowering the barriers between them. A quick bit of math reveals that we would still get less than a 50 percent reduction in total development time. That would take an 18-month development time and reduce it to around 10 months.

The best time reduction might be 50 percent

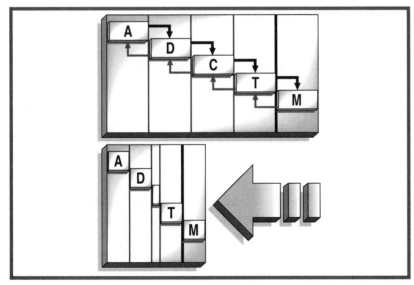

Compressing the Waterfall

That's not good enough	If realizable, a 50 percent reduction in development time would certainly be a major improvement. But it wouldn't be good enough to get us out of the software development crisis. For this, we need order-of-magnitude improvements not just in coding time, but also in the total development life cycle. We need to get that 18 months down to a month or two at most.
How do we get a 10:1 improvement?	How do we get a 10:1 compression of the software life cycle without making a total shambles of it? We can't collapse all the stages by 90 percent without creating chaos. On the other hand, we can't skip any stages without reducing the development process to mere hacking. The waterfall method was developed out of hard experience, and every step in it is essential to building quality software.
We need to look deeper for a solution	What we need is an alternative to the waterfall approach that preserves all of its good qualities yet overcomes its increasingly apparent limitations. Switching to object technology will not, in itself, provide that result. We need to look deeper into the way software is constructed to find a solution to this dilemma.

Rethinking the Goal of Software Development

We need to rethink our goals	Finding an answer to the development dilemma requires that we rethink the goals that led to the traditional development methodology. If we can identify a better goal, we may be able to figure out how to fix the methodology.
The goal has always been a monolithic application	Throughout the history of programming, the goal of software development has always been the monolithic application—a closed, self-contained software system that is created from scratch to respond to a specific set of application requirements.

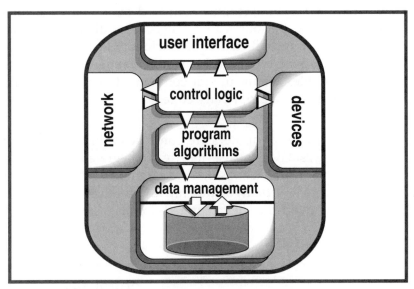

The Monolithic Application

This was a reasonable goal 40 years ago, but it no longer makes sense in today's computing environment. Much has changed in those 40 years, not the least of which is the advent of object technology, and it is time to rethink our goals in light of those developments. As Mitch Kapor put it:

It's time to rethink that goal

> If we had object-oriented applications, there would be a different application ecology. It would mean the end of the era of monolithic applications. (Quoted in Winblad, Edwards, and King, Object-Oriented Software: Addison-Wesley, 1990, p. 4.)

LAYERED SOFTWARE DEVELOPMENT
Layered Development of Hardware

The way computers are built has changed dramatically in the last 40 years. They, too, were once monolithic creations built from scratch to serve a specific set of needs. In most cases, this is no longer true.

Computers were once monolithic machines

Now they are designed from existing components

When computer manufacturers want to design a new machine today, they don't start out with a collection of diodes, resistors, and transistors, then build a unique machine from the chassis up. Rather, they assemble the machine from standard components wherever possible, creating unique components only when doing so would give them a proprietary edge.

Computers are built up in layers

In most cases, new computers are constructed in three distinct layers. The lowest layer consists mostly of integrated circuits, collections of low-level functions that are assembled into a standard package or "chip." Virtually all the chips a computer maker would use are standard, off-the-shelf itegrated circuits (ICs), selected out of a catalog.

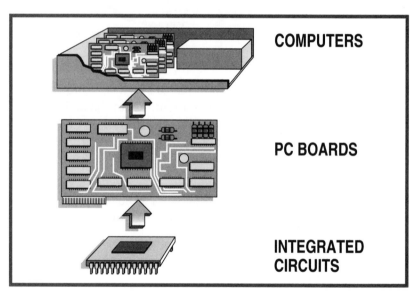

Layered Hardware Construction

Each layer uses standard components

The next layer is the printed circuit board. Typically, computer manufacturers create at least one of these boards working from standard chips, but the rest are usually standard, off-the-shelf boards that carry out specific functions. The highest layer is the computer itself, which is an assemblage of boards and other high-level hardware such as power supplies and disk drives.

This final package is not a closed, fixed system. Closed hardware systems were once the norm, at least for personal computers, but buyers overwhelmingly rejected that approach. The clear choice of the marketplace was an *open* system in which end users could adapt their machines to their own needs by adding new boards and devices.

The final system is open to modification

This process of designing new computers differs from the way software is presently constructed in some very important ways:

This is very different from software

- **The goal is different.** Where software vendors create monolithic, closed systems, hardware vendors build modular, open systems.

- **The architecture is different.** Where software vendors use highly interconnected program components with little or no layering, hardware vendors use a loosely coupled collection of modules that interact on three distinct levels.

- **The process is different.** Where software vendors build virtually all their components from scratch for each program, hardware vendors buy standard components wherever possible and build their own components only when they can gain a proprietary advantage.

- **The result is different.** Where software vendors usually produce unreliable, rigid systems that are suited only for specific applications, hardware vendors produce robust, modifiable systems that can support a virtually infinite range of applications.

Building Software Like Hardware

Clearly, the hardware approach has some powerful advantages. It offers far more reliable, adaptable functionality while getting maximum reuse out of existing components. The results are better for everyone, from the vendor to the reseller to the end user.

The hardware approach is much better

Software vendors have tried to close the gap

This embarrassing contrast has not been lost on software vendors, who have often envied the hardware vendors' advantages. There even have been some attempts to emulate hardware construction in software, but the basic technology hasn't been up to the task.

Object technology can provide the required tools

Object technology offers a new opportunity to move software out of the era of monolithic applications, as Kapor puts it, and to begin to emulate some of the successes of hardware. Using this technology, we can take a layered approach to software development, using standard components wherever possible in each layer.

We consider a three-layered model

In the approach considered here, we assume there are three layers, just as with hardware. The layers are *classes, models,* and *applications.* But there's nothing magical about three layers; it's certainly possible to use four or more layers, particularly with larger systems. However, a three-layered model is sufficient to convey the basic ideas.

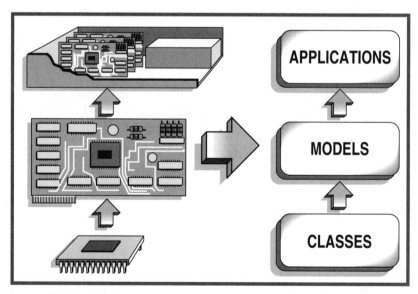

Layered Software Development

Layer 1: Classes

The lowest level of software in this approach is made up of classes that offer standard packages of functionality. These are comparable to the integrated circuits that make up the lowest level of hardware, and they are sometimes called "software ICs" by analogy.

Layer 1 consists of standard classes

The accompanying illustration shows a few examples of the kinds of reusable classes that will form the foundation of future information systems. Some of these are very simple classes. Others, such as the bill of materials, might be deeply nested composite objects containing thousands of component objects.

Classes can reflect business objects

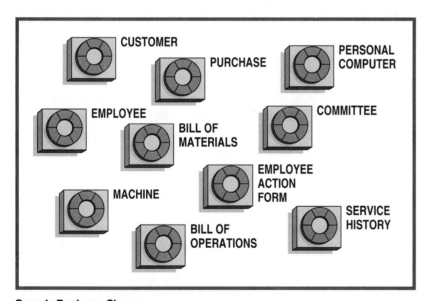

Sample Business Classes

Layer 2: Models

The intermediate layer is made up of reusable models of business operations. Just as printed circuit boards handle such basic functions as printing and display control, business models handle routine business functions such as purchasing, inventory control, and customer billing.

Layer 2 provides reusable models

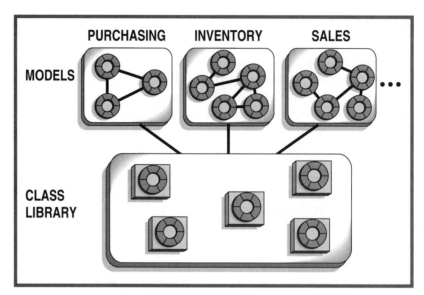

Examples of Models

Intermediate layers maximize reuse

The use of intermediate layers is not yet a universal practice in object development, but many companies are turning to it because it allows many different applications to be built on the same basic structures. As the case studies in Chapter 12 illustrate, the use of business models is especially prevalent in full-scale information systems.

They also increase stability

Also, since reporting and control requirements typically change faster than basic business operations, building separate models to handle routine operations can make information systems more stable. This contrasts sharply with monolithic systems that bind together knowledge of every level, from basic computing resources to immediate business needs. If there is a change at any of these levels, a monolithic application has to be rebuilt.

Layer 3: Applications

The top layer contains the actual applications

The top layer in a layered system consists of the actual applications that fulfill current business needs. This is the code that performs inventory aging analyses, prints out inventory reports, and performs other business tasks.

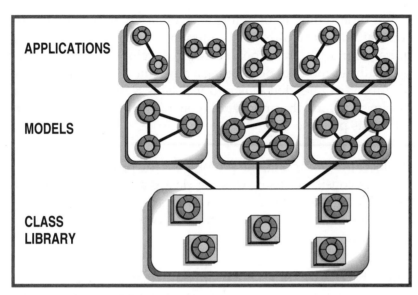

Applications on the Models

These applications are very different from traditional, monolithic applications. Most important, they require very little new development. Just as a computer is mostly an assemblage of existing PC boards, object applications may be no more than new ways of exercising existing business models.

These differ from monolithic applications

Also, these applications are largely independent of the details of how the business functions. For example, if a company changes the way it tracks customer addresses and does its mailings, the applications that depend on these activities would normally adjust to the new procedures without requiring manual modifications.

They are independent of underlying models

RAPID PROTOTYPING
A New Kind of Prototyping

Because applications require relatively little new construction in the layered approach, they typically can be generated and deployed very quickly in comparison to traditional, monolithic applications. Assembling new applications is accomplished through a process known as *rapid prototyping*.

Applications are built through rapid prototyping

This is not traditional prototyping

Rapid prototyping is an unfortunate choice of terms because the word *prototyping* is already in common use and means something quite different. In traditional software development, prototyping is usually a process of developing a quick mock-up of the product to convey its intended look and feel. This is usually done at the design stage, and the prototype is generally thrown away once it's served its purpose.

Object prototypes are real programs

In object programming, the prototype *is* the program. Rapid prototyping consists of using existing classes and models to quickly assemble a working version of the program. That working version is then extended and refined until it fills the stated business requirements.

They are rarely thrown away

Object-based prototypes rarely are thrown away. Object-oriented software is sufficiently malleable that even relatively deep design decisions can usually be revised without reconstruction, allowing an early sketch of a solution to evolve gracefully into a polished application.

They can be assembled quickly

As the next illustration suggests, object-based applications can usually be developed very quickly. In fact, if a company has a solid foundation of classes and models to build on, complete working systems can often be delivered in less time than it would take to complete a traditional requirements analysis.

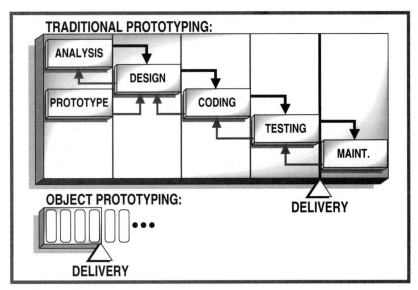

A New Kind of Prototyping

Even after making the transition from prototype to production system, an object-oriented application can keep on growing. As the business needs change, the application continues to evolve to meet those needs — without going back through the entire development life cycle. This capacity for evolutionary change is a valued advantage of object technology.

Object prototypes continue to evolve

The Benefits of Rapid Prototyping

To summarize, rapid prototyping has some important advantages over traditional software development:

Rapid prototyping has advantages

- **Rapid prototyping is fast.** Given that the required classes and models are in place, applications can often be generated up to ten times faster than traditional programs.

- **Development is more flexible.** A small team of managers and prototypers working together can conceive, design, and build the application interactively, shaping it as they go. With this partnership, the delivered system is virtually guaranteed to meet the business requirements.

- **Prototypes are easily extended.** Because an object-oriented application uses a relatively small collection of code compared to a monolithic application, it is easily modified to meet changing needs.

The speed comes from what isn't done

It's important to emphasize that the increase in speed gained from rapid prototyping doesn't come from doing anything faster. Instead, the speed is gained by doing less. Given all the groundwork that's already been laid, the final application takes only a fraction of the code of a full, monolithic application. So the speed advantage comes not from working faster but from doing less.

Maintaining Traditional Controls

Rapid prototyping can be dangerous

Rapid prototyping is an important advance in software development, but it is not without its dangers. Improperly managed, rapid prototyping can quickly degrade into a form of hacking that is often referred to as "rabid prototyping." It is generally so easy to add new functionality to object-oriented prototypes that end users rapidly escalate their demands, a problem that is vividly portrayed in two of the case studies in Chapter 12.

Rapid prototyping still needs controls

The solution to this problem is, of course, to maintain the same management controls over software development that we have in the past. But this conclusion brings us right back to the fundamental dilemma we began with: We can't afford to skip any of the stages in the traditional software life cycle, but we can't afford the time it normally takes to move a project through all these laborious stages.

These controls are all preserved

Here is where layered software development shows its real strength. With layered development, all the traditional controls can be preserved, and they can work more effectively than ever before. The trick is simply to replicate them at every level of development:

- The **development of every class requires all the traditional stages** of analysis, design, implementation, testing, and maintenance to ensure that they include the right functionality, construct the class correctly, and so on. These steps may occur very quickly when only a single class is involved, but all of them are essential.

- Similarly, **model builders must go through the entire life cycle** as well, assuring that their models meet business requirements and are properly designed, implemented, tested, and maintained.

- **Each prototype must go through these same stages,** and it may do so many times as the prototype is revised and enhanced. But because so much work has already been done at the lower levels, the process is very rapid.

In short, all the traditional controls are preserved in this new methodology. Instead of being applied to a monolithic application, however, they are "miniaturized" and replicated at every layer in a layered object architecture.

Controls are replicated at every level

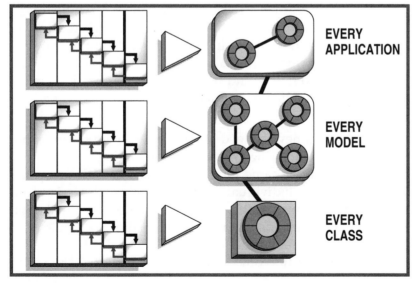

Controls at Every Level

All the stages are reused

Here, then, lies the resolution to the dilemma of realizing order-of-magnitude benefits while maintaining traditional controls. We are not just reusing code. We are reusing analysis, design, testing, and maintenance as well. *All* stages of the development cycle are reused, so all of them are compressed by the same factor.

MAXIMIZING REUSABILITY
An Industrial Revolution for Software

The Industrial Revolution is a useful analogy

The essence of object technology is the construction of new software out of standard, existing components. Brad Cox has compared the shift to this new kind of construction to the Industrial Revolution that led to the modern method of manufacturing (*Object-Oriented Programming: An Evolutionary Approach*: Addison-Wesley, 1986). The comparison is useful in providing a context for understanding both the magnitude of the transition involved and the long-term benefits that could be realized.

Products used to be handcrafted

Two hundred years ago, all products were crafted by hand, starting with the most basic raw materials. A gunsmith, for example, would create all his own screws out of rod stock, carefully threading each individual screw uniquely to fit its location in the finished weapon. As you might imagine, this was a painfully slow and expensive way to make rifles. It was also hard to control the quality of the finished goods, and the lack of standardization made it very difficult to maintain products in the field.

Eli Whitney changed all that

Inventor Eli Whitney changed all this in 1798 with the invention of modern manufacturing. Instead of handcrafting products from raw materials, these same products were assembled from standard components. Individual specialists made each kind of component, and all components were carefully checked to make sure they met rigorous standards for form and quality. The result: Products were created faster and less expensively; quality became more consistent; and repairs could be made easily in the field by replacing standard components.

Over time, as Whitney's new method caught on, the creation of standard components spawned an entire new industry. Instead of each manufacturer making its own screws, new companies arose that specialized in making screws in a variety of standard shapes and sizes. This development simplified the manufacturing process even further because manufacturers of finished goods could buy many of their components rather than fabricating them in-house.

A new industry was created

Today, the idea of handcrafting complex products seems ludicrous given our understanding of modern manufacturing techniques. Yet that is precisely how we continue to build complex software systems. Viewed in this light, the move to object technology is, in effect, an attempt to bring about an industrial revolution for software. The goal is to assemble software out of standard components (rather than handcrafted pieces) that are purchased from outside vendors whenever possible.

The same changes are happening in software

Making this transition requires a whole new way of thinking about software. That is why the shift to object technology is often referred to as a *paradigm shift*. A paradigm is simply an established way of thinking and acting in a given context; a paradigm shift is what happens when that set of ideas is displaced by a new one. The transition from handcrafting to manufacturing 200 years ago was a paradigm shift that transformed society. Although the jury is still out, it is quite possible that the transition from handcrafting software to programming by assembly will have a comparable impact on how we view software and information systems.

Object technology is a new paradigm

Sources of Reusable Classes

The idea of building software out of standard, reusable classes raises an important question: Where do these classes come from? Many companies assume they will have to build all the classes themselves, but that shouldn't ordinarily be the case. These classes can come from three different sources:

Reusable classes can come from three sources

- **Language vendors** often include an extensive array of classes as part of their language offerings. Smalltalk is the best example of this.

- In other cases, these classes are **developed in-house** by companies using object technology.

- Increasingly, however, reusable classes are being purchased from software development companies known as **class vendors**.

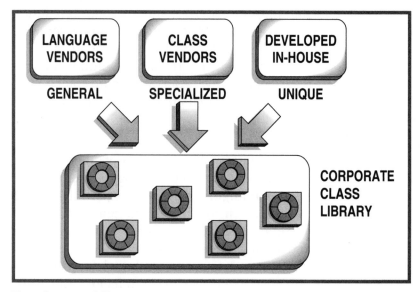

Three Sources of Classes

Class vendors will be important

Just as modern manufacturing created a new industry for components suppliers, object technology is spawning a new type of company called a *class vendor*. Within the next decade, standard commercial classes should be available for a broad range of applications. By that time, application developers will typically do very little programming of new classes. Just as computer designers create new chips only when they can gain a proprietary advantage, programmers will develop their own classes only for specialized functionality that reflects unique aspects of their business.

The commercialization of standard, application-level classes faces many obstacles, and some advocates of object technology are disappointed that the class-vendor business is still in its infancy. However, supporting industries always take years to develop. It's a chicken-and-egg problem: The demand for classes has to be great enough to support corporations who do nothing but create and sell classes, yet wholesale conversion to object technology depends in part on the availability of commercial classes.

There aren't many class vendors yet

The natural solution to this problem is to follow the example of the Industrial Revolution, creating standardized components in-house and then gradually converting to external vendors as they become viable.

But that shouldn't hold up the process

Leveraging Business Models

Business models are very important to maximizing reusability. It's a big jump from base classes to end-user applications, a jump that can be bridged only by creating new classes. Every class that's invented to solve a single application problem runs counter to the goal of reuseability. Ideally, all of these intermediate-level classes should be reusable as well. Business models make this possible.

Business models are vital

Here's a concrete illustration of the value of modeling. Suppose a company builds a program to handle accounts receivable. This company has adopted object technology, so it reuses existing base classes for customers, bills, and other fundamental elements. But it must to develop many new classes to build the accounts receivable program.

Example: An accounts receivable program

Now let's imagine that the marketing department decides to do regular mailings to the company's customers. The accounts receivable program already mails invoices to customers, so marketing would like to use that program to handle its mailings as well. But the accounts receivable program wasn't designed to handle anything other than invoices and overdue notices. It can't be extended to do new kinds of mailings without being significantly redesigned.

This program can't be used for mailings

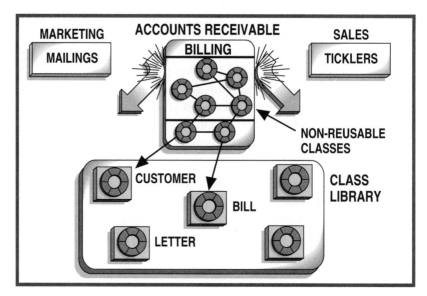

A Traditional Accounts Receivable Program

*Nor can it be used
for sales reminders*

Let's up the ante. Suppose the sales department decides it wants to have automatic reminders from accounting whenever customers change their buying patterns or have some other change in status that would suggest cross-selling opportunities. The accounts receivable package has all the right information, but it wasn't designed to serve this need. Again, a major redesign would be required.

*The model is there,
but it's hidden*

The irony of this situation is that the accounts receivable program contains an implicit model of customers, their buying history, and their financial interactions with the company. The problem is that that model is not explicit, and it's not available outside the program.

Let's make the model explicit and accessible using an intermediate layer in the system. At the lowest level, we have the same reusable classes for customers, bills, letters, and other common objects. At the next level, we have a model of the interactions with our customers. Being a separate layer, this model can be used by many different applications for many different purposes.

Here's how a separate model would look

At the highest level, we have a variety of simple application programs that address specific operational problems. In fact, these different applications are no more than different ways of using the model. Sending out bills is one way of using the model, and doing marketing mailings is another. Because the model is available to any application that needs it, new applications can be built on top of the model with relative ease.

Applications are just different uses of the model

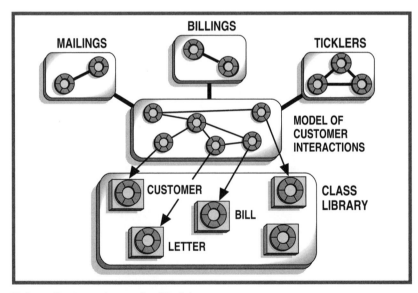

Using a Customer Interaction Model

6

Creating an Object-Oriented Information System

This chapter provides a concrete illustration of an object-oriented information system to show how the methodology described in Chapter 5 can be applied to create more flexible, dynamic systems.

This chapter presents a concrete example

I have, of necessity, kept things fairly simple—otherwise, the example could easily consume the rest of the book. To this end, I focused on design issues and avoided most implementation questions, leaving the discussion of specific tools and their use to the next three chapters. Also, I restricted myself to a model that is just complicated enough to illustrate the essential design principles, but not so complex as to lose anyone in the details.

The example is very simple

I also used simple, generic diagrams to illustrate the system. While the intricate notational systems of some analysis and design methodologies may be useful for larger-scale systems, they would only complicate matters in this example.

I used generic diagrams

GETTING STARTED
The Challenge

The company for this example is a distributor of electronic components. Its selection is fairly arbitrary; we just need a reasonably manageable example to illustrate the basic design principles. Distribution companies have a relatively simple business structure that is readily generalized to more complex operational models.

We are building a system for a distributor

It must be efficient, maintainable, and modifiable

The goal of the effort is to construct an object-based information system for this company using the layered methodology described in the preceding chapter. From the company's point of view, this system should be as efficient, maintainable, and modifiable as possible.

This is not a traditional starting point

By conventional standards, this goal is so oversimplified as to be virtually useless for starting system development work. We haven't said anything about what kinds of data we need to manage or what types of end-user problems we have to solve, nor have we wrestled with any of the other decisions that usually precede a software development effort.

But it's correct for the methodology

We aren't skipping essential steps here. This is, in fact, the right level at which to start the project. Certainly with more complex systems it would help to anticipate the demands that some of the applications will place on the system, but these considerations should not be the driving force behind the design of the system. With the layered approach to software, you don't build systems to solve specific problems — you build them to solve a wide range of problems. Since you can't anticipate every problem a system may have to solve in the future, you want to make it as flexible and general purpose as possible.

The Plan of Attack

We start by building a model

In keeping with methodology described in the preceding chapter, we will build the system in three distinct layers: classes, models, and applications. However, we won't construct the layers in quite that order. The overall model of the business is the driving force, so we will start with the model and develop both upward and downward from there. The actual sequence we will follow is:

1. **Develop a model** of the business that identifies the required objects and their relationships to each other.

2. **Design the classes** to support these objects and fulfill their responsibilities within the model.

3. **Build applications** on top of the model using rapid prototyping.

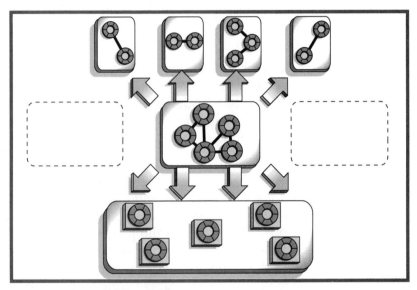

Building from the Model Outward

In our example, we will build a single model to represent the entire enterprise. We can do this because the example is so simple. But don't be misled into thinking this is the right way to proceed with large-scale systems.

We will use a single model for this example

In a real development situation there would be a large number of models, each describing a different aspect of the business. For example, there might be models of sales, purchasing, manufacturing, personnel management, and customer service. These models would provide large-scale modularity in that each could be developed and modified independently. Woven together through high-level, message-based interactions, these component models would form an overall working model of the enterprise.

Normally there would be many models

Classes and applications follow from the model

Once the model has taken form and defined the roles played by the various objects, we can drop down a level and start defining the internals of these objects. After we get the classes working and tested, we can plug them together and actually run the model to see how it works. Once we are satisfied that we have a realistic working model of the company, we can begin prototyping applications on top of this model.

In practice, this process is iterative

This sequence sounds quite linear, but in practice it's highly iterative. We don't really expect the model or its underlying classes to be correct on the first pass. We define the classes by the roles they play in models, but the needs of new applications will change the requirements for the models, which may call for revisions of the classes, and so on.

The goal is to stabilize the model quickly

This iteration is not only normal, it's essential to building a good system because it allows models and classes to evolve in response to real-world demands. The important thing is to strive to make the design as generic as possible at each iteration. Classes and models that are created to solve particular application problems usually have to be reworked considerably before they can be reused. On the other hand, classes and models that are direct, unbiased descriptions of the operations of the business generally stabilize fairly quickly and provide maximum reuse in building applications.

DESIGNING THE MODEL
The Basic Business Cycle

The starting point is the business cycle

We start the design process by examining the basic business cycle for the company. At the broadest level, this cycle consists of the following three steps:

1. Buy products from various suppliers.

2. Maintain an inventory adequate to meet the anticipated demand for these products.

3. Sell the products to corporate customers.

Now we must translate this business cycle into software. The most obvious way to do this—the way that years of experience tell us is the only correct way — is to start decomposing the overall cycle into component processes. But that path will never lead us to objects. It will only lead to smaller and smaller processes.

Functional decomposition is a false start

Functional decomposition doesn't lead us to objects because it focuses on operations, which are typically expressed as verbs. We need to look for objects, which usually appear as nouns. Then we figure out how these objects interact to produce the operations of the company.

Object design begins with nouns

Finding the Basic Objects

When we look at the description of the business cycle and highlight the nouns, we get the following:

Here are the nouns in the description

1. Buy **products** from various **suppliers.**
2. Maintain an **inventory** adequate to meet the anticipated **demand** for these **products.**
3. Sell the **products** to corporate **customers**.

We obviously have five candidate objects for our system: products, suppliers, inventory, demand, and customers. It isn't immediately clear whether all of these are objects, and it's a sure bet that we don't have all the objects we need yet. But we have a place to start.

We have five candidate objects

The best way to see which of these candidates qualify as objects is to draw a rough diagram of the business cycle and see which of the names pop up. This is actually the initial step in building a working model. The following illustration shows a first pass.

Here's how some of them fit together

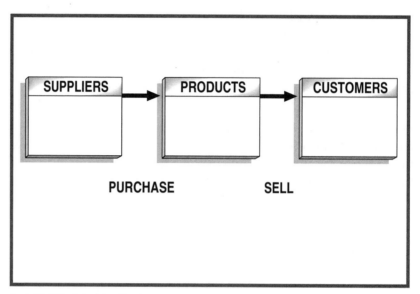

An Initial Model of the Business

*A couple of candi-
dates don't appear yet*

Only three of our candidate objects appear in the initial diagram. Two are missing:

1. There is no obvious place for *demand* yet. That's not a concern—depending on its importance and role, it may appear as an object later, it could be a variable within an object, or it might not enter into the model at all.

2. We have no object for *inventory*. Tracking inventory is obviously critical to the model, so we have to find a place for it. But the term actually refers to the *products* the company has on hand, which are already in the model. So in one sense, inventory *is* in the model. This ambiguity will be resolved shortly.

Identifying Additional Objects

*We need to identify
more objects*

This is a start, but we clearly need more objects than this to model the business cycle. Are there other aspects of the cycle that suggest additional objects?

I drew some arrows in my sketch and called them "purchase" and "sell." These aren't nouns, so we didn't pick them up as objects on the first pass. But do objects always have to be nouns? Can verbs qualify?

What about "purchase" and "sell"?

Obviously, we are probing a deeper question here, one that goes beyond the superficial distinction between nouns and verbs. What we'd really like are some criteria to help us decide when something should be represented as an object as opposed to a method or a variable within an object.

We need criteria for recognizing objects

Here are some suggested criteria for recognizing objects. As a rule, if a candidate object meets two or more of these criteria, it's probably best to represent it as an object:

Here are some suggested criteria

- It **can be viewed as a thing** (noun) even if it's expressed as a verb.

- It **contains information** of some kind.

- It **has procedures** associated with it.

- It **has special cases**, or is likely to in the future.

- It **shares properties with other potential objects**, such that it might be a special case of some higher-level class.

- It **contains things that are already defined as objects**.

Let's look at the verb "purchase" in this light. Note as we tick off the criteria that the same conclusion applies to "sell" in each case if we change this verb to the noun "sale."

We apply these criteria to "purchase"

- "Purchase" can certainly be viewed as a noun; it's a type of transaction between two parties.

- A record of a purchase would normally contain a fair amount of information about the purchaser, seller, items purchased, quantities, selling amount, sale date, and other particulars.

- Purchases have a fair number of procedures associated with them. These include recording the purchase, calculating the amount due, logging the date and type of payment, and similar operations.

- We can readily imagine special kinds of purchases, such as cash or credit purchases, standing orders, and special orders. We may not need these special types now, but the possibility for specialization certainly exists.

- A purchase is a kind of transaction. If it turns out that we have other transactions in our systems (a sale is certainly a candidate), a purchase may well turn out to be a special case of a higher-level class.

- Purchases will naturally include a list of products purchased. We have already decided that products are going to be represented as objects, so purchases are definitely going to contain objects as components.

So purchases and sales qualify as objects

In short, "purchase" qualifies as an object on every single criterion, and "sale" also qualifies on all counts. When we add these new objects to our sketch, we have a design that looks something like the following illustration.

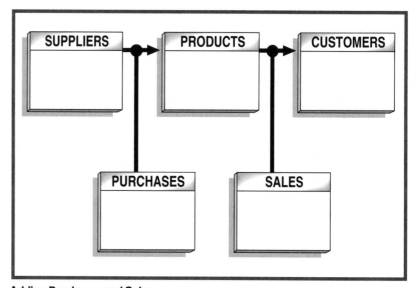

Adding Purchases and Sales

Introducing Collections

We now have five basic objects with which to build our model, and they all have something curious in common—they all appear in the plural form. That's because we're dealing not just with a single object in each case, but with groups or collections of objects. The next step in building the model is to figure out how to handle multiple objects in each box of our diagram.

All our objects seem to be plural

This problem is easy to solve with object technology. Objects can "contain" other objects, so it's not hard to build an object that's dedicated to containing collections of similar objects.

We let objects contain other objects

In fact, in virtually all object languages there are standard classes, called *collection classes*, which are dedicated to performing this service. These classes have methods for storing a variable number of similar items, retrieving specific items from the store, adding new items, and so on. The items themselves are typically objects, but they may be simpler data types such as names or numbers in some languages.

Collection classes do just that

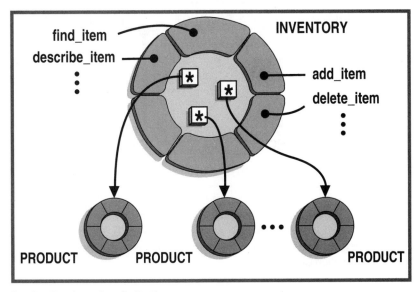

Storing Products in a Collection

We just create instances of the collection class

To build a collection, then, we only need to create a new instance of an existing collection class. This new collection object then takes care of all the details of storing objects, sorting them, retrieving them, and so on. The code is already written for us and the variables are all set up. We can create the collection and initialize it using no more than a single instruction. Once created, the collection is totally self-managing.

Using Collections in the Design

Here's how to add collections

Let's put collections to work in our model. We need five different collection objects: *suppliers, purchases, inventory, sales,* and *customers.* Notice that in all but one case I named the collection using the plural form of the objects it will contain. This convention makes it easy to remember what's in the container. The only exception is *inventory,* which is a more precise term for the collection of objects currently on hand for immediate sale.

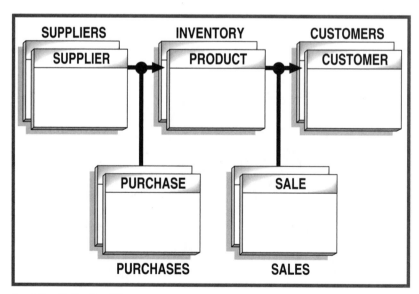

Applying Collection Classes

When using collections, it's important not to confuse the collection object with the objects it contains. If you wanted a list of all the products currently in inventory, you would ask the *inventory* object to give you that list. If you wanted to know the current values of all the products in the inventory, you would have to ask each of the *product* objects in turn to report its value. The *inventory* object knows only how to manage collections; it knows little or nothing about the objects it contains.

A collection is just a smart container

In fact, it's a key element of good design that the *inventory* object be smart about collections but ignorant of its contents. That's what allows a single *collection* class to provide containers for any kind of object without requiring modification or subclassing.

This is good, modular design

ASSIGNING RESPONSIBILITIES
An Approach to Designing Classes

Our model of the business is still pretty rough, but it provides enough guidance that we can begin to design the classes we've identified so far. We will assume that we don't need to do anything about the collection class because it's already provided. That leaves us free to concentrate on the actual business objects.

We now know enough to define classes

We have several options in designing our classes. One approach would be to start by thinking about the kinds of information each object will have to contain, then derive methods for managing this information. That would be a natural approach from a database perspective.

We could define classes according to their data

Alternatively, we could start with the methods and then develop the data structures to support these methods. This approach would probably feel more natural for application developers, who are accustomed to modularizing software based on functionality.

Or we could define them by their methods

Neither of these approaches is optimal

While both of these approaches are viable, neither of them is likely to produce optimal class definitions. Each biases class design along traditional lines, often leading to classes based on data-flow analysis on the one hand or functional decomposition on the other. Worse yet, both plunge into the internals of objects much too quickly.

We need to consider objects as integral wholes

A much more effective approach is to consider each object as an independent, self-managing entity. As such, it carries out a set of assigned tasks. Our first job is to define those tasks for each of the various objects, without being concerned with the internal structure of the objects.

This is essential to information hiding

This is, after all, the essence of object technology; objects hide their own internals through encapsulation, leaving these internals free to change over time without disrupting other objects. Given this principle, violating encapsulation and defining classes in terms of their internal structure would hardly be the best way to start off.

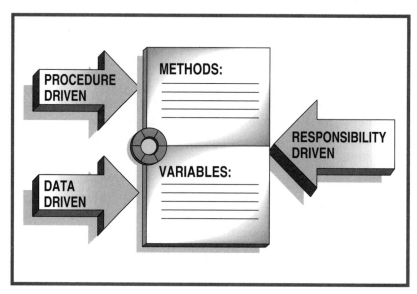

Three Approaches to Designing Classes

The general approach we take here is known as *responsibility-driven design*. The most authoritative text on this approach is by Wirfs-Brock, Wilkerson, and Wiener (*Designing Object-Oriented Software*: Prentice Hall, 1990), who provide detailed techniques for each stage of the process. The approach illustrated here is loosely based on their techniques but is highly simplified.

We will use responsibility-driven design

In responsibility-driven design, we determine what the responsibilities are for each class by clarifying the role that each plays in the model. Our goal is to make the model work based on each class fulfilling its responsibilities. Only when we have achieved that goal is it time to begin looking at the internals of the classes.

This approach defines objects from the outside in

The Responsibilities of Product Objects

For example, let's consider the responsibilities of a product object within our distribution system. At the very least, a product should know certain things about itself, such as its part number, type, package quantity, current price, shipping weight, package dimensions, and stock on hand. It should also be able to report this information on demand and to modify it as requested.

Example: Product objects

There are some other things you might want product objects to know about themselves. A product could keep track of where and when it was purchased, how much it cost, and how long it has been held in inventory. At first these responsibilities may seem to make sense, but on reflection they reveal an ambiguity in just what the term "product" means in our system.

"Product" is an ambiguous term

Is it a type of component or a individual component?

On the one hand, we might want to define a "product" to represent a single physical object, such as an individual math coprocessor. In this case, it would make sense for the object to know where and when it was purchased. Alternatively, a "product" could be defined as a generic type of component, such as "80287 math coprocessor." By this definition, it would make sense to track the current number of 80287's in stock, but not to store when each one was purchased, because there would be no representation of individual coprocessors in this model.

This is a design decision

There is no overall right answer to resolving this ambiguity. It's a design decision that depends on how you want your system to work. If we were dealing with cars and trucks, which have serial numbers and exhibit individual characteristics, it would make sense to define a unique instance for each car and truck we handled. But with electronic components, there could be hundreds of thousands of equivalent, nonserialized products, so it wouldn't be very helpful or efficient to create an instance for each and every one of them. Accordingly, we will consider "product" to mean a particular *kind* of electronic component, not an *individual* component per se.

Responsibilities clarify roles

Note that thinking through this object's responsibilities helped us clarify what a product object actually represents. This is one of the benefits of the responsibility-driven approach. It forces clarity in our thinking before we can begin to design or code conflicting characteristics into a class.

Here are the responsibilities

Given our choice, the following illustration is a reasonable allocation of responsibilities to the product object:

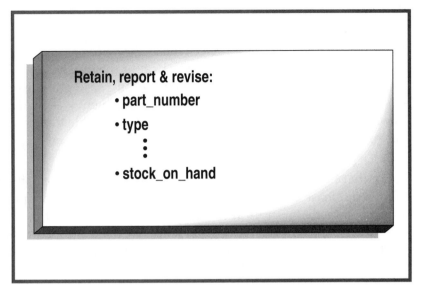

Retain, report & revise:
- part_number
- type
- stock_on_hand

Responsibilities of a Product Object

Responsibilities for Purchase Objects

All the responsibilities we identified for product objects have to do with information management. There is hardly any process here at all. That's largely a result of the object we chose—products aren't responsible for carrying out many processes in our system. If we consider a purchase object, however, we get a very different result.

Product objects don't do much

What should a purchase object be responsible for? This object represents an individual transaction in which some quantity of a product is ordered from a supplier, subsequently received, and then paid for. Clearly, there are many opportunities for processing operations here.

Purchase objects are much more active

They contain much information

Let's deal with the informational aspect first. A purchase object has to manage a variety of data: type and amount of product purchased, the supplier used for the purchase, the price per unit, any discounts applied, the total extended price for the purchase, and the dates for such key events as when the purchase order was issued, when delivery was taken, and when payment was made. As with product objects, purchase objects must be able to record this information, retain it over time, and report it on request.

This information implies new objects

Notice that in describing some of the informational responsibilities of a purchase object, several new nouns popped up, a couple of which immediately appear to satisfy the criteria for objecthood: namely, "purchase order" and "payment." We mark these as candidates for objects to add to the system if needed when we design the internals of purchase objects.

Objects should be self-managing

On the processing side, purchase objects should be as self-managing as possible. If we opt to make them passive containers of data, then we are going to have to create higher-level objects that operate on purchase objects to make them do things. But that's a dangerous path; if we continue along those lines, eventually we will reach a program called "main" that contains all the intelligence of the system.

Purchase objects model a complete transaction

Part of the spirit of object technology is to distribute intelligence as much as possible so that objects can interact with each other directly, without the benefit of an overall "control" program. In fact, one of the benefits of responsibility-driven design is that it encourages us to delegate responsibilities throughout a system rather than centralizing them in one place. So we want to build as much self-management into the purchase object as we can. This is, after all, the object that captures the critical information about a multi-step transaction.

In order to manage the complete transaction, a purchase object must know what state it is in at any given time and have methods for moving the transaction from state to state. Suppose there are five states any given purchase moves through: request for a purchase, approval of the purchase, issuance of a PO, receipt of the order, and payment for the order.

This involves maintaining state information

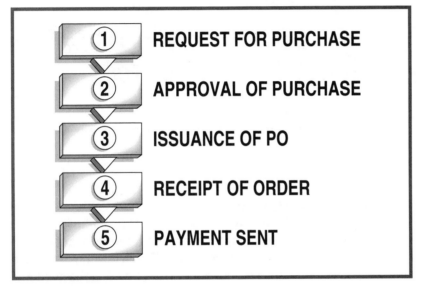

A Five-Step Purchase Cycle

To make this idea of self-management more concrete, imagine that a user selects a menu item to request that a purchase be initiated. This selection would trigger a message to the purchase class to create a new instance of this class, giving us a new purchase object to work with. During the initialization of this object control would pass to it, and it would immediately put up an input screen to get the required information about the purchase from the user.

Here's the actual sequence of events

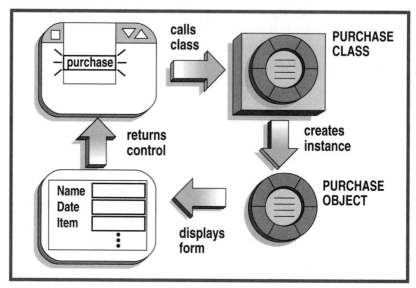

The Birth of an Object

The object would be fully self-managing

Once all the necessary information had been gathered, the purchase object would strive to move through its five stages as efficiently as possible. First it would seek the approval of someone with the required signature authority, then it would print out the approved purchase order or send it via EDI (electronic data interchange), and so on. Once the merchandise had been received and checked, the purchase object would simply count days until the term of the PO had expired and then cut a check.

Here are the responsibilities

In sum, the responsibilities of a purchase object would be roughly as shown.

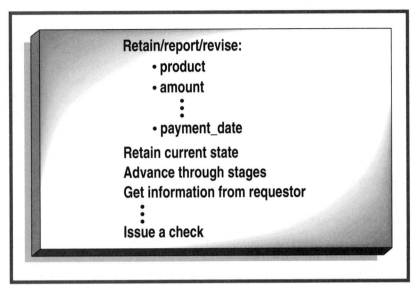

Retain/report/revise:
- **product**
- **amount**

⋮

- **payment_date**

Retain current state
Advance through stages
Get information from requestor

⋮

Issue a check

Responsibilities of a Purchase Object

Testing the Allocation of Responsibility

Once the responsibilities have been defined for all the component objects, it's time for an informal walk-through. The goal of this exercise is to see if the model works given the allocation of responsibilities to objects. The best way to conduct the walk-through is to have different people act on behalf of the individual classes, acting out their parts as their responsibilities dictate.

Responsibilities are tested in a walk-through

As each possible scenario is acted out, people tend to identify with their objects and argue over who's responsible for what. When the various debates finally settle down to a state of violent agreement, you know that the responsibilities have been reasonably allocated.

Arguments are to be expected

Incidentally, the originators of responsibility-driven design, Kent Beck and Ward Cunningham, originally developed this technique using old-fashioned index cards to represent objects. Later, they developed a more sophisticated, computerized version of the technique, in which objects could be represented on the screen, moved around, and manipulated in other ways.

This kind of design can be done electronically

But it works much better with people

Unfortunately, the computerized version didn't work very well. It turns out that getting people in a room together and encouraging them to identify their roles with objects in a physical, tangible way is essential. In a typical session, people grab their cards and wave them at each other, rearrange the cards on a table or cork board to show their relationships, walk the cards from place to place to act out transfer of control, and engage in other physical activities not possible with a computer screen.

Defining the Interfaces

Responsibilities structure interfaces

Once responsibilities have been established, the next step is to define the interfaces required for each object to fulfill its responsibilities. In effect, this means we have to define the messages to which an object will respond. This includes creating names for the methods that can be invoked by other objects, deciding what parameters each method will require, and determining what kinds of responses the method will make in response to each message.

Example: Products

For product objects, the message protocols might read something like the following illustration.

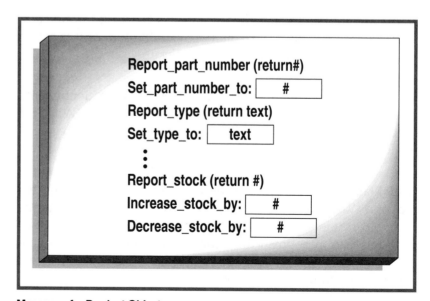

Report_part_number (return#)

Set_part_number_to: `#`

Report_type (return text)

Set_type_to: `text`

⋮

Report_stock (return #)

Increase_stock_by: `#`

Decrease_stock_by: `#`

Messages for Product Objects

The interface for product objects is pretty obvious. That's because a product object is relatively passive. For each type of information it maintains, we need a message to set that information and another to retrieve it. The only exception is tracking the stock on hand. In this case, we are more likely to want to increase or decrease the stock count based on purchases and sales rather than setting it to an arbitrary value, so our interface supports this preference.

The messages for products are obvious

For purchase objects, the interface is much less obvious. The internal functioning of a purchase object is fairly sophisticated. How much of that sophistication must be reflected in the interface? In keeping with the principles of modularity, we want every object to have the simplest possible interface. So the answer is clear: Purchases should hide virtually all of their internal processes. One interface that would do this is shown in the following illustration.

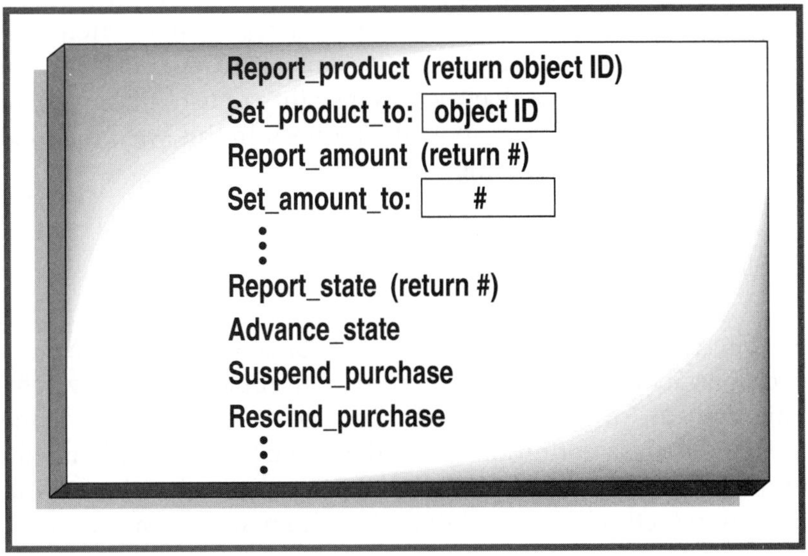

Example: Purchases

Report_product (return object ID)
Set_product_to: object ID
Report_amount (return #)
Set_amount_to: #
⋮
Report_state (return #)
Advance_state
Suspend_purchase
Rescind_purchase
⋮

Messages for Purchase Objects

Purchases hide their internal state

In short, a purchase object can report its current state if asked to do so, and it can be suspended or rescinded if necessary for business reasons. But left to its own devices, it will simply move through its stages in a timely manner with no outside intervention. All that's required is that it receive a periodic message to check its state and take action if appropriate. And in languages that support multi-threaded execution, as described in the next chapter, even this little prod is unnecessary.

These messages define the interface only

The protocols shown above describe only the external interface of the object—they make no assertions about how these interface methods are carried out or what information is stored inside the object. Nor do they rule out the existence of additional methods that are used within the object but aren't part of the interface.

Interfaces are tested by another walk-through

Once the actual interfaces have been defined, most design teams do another walk-through to make sure that each interface fully meets the responsibilities of the object it represents. Often, one person will insist that someone else's object carry out an action that is clearly the other object's responsibility, only to discover that there is no message to support the request. In this way, the final gaps in the interface are filled.

DESIGNING THE CLASSES

It's time to look inside the classes

It is interesting to note how far we have come without making any decisions about the internal structure of the objects in our system. This is ideal for modularization because it assures us that the model and class definitions are independent of the implementation details. However, the time has come to make decisions about the actual methods and variables that will make up each class.

Creating the Classes

Given the work done to this point, designing the internals of the classes requires little more than declaring variables and adding any methods that were not included in the external interface. In the case of methods, we will state the purpose of each method but avoid getting into the actual, language-dependent implementations.

We have to declare variables and methods

The product class is fairly easy to define. None of the information it manages requires recalculation or other complex manipulations, so the natural solution is simply to store it all in variables. Moreover, since the class is relatively passive, it doesn't need any methods other than the ones already declared for the interface. Here, then, is an illustration of the reasonable definition for the product class.

Example: The product class

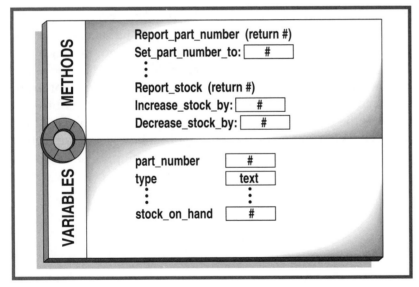

Definition of the Product Class

Persistence is implied

One responsibility of the product object does not appear in this definition—the responsibility to retain the required information over time. This responsibility implies *persistence* of the information from one session to the next, which means it will have to be stored in some external medium when the software is not actually running.

Persistence does not affect the design

We explore alternatives for storing object information in Chapter 8. The important point here is that the need for persistence does not affect our design in any way. Unlike traditional approaches, which have very different techniques for designing databases versus programs, object technology takes the same approach to both persistent and transient objects. This enables developers to concentrate on good design and allow persistence to simply fall out of the design where it's required rather than making arbitrary decisions early in the design process.

Example: The purchase class

In contrast to the product class, the purchase class has a much richer internal structure. In addition to the interface methods defined earlier—generally referred to as *public* methods since they are available to other objects—there are also *private* methods that can only be called by other methods within the object. For example, when a purchase object is activated to advance its progress through the purchasing cycle if it is ready, it will invoke methods to check its current state and attempt to take appropriate action. None of these methods is public because the purchase object is entirely self-managing.

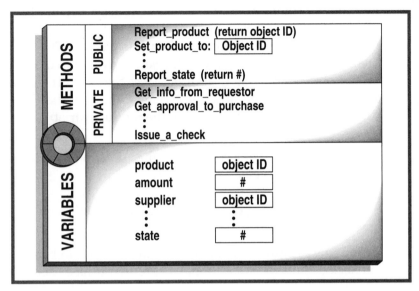

Definition of the Purchase Class

Looking at the data components of the purchase class, we find something new here as well. Purchases refer to other objects in the system. Specifically, each purchase makes reference to a specific product and a particular vendor. How we handle this kind of cross-referencing is a key aspect of object technology.

Purchases reference products and suppliers

Linking Objects Together

One way of making the connection would be to store some text in each purchase object that uniquely specified the supplier. Such text is called a *foreign key*, and it's the basic technique that relational databases use to link entries together.

We could do this with foreign keys

This approach gets the job done, but it requires considerable overhead: You have to store the foreign key in both the purchase object and the supplier object to make the connection between the two; you have to make sure that the key is unique; and you have to search for the key each time you need to make the connection. The first two concerns are largely nuisance factors. The third concern is critical because the search process can be fairly time consuming.

But they carry significant overhead

Object identifiers offer a better alternative	Object technology offers a simpler solution. As described in Chapter 3, every object in an object-oriented system is automatically assigned a unique object identifier when it is created. The existence of object IDs makes it easy to link objects together. In the case of purchase objects, the system simply places the object ID of the appropriate supplier in the supplier variable. Similarly, the object ID for the product ordered is placed in the product variable.
Object IDs have several advantages	Using object IDs to link objects together has several advantages over the use of foreign keys:

- **Selection is automatic.** The programmer doesn't have to invent a new name for every entity in a system.

- **Uniqueness is guaranteed.** The programmer doesn't have to check each new name to make sure that it hasn't been used before.

- **Storage requirements are minimized.** Object IDs usually take up less storage space than foreign keys, which are typically many characters long.

- **Access is fast.** Because object IDs give direct access to the address of another object, retrieval is very quick. There is no need to carry out a search and comparison to match foreign keys against each other.

Object IDs are also content independent	The fact that object IDs are independent of content gives them another important advantage over foreign keys. You can literally change the value of every single variable in an object and the system will still recognize it as the same object. This can be a major advantage if you decide to modify serial numbers or other identifying information.
Here are the actual references	Given these object identifiers, we can actually assemble a complete model of our distribution operation by making the appropriate links among products, suppliers, customers, purchases, and sales. Here is a simplified illustration representing how the model would look, with the basic variables for each class of object filled in along the lines of our previous efforts for products and suppliers.

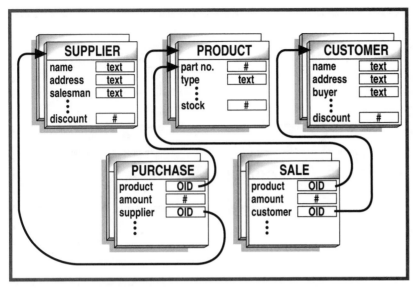

Connections through Object IDs

As you examine this illustration, notice that purchase and sale objects are now different from supplier, product, and customer objects in an important way. Purchases and sales are composite objects because they include, by reference, other objects in the system.

Purchase and sale objects are composite objects

Introducing Abstract Classes

Now that the model is taking shape, let's look at its classes more closely and see if we detect any similarities. It's fairly obvious from the preceding illustration that suppliers and customers are quite similar—there's just one variable that's different, and the corresponding methods show a comparable similarity. By the same token, purchases and sales are also very similar. How can we take advantage of these similarities?

There are similarities among the classes

We define two higher-level classes, or superclasses, of which these classes are special cases, as shown in the illustration.

High-level classes capture similarities

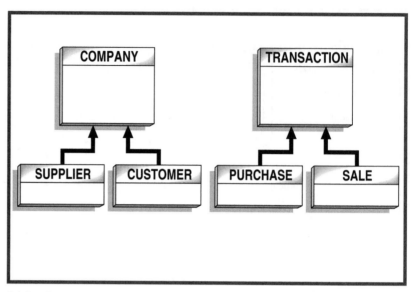

Adding Company and Transaction Classes

These classes have no instances

These new classes, company and transaction, have no instances. That is, any given instance of company would actually be either a supplier or a customer. This, too, is similar to the patterns in nature—there are no instances of the class mammal, just instances of particular kinds of mammals such as wolves, cheetahs, and elephants.

Such classes are called abstract classes

A class that has no instances and is introduced to give structure to existing classes is called an *abstract class*. Basically, abstract classes are used to group other classes and capture information that is common to the group.

Abstract classes can always get instances later

There's no reason why we *couldn't* create instances of these particular classes. For example, we might want to have entries for competitors, potential clients, and other kinds of companies that don't qualify as either suppliers or customers. We could create new subclasses for these, or we could simply assign them all to the company class—it depends on whether we need specialized information and behavior for these new types of companies.

Using Abstract Classes to Advantage

Now let's see how we can use these new abstract classes to advantage. We can put all the variables and methods that are shared by both suppliers and customers up into the company class, where they will be shared by both of the special cases. This eliminates the duplication we would otherwise have, and it makes it much easier to make global changes in these variables later.

We can use abstract classes to eliminate variables

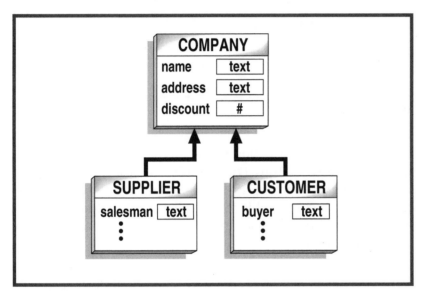

Abstact Class for Companies

Of course, we would do the same thing for transactions, pulling up all the information that is generic to both purchases and sales into the abstract class.

We can do this with transactions as well

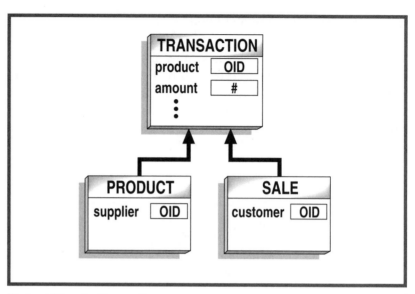

Abstract Class for Transactions

Picking the right level isn't always easy

Knowing which information to elevate to an abstract class may take considerable analysis. For example, the variable and methods for discount were moved up to the company class because they appeared to be comparable for suppliers and customers. But in actuality very different discount schedules and procedures might apply in the two cases.

But decisions are easily reversed

Fortunately, such decisions are easily reversed. If the discount information is different for the two kinds of companies, it can simply be moved back down a level. Given the way inheritance works, no other object in the system will even know that a change has been made. The fact that a message is handled at the level of a supplier or customer rather than at the company level is completely transparent to the sender of that message.

BUILDING APPLICATIONS

Applications put the model to work

At this point, our model of the distribution company is sufficiently complete that we can begin to build some applications on top of it. Let's see how we can apply the model to solve business problems.

In thinking about the kinds of applications we need to build, the most important thing to realize is that the really big applications are already complete within the model. This is one of the great advantages of building business models into object-oriented software.

The big applications are already done

For example, we might decide to start out by building a purchasing program. But we've already built the basic functionality of a purchasing application by creating the right basic objects and having them manage their own affairs. We don't need a master program to accept purchase requests, create purchase orders, cut checks, and the like; purchase objects already do these things for themselves.

Example: A purchasing program

So the applications we build will necessarily be small and simple, addressing very specific needs that are not handled directly in the model.

Applications are small and light

Performing Routine Maintenance

Most of what we might think of as application functionality involves adding a user interface to interact with the model in appropriate ways. For example, to use our system, we need to be able to add new suppliers, customers, and products. We may also need to modify the information for existing companies and products from time to time, and we should be able to delete them as well.

Example: Maintaining companies and products

Implementing this maintenance function is mostly a matter of building the right interface. Imagine that there is an item on a menu labeled "update products and companies." When you select this item, a message is sent to a maintenance object that puts up two successive menus that let you decide whether you want to add, modify, or delete a product, supplier, or customer.

You start the process via menu selections

Putting up these menus is trivial; most object languages come with numerous classes for displaying pop-up, pull-down, and other types of menus, and for accepting user input via a keyboard, mouse, or other device. You only have to create new instances of these menus and type in the text for each selection.

Adding menus is easy

Example: Add a product

Take "add a product" as an example. Your method for that selection sends a message to the product class to create a new instance of a product. The newly created product object puts up a form to get the required information, then sends a message to the product collection to add itself to the list. Typically, all of this can be done in five to ten lines of code.

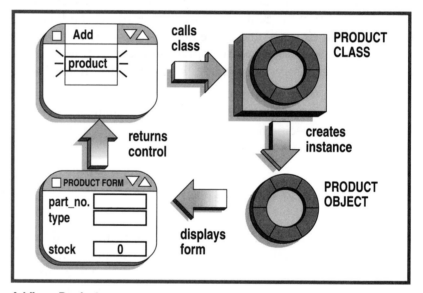

Adding a Product

Other choices are comparable

Adding suppliers and customers is equally straightforward. Modifying existing products and companies is even easier—all we do is pull up the input screen with the existing data in it and allow the user to modify it. For deletions, you would specify the product or company to be deleted, either by entering a name or by picking an item off a list of choices. A message would be sent to remove the object from the collection that contained it, then the object's class would be called to destroy the object and reclaim the memory it occupied.

Recording Transactions

At this point, you can readily imagine how transactions would be handled in this system. To record a sale, for example, a menu selection would send a message to the sale class to create a new sale object, which would put up an input screen to gather the required information. Once completed, the sale object would send a message to the sales collection to add itself to that collection.

We can also record transactions

We can, of course, elaborate this transaction process to make life easier for the end user. For example, we could provide pop-up "pick lists" of suppliers and products so that the user doesn't have to type this information when recording a sale. Again, this is easily achieved using messages.

We can easily add features to this interface

For example, when the user pressed a key to get a list of vendors, a message would be sent to the suppliers collection to return an alphabetized list of the vendors. This list would be presented in the form of a scrolling menu, using a standard menu class. Once the user made a selection, a new message would be sent to the suppliers collection to get the address, discount, and other information for the selected vendor. This information would then be automatically entered into the proper fields on the input form.

Example: Filling in supplier information

In reality, you probably wouldn't even code these procedures by hand. Instead, you would use an object-oriented screen tool to draw the input form for recording sales, then attach the various fields to the objects that manage those fields. In practice, this effort would differ little from the use of existing screen tools. The result, however, would be a smaller screen module because most of the operations would already be provided by the referenced objects.

You would probably use a screen tool

Reports, Queries, and Other Activities

Another type of application would be extracting management reports from the accumulated data. In fact, once a basic system has been set up, this is by far the most common kind of application and the one that tends to change the most frequently.

We can also build reports

Information is gathered by the model

Once again, many of the procedures for constructing reports are already provided by the objects in the model. For example, you can send a message to the sales collection to locate sales that meet a given set of criteria, and it will return a list of the sales that satisfy those criteria. Finding out how many products of a given type have been sold in the last six months is a relatively easy task.

Object-oriented report tools are available

Most of the effort in building up reports has to do with formatting the report, taking totals, and other such mundane activities. As with input screens, you probably wouldn't bother to code these processes by hand. Instead, you would use an object-oriented report package to create the reports for you. Alternatively, you could use an object-oriented query language, such as object SQL, to form questions on the fly. We examine screen, report, and query tools in more detail in Chapter 9.

Object-based applications really are easier

By this point the conclusion should be clear: Building "applications" on top of a solid, well-constructed model is considerably easier than building them from scratch, which is why model-based rapid prototyping has proven so effective. By building an intelligent, self-managing model of your business, you reduce applications to mere interfaces that request the model to carry out certain actions.

EXTENDING THE SYSTEM

The model is easily extended

The model we've constructed is necessarily a simple one, but it easily can be extended to become more sophisticated. Here are a few examples of possible extensions.

Using Hierarchies for Special Cases

Products don't all follow the same form

In modeling products, we naively assumed that all products could be described by the same set of variables. This is obviously not true—integrated circuits would need variables to represent pin configurations, power supplies would require voltage and wattage ratings, and so on.

This is an obvious case where subclasses should be created. We need to break down the product line according to major categories, then divide each category down into subcategories, until an adequate level of description is reached for each product. How deep the hierarchy goes depends entirely on the needs of the business.

The solution is subclassing

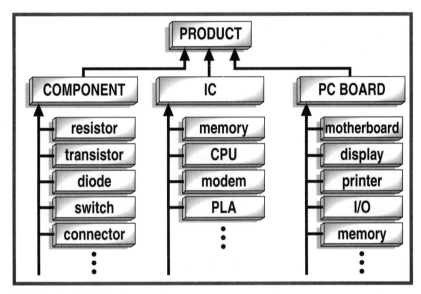

Subclasses of Products

Similarly, there may be important distinctions we want to represent among different kinds of suppliers, purchases, customers, and sales. In each case, the solution is to construct special cases and add to or override the more generic information contained in the high-level class.

Hierarchies may be useful for other classes, too

Subclassing doesn't disturb applications

Adding subclasses offers new opportunities for enhancing the model, but it doesn't disrupt the model in its present form. For example, all the methods and variables in the high-level classes will continue to function just as before. If some of these methods and variables are overridden in subclasses, these more specialized cases will automatically be used in place of the more generic ones. In each case, all applications will continue to run without disruption. You only have to modify other classes and application code when you want to use new information not anticipated in the original model.

Adding Intelligence to Products

Products aren't very responsible

We observed earlier that our product objects are rather passive; all they do is contain information and allow us to view or modify it. Yet one of the tenets of responsibility-driven design is to make every object as responsible as possible for its own state. Is there any way we could apply this principle to products to make them more self-managing?

Products could monitor their stock levels

A bit of reflection suggests an obvious way to do this. One of the things that product objects do is keep track of stock on hand. But they don't actually *do* anything about the stock on hand; left to their own devices, they will sit there passively until the stock runs out. A product object with even a modicum of intelligence should be able to prevent that from happening.

They would do this by issuing purchase requests

Extending product objects to handle this responsibility is easy. First, we add two variables, which we'll call *minimum_stock* and *order_quantity*. As the names suggest, we make the product responsible for ensuring that the stock on hand stays above the minimum level. If it falls below the minimum, the product object automatically orders a preestablished economic order quantity, as specified in the second new variable. It does this by creating a purchase object, triggering the same sequence of events that we previously initiated through a menu selection.

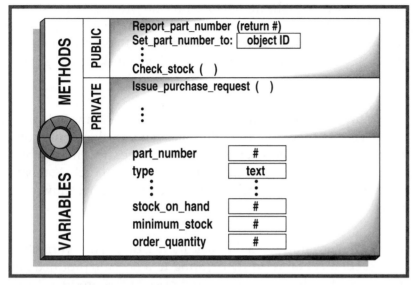

A More Responsible Product Object

As an aside, notice that we have finally dealt with the noun *demand* that appeared in the original description of the business cycle. Demand would be reflected in the minimum quantity variable; if we tend to run out of a given item frequently, we increase this value. If we tend to have inventory sitting idle on the shelf, we lower the number.

This extension captures the "demand" consideration

In fact, now that we finally see how demand fits into the picture, we could make product objects even more responsible by having them monitor their average stock level and the frequency with which they run out of stock, automatically adjusting the minimum quantity variable to maintain an optimal level of stock.

Products could monitor their own demand

Adding Line Items to Purchases and Sales

Here's another potential extension to our model. In describing purchases and sales, we made the rather simplistic assumption that a single product was involved in the transaction. This may happen from time to time, but most transactions involve a mixture of products in varying quantities. This mixture is generally handled by having line items in transactions, using a different line for each product.

We could add line items

This is easily done

How can we extend the model to handle line items? A very simple fix will do the job. You may want to pause a moment to see if you can think of the answer before reading on. If you can solve this problem, you are well on your way to being a skilled object designer.

Adding multiple product slots isn't the answer

One solution is to create multiple "slots" for line items in a transaction. That's a time-honored solution, but it's a rather limited one. If you don't use all the slots, you waste storage space in the transaction object. And if you need more, you're out of luck. You have to create a separate transaction object to handle the overflow, even though only one transaction is actually involved.

The solution is to add a collection

Here's a better solution. In the basic model, the *product* variable in a transaction contains an ID pointing to a specific product, and other variables give the quantity and price of this product. To get line items, we need to do two things:

1. Pull the variables for a specific product out of the transaction class and put them in a new class called *line_item*.

2. Create a new instance of a collection to hold a variable number of these line items and store the pointer to this collection in the transaction object.

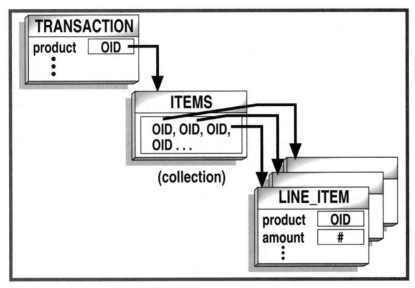

Adding Line Items

Now we have complete freedom to include any number of products in any given purchase, and the same holds true for sales. If there is only a single product, then the collection contains only a single item and everything works as before. If there are multiple products in the transaction, they appear as multiple line items. There are no limits on the number of products, and you never waste space on line items.

This gives you maximum flexibility

Another advantage of this solution is that it allows a transaction object to be modified extensively without actually changing it. For example, you can create a sale object for a particular customer, then experiment with various combinations of products to get the right configuration. The original sale object is impervious to these iterations because all the changes take place down in a separate collection object, which is designed to change its size and composition dynamically.

It also protects the transaction object

Embedding Intelligence in Workflow Management

Workflow automation programs are becoming popular

As a final example, let's tackle a more ambitious extension. One of the hot topics in business software today is *workflow automation*, in which routine business processes are automated in software. Typically, this is done through the use of separate programs, generically known as *groupware*, that examine documents, calendars, and other software entities, check their current status, and attempt to advance them through corporate channels.

Object technology supports embedded workflow

With object technology, workflow automation can be built right into the objects that represent the work to be done. In fact, our simple model already contains a healthy dose of workflow automation. A purchase object, once created, knows what stages it must go through to consummate the intended transaction. It constantly monitors its current stage and attempts to move itself to the next stage at the appropriate time.

The real goal is to add intelligence

But workflow automation alone is not much of a breakthrough—it just means that the computer pushes forms from desk to desk rather than requiring people to do that. The real challenge is to build intelligence into workflow management so we can minimize the human effort involved in getting a job done. As it happens, objects offer some excellent opportunities for embedding this intelligence.

Example: Picking a supplier

Consider the purchase object as an example. This object's first task is to gather the required information, which it does through a data input screen. Pick lists and other aids can ease the task of filling out that screen, but that's a rather superficial level of assistance. For example, entering the name of a supplier is easy—the hard part is deciding which vendor to use for any given purchase.

Because objects contain methods, they can execute anything from simple rules to complex inferences, perhaps querying other objects to fill in missing information. Given a set of criteria, a purchase object could analyze the suitability of various suppliers. The criteria could include the product required, current price and discount information, projected delivery date, quality measures, and anything else that would influence the choice of vendor.

The purchase object could perform this task

Instead of putting up a pick list of all the vendors in the system, the purchase object would present a short list of potential vendors ordered by how well they fit the criteria. Ordinarily, the purchasing agent would simply press a key to select the top vendor on the list.

The user would get a prioritized list

Similarly, a purchase object could use rules to reach its second stage, approved purchase, as quickly as possible. Based on the type of product, the size of the order, and other factors, it would determine who had the appropriate signature authority and seek that person's approval by popping up on his or her to-do list. If it failed to get the attention it needed, it could issue a few nags, try someone else with equivalent authority, report its lack of success back to the original requestor, or use any combination of these tactics.

Purchase objects could accelerate their own approval

Even after the purchase order had been issued and the merchandise received, the purchase object could bring a little more intelligence to bear. While counting down the days to the payment due date, the purchase object could check the cash on hand to determine whether a little extra float would be helpful. If so, it would query the supplier object to find out what this particular supplier's tolerance was and then add as many days as it could get away with before cutting the check.

They could even look for float on payments

As with many other kinds of changes, adding intelligence to workflow automation is relatively easy to do because it has little impact on the rest of the system. No other object in the model knows anything about how a vendor is selected within a purchase object, so increasing the intelligence of that process has no effect on the structure or functioning of the model.

None of these changes disrupt the model

Evolutionary Information Systems

*Our system can
evolve over time*

The conclusion from these few examples is clear: Object technology allows complex systems to be extended over time rather than rebuilt to accommodate new functionality. This is one of the most vital advantages of this technology. In short, it means we can build simple systems that solve today's problems and grow them along with the business to solve the problems that arise in the future. It means we now have the means to build truly evolutionary information systems.

7

Object-Oriented Languages

THE ORIGINS OF OBJECTS
Simula—the First Object Language

Smalltalk is often depicted as the original object language, but it's not. The grandfather of object languages is Simula, which is an acronym for "simulation language." Simula was developed in Norway during the 1960s to handle complex simulation problems. Simulating complex real-world interactions also turned out to be a very good way to build software. And so began the evolution of object languages.

The original object language was Simula

Simula is often described in the past tense, as though it were the Latin of object languages. In fact, Simula is very much alive today. It is available from at least eight different vendors, and it has a significant installed base in Europe. However, as far as mainstream business computing is concerned, Simula has very little market presence in the United States.

Simula is still alive

The Evolution of Object Languages

From its origins in Simula, many branches developed in the family of object languages. Here's a rough genealogy of the descendents of Simula.

Object languages have evolved over 25 years

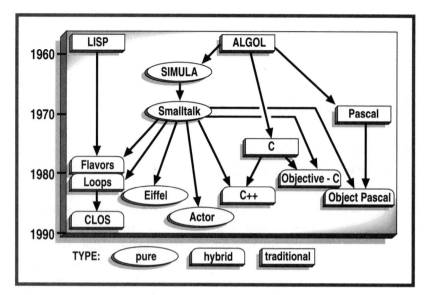

A Genealogy of Object Languages

Smalltalk went well beyond Simula

Simula inspired the development of Smalltalk, the first true object language developed from scratch and still the preeminent member of that class. Smalltalk was developed at Xerox's Palo Alto Research Center (PARC) in the 1970s as part of an effort to redefine computing as a more personal, interactive activity.

Smalltalk spawned many other languages

Smalltalk, in turn, begat other pure languages, such as Eiffel and Actor. It also inspired the addition of object features to a variety of traditional languages such as LISP, C, and Pascal.

We focus mostly on Smalltalk and C++

In this chapter, we focus primarily on the two most commercially viable alternatives for the mainstream business market: Smalltalk and C++. Both of these languages are available from multiple vendors, both are rapidly becoming standardized, and both are enjoying major commercial acceptance. We do, however, take a brief tour of some of the other object languages later in the chapter.

TRADEOFFS IN LANGUAGE DESIGN

Designing an object-oriented language involves making choices on a series of dimensions, with each choice implying cost-benefit tradeoffs to the language user. The best way to understand the differences among the various object languages is to examine the basic tradeoffs and what they imply. Armed with this information, it will be much easier for you to make intelligent decisions about which language is right for any given application.

Object languages involve many tradeoffs

Pure vs. Hybrid

There are basically two different types of object languages, loosely called *pure* and *hybrid*. A pure language has been built from the ground up to be object-oriented. Everything in it consists of objects, methods, and classes. A hybrid language, on the other hand, is built on top of an existing programming language such as C or Pascal. It has all the features of the existing language plus an overlay of objects, methods, and classes.

Languages fall into two categories

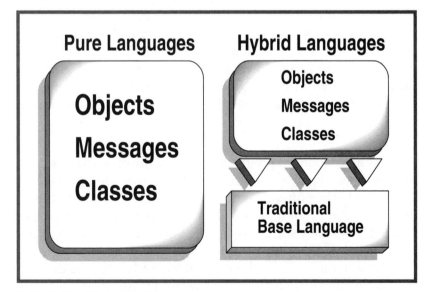

Pure vs. Hybrid Languages

Pure languages may be more powerful	Each type has its strengths and weaknesses. Pure languages typically deliver the full power of object technology, in terms of supporting all the features of this new approach to programming. They also give you maximum flexibility to change the underlying language. Because everything in the language is built out of objects, you can make very deep changes if you need to.
They may not be as fast as hybrid languages	However, there is often a price to this power and flexibility. Most pure languages are not as fast as hybrids at carrying out the kinds of operations that are normally "hard-coded" in traditional languages, such as addition and multiplication. However, many pure languages are nearly as fast as hybrid languages when object-oriented features are in full use.
Hybrid languages are more restrictive	By contrast, hybrid languages are often missing some of the features of pure object languages, and they generally don't let you alter characteristics that are built into the base language. But they are typically faster for operations that are built into the base language.
Pure and hybrid languages differ in ease of learning	Pure and hybrid languages also differ in ease of learning, though which is easier depends on the starting point. For a nonprogrammer, learning a pure language usually is easier because it's simpler; there is only a single language to learn, not a base language plus an object overlay. However, for an experienced programmer, moving to a hybrid language may be easier if the base language is already familiar because only the object extensions must be mastered.
Pure languages force a more complete conversion	Although experienced programmers typically pick up hybrid languages faster than pure ones, there is a downside to this faster adjustment: They often make only a partial conversion to the object approach. A common result is that they use the new object features when they seem convenient, but continue to think in procedural terms. By contrast, learning a pure language generally forces a programmer to fully understand and adopt the different mindset behind object-oriented programming.

Compiled vs. Interpreted

Another important distinction among object languages involves the way that the human-readable, object-oriented instructions are converted into machine-level instructions that the computer executes. There are basically four strategies:

Object languages are implemented in different ways

1. **Interpreters** convert each instruction into a compact, internal byte code as new methods are defined. Later, when the program is run, a run-time interpreter translates these byte codes into machine codes that will run on the target computer.

2. **Dynamic compilers** are variants of the interpreter scheme that increase the speed of execution. Instead of translating byte codes one at a time, an entire method is compiled into machine code whenever it is encountered. A running pool of recently compiled methods is cached in main memory to avoid recompilation whenever possible.

3. **Preprocessors** convert object-level instructions into a traditional high-level language, then pass this converted text on to a standard compiler for further conversion. Many hybrid languages were originally implemented in this way.

4. **Conventional compilers** convert all the object-level instructions in a program directly into executable instructions. Hybrid languages take this approach more often today. The term "conventional" is introduced to distinguish this type of compilation from the dynamic compilation strategy, which has a run-time component.

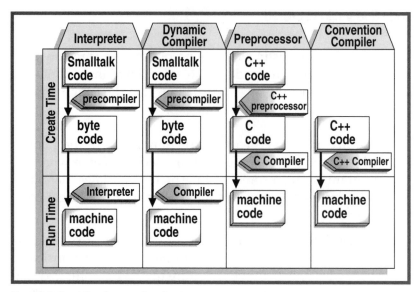

Four Schemes for Converting Code

Interpreted languages favor development

Interpreted and dynamically compiled languages are the most flexible and convenient to use because a minor change in a program can be tried out immediately, without having to wait while the entire program is relinked. The cost of this convenience is that interpreted languages typically execute more slowly than compiled ones because they are doing more work at execution time.

But they can still be fast at run time

However, interpreted languages for production systems have been optimized to the point where the performance penalty is usually quite small. Systems that use the dynamic compilation scheme are especially efficient at run-time execution.

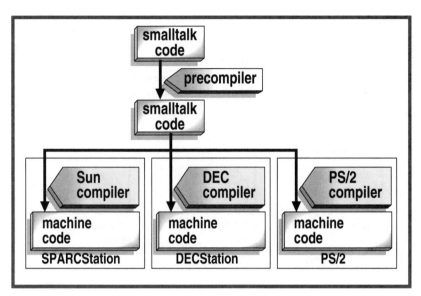

Dynamic Compilers

The use of translators originally arose as a way of bringing hybrid languages online quickly. Instead of modifying an existing compiler, it only required writing a translator that converted the object extensions into the standard form of the native language. A further advantage of this approach was that it made programs more portable, as the translator could be used in combination with a wide variety of machine-dependent compilers. However, the use of a translator plus a compiler is somewhat tedious, and most hybrid languages tend to migrate into compiler form as they become more widely used.

Translators aid portability

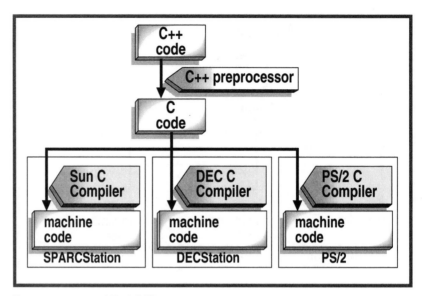

Preprocessors and Portability

Compiled languages favor delivery

By comparison with interpreters, conventionally compiled languages are less convenient to use because each small change requires relinking the whole program, a process that can take anywhere from a few seconds to several hours. But compiled languages typically execute more quickly than even the most optimized interpreters or dynamic compilers. Also, compiled languages are simplest for delivery because there is no need to include a vendor-supplied run-time execution component.

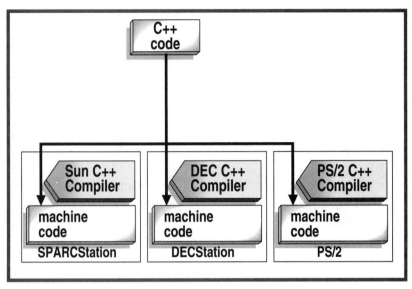

Dedicated Compilers for Each Platform

Strong vs. Weak Typing

"Typing" is the process of declaring what kind of information a given variable may contain. For example, a variable might be typed to contain a single character, a string of characters, an integer number, or a floating-point number. Once typed, the variable is restricted to containing that kind of data. Any attempt to place another kind of data in the variable will produce an error message.

Typing restricts the contents of variables

Some object languages require that all variables be assigned a type before they can be used. Other languages make no such requirement, allowing variables to take on whatever type may be convenient at any given time. These two options are called *strong* and *weak typing*, respectively.

Not all languages require typing

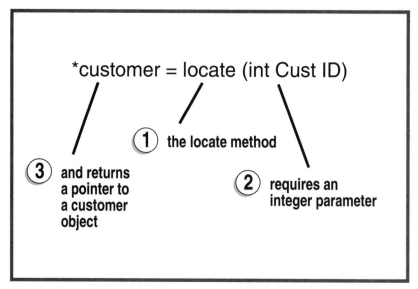

*customer = locate (int Cust ID)

① the locate method

③ and returns
a pointer to
a customer
object

② requires an
integer parameter

An Example of Typing in a Message

The value of typing is much debated

There is an ongoing debate over the relative merits of strongly and weakly typed languages. Weak typing is much more flexible in that new kinds of variables can be introduced that weren't envisioned at the time a program was written, and these can often be infused into the program without revising it. By contrast, strong typing is less flexible but safer because the language can perform routine checks to make sure that the parameters of messages are of the correct type, something that weakly typed languages can't do. Strong typing also permits stronger compiler optimizations, resulting in tighter, faster programs.

Pure languages often use weak typing

Pure object languages often use weak typing because this approach gives them maximum flexibility, especially during development when new object types are being created frequently. In fact, advocates of pure object languages reject the concept of typing altogether and tend to dislike the term *weak typing* because it suggests that they are doing something poorly. Their belief is that typing is simply not appropriate to a true object language, and they prefer to think of object languages as *untyped* languages.

Hybrid languages, by contrast, tend to be built on top of strongly typed languages, and most carry the requirement for strong typing into their object-oriented extensions. It is possible to specify the type of an argument so that there is some flexibility at run time, but special efforts are required to do this.

Hybrid languages are usually strongly typed

Static vs. Dynamic Binding

A distinction that is closely related to strong and weak typing is the difference between *static* and *dynamic binding*. This can be a confusing distinction, and the confusion is heightened by the fact that the distinction goes by several different names. Static binding is also known as "early" or "compile-time" binding. Dynamic binding is often referred to as "late" or "run-time" binding.

Languages may use static or dynamic binding

Binding is the process whereby the receiver of a message is determined. In languages that require static binding, the identity of the receiver must be specified when the program is created. If a language supports dynamic binding, the identity of the receiver may be left undetermined until the message is actually sent at run time.

Binding determines the identity of a receiver

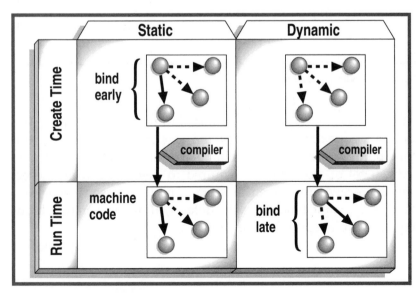

Static vs. Dynamic Binding

Dynamic binding supports polymorphism

Dynamic binding is generally believed to be an essential property of an object language because it makes polymorphism possible. For an illustration of this, think back to the example of evaluating financial instruments described in Chapter 4. For the example to work without the use of a case or switch statement, the object that will receive the message can't be known until run time. In fact, the receiver object may well be something that was added since the program was written, in which case it couldn't *possibly* be known when the program was created.

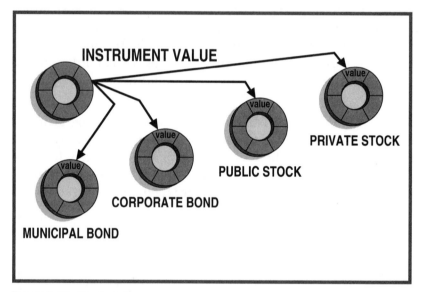

Dynamic Binding in Action

Most object languages support dynamic binding

Many object languages use dynamic binding for all messages, providing for maximum flexibility and extensibility. However, run-time binding does extract a small performance penalty in that an extra level of "look-up" is required to determine which object should receive any given message. For this reason, some languages use static binding as the default, allowing dynamic binding only under special circumstances.

Single vs. Multiple Inheritance

As described in Chapter 4, there are two types of inheritance in object languages: single and multiple. In single inheritance, each class may have, at most, a single superclass. With multiple inheritance, a class can have two or more superclasses, and it inherits all the methods and variables of all its superclasses.

Classes may have one or more superclasses

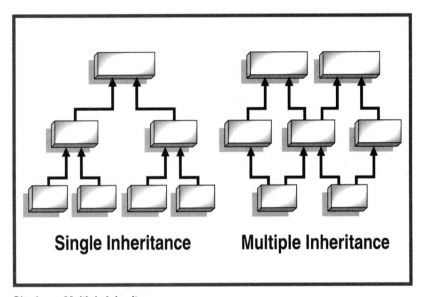

Single Inheritance   Multiple Inheritance

Single vs. Multiple Inheritance

The use of multiple inheritance is strictly language-dependent. Some languages support only single inheritance. Others support multiple inheritance, giving the user the option of using either single or multiple inheritance in any given situation.

Not all languages permit multiple inheritance

Multiple inheritance is another hotly debated feature of object-oriented languages. Those who favor it argue that it is necessary to represent many real-world situations, and that restricting a programmer to single inheritance can require extensive duplication of code. Duplicating the same code in more than one class is, of course, a clear violation of object-oriented principles.

Multiple inheritance can avoid duplication

But it is often
unnecessary

By contrast, the opponents of multiple inheritance argue that most, if not all, situations that appear to require multiple inheritance are examples of poor design that could be adequately handled by single inheritance with a little restructuring.

And it does
introduce
complications

They also point out that multiple inheritance involves much overhead for both the programmer and the language. For example, suppose a class inherits two or more methods with the same name. How does the class decide which one to use? Techniques are available for handling these conflicts, but there is no elegant, universal solution to the problem.

Language Only vs. Full Environment

Some languages
include environments

One more tradeoff to consider is that some languages come with extensive development environments, whereas others provide only a bare-bones compiler or interpreter. Again, there are arguments in favor of both approaches.

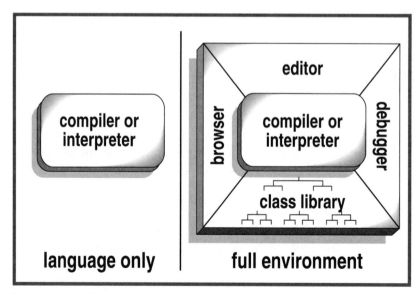

Languages vs. Environments

Languages that provide extensive development environments are typically much more convenient to use because all the tools and classes needed to work with the language are immediately available. An additional advantage is that there is typically a high degree of internal consistency to the environment. Also, because the environment is the same for everyone who buys the language, it may be easier to exchange classes and objects among multiple programmers.

Full environments are convenient

The argument for providing a language separately from its environment is that the choice of development environment should be left to the programmer or company using the language. This is less convenient initially, but it may ultimately allow a much tighter fit to the needs of the company.

But they can be constrictive

A SMALLTALK PROFILE
The Origins of Smalltalk

Smalltalk, the first language ever developed as a pure implementation of object technology, was created by a team of researchers at Xerox Corporation led by Alan Kay and Adele Goldberg. The vision behind their efforts was to create a personal computing environment that overcame the impersonal barriers that surrounded mainframe computers.

Smalltalk was derived from Simula

As it turned out, their vision was nearly 20 years ahead of the capabilities of the prevailing technology. Little wonder, then, that it took a few years for Smalltalk to make it into the mainstream of computing!

Their vision was well ahead of the hardware

The Basic Smalltalk Profile

In terms of the design tradeoffs described above, the profile of Smalltalk is as follows:

Smalltalk has a unique profile

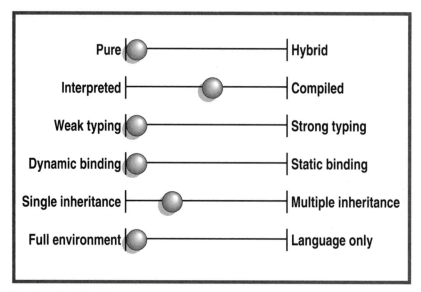

The Smalltalk Profile

Early versions of Smalltalk were limited

Early versions of Smalltalk were primarily research vehicles, and were not designed for production environments. The limitations of these early versions gained the language a reputation that it is still trying to shrug off. Specifically, the early interpreters were slow, imposing a significant penalty on run-time performance, and the extensive environment included with the language required many megabytes of memory that few personal computers could provide back in the late 1970s and early 80s.

They were also closed systems

Moreover, the Smalltalk environment was closed, in the sense that Smalltalk took over the entire machine and did not interoperate easily with other software. This restriction was of little consequence in research environments, but it created considerable frustration as the language moved into the commercial arena.

These limitations have been overcome

These limitations have been overcome in recent years. Most versions of Smalltalk are now optimized to the point where run-time performance is quite good, often coming reasonably close to the performance of conventionally compiled languages. Full-featured versions of Smalltalk are also available on smaller PCs with only a few megabytes of memory, and these systems can create run-time copies of applications that require even less memory.

Smalltalk has also been liberated from the confines of a closed environment. New versions of Smalltalk can operate across a variety of operating systems and under a number of different window interface managers. They can operate at the same time as other programs and share data with other programs to participate in higher levels of system integration.

Smalltalk can now work in an open environment

Everything is an Object

Because Smalltalk is a pure object language, *everything* is an object, and all work is carried out through messages. There are no "built-in" operators with fixed definitions.

Smalltalk contains only objects

For programmers schooled in traditional languages, this can lead to some surprising results. For example, the expression *count + 1* in Smalltalk is not an instruction to the compiler to set up an addition operation between a variable and a constant. Rather, it's an instruction to send the message + to the object count with a parameter of *1*, so that count will increase its value by one.

This can lead to some surprises

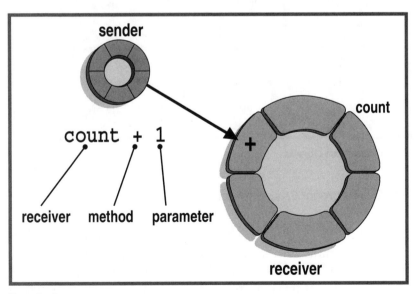

Count + 1

Even classes are objects

Here's another surprise. Since everything is an object in Smalltalk, classes must themselves be objects. That raises an interesting question. If every object is a member of some class and classes are defined as objects, then classes must, in turn, be defined by class-defining classes. But these class-defining classes, being objects, would have to be defined by classes as well, which rapidly leads to an infinite regress.

Metaclasses solve this problem

The designers of Smalltalk avoided this infinite regress by arbitrarily declaring that all classes are defined by things called *metaclasses*, and that all metaclasses belong to a single class named *metaclass*. The buck stops there.

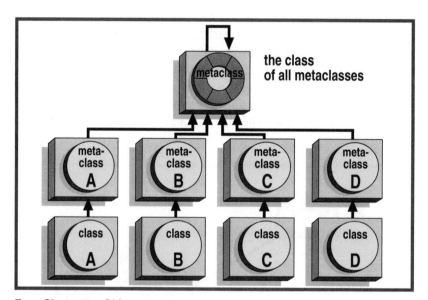

Even Classes are Objects

The Development Environment

Smalltalk has an extensive development environment

Smalltalk comes with a very extensive and sophisticated development environment. In fact, the Smalltalk environment pioneered the multiwindowed interface with mouse control, popup menus, and other ease-of-use features that were subsequently adopted by Apple in its Macintosh products and are now becoming the standard interface in all brands of PCs and workstations.

Developing applications with Smalltalk tends to be very fast. Because Smalltalk code is incrementally compiled, new class and object definitions become effective as soon as they are entered. There is no lengthy edit, compile, and link cycle as with conventional compiled languages. The immediate feedback and high degree of interactivity of the Smalltalk environment makes it very productive for rapid development.

Development in Smalltalk is fast

The other characteristic of Smalltalk that makes it a highly productive environment is the extensive library of classes that comes with the language. Initially this wealth of classes is daunting, and it may take programmers weeks or months to become familiar with them. But once they do, they find that much of their programming is done for them. They begin building applications by assembling classes, developing new classes only as required to "glue" existing classes together.

Smalltalk provides many classes

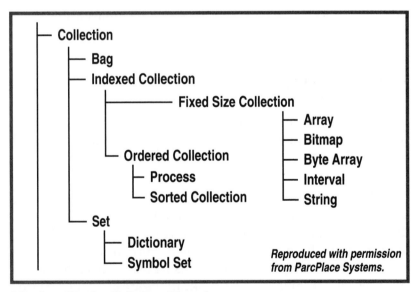

A Portion of the Smalltalk Class Hierarchy

All code is stored in an image file

Another unique aspect of Smalltalk is the way it handles persistence. Whenever a working session is completed, the Smalltalk kernel saves the entire state of the environment to disk in the form of an *image file*. The next time Smalltalk is started up, this image file is reloaded, and the programmer resumes precisely where he or she left off. All variables are set just as they were, and every window is laid out as it was.

Smalltalk can be easy or hard to learn

The Smalltalk language is very simple and quite close to English. People with little or no programming experience tend to learn the language rather quickly. On the other hand, experienced programmers may find Smalltalk hard to learn because it is so different from what they are used to.

The language is actually very simple

Because the Smalltalk language is simple and similar to natural language in its structure, learning the language itself is rarely a problem. Most of the work of learning Smalltalk is mastering the extensive collection of built-in classes and the sophisticated development environment.

The Commercialization of Smalltalk

Smalltalk has two vendors

At present, Smalltalk is sold by two vendors: ParcPlace Systems, which markets high-end products for workstations; and Digitalk, which sells smaller, leaner products for personal computers.

ParcPlace's product is very portable

ParcPlace's Smalltalk product, Objectworks\Smalltalk, is the descendent of the Xerox Smalltalk-80 language. Smalltalk-80 uses a dynamic compiler strategy, which gives it all the benefits of an interpreter while gaining most of the performance advantages of a conventional compiler. Also, because it uses a machine-specific run-time engine, Smalltalk-80 applications are easily ported from one type of workstation to another. In fact, in most cases a single Smalltalk-80 image file can be carried from one type of computer to another with no changes whatever.

For most of its product line, Digitalk uses the interpreter model for implementing execution. This strategy is used in its classic Smalltalk/V and /V286 products, as well as its Smalltalk/V for Windows. In the OS/2 Presentation Manager environment, however, Digitalk took a different approach. In development mode, the product runs as an interpreter. For delivery, the final code is processed by a conventional compiler to produce a fast, stand-alone run-time package.

Digitalk's product comes in various forms

Both ParcPlace and Digitalk are relatively small companies, which may raise concerns in large organizations about the stability of the language in the marketplace. Another concern is that the two vendors do not agree on the precise definition of the language and its class hierarchy, which makes it difficult to move programs from one vendor's product to the other.

Both vendors are relatively small

These concerns are currently being addressed by a mutual effort between the vendors to produce a single, standard version of the language. In addition, a third vendor, Enfin Corporation, is joining this standardization effort to provide yet another source for the Smalltalk language and its accompanying tools. Moreover, Smalltalk has recently received a major industry endorsement from IBM, which has entered into agreements with both Digitalk and ParcPlace and has adopted Smalltalk/V PM as its development environment for Presentation Manager applications.

However, standards are emerging

So Smalltalk is rapidly becoming an accepted language in corporate development environments. In fact, the informal survey of commercial applications in Chapter 12 suggests that the majority of object-oriented development for mainstream business applications is now taking place in Smalltalk.

Smalltalk is gaining corporate acceptance

A C++ PROFILE
The Origins of C++

C++ is a hybrid language from AT&T

C++ is a hybrid language based on C, currently the dominant development language in the PC and workstation market. C++ was developed in the early 1980s by Bjarne Stroustrup at AT&T's Bell Labs. The rather strange name of the language is a programmer's play on words. In C, the "++" operator increases a variable by one, implying that C++ represents an incremental step beyond C.

C++ was readily accepted

Once released, C++ quickly gained widespread acceptance in the marketplace. Because it's based on a language that is already a standard in the market and available from many vendors, it is generally regarded as being secure from vendor failure. The large population of skilled C programmers also makes adoption of C++ a natural migration path to object technology.

The Basic C++ Profile

C++ is very different from Smalltalk

C++ and Smalltalk are at opposite poles on most of the basic design tradeoffs established previously. In addition to being a hybrid language, C++ is strongly rather than weakly typed, supports dynamic binding only in a limited form, offers multiple inheritance, and does not include development environment as part of its basic definition. Also, the language is typically implemented using a preprocessor or conventional compiler rather than an interpreter or dynamic compiler.

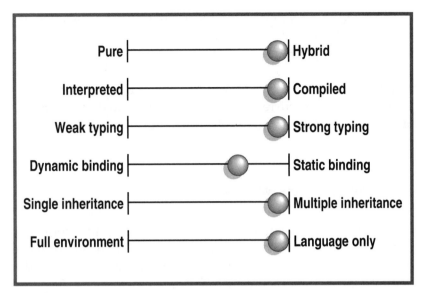

The C++ Profile

In its early releases, C++ was implemented as a preprocessor. This tactic allowed C++ to be used on any machine that supported a C compiler, providing immediate portability and leveraging the robustness of proven C compilers. However, this approach required programmers to write in C++, run a program to translate the C++ code into C code, run a C compiler to generate machine code, and then run a linker to create an executable file. Another drawback of this approach was that early debugging tools typically worked only on the generated C code, making it very difficult to think in object-oriented terms during the debugging process.

C++ was introduced as a preprocessor

As the market for C++ expanded, vendors began to introduce true C++ compilers, eliminating the translation step. Most C++ vendors also offer debuggers that work directly with C++ code, allowing programmers to write and debug their code in the same language.

Compilers are now available

The latest development is the introduction of C++ interpreters and dynamic compilers. These operate similarly to Smalltalk, allowing programmers to avoid the edit, compile, and link cycle required by conventional compilers. For example, Objectworks\C++ from ParcPlace is a comprehensive development environment that offers many of the advantages of its Objectworks\Smalltalk product, including dynamic compiling of C++ code.

Interpreters are also becoming available

Development environments are improving

With regard to development environments, most C++ language vendors make up for the minimalist character of C++ by marketing integrated environments of their own. At present, these environments do not provide the same degree of integration that Smalltalk does, but they are rapidly closing the gap. ParcPlace's Objectworks\C++ currently comes the closest to duplicating the Smalltalk environment given the inherent differences in the languages.

Converting to Objects with C++

C++ can ease the transition to objects

One of the great advantages of C++ is that, like all hybrid languages, it eases the transition from traditional to object-oriented programming. However, it can also make this transition more difficult, because it's all too easy for programmers to use C++ as a better version of C and miss the essence of object technology altogether.

Education in object technology is essential

To avoid this pitfall, it is essential to provide liberal doses of education in object technology. Simply handing a C programmer a C++ compiler will often do more harm than good. A much better approach is to provide extensive training in the new methodologies described in Chapter 5 first, then introduce the extensions to C that allow the language to support these methodologies.

There is one other alternative

There is a third option you might want to consider, at least for a few key people. Instead of moving these programmers directly from C to C++, have them learn Smalltalk first. Assuming they make the transition successfully, they will definitely convert to the object-oriented approach. Then, when you introduce them to C++, they will be much more likely to use its object capabilities. There is, however, a risk associated with this strategy: Some C programmers may decide that they prefer the Smalltalk environment and refuse to go back to a C-based language.

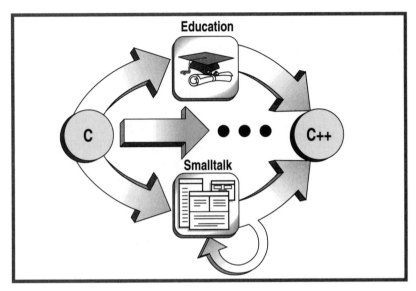

From C to Shining C++

Tradeoffs in C++ Design

Like its predecessor, C++ is a fast, compact language. C itself is finely tuned for high-speed execution, and the object extensions to C were designed to have as little impact on that speed as possible. Both languages also create executable files that are typically smaller than those of pure object languages, particularly where interpreters and run-time packages are involved.

C++ is a fast, compact language

However, C++ doesn't provide as complete an implementation of object principles as a pure language like Smalltalk does. Certain useful features are either missing or implemented rather awkwardly. To cite a particularly sore point, dynamic binding is available in C++ only as an option, and then only for classes that belong to the same superclass. While it's nice to have static binding as an option, getting the full benefits from polymorphism depends on having flexible, efficient dynamic binding.

But it lacks some object features

*C++ is a complex
language*

Also, C++ is a complex language that is difficult to learn and use. C is a complicated language in its own right, and the object-oriented extensions add another layer of complexity that can make learning C++ almost as challenging as learning two completely different languages.

*And it's a bit
dangerous to use*

Finally, compared to other high-level languages, C (and therefore C++) is actually a very low-level language that gets quite close to the machine. In fact, its original purpose was to build operating systems, which require intimate access to machine resources. This makes it a rather dangerous language for application programmers, who can easily "crash" a computer or corrupt a database if they experience what is fondly known as a "wild pointer."

*C++ adds options for
encapsulation*

Here is another tradeoff with C++. Unlike the fixed definition of encapsulation provided by Smalltalk, in which methods are public and data are private, C++ introduces a more flexible mechanism for encapsulation. In C++, there are actually three levels of privacy: *public* (available to anyone), *protected* (available only to subclasses), and *private* (available only within the class). The programmer has complete flexibility in terms of declaring the protection level for each method and variable.

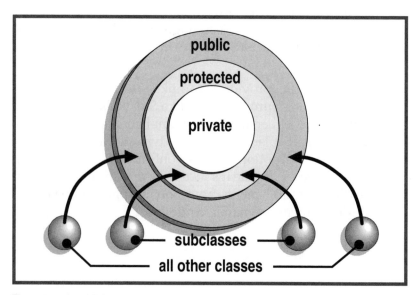

Three Levels of Privacy

This flexibility is a mixed blessing. As we saw in the sample system in Chapter 6, there are often methods that are to be used only within an object. Being able to declare such methods as private is an improvement over Smalltalk, which must rely on programming disciplines to achieve this result. On the other hand, placing variables in the public area of an object, which many C++ programmers do routinely, is a violation of information hiding. Given that programmers are less than perfect and will often bypass discipline in favor of quick solutions, it may be better to have a language enforce the fundamental tenets of object technology.

This is a mixed blessing

The Commercialization of C++

There are many different vendors for C++, including some major software companies that have the size and stability that tend to inspire trust in Fortune 500 companies. Moreover, the language is virtually standardized right now as it is defined by AT&T, and a formal standardization effort is underway.

C++ is available from many vendors

Given these considerations, many large organizations consider C++ a very safe "bet" compared to most other object languages. From the day it was introduced C++ has sold well, and it continues to be the best-selling object-oriented language on the market.

This has led to rapid acceptance

OTHER OBJECT LANGUAGES

Smalltalk and C++ are the most widely used object languages today, but they are hardly the only languages available. In fact, there are a wealth of choices for the company that requires something a little different. However, each of these choices requires giving up generality and standardization for special features, a choice many companies are reluctant to make.

There are many other object languages

Languages are intro-
duced chronologically

To help bring some order to the apparent chaos of offerings, the languages are introduced here in roughly chronological order. The timing gets a little close toward the end of the section as Eiffel, CLOS, and Actor were all introduced within the last few years.

Ada

Ada was mandated
by the DOD

Ada is a language with a unique history. The development of Ada was commissioned by the United States Department of Defense to provide a standard language for all product development under government sponsorship. The language was defined by a committee rather than an individual, and the effects of committee thinking are reflected in the result. Ada is generally regarded as a complex, cumbersome language. It is very powerful, but the price of that power is a steep learning curve and programs that are often difficult to understand and maintain.

Ada is only partially
object-oriented

Because Ada was developed before object technology became a major force in the industry, object concepts had relatively little influence on its design. However, it is possible to "retrofit" these concepts to Ada. Of the three basic mechanisms of object technology, the language already supports two: objects, which are called "packages" in Ada, and messages. Ada lacks the concept of classes, however. Every package must be uniquely defined, and there is no inheritance or other logical relationship among the packages.

Classes can be added

Strictly speaking, then, Ada is not an object-oriented language. Rather, it is what computer scientists call *object-based*, implying that is has objects but not classes. But it is possible to add class constructs to Ada through the use of a preprocessor, and there is presently one product on the market—Classic Ada from Software Productivity Solutions—for doing just that. So while Ada is less than ideal for developing object-oriented systems, it can be made to play the role with reasonable grace.

Because it is government-mandated, Ada is strictly standardized, and there are numerous vendors of the language. This relieves the concern of large organizations about the stability and viability of the language. However, the limitations of Ada are such that it is used primarily by defense contractors, who have little choice in the matter. It has made few inroads into the general commercial marketplace.

Ada is standard-ized and multi-vendor

Objective C

Objective C is a hybrid language developed by StepStone Corpo-ration that attempts to combine the best of C and Smalltalk in a single language. It holds a special place in the history of object languages because it was the first attempt to create a C-based object language. Technically, it is in many ways superior to C++, offering more graceful solutions to the problems of dynamic binding and other object features.

Objective C was derived from C and Smalltalk

Objective C is implemented as a precompiler that translates Objec-tive C source code into C code, which is then compiled in the tra-ditional way. The language also comes with an interactive devel-opment environment that offers some of Smalltalk's rapid development capabilities.

It uses the pre-compiler strategy

Given its effective addition of object concepts to a standard lan-guage, Objective C enjoyed considerable acceptance among large development organizations. It was also adopted as the core lan-guage of the NeXTStep environment in the NeXT computer. When IBM invested in NeXT, the future of Objective C appeared to be very bright.

Objective C was well received

Unfortunately, Objective C suffers from the classic single-source problem, and the indirect endorsement from IBM did little to offset that problem. When AT&T introduced a standard extension to C and allowed multiple vendors to market it, Objective C was quickly overshadowed in the marketplace despite its technical merits.

The future of the language is in doubt

Object Pascal

*Object Pascal
extends Pascal*

Another effort to graft object concepts on a traditional language is Object Pascal. Like C++, it is a compiled, strongly typed language that requires a separate suite of development tools. Its primary advantage is that it represents a relatively simple extension to an already simple language, providing a reasonably easy migration path to object technology. Object Pascal also implements the object approach more completely than C++ does, offering full polymorphism, dynamic binding, and other critical features.

*It is not a major
commercial success*

Versions of Object Pascal are currently offered by Apple, Borland, Microsoft, and Symantec. But the implementations are vendor-specific, and there doesn't appear to be much energy directed toward a standardization effort. In general, sales of Object Pascal have been eclipsed by the increasing dominance of C++.

Actor

*Actor is a Windows
language*

Actor is a C-based language that is dedicated to facilitating the development of applications to run under the Microsoft Windows environment. Although it retains some of the flavor of C, Actor is very similar to Smalltalk in its look and feel. It is a very efficient and productive tool for Windows development.

*Actor is popular
with application
vendors*

While Actor has enjoyed commercial success among software developers, it has little recognition or presence among Fortune 500 companies. Although an excellent, well-crafted language, its appeal is limited by the fact that it is a single-vendor product dedicated to a specific operating system and user environment.

*There is now a C++
variant*

The Whitewater Group, the maker of Actor, has recently introduced a version of its Windows class library that works with Borland's C++ product. This combination of an elegant Windows interface with a standard language is attracting much attention and may well represent a more attractive package for corporate buyers.

Eiffel

Eiffel is a pure object language developed by Bertrand Meyer (*Object-Oriented Software Construction*: Prentice Hall, 1988). Its design was inspired by Simula, but it also shows the influence of Smalltalk and Ada. In addition, it incorporates some modern techniques of software engineering that have been developed since the introduction of these earlier languages.

Eiffel offers unique features

One of the unique features introduced by Eiffel is the concept of *assertions*. Classes can contain general statements about the conditions under which each method may be executed, and these assertions are automatically checked whenever the method is invoked. For example, a precondition for removing a part from inventory is that the inventory actually contain one or more parts of the specified type. Assertions such as these can be quite useful in assuring software quality.

One of these is the concept of assertions

Eiffel also offers a unique combination of static type checking with dynamic binding to offer both compile-time checks on variable types and the real-time flexibility required by polymorphism. Storage allocation and deallocation are also handled automatically, as in Smalltalk, freeing the programmer from having to deal with these matters.

Eiffel offers other advantages as well

Despite these advantages, Eiffel still suffers from the single-vendor problem. It has been used in a few major commercial development projects, but it has relatively little market share among the Fortune 500.

But it's still a single-vendor language

CLOS

CLOS is a very flexible object language based on LISP, a language that has been the standard for artificial intelligence programming for nearly 20 years. CLOS is the descendent of a number of object-oriented LISP variants, and its name derives from a desire to converge these efforts: CLOS is an acronym for *Common Lisp Object System*.

CLOS is based on LISP

CLOS is used mostly in AI work

Like its parent language, CLOS is used primarily for developing applications in artificial intelligence (AI), particularly expert systems. In this arena, it has enjoyed considerable commercial success. CLOS is currently available from at least six vendors, and more introductions are expected within the next year. This makes CLOS a relatively stable, standard product that doesn't suffer from the single-source problem that plagues many other object languages.

It won't play a major role in mainstream systems

However, CLOS's focus on AI and its roots in LISP have tended to limit its acceptance for mainstream business applications. It will no doubt continue to be an important tool for building commercial expert systems, but it is not likely to play a significant role in the construction of large-scale corporate information systems.

Object COBOL

Object COBOL is on the horizon

The last language we consider is difficult to describe in detail because it is still under development. However, object extensions to COBOL are imminent, and MicroFocus is already testing a product that should be on the market in 1992. More important, there is an ANSI standards committee that is close to releasing an initial specification for the language, which should greatly accelerate its market acceptance.

Object COBOL has a ready market

Object COBOL seems destined to play a significant role in the evolution of object languages. Although there is some question about how gracefully COBOL can be extended into the object arena, Object COBOL already enjoys a large and highly receptive market in Fortune 500 companies, who are keenly interested in protecting their vast investment in COBOL programs and programmers (*IDC Survey of Object-Oriented Systems*, 1991).

CHOOSING A LANGUAGE
Moving Toward a Standard Language

In sum, there are now two major contenders for a standard, multi-vendor object language: Smalltalk and C++, with a third contender about to enter the scene. This conclusion naturally leads to the question of whether one of these languages will emerge victorious and become the industry standard.

There are two major contenders

Some believe that the market has already spoken on this matter. To date, sales of C++ compilers and related tools are exceeding sales of Smalltalk by a considerable margin. According to the IDC study of Fortune 500 companies, 53 percent of the Fortune 500 are considering, evaluating, or using C++, compared with only 22 percent for Smalltalk (*IDC Survey of Object-Oriented Systems*, 1991).

C++ is outselling Smalltalk

Many believe that percentages such as these demonstrate that C++ will soon dominate the market and become the de facto standard object language by end of the 1990s. However, these early sales figures should be interpreted with caution for two reasons:

But it's not yet the "standard"

1. There is no way to tell how many of the C++ buyers are simply **upgrading to new C features** as opposed to using the language for object-oriented programming.

2. The early adopters of object technology have been primarily in the **scientific and engineering** markets, where C is already an established standard. C has virtually no presence in corporate MIS departments.

There is a distinct possibility that as object technology moves into the mainstream of corporate computing, we will see a shift in dominance from C++ toward Smalltalk. Indeed, there are clues that this has already begun to happen. In my experience as a consultant, I have found far more Fortune 500 companies working with Smalltalk than with C++ for office applications, and a quick tally of the corporate case studies in Chapter 12 reveals that more of them are based on Smalltalk than any other language.

Smalltalk may win out for information systems

And then there's
Object COBOL...

Of course, there's still that dark horse in the back of the pack, the invisible one named Object COBOL. It remains to be seen whether object mechanisms such as dynamic binding and polymorphism can be successfully grafted onto such a venerable language. Then there's the question of whether COBOL programmers will actually make the transition to object-oriented programming given these extensions. The jury won't come back with a verdict on this one for some time. In fact, the case won't even come to trial for at least a year.

You Can Choose More than One

When in doubt,
choose more than one

The common question "Which language should we adopt?" is based on a hidden assumption—that a company or team only gets to choose one. While some companies may enforce strict standards across the entire organization, they will probably be doing their developers a disservice.

Different languages
have different
strengths

Because it runs close to the machine and is very fast, C++ is probably a better choice for system programming, real-time transactions, and applications in the scientific and engineering arena. On the other hand, Smalltalk's high-level syntax and transparent memory management make it better suited to mainstream business applications such as manufacturing management and customer service systems. And some of the other languages discussed may find special niches within the organization where their unique qualities give them extra leverage.

We will undoubtedly
see a mix of
languages

Real-world experience to date suggests that just such a mixture of languages will take place. In fact, one of the summary conclusions of the case studies in Chapter 12 is that companies are not only mixing object languages but also combining object technology with conventional languages and database systems. So long as the interactions of these heterogeneous systems are well managed, picking the best language for any given task may be a better strategy than worrying about settling on a standard at this early date.

8

Object Databases

Object DBMSs are basically similar to previous generations of DBMSs; they have mechanisms for storing and retrieving information, handling concurrent access, securing information, backing up and restoring data, and performing other traditional DBMS services. What makes them different is that they store objects rather than hierarchies, networks, or tables.

Object DBMSs are like previous DBMSs

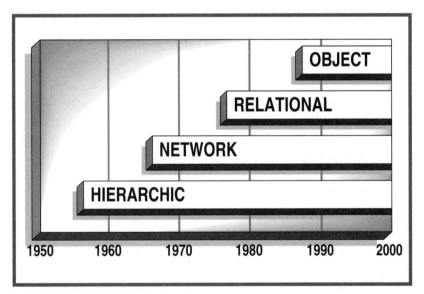

Generations of DBMS Structures

Given their similarity, object DBMSs may be viewed as one more step in the evolution of information structure in DBMS technology. But the implications go much further than that because objects contain not only data but procedures as well. This is an important break from the traditional role of a DBMS, and it is bound to have significant effects on the role of DBMSs in corporate information systems.

Yet they are also very different

THE ORIGINS OF OBJECT DBMSs
The Driving Forces Behind Object DBMSs

There are three motivations

There are three distinct reasons for adopting object DBMSs, and these reasons have evolved in roughly the following order:

1. **Better DBMS capabilities**—The original motivation was the need for a better kind of DBMS, one that overcame the structural and performance limitations of relational systems.

2. **Persistent objects**—With the increasing availability of object-oriented programming languages, a second motivation arose: the need to store and retrieve objects that outlast the execution of a single program.

3. **Reusable components**—Finally, as object programming matures, there is an increasing need for a common repository to contain reusable classes and other software components.

The latter two aren't the same

The latter two uses for object DBMSs are sometimes confused, but they are quite distinct. When used as a persistent object store, the object DBMS stores actual data instances created by running applications. When used as a component repository, the DBMS stores class definitions that are used to build new applications.

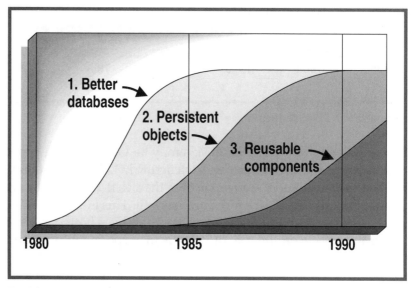

Evolving Needs for Object DBMSs

All three needs are well met by the new breed of object DBMSs. However, there are some difficult tradeoffs among these motivations. The following sections show how each of these differing needs is met by object technology and how the tradeoffs are being dealt with.

Object technology meets all three needs

The object DBMSs currently on the market represent these three motivations to varying degrees. To help you discriminate among these products, I mention a number of them by name in the next few sections. At the end of the chapter, after the basic concepts have been established, I provide a thumbnail sketch of all the products mentioned in the chapter to give you an overview of what's available today.

Current products represent a mix of motivations

1. A Better Kind of DBMS

Considered solely as a new kind of DBMS, object DBMSs may represent a genuine breakthrough in information storage. In fact, a plausible case can be made that object DBMSs combine the best of all the preceding generations of data-management technology.

Objects combine the best of prior generations

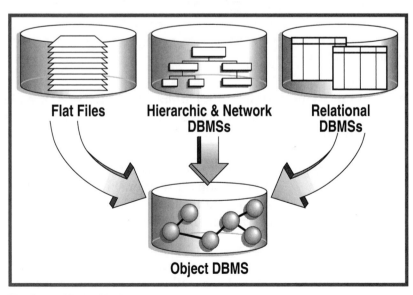

The Best of Three Worlds

They have the flexibility of flat files...

As with flat files, object DBMSs give you the freedom to store any kind of data you like, but with all the structure and access controls that DBMSs offer. Object DBMSs place no restrictions on the types or sizes of data elements that can be stored, and users are free to invent new data types of any complexity. In fact, object DBMSs can store anything that can be digitized, making them ideal for multimedia and other advanced applications.

Multimedia Database

...the structure and speed of network DBMSs...

As with hierarchic and network DBMSs, object DBMSs provide rich data structures with fast access, but without the rigidity of these early DBMSs.

- The **rich structures** are provided by composite objects, inheritance trees, and other object relationships. In fact, the object model is a superset of the hierarchical, network, and relational models, so it is guaranteed to support structures of arbitrary complexity.

- The **fast access** comes from the fact that objects are linked together through object IDs rather than foreign keys or other associative mechanisms. Object IDs provide direct access to other objects, without the need for tedious search-and-comparison operations.

At the same time, object DBMSs provide all the flexibility of relational DBMSs together with their powerful capability for multiple views of the same information.

...and the flexibility and views of relationals

- The **flexibility** is a product of encapsulation. Instead of "hard-wiring" structural information into the database system, as network and hierarchical systems do, this information is packaged inside each individual object. Given this local packaging, information structures can be modified on the fly without shutting down the database or disturbing other running applications.

- The **multiple views** are made possible by composite objects, which combine lower-level objects into meaningful, integrated structures. Because individual objects can participate in any number of composite objects, there is no limit to the number of "views" that can be created for any given collection of data. Moreover, since composite objects contain the actual IDs of the objects they encompass, these composite views can be used for any database operation, including updating.

Here's an example of how much more efficient an object DBMS can be relative to a relational DBMS when storing complex information. The U. S. Navy is developing a system for materials acquisition that requires it to maintain a feature-based parts information database. It found the relational DBMS it had originally selected to be painfully slow at manipulating these data structures. For example, storing the geometry necessary to display a printed circuit board consisting of 2,500 components in a CAD system required a quarter of an hour with the relational system.

Example: A bill of materials

To see if an object DBMS could help with this problem, the Navy loaded the same information onto an ODBMS and ran a comparison test. The object DBMS performed the same storage in just nine seconds—a speed improvement of two orders of magnitude. The same degree of improvement was obtained with retrieval as well.

An object database can be 100 times faster

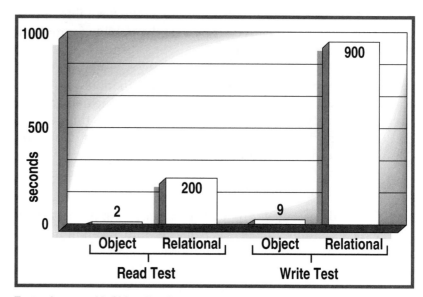

Faster Access with Object Databases

These results are typical for complex data

While these results are dramatic, they are generally typical of the performance improvements that can be gained with complex data. Relational systems typically handle simple transactions faster than object databases, and they are better suited to associative queries. But when it comes to handling complex data structures, object databases are consistently faster. A study by Sun Microsystems established a benchmark for dealing with structured information and found that every object DBMS tested outperformed all of the leading relational systems (Cattell, *Object Data Management*: Addison-Wesley, 1991).

Object DBMSs handle exceptions well

Object DBMSs also offer the ability to handle exceptions to normal information structures by creating subclasses. For example, if you must store foreign addresses in a database that's designed for domestic addresses, you can create a subclass of the address class to handle the additional information. That allows you to handle the special case without restructuring all the existing addresses.

Because the earliest object DBMSs were motivated primarily by the desire to build a better kind of DBMS, their design was driven by DBMS considerations. These considerations included concurrency control, security, integrity, and other traditional DBMS features.

DBMS considerations dominated

In keeping with the historical trend in DBMSs, these early object DBMSs defined their own proprietary data-definition (DDL) and data-manipulation (DML) languages. For example, Servio's GemStone uses Opal, a proprietary version of Smalltalk, for both its DDL and DML. Ontologic's VBase product used two C-based languages to play these roles: *TDL* for the DDL and *COP* for the DML.

Proprietary languages were often used

2. Persistence for Object Languages

For single-user applications written in Smalltalk, providing persistence for objects was not a problem. As described earlier, Smalltalk concludes each session by saving a complete image of its current state, including the values of all the variables in its objects. When Smalltalk is started up again, everything is just as it was. Object persistence is entirely automatic and completely transparent.

Smalltalk provides automatic persistence

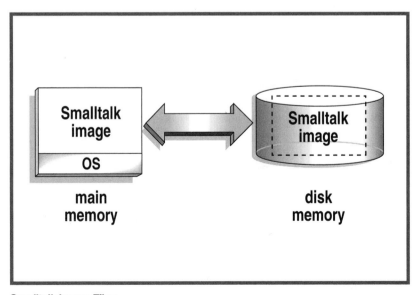

Smalltalk Image Files

Flat files and relational DBMSs don't work well

For multi-user applications, something more than image files is required. Several alternatives to image files have been explored. It is possible to store object information in flat files, but flat files are inadequate for multi-user access. Another option is to store objects in relational DBMSs, but performance with this option is generally poor—objects must be decomposed into simple record structures to fit the format of a relational system, then reconstructed again upon retrieval.

Object DBMSs are the best solution

The obvious and most viable alternative is to use a new kind of DBMS for storing and sharing objects, one built exclusively for this purpose. This gives rise to the second motivation for adopting object DBMSs.

This new use shifted the emphasis to languages

This emerging use of object DBMSs placed new demands on their design. Whereas the initial motivation was driven by DBMS concerns, this second wave of interest was driven by language concerns. With this shift, the traditional approach of using a proprietary DDL/DML became less attractive because it required translation between the application language and the language of the database with every transaction.

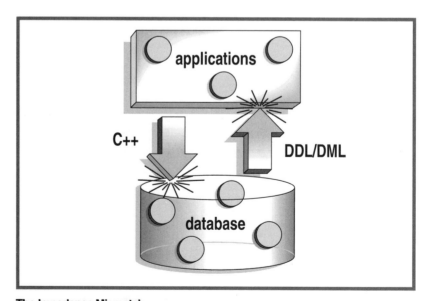

The Impedance Mismatch

For example, suppose applications are programmed in C++. Translating C++ objects into Opal or COP objects requires an extra step on the programmer's part, one that slows both development and run-time performance. This mismatch led to a second wave of object DBMSs that were designed as extensions of existing languages. The most common choice was C++, with LISP coming in as a distant second.

The result was a wave of C++ DBMSs

In keeping with this trend, Ontologic withdrew its VBase product from the market and replaced it with a C++ compatible DBMS called Ontos. Servio, with its Smalltalk-like Opal, continued to support its Smalltalk interface but also added an interface to C++.

Early companies revised their products

Given the new concerns about language compatibility, some of the new entrants in the object DBMS arena were a bit less concerned about the traditional DBMS functionality of their products. For example, Object Design's ObjectStore provides very fast, efficient access to persistent C++ objects through a virtual memory scheme. While this approach has tremendous performance advantages, the idea of C++ programmers gaining access to corporate databases through direct pointers would strike terror in the hearts of most traditional database administrators.

DBMS concerns became secondary

3. Repositories for Software Components

As the market for object technology continues to mature, yet another role is emerging for object DBMSs. If software is to be constructed from a library of reusable classes, there must be some repository for storing those classes and sharing them among many programmers.

A repository is needed for shared classes

The early solution to this problem was to use the same source-code control systems that had worked for storing functions for procedural programs. That approach was adequate for small teams, but large-scale reusability requires more sophisticated concurrency controls, extended checkouts, versioning systems, and other DBMS features. Object DBMSs represent the obvious choice for storing and sharing reusable classes.

Source-code control programs aren't sufficient

This use introduces a new requirement

This newest application of object DBMSs threatens to place yet another requirement on the technology: the ability to store objects written in different languages. At present, most object repositories require that all objects be written in the same language. While this assumption may hold for relatively local development efforts, it seems unlikely that entire enterprises will standardize on a single object language.

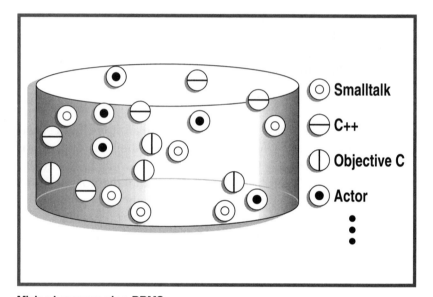

Mixing Languages in a DBMS

Some support is available now

At present, there is some support for this option. Servio's Gem-Stone stores all classes in its own Opal format, allowing translation to and from either Smalltalk or C++ when the objects are stored and retrieved. By contrast, the VERSANT system stores C++ and Smalltalk objects in a form similar to their native format. However, each type of object currently can be accessed only from its original language or from C.

Better class locators will also be necessary

Finally, large repositories of reusable components will have to provide something more than the prototypical Smalltalk browser to help programmers find classes. While browsers are helpful, they are simply too slow and cumbersome when thousands of classes must be scanned and reviewed. Programmers will need active assistance from their repositories to find the classes they need.

In the ideal repository, a programmer could list a set of responsibilities a class must fulfill. The repository would then perform a similarity match against all its classes and return the ones that met the programmer's needs most closely. The programmer could then decide whether to use an existing class, subclass one of the existing classes, or create a new one from scratch.

Example: Similarity matching on responsibilities

APPROACHES TO BUILDING AN OBJECT DBMS

Now that the emerging roles of object DBMSs have been examined, it's time to look deeper into the technology and consider how object DBMSs are actually constructed. The first and most obvious discovery is that, like object languages, object DBMSs come in two basic forms: pure and hybrid. Pure object DBMSs are built from the ground up to handle the storage of objects. Hybrid object DBMSs are constructed by adding a layer of object features on top of an existing database engine.

There are two main approaches

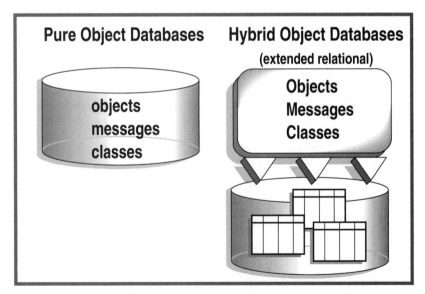

Pure vs. Hybrid Object Databases

Pure Object Databases

Pure object databases are dedicated to objects

As with languages, pure object DBMSs are designed and constructed for the sole purpose of dealing with objects. In general, DBMSs of this type are marketed by startup companies who specialize in this new form of DBMS. All of the products mentioned so far in this chapter are examples of pure object DBMSs.

Pure systems get a fresh start

Vendors of pure object DBMSs have the advantage of being unencumbered with the philosophy and technology of earlier generations. By starting from scratch, they can create products that are precisely tuned to the requirements of object management, while also taking advantage of the latest developments in DBMS technology. For example, most object DBMSs were designed from the beginning to offer distributed information storage. By contrast, this is a feature that is being slowly grafted onto existing relational systems.

The Hybrid Approach

Objects can be added to traditional systems

The second approach is to add object extensions to an existing type of DBMS. All the efforts I'm aware of in this arena are based on the relational model, and it seems unlikely that the network or hierarchical models will be recalled to service at this late date.

Relational systems can store objects as records

A relational DBMS stores objects by breaking their components down into table entries. This approach is equivalent to the "hybrid" approach to languages. DBMSs of this type are coming from established relational vendors who want to offer the advantages of objects without abandoning their established technology base.

In simple cases, this works fine

In some ways, using a relational DBMS to store objects makes a lot of sense. As explained in Chapter 4, classes are analogous to tables, and instances are analogous to rows. So pulling the values out of instances and placing them in records is a straightforward solution to storing objects.

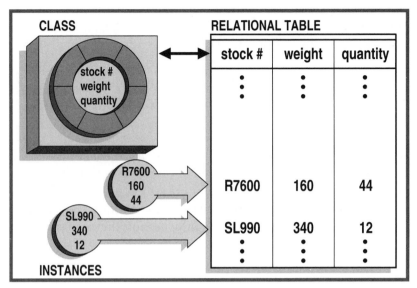

Storing Instances as Records

There are, however, some rather difficult problems with this scheme. To mention just a few:

But there are problems with this approach

- It **only works with strongly typed languages**. Relational DBMSs require that all entries in a column of a table have a fixed type and length. C++ variables meet this criterion, but Smalltalk plays havoc with this requirement.

- There is **no facility for user-defined types**. Information in relational systems has always been restricted to a fixed set of predefined data types. The ability to define new data types, in the form of classes, is a key aspect of object technology.

- Relational DBMSs **aren't well suited for storing complex procedures**. This is a crucial problem because the essence of object technology is to encapsulate related procedures and data.

- Relational DBMSs are **poor at navigational access**. Object technology depends heavily on accessing objects through their IDs. Relational systems were designed to use content-based, associative access.

All these problems are being addressed

Relational vendors are addressing these problems through what they call the *Extended Relational Model* (Cattell, *Object Data Management*: Addison-Wesley, 1991). In an extended relational system, untyped data can be stored, users can define new data types, and procedures can be stored either directly in the database or as references to separate files.

The BLOB plays a central role

One of the mechanisms for achieving these extensions is known as the BLOB, an acronym for a *binary large object*. Basically, BLOBs are files that contain binary information representing an image, a procedure, a complex structure, or anything else that doesn't fit well in a relational database. The database contains references to these files, so it does manage the information they contain, albeit indirectly.

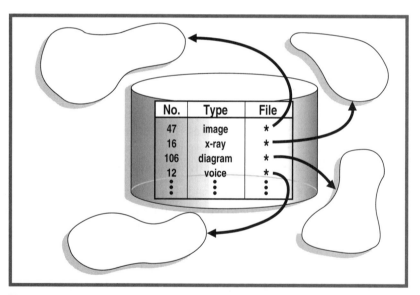

The Invasion of the BLOBs

But BLOBs aren't a very good solution

The use of BLOBs is not an elegant solution to the problem of storing multimedia information. Storing this information in external files denies it many of the protections naturally afforded by the DBMS. More important, BLOBs can't contain other BLOBs, so they can't take the form of composite objects. Also, BLOBs generally ignore the behavioral aspects of objects.

Tradeoffs Between the Two Approaches

Despite these reservations concerning BLOBs, both approaches to building an object DBMS are viable, and each offers distinct advantages:

Both approaches are viable

- **Pure object DBMSs provide a richer set of features for dealing with objects, messages, and classes,** the basic mechanics of object technology.

- **Pure object DBMSs are better at pointer navigation**, which is what gives object DBMSs their superior retrieval speed with complex information structures.

- **Extended relational systems are better for associative access,** and they are currently faster at transaction processing with simple data structures.

- **Extended relational DBMSs currently provide better tools** for defining databases and building applications.

These are a few of the tradeoffs to be considered in choosing between a pure object DBMS and an extended relational system. There are other considerations, but it would be premature to discuss them because the technology is changing so rapidly.

Both technologies are changing fast

Although there are a couple of products on the market, extended relational DBMSs are primarily theoretical at this point, so it's hard to argue their merits in any detail. Similarly, the pure object DBMSs are maturing so fast that some of their limitations are already being eliminated.

Extended relationals are just now appearing

Further complicating the comparison is that the two approaches are converging fast. Most pure systems now offer mechanisms to support efficient associative access, and their tools are becoming richer all the time. Extended relationals, on the other hand, are adding increased support for procedures, inheritance, and other object-oriented features. In fact, relational vendors are actually beginning to add object IDs to their tables and introduce pointer navigation as an alternative to associative access.

The two approaches are converging

Eventually there may be no difference

Eventually, pure object DBMSs and extended relational DBMSs may converge to the point where they are indistinguishable. At this point, the term "extended relational" may no longer make much sense because the relational vendors will have left the original relational model so far behind that it no longer applies. The simple act of adding pointer navigation to a relational system brings into question the mathematical foundation of relational technology.

Relational vendors will sell pure object DBMSs

By the time they go this far, relational DBMS vendors will, in effect, be in the object database business. Many of them recognize this fact and are quite open in acknowledging that the future belongs to object DBMSs, so long as they are arrived at by extending the relational model!

In the mean time, buy the features you need

The convergence between the pure and hybrid approach will take years to complete. In the meantime, your choice of technology should be based on your current needs. If transaction processing and SQL access are your primary concerns, then extended relational DBMSs offer a way to move toward objects without compromising your existing needs. On other hand, if you want full support for object technology in a fast, effective manner, your only option at this point is to go with a pure object DBMS.

We focus on pure systems

Object-oriented information systems require the full power of object technology from every component. For this reason, the remainder of this chapter focuses on pure object DBMSs. This focus is not meant to slight the extended relational systems, but to reflect current realities. If the day comes when a relational vendor can offer a product that matches the functionality and performance of a pure object DBMS, then you should seriously consider that product as a central component of your object-based information system.

COMPONENTS OF AN OBJECT DBMS

The Basic Architectural Components

Every vendor of object DBMSs takes a different approach to constructing its product. There are, however, a few components that nearly all of them have in common. An overview of this common architecture will help you understand how object DBMSs work. It should also make you a more informed consumer as you compare the claims of the competing vendors.

Object DBMSs have a common architecture

Essentially, there are three basic kinds of components to an object database management system: object managers, object servers, and object stores. As shown in the following figure, they are layered in roughly that order: Applications interact with object managers, which work through object servers to gain access to object stores.

There are three basic components

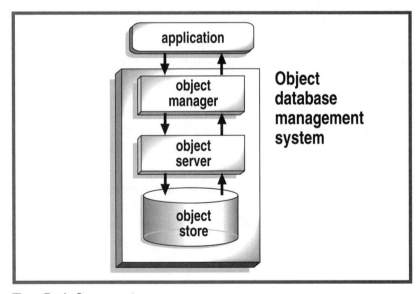

Three Basic Components

There are many combinations

The reason these components are separated is that they can be mixed and matched to provide a wide variety of options for managing shared objects. The illustration shows the simplest case, in which a single-user application requires only one of each component. After the roles of the various components have been defined in this context, we will examine more sophisticated ways of combining them.

We focus on the manager and server

Most of the discussion focuses on the two higher-level components. The object store, the actual database on the disk, consists of a physical storage system that places objects in database files working through the local operating system. Although its role is obviously indispensable, the functions it performs are very low level and of little interest to this discussion.

Object Managers

Object managers provide a local cache

The basic role of the object manager is to manage a local cache of objects for an individual application. Essentially, applications check out objects from the database, using the services of the object server to gain access to the store of objects, then check the objects back in when they are done with them. Typically, the local cache is implemented as virtual memory to avoid size limitations, paging to the disk as needed to bring in the actual objects.

This cache is a temporary workspace

The local object cache acts as a temporary workspace for dealing with objects outside the database environment. As a rule, all new objects are created in the cache first, then committed to the database when completed. The same is true for modifications of existing objects.

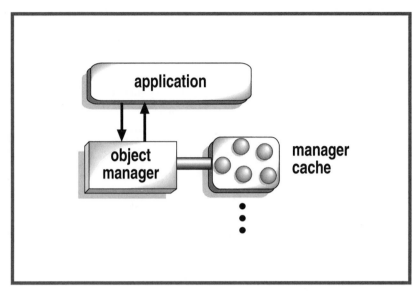

Object Manager with Local Cache

The object manager also works with an object server to provide other types of services. These include managing the log-in and log-out processes, committing new or modified objects to the database, and performing any necessary translations between program object formats and database object formats. An example of this last service would be converting program objects from C++ form to the Opal format used internally by the GemStone DBMS.

The object manager provides other services

Object Servers

The role of the object server is to manage a separate, shared cache of objects. This cache is implemented in shared memory so that it can be accessed by many different applications simultaneously. Essentially, the server uses this cache to coordinate access to the object store.

The object server manages its own cache

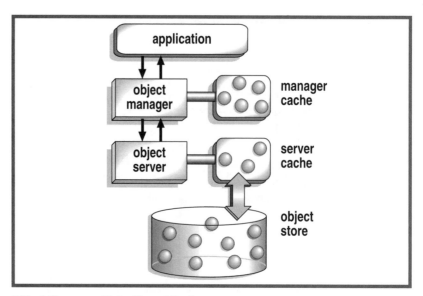

Object Manager with Its Shared Cache

The object server handles locking

For example, all locking operations are performed by the object server using this shared cache. Locks are used to avoid conflict when different applications attempt to access the same objects. Locking and transaction management are among the primary responsibilities of the object server.

Object servers translate object formats

Object servers also handle the different physical data formats among the various machines they may be serving. For example, if an object manager is running on a Sun 4 and a server is running on an IBM RS/6000, the object server would automatically translate the data storage formats so that the Sun would read the objects correctly. This facility allows object DBMSs to run in a distributed manner across heterogeneous hardware platforms.

Combining Object Managers and Servers

Managers and servers can be linked in many ways

Most object DBMSs allow very sophisticated combinations of object managers, servers, and stores. In addition, they permit a wide range of configurations such that these various components may be run on the same or different machines in order to optimize computing resources.

In one common configuration, many different applications would access a single database. In this case, each application would have its own object manager and object server, but the various servers would all interact with the object store through the shared cache maintained by the object servers.

Multiple applications may access a single DBMS

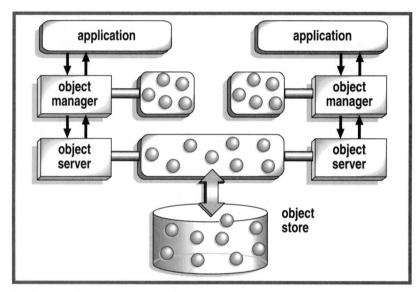

Multiple Applications on a Single DBMS

Conversely, a single application could access multiple databases, using a separate object manager and server for each. This is actually a limited form of distributed object management. We will consider more sophisticated forms of object distribution in the next section.

A single application may access multiple DBMSs

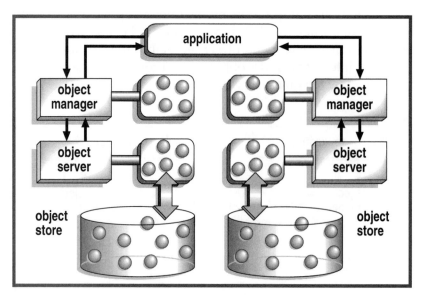

One Application Accessing Multiple Object DBMSs

Many combinations are possible

Between these two extremes, many intermediate combinations are possible. For example, multiple applications could access multiple databases in an overlapping manner.

Linking vs. Remote Procedure Calls

Managers and servers can be linked to applications

However many object managers and servers may be involved in a system, there are various options for how they are actually coupled together. The simplest option is to link an application, object manager, and object server into a single process, using standard program-linking techniques. This option provides maximum speed because the various components interact through direct function calls. This configuration is typically used for single-user environments, such as Computer-Aided Design (CAD) and other engineering applications.

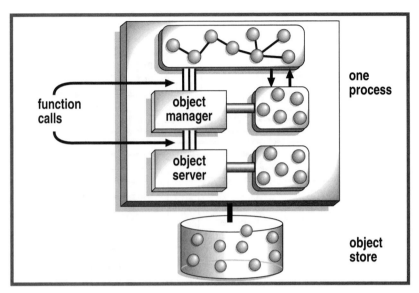

Fully Linked Configuration

Other options come about by moving various components into other processes, either on the same or different machines. These processes communicate through *remote procedure calls* (RPCs), which are slower than direct function calls but offer more flexibility in the allocation of computing resources.

They can also be connected through RPCs

Let's take this option to its logical extreme. An application, its object manager, the corresponding object server, and the object store could all run on different machines. This kind of distribution is most common in multi-user applications that need to optimize the use of existing computing resources. Some database products even allow the communications among these components to take place over different network protocols simultaneously.

Example: Every component on a different machine

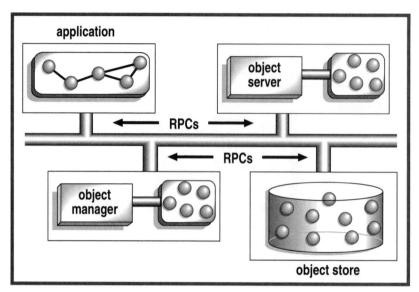

Fully Distributed Components

UNDERSTANDING OBJECT DBMS DESIGNS

An object DBMS is a combination of tradeoffs

There is no one right way to build an object DBMS. As with object languages, designing — and selecting — an object DBMS is a matter of making a series of tradeoffs on a number of dimensions. The combination of these decisions defines a unique product. In this section, we consider some of the more important decisions and their possible consequences.

Proprietary DDL/DML vs. Language Extension

Traditional DBMSs have DDLs and DMLs

As described previously, early object DBMSs were driven by the desire to create a better kind of DBMS. Traditionally, database management systems have contained their own data definition and manipulation languages (DDLs and DMLs), and early object DBMSs were no exception. However, unlike earlier databases, the languages provided by these object DBMSs were computationally complete, allowing tremendous flexibility in expressing operations on data.

Having a self-contained language increases the power of an object DBMS in several ways. First, it provides a single canonical form for dealing with persistent objects regardless of the language in which they were originally defined. Moreover, since all methods are defined in a single language maintained as part of the database, it is possible in principle—although not always in practice—to execute methods directly in the database environment.

A built-in language has many benefits

On the downside, having a separate DDL/DML for the database represents yet another language to learn. For corporate database administrators, who are accustomed to having their own database language, this is not a problem and may be perceived as a benefit. But for programmers who simply want persistent objects, having to deal with two different languages is not a welcome prospect.

But two different languages are required

Closely related to the dual-language issue is the problem of dual object spaces. Given different application and DBMS languages, all classes have to be defined twice, once in each form, and any changes to these classes must be maintained in both places.

Dual object spaces are also required

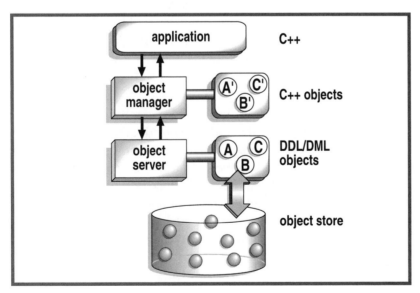

Dual Object Spaces

And objects are not always identical	Moreover, the objects in the database are rarely identical to the program-based objects because the demands of persistence and shareability often require different representations. This complicates the management of the two object spaces even further.
Language extensions simplify matters	By contrast, object DBMSs that extend existing languages such as C++ and Smalltalk avoid these problems. Classes are defined only once, and no translation is required to go from database form to application form. Moreover, the schema definitions for database objects can often be captured directly from the application source code rather than being defined by special DBMS tools. This is a real convenience, especially when building complex applications.
Persistence can be fully transparent	In some implementations, application methods can actually access persistent objects transparently, without regard to whether objects are currently in the application or the database. This can simplify the coding of objects because programmers need not be concerned with the issue of persistence at all.
But there are costs to this simplicity	However, the lack of a separate DDL/DML removes a level of protection and control over the database that traditional database administrators may be reluctant to give up. Also, getting existing object languages to handle persistence transparently requires changes to those languages.
Persistence can be added in two ways	These changes can be accomplished by creating a new compiler for the base language that adds new, database-oriented commands. But programmers are usually reluctant to give up their preferred compilers and convert over to one supplied by a DBMS vendor. More commonly, the persistence is achieved by running a preprocessor on the source code, then applying the customer's preferred compiler. This is often regarded as the better option, but it's still an unwelcome complication of the compilation process.

Techniques for Handling Procedures

Object DBMSs handle procedures in two different ways. Some store procedures in external files, while others keep them right in the database. The first technique is typically used with DBMSs that are extensions of existing languages, particularly compiled languages such as C++. The second approach, which is less common, is more likely to be found with DBMSs that have their own DDL/DML.

Procedures are handled in two ways

The first strategy is similar to the procedure libraries of traditional DBMSs, in which application programs interact with a DBMS by linking in special subroutines from a library of access procedures. Of course, with objects the procedures handle much more than simple access.

The first approach resembles access libraries

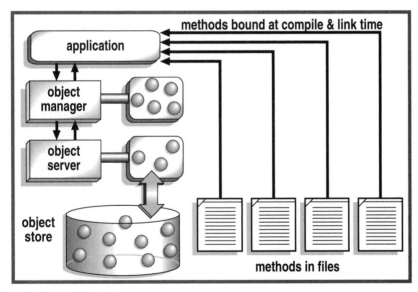

Storing Methods in Files

Moreover, one of the major problems with traditional access libraries—finding the right procedure to access a given piece of data—is eliminated. Given the relationship of procedures to data in object technology, if you know the data you want, the procedure is immediately determined.

There's no problem finding the right procedure

But updating is not automatic	However, as with database access libraries, updating methods stored outside the database can become complicated. If you modify the definition of a stored class, then every model or application that uses that class has to be relinked and redeployed. Moreover, the changeover has to be all-or-none; if any application is missed, old methods could be used to access new instances, producing faulty results and possibly corrupting the database.
Versioning helps somewhat	This problem can be reduced through the use of versions, as discussed below. However, all versions do is allow you to make sure that old methods aren't applied to new instances. You still have to relink and redeploy all the affected applications.
Security and concurrency controls are sacrificed	Another problem with storing method definitions outside the database is that they are much less secure. In most contemporary systems, the methods are stored in standard Unix files that, by traditional IS standards, have rather limited security controls. Moreover, this approach eliminates any concurrency controls over methods. Without these controls, different developers could create conflicting modifications of the same methods and unknowingly create inconsistencies in database access.
So the first approach is less than ideal	In short, storing methods outside the database breaks down encapsulation and treats methods as second-class citizens, denying them the protections and services of the DBMS. If your models and applications change only rarely and your primary concern is with storing instance variables, this need not be a serious concern. However, this approach definitely falls short of meeting the full promise of object-oriented DBMSs.
The second approach stores methods in the database	The alternative approach to handling methods is to store them directly in the database, making them an inseparable part of the stored information.

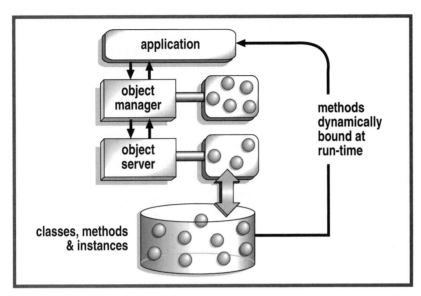

Storing Methods in the Database

It is clear from the preceding paragraphs that this approach offers several advantages:

This approach has several advantages

- **Methods can be updated automatically.** If a method is changed, applications can automatically access the new method and apply it. Not every system can do this because it requires dynamic binding, which is not fully supported in all object-oriented languages.

- **Methods are more secure.** Because they are stored directly in the database, methods benefit from the various levels of security built into DBMSs. As the methods of database objects begin to express more of the intelligence and proprietary procedures of an organization, this security will become increasingly important.

- **Methods enjoy concurrency controls.** Like security, this benefit is taking on increasing importance as object DBMSs begin to play a central role in corporate information management. In a fast-changing environment, methods and data structures may be altered quite frequently. Controlling concurrent access to methods will be essential to maintaining database integrity.

- **Methods enjoy other DBMS benefits.** With this approach, methods are treated as corporate assets of equal value to data. Not only are they protected by security and concurrency controls, they also receive routine backups, transaction management for multiple changes, and other benefits normally provided by database management systems.

This approach is best for component repositories

These advantages are important for all three of the major uses of object DBMSs, but they are particularly relevant to using object DBMSs as repositories for reusable components. In this role, the primary responsibility of the DBMS is to manage class definitions as opposed to instance values. So it is vital that the DBMS provide change management, concurrency controls, security, and other DBMS features for methods as well as data.

Locking and Transaction Management

Locks avoid conflicting access

As with conventional DBMSs, locks are used to control concurrent access by multiple users. By allocating locks, object servers ensure database integrity by preventing one application from changing objects that another application is currently accessing.

Locking can be done at multiple levels

Depending on how an object DBMS is implemented, objects can be locked on various levels of granularity. Most products allow objects to be locked individually. Virtually all products also support locking of larger groupings of objects called *pages* and *segments*. Although the precise definitions of these terms vary, they generally refer to how objects are organized on the disk.

Each has its advantages

Each level of locking has advantages. Locking individual objects gives fine granularity and minimizes concurrency conflicts. But page and segment locking are more efficient when objects that go together are stored together and need to be checked out as a unit.

Example: Composite and collection objects

For example, many systems allow users to store all the elements of composite or collection objects on the same page or in the same segment. Being able to lock and load this entire structure of objects minimizes both access time and network overhead.

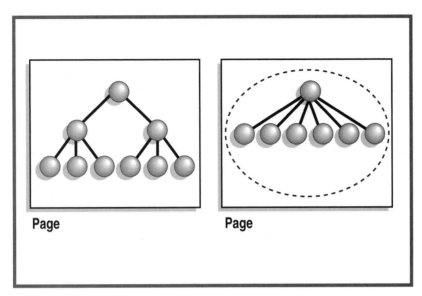

Clustering Objects

The preceding description of locking is highly simplified. Commercial object DBMSs provide many different forms of locking mechanisms, including write locks, read locks, dirty read locks, write with notification, read with notification, and others.

There are many variations on these themes

These flexible locking mechanisms are required to support the greater complexity of information in object databases. With just the traditional read/write locks, there could easily be too much contention for access to complex, nested structures, and database performance would suffer.

Object technology requires sophisticated locking

Managing Short and Long Transactions

Object DBMSs typically provide two options for locking to support what are known as *short* and *long* transactions. In short transactions, the locks do not survive a database session—when a user disconnects from the database, the locks are automatically removed. Short transactions are typically used to do quick updates to stored values, which is the way most traditional DBMSs are used.

Short transactions use temporary locks

Long transactions need persistent locks

By contrast, long transactions take place over multiple database sessions, so their locks are preserved from one session to the next. Long transactions are typically used for applications such as computer-aided design (CAD), in which large groups of objects are worked on for hours or days at a time, then returned to the database in a modified form.

Locks may be obtained early or late

In most cases, locks are requested from the object server at the time objects are brought into the local cache, which assures that no other application can change them in the meantime. However, objects can be brought into the local cache without locks, leaving the objects available for others to lock and possibly modify. When such objects are returned to the database, the object server attempts to allocate locks at that time to see if all the changes can be stored in the database.

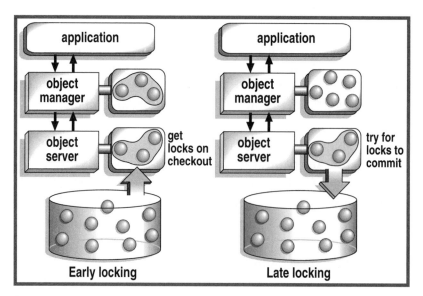

Early and Late Locking

If an application changes multiple objects without previously obtaining locks on all those objects, there's a possibility that it can't commit all of its changes due to other users locking some of the affected objects. Object servers protect against this problem by treating all the changes as a single *transaction*, ensuring that either all the changes are made or none are made. If some are completed but others fail, the object server will perform what is called a *rollback* to undo any changes that were made and restore the database to its previous state.

Changes are committed as transactions

Distributed vs. Nondistributed DBMSs

Being able to distribute data transparently across a variety of hardware platforms is an increasingly important feature for corporate databases, and most object DBMSs have been constructed with this feature in mind. The basic approach to implementing this feature is to provide a single object manager interacting with multiple object servers, each of which can access a separate physical database.

Most object DBMSs permit distribution

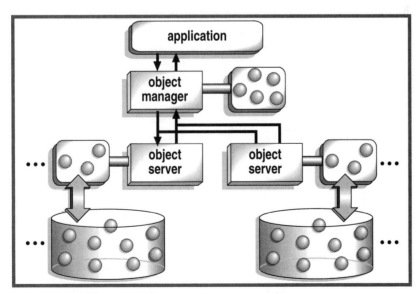

Access to Distributed Objects

Full transaction management is provided

In each case, the actual location of any given object is transparent to the application program. In addition, the shared object server handles all concurrent access, including locking, transaction rollbacks, and other facilities for supporting distributed data.

Two-phase commits are essential

A particularly important feature in managing distributed data is support for two-phase commits. In a *two-phase commit*, the object servers first check to see if they can obtain locks on all the affected objects in the various databases involved. If they all succeed, they then proceed to the second phase and commit the changes for all objects. If one or more servers fail, or if the second phase can't be completed for some reason, the object servers will back out of the transaction and return all objects to their previous state.

Support for Workgroups

Personal databases are fast and convenient

Some object DBMSs provide the ability to support personal databases in addition to shared or group databases. The advantage of a personal database is that it can be accessed more quickly because it avoids the overhead of network transfer and bypasses locks and other concurrency mechanisms.

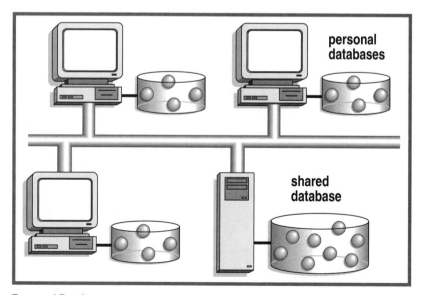

Personal Databases

Personal databases are particularly valuable for applications where individual users need access to large groups of objects for extended periods of time. This requirement is typically supported using check-out procedures with long-transaction support. For example, a CAD program could check out the objects for a part diagram, then check them back in two days later after the diagram was revised.

They are best for long transactions

In the meantime, however, the CAD user would need someplace to store the objects when the CAD program wasn't running. They could be kept in a local file, but that approach sacrifices many of the benefits of tying the CAD program into an object DBMS in the first place. Having a personal object database to hold the objects locally is a much better solution.

They provide a place to keep checked-out objects

Versioning of Objects

Support for versioned objects is another important feature for object DBMSs. The main use of versioning is to track the evolution of object states and definitions in the database rather than in application programs. For example, as a part undergoes successive engineering changes, it is important that earlier versions be available to existing assemblies even as the new versions are incorporated into subsequent releases.

Versioning permits tracking evolution

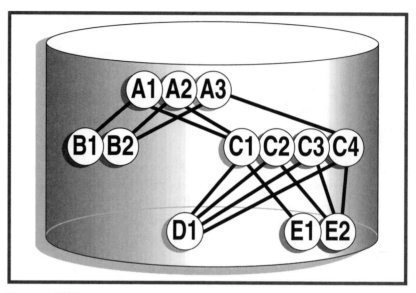

Versioned Objects

Versioning also permits alternatives

Another important use of versioning is to provide an alternative solution to locking mechanisms such that multiple designers can store alternative definitions of a part without conflict. After a decision has been made about the final design, one version is preserved and the others deleted or, if they show promise for other situations, archived for later use.

Single vs. Multiple Inheritance

Some DBMSs support multiple inheritance

Object DBMSs differ in their support for multiple inheritance. While it is certainly preferable to have multiple inheritance available if it is truly required by a complex situation, this facility can be even more dangerous in databases than it is in languages. The problem is that groups of people are accessing persistent data and changing the multiple ancestors to objects, often with confusing and conflicting results.

Use it with caution

As with languages, the rule of thumb is that multiple inheritance should be used only if it truly simplifies a problem or eliminates a significant amount of redundancy.

Support for Queries

Object DBMSs are founded on the idea that pointer navigation is the dominant access mechanism to the data. This is in contrast to relational systems, which are based on the notion that associative accesses are preeminent. In this regard, object DBMSs actually represent a return to the earlier network and hierarchical models, which were entirely based on navigational access.

Object DBMSs use pointer navigation

However, object DBMS vendors recognize the importance of associative access, and virtually every one offers facilities for this kind of access. To date, associative access in object DBMSs is generally not as fast and efficient as it is in relational systems, but that has more to do with the maturity of the technology than with any architectural limitations. As object DBMSs become more finely tuned over time, their performance on associative access may well match that of relational systems.

They also provide associative access

Of course, one of the benefits of associative access is the availability of declarative query languages, especially the now-standard structured query language (SQL). While SQL is not naturally suited to object retrieval, most vendors of object DBMSs are extending the SQL model to create an object SQL for accessing their systems. At least one vendor has an OSQL on the market today, and an informal effort is now underway to standardize this extension of SQL.

OSQL is on the way

Although object DBMS vendors are eager to add associative access to their systems, they are typically doing so in a way that violates one of the basic tenets of the technology—namely, the encapsulation of data. In order to get reasonable performance for content-based access, they bypass methods entirely and examine variables directly, building B-trees, hash tables, and other structures based on the values they find. This compromises the value of encapsulation because changes in the data structures are no longer isolated to the object, but require changes in the associative access code that has been built on those structures.

Associative access violates encapsulation

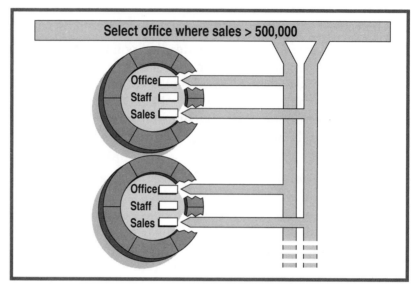

Violating Encapsulation

A SURVEY OF CURRENT PRODUCTS

Here is a snapshot of current products

The following section provides capsule reviews of the major object DBMSs on the market today. While this information is bound to become dated as these products evolve and new offerings enter the market, it may nonetheless be helpful to take a snapshot of the current state of the market and see how the different vendors are dealing with the design issues described previously. In the interests of objectivity, the products are described in roughly historical order.

Servio: GemStone

Servio's GemStone has its own DDL/DML

One of the earliest multi-user object DBMSs on the market was GemStone from Servio Corporation. GemStone has its own proprietary DDL/DML called Opal, which is essentially a DBMS-oriented version of Smalltalk. All DBMS methods are written in Opal; definitions of persistent classes must be defined in both Opal and the application language.

GemStone supports C, C++, Smalltalk (from both ParcPlace and Digitalk), and any language with C foreign function calls. Following Smalltalk, GemStone supports single inheritance only. The DBMS does not support distribution or versioning, although versioning can be achieved artificially by defining an abstract class *versioned object* and subclassing it.

GemStone supports multiple languages

GemStone is one of only two commercial object DBMSs that store their methods directly in the DBMS and dynamically bind them to applications whenever objects are accessed. If a DBMS method is changed, all applications automatically use the new version. It is also possible for GemStone to execute methods directly in the DBMS environment, bringing it closer to supporting active objects than most other products currently on the market.

GemStone stores methods in the DBMS

Ontos: Ontos

Another pioneer in the object DBMS world is Ontos Corporation, formerly known as Ontologic. Ontos originally introduced a product known as VBase, which had its own C-based DDL and DML. It subsequently removed that product from the market and introduced Ontos in its stead.

Ontos began with its own DDL/DML

The new product provides a C++ class library of DBMS interface objects that supports multiple inheritance. Like most C++ products, it also has a C interface that allows access from languages that support C foreign function calls. Ontos uses an independent object space for the DBMS, in that objects must be explicitly stored and retrieved to gain persistence.

Ontos is based on C++

Objectivity: Objectivity/DB

Like Ontos, Objectivity/DB from Objectivity is also based on C++ and supports multiple inheritance. It, too, has an independent object space and requires explicit storage and retrieval of objects. The product supports fully distributed data and offers good performance. It provides good support for long transactions.

Objectivity/DB is also based on C++

It is specialized for ECAD

Of the various object DBMS vendors, Objectivity has the most sharply defined market niche. Its product and services are specifically targeted to the computer-aided design market, with a distinct emphasis on electrical and mechanical CAD, and the staff is uniquely qualified in this area.

Versant: VERSANT ODBMS

Versant combines C++ and Smalltalk

Versant Object Technology, formerly known as Object Sciences, markets another product based on C++. Like other C++ DBMSs, it supports multiple inheritance and also provides a C interface for interacting with traditional languages. Unlike most C++ DBMSs, it is also capable of access from Smalltalk-80, and it can store Smalltalk methods in their native form directly in the DBMS.

Versant supports private DBMSs

VERSANT ODBMS is fully distributed and provides support for both personal and multiple group DBMSs. VERSANT supports versioning and offers a wide range of locking options for both short and long transactions.

Versant offers good tools

Versant is now rolling out an extensive array of tools to complement its DBMS technology. These tools include object modelers, schema designers, screen and report tools, support for database administrators, and an object SQL tool based on research done by Texas Instruments. Versant also offers transparent integration with relational DBMSs through its VERSANT Star product, and extensions for integrating hierarchical and network DBMSs are planned.

Object Design: ObjectStore

ObjectStore uses virtual memory

Object Design's ObjectStore is an extension of C++ that takes a different approach to object persistence. Rather than maintaining a separate object space that requires explicit store and retrieval operations, ObjectStore handles persistent objects automatically, using a virtual-memory scheme to create sufficiently large object spaces.

This approach is simple for programmers and leads to fast execution. However, it does require the use of either a modified C++ compiler or a preprocessor to distinguish between persistent and transient objects. It also makes the database more vulnerable to wild pointers in application programs, which may be a concern for database administrators.

This makes it fast and easy to use

ObjectStore also provides a C interface for direct calls from traditional languages. It offers good support for both long transactions and nested transactions within long transactions. The DBMS supports distributed objects.

ObjectStore supports long transactions

Itasca Systems: Itasca

Itasca is a newly released, commercial version of Orion, an object DBMS developed as a research project by the MCC consortium in Austin, Texas. Its commercialization is being funded in part by Control Data Corporation, a member of MCC.

Itasca began life as Orion

Itasca is a distributed object DBMS that supports both private and shared databases with long transactions between the two. Object versioning is also supported.

Itasca supports private databases

Like GemStone, Itasca is exceptional in that methods are stored in the database rather than in external files. As with GemStone, updated methods are automatically accessed by existing programs without recompiling. Primary access is through LISP, although the usual C interface is also provided.

Methods are stored in the database

9

Supporting Systems

It takes more than a language and a database to develop object-oriented systems. Specially designed tools and supporting systems are also required. This chapter provides a brief overview of the kinds of tools now on the market.

Good tools are essential

The emphasis of this chapter is on defining the different categories of tools and support systems that are important to object-oriented systems. I mention a few products by name to provide concrete examples, but I won't make any attempt to do a serious survey. There are too many products to evaluate, and the market is changing so fast that a survey would soon be dated in any case.

The emphasis will be on categories

In keeping with the conclusions of Chapter 7 on languages, we focus primarily on tools and systems that support Smalltalk and C++. These products are the most likely to dominate mainstream software development, and the offerings for these products are often leading indicators of what will be available for other products later on.

We focus on Smalltalk and C++

USER INTERFACES

The first point of contact between the user and an object-oriented system is the user interface. Unfortunately, there is a lot of confusion about the relationship between icons and object technology. So our first task is to clear up that confusion.

User interfaces are the first point of contact

Icons vs. Objects

People equate icons and objects

Perhaps the most common confusion about object technology is that it corresponds to the use of icons in the user interface. The popular equation is simple: If a program has little pictographs on the screen, it must be object oriented.

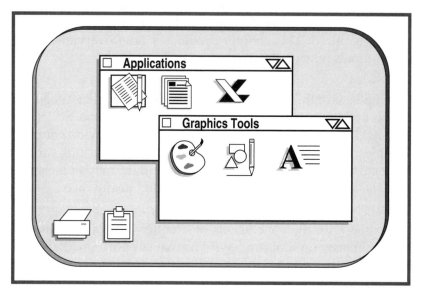

An Iconic Interface

Icons don't imply objects

While it's true that many object-based systems use iconic interfaces, there is actually no direct correspondence between the two. The choice of a user interface is essentially independent of whether the software behind the interface is programmed using object technology.

But icons often do represent objects

However, object technology and the iconic interface do have common roots in the original Smalltalk development effort, so it's natural to associate the two. And, in fact, most object systems with end-user interfaces do make extensive use of icons. This is because icons provide an excellent means of representing objects so that users can access and control them. It is much simpler to just click on an object than to type commands to that object at a command prompt.

Windows into Computing

One of Smalltalk's great contributions was that it popularized the concept of *windows*. Windows are simply rectangular areas on a screen that provide an interface to a particular program or aspect of a program. Users are typically able to have any number of windows open at a time. One of these windows is the "active" window —the one that the user is interacting with at any given moment. Depending on the system, the other windows may continue processing in the background or simply wait on screen, preserving their current state until the user reactivates them.

Smalltalk opened up windows on computing

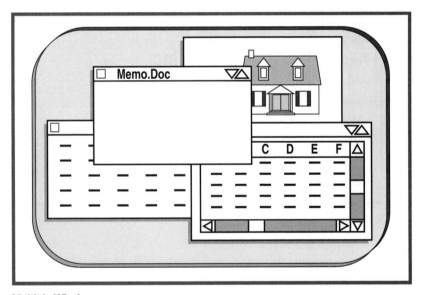

Multiple Windows

Smalltalk also demonstrated the value of a new device for controlling computers—the *mouse*. The mouse is nothing more than a simple pointing device with one to three buttons on it. As the mouse is moved about, a pointer moves on the screen. By clicking, double-clicking, dragging, and performing other mouse gestures, a wide variety of events can be caused to happen on the screen without ever touching the keyboard.

Mice permit direct manipulation

Menus avoid typing commands

One of the most common things to do with a mouse is to click on *menus*, which can cause other menus to pop up on the screen, open or close windows, select program options, or perform other tasks. Back in the 1970s, menus were a major breakthrough as compared to the typical command-line interface, in which users had to recall instructions from memory and type them letter-perfect at a command prompt.

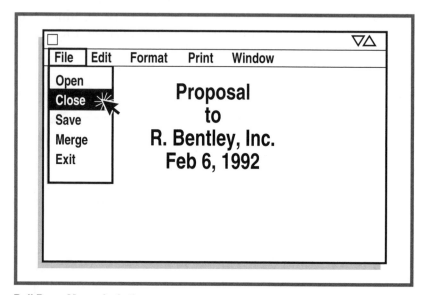

Pull-Down Menus in Action

Graphical interfaces are known as GUIs

Combinations of graphical components such as windows, icons, and menus, together with other visual controls such as radio buttons, slider controls, and scroll bars, are known as *graphical user interfaces*. GUIs, as they are fondly known, have now become the standard user interface.

GUIs come in many forms

In fact, the GUI is such a good standard that it comes in a seemingly infinite variety of forms. The major variants are Apple's Macintosh interface, Microsoft Windows, IBM's Presentation Manager, Sun's Open Look, and OSF Motif for Unix. Although these all differ in detail, there is a gradual convergence taking place in the industry that may ultimately lead to a standard, platform-independent interface.

Coping with Multiple GUIs

Having a graphical user interface simplifies the task of making objects available for direct user control. But the current situation of multiple, contradictory GUIs creates a new problem—objects have to know which GUI they are running under in order to behave properly. It's not just that the commands are different, a problem that could be solved with relatively simple translations. The harder problem is that the actual functionality differs among the various GUIs. Things that are possible under one GUI are impossible under another.

Multiple GUIs present a new problem

If a program is to run only under a single interface, there's no problem. But if it's going to run under multiple GUIs, as most programs must now do, it needs some form of insulation from the variations among GUIs. Programmers can achieve this goal by creating a layer of objects just beneath the GUI to act as an interface to the interface. In effect, an object sends a window object a message that says "I'd like to have a window that does such-and-such," and the window object calls the appropriate functions to get the current GUI to do the job.

Objects act as interface buffers

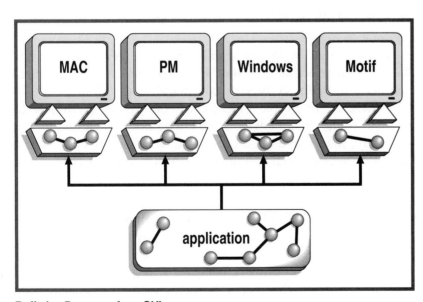

Buffering Programs from GUIs

Programs often use the lowest common denominator

If the desired function isn't available under a given GUI, the window object will provide the closest possible result. If it can't come remotely close, it will return a gesture of hopelessness to the requesting object. Typically, programs that have to run under multiple GUIs are designed to the least common denominator so that all desired operations can be carried out one way or another.

Class libraries can help

The problem of dealing with multiple GUIs is sufficiently common that class libraries are now available for buffering applications from the differences. For example, Glockenspiel makes a C++ library called CommonView that provides interface objects to deal with the differences between Windows and Motif.

Objects for Process Animation

Process animation helps the user

One of the most difficult aspects of building usable software is communicating to the user what's going on inside an application. While it is possible to provide a textual description of events in the form of a transaction log, few users are equipped or motivated to sort through such logs. A much more natural way to help users understand what's happening is to provide the feedback visually, through a technique called *process animation*.

Example: Deleting a file

A simple example of process animation can be seen in the way the Macintosh interface handles the deletion of files. In a nongraphical interface, you would type a command like "DELETE PROPOSAL.DOC." In a typical GUI, you would move the mouse to the appropriate document icon and click a button to highlight the document, then move the mouse up to a menu bar, click on the *File* option to pull down a submenu, then click on the *Delete* option on that list.

The Mac animates this operation

With the Mac, you simply use a mouse gesture to grab the document, drag it over to a trash-can icon, and drop it in. You see the file moving across the screen, and you watch it go into the trash can. Not only is this gesture a faster way to delete a file, it's also much easier to see what's actually going on and be sure that the action you intended took place.

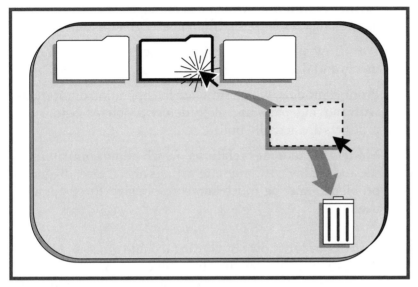

Deleting a File

Traditionally, process animation is accomplished by writing a separate set of routines to draw images on the screen and make them move. But with object technology, the methods for animating objects can be built right into the objects themselves. This makes it much easier to add animation capabilities to a program, and the encapsulation it provides greatly simplifies maintaining this animation capability as the system evolves.

Objects allow integrated animation

Applications of Process Animation

Deleting a file is, of course, a rather superficial example of process animation. Where process animation really comes into its own is in showing events deep inside the software that the user would never be able to "see" otherwise. Alternatively, process animation can be used to provide overviews of real-world processes that otherwise could not be monitored in a single graphic image. Here are a few examples of this technique in action:

Process animation can be very sophisticated

- **Factory simulation**, which lets managers monitor what's happening on the factory floor at any given moment

- **Workflow automation**, which manages the flow of documents and decisions within a company

- **Product models**, which simulate the operation of products with moving parts and help detect problems before the products are actually built

- **Models of customer relations**, which allow companies to see and replay customer interactions at a glance, diagnose problems, and be much more responsive to customers' needs

Example: Factory automation

Here's an example of how objects can facilitate process animation. A few years ago, a large manufacturer invested millions of dollars in a process animation system for its plants. The animation was wonderfully detailed, visually dazzling, and an excellent aid to management. Then a change was made in the layout of the plants, and the software had to go back for a major rework. After a few rounds of this, the manufacturer discovered that the cost of keeping the system in sync with the ever-changing manufacturing process was prohibitive. Ultimately, it abandoned the system.

Object animation facilitates change

Object technology doesn't provide an instant cure for this problem, but it does make it easier to keep the model in line with the real world. Every object is responsible for projecting its own image and actions. If you relocate machines, they draw themselves at their new coordinates. If you add new machines, they add themselves to the image. If you reroute a process, its physical movement on the screen will change to reflect its new route. In short, the process animation is fully coupled with the actual, working model of the manufacturing process, so changes tend to be incorporated automatically.

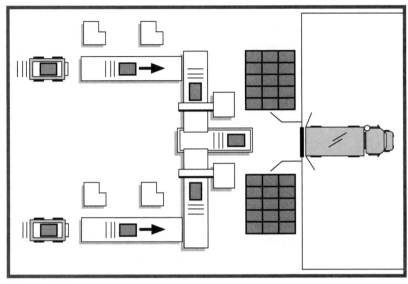

A Factory Animation

TOOLS FOR SMALLTALK

Once we penetrate beyond the user interface, tools and support systems become very language dependent. In particular, Smalltalk is unlike any other system in the philosophy behind its development environment. Given this, it is simpler to just describe the Smalltalk environment, then consider the tools and environments for C++.

Environments are language dependent

An Integrated Development Environment

Throughout the history of computing, programmers have been much like traditional craftspeople, assembling their own sets of tools to do their jobs as best they could. But the range of tools available for efficient programming is growing rapidly, and the problem of getting all these tools to work together is growing more serious. An emerging solution to this problem is to offer integrated environments with seamless connections among compatible tools. This approach limits the choices of individual programmers, but it rewards them with a system that can significantly increase their productivity.

The value of an integrated environment

Smalltalk pioneered the full-featured environment

Smalltalk pioneered the integrated development environment nearly 20 years ago. In fact, you can't buy Smalltalk just as a language; it's only available as a complete package. This package includes an editor, an interpreter and/or compiler, a class browser, a debugger, a rich variety of ancillary tools, and an extensive array of reusable classes.

The Editor

Smalltalk's editor is elementary

Smalltalk's editor is not its strongest feature. It's a full-screen text editor with enough features to satisfy basic programming needs, but it's rather primitive compared to the dedicated editors available for other languages. On the other hand, a Smalltalk editor need not be very sophisticated because the biggest thing you ever edit is a single method, and methods are rarely more than 10 to 20 lines long.

It supports direct execution

Although functionally simple, Smalltalk's editor offers a unique and powerful feature: You can highlight any sequence of commands and execute it right in the editor with a click of the mouse. If the highlighted code doesn't work, you can fix it on the spot. If it does work, you can easily "paste" it into a permanent method.

And it's always available

Then again, you may not have to do even that much. One of the unusual features of the Smalltalk editor is that it's automatically available anywhere you can view your code. If you are examining a method in the class browser, for example, you can change that method on the spot without having to call up a separate editor.

The Class Browser

The browser lets you scan classes

One of the challenges that object programmers face is keeping track of all the classes they and other programmers have created. To ease this task, Smalltalk provides what is called a *class browser*. The browser is a special window that includes multiple sections, called *panes*. Each pane contains a different kind of information. For example, the Digitalk browser looks something like this:

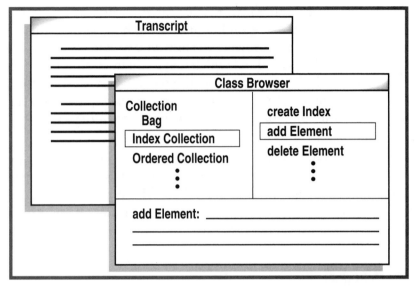

The Class Browser

The upper-left pane contains the list of classes that have been defined so far. This list uses indentation to show the position of each
class in the class hierarchy. As with outline processors, you can
expand or contract high-level classes to view or hide their subclasses, allowing you to focus down on the branch of classes that
interests you. As with most operations in Smalltalk, you highlight
a class by clicking the mouse on it.

*One pane
contains the
classes*

When a particular class has been highlighted, the names of its
methods show up in the adjacent pane. By moving the mouse to
this pane, you can scroll through these methods and highlight
whichever one interests you.

*Another pane
contains methods*

A larger pane below the lists of classes and methods shows the
actual code for the highlighted method. This lower pane is actually
the editor popping up again, so you can change the code on the
spot if you like. As usual, any changes you make take effect immediately.

*A third pane
contains method
definitions*

The browser locates related classes

The browser offers other features that can be very convenient. For example, once you have highlighted a method, you can use a mouse click to ask the browser to show you all the classes in the system that call this method, which helps you trace object interactions. Alternatively, you can have the browser list all the classes that implement a method with the same name, helping you keep track of how a polymorphism is being used in your system.

It also lets you work on these classes

If the browser shows you a class or method that interests you, you can simply click on its name and another browser window will come up set to that class and method. These browser services make it very easy to trace relationships among classes and repair those that aren't working properly.

The Debugger

Errors produce a walkback window

Whenever an object runs into a problem, it halts execution and brings up a message window telling you the nature of the problem. This window also shows you a list of the message-based interactions that led up to the error, to help you figure out what went wrong. In fact, this list can be scrolled, so that you can examine the entire history of the execution sequence if you like. This window is called the *walkback window* because it lets you trace back through the events that led up to the error.

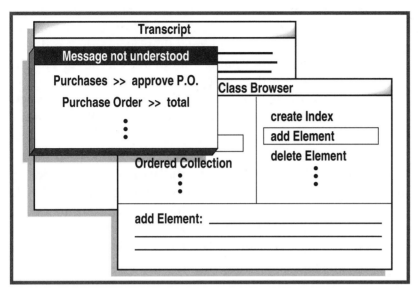

A Walkback Window

Sometimes, simply examining this history may give you enough information to fix the problem on the spot. If not, you can go into an interactive debugging mode by pulling up the *debug window*. This window also shows the walkback list, but with a new feature added: As you scroll back through the list of messages, you can see the definition of each method and you can inspect the contents of any variables it was operating on.

You can switch to the debug window

As with the class browser, the pane showing the method definition is actually an editor. You can make changes to the definition of the method, then resume processing from that point forward just as though the succeeding steps had never taken place. You can also change the values of the variables to see how this would affect execution. In either case, Smalltalk automatically takes care of resetting itself to the state it was in when the message you selected was actually executed, then makes a fresh start from that point.

You can modify code or values

Other debugging features are available

The debugger window also provides many of the standard facilities you would expect to find in a good debugger. For example, you can set breakpoints that will cause the system to halt and show you a walkback window. Again, you can inspect the current state of the system or go into debugging mode. You also have the option of stepping forward one message at a time after execution has been halted, allowing you to examine the actions of your program in close detail.

All this makes for fast debugging

The fact that changes to methods and variables take effect immediately, combined with the extensive debugging facilities described above, make debugging a highly interactive and rapid process in Smalltalk. This is arguably the main reason that Smalltalk is one of the most productive development environments available.

Pluggable Tools

Tools are programmed in Smalltalk itself

Other tools are available in the Smalltalk environment, but the three described previously should give you a good feeling for the environment. What is striking about all these tools is that they are not part of an external environment that surrounds the Smalltalk language, nor are they programmed into the compiler or interpreter. Rather, they are programmed in Smalltalk itself. In effect, they are extensions to the Smalltalk environment.

Smalltalk is fully extensible

This is a very important aspect of Smalltalk. With the exception of some basic primitives, everything in the Smalltalk environment, including the language itself, is programmed in Smalltalk. By its very nature, Smalltalk is a fully extensible language. In fact, you don't so much program in Smalltalk as extend the environment by adding new functionality. You are completely free to modify the editor, browser, or debugger if you are so inclined. You can also add new tools that suit your special needs. Alternatively, you can buy class libraries that, when loaded into your Smalltalk image, give you additional functionality.

For example, some class vendors offer graphical browsers that let you view your class hierarchy as a tree structure rather than an indented list. This can make it much easier to see the structure of your hierarchy and locate classes of interest.

Example: Graphical browsers

There are also classes that extend the language by adding buttons, scrollable display windows, and other useful tools informally known as *widgets*. Some of the more interesting widgets are pluggable gauges. Once you have one of these gauges in hand, you can "plug" a stream of data into it and a graphical image of a dial or linear gauge will appear that changes in real time as the numbers come in.

You can buy lots of widgets

For example, suppose you wanted to monitor the production rates of various machines on a factory floor. Using whatever sensors were required, you would collect a data stream from each machine, feed it into your computer, and pass a copy of the data to a gauge. If you arranged these gauges on the screen in the same layout as the factory, you could watch the flow of work move around the floor in real time, instantly spotting slowdowns or breakages. You could even attach running averages to the gauges, or instruct each gauge to sound an alarm and flash if its rate fell below a certain level.

Example: Monitoring a factory floor

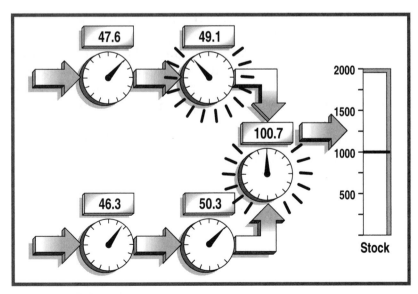

Monitoring a Factory

Building Applications

Programming consists of extending the environment

Throughout this discussion of the Smalltalk environment, I haven't even mentioned building applications. But in a sense, I actually have. The only way in which building applications with Smalltalk differs from working with the environment is that the tools and widgets you add are more focused on satisfying a particular set of business requirements. The basic activity is still the same. All programming in Smalltalk consists of extending the environment.

You have complete freedom in how you do this

It's a rather Zen-like concept if you think about it for a while. Smalltalk is nothing more or less than a fully extensible environment. You can specialize this environment to become whatever you want. You can add tools; you can extend the language to specialize it for factory automation; or you can build a stand-alone billing application. It's all the same to Smalltalk. As Chuck Durrett of EDS puts it, "There are no programs in Smalltalk—only objects behaving."

TOOLS FOR C++
C++ is a Minimalist Language

C++ is very different from Smalltalk

C++ could hardly be more different than Smalltalk and still fall within the same broad category of programming languages. Unlike Smalltalk, which was conceived from the beginning to provide a comprehensive, interactive environment for developing applications, C++ has its origins in systems development work. Its predecessor, C, was developed primarily for building operating systems. As such, it was conceived to be a small, fast language that ran very close to the machine, providing maximum control of system resources. C++, as an extension and superset of C, inherits these qualities.

Part of this inheritance is a philosophy of linguistic minimalism. The original idea was that nothing should be built into C that could be added through function libraries. C++ carries this tradition forward by insisting that everything that can possibly be divorced from the language be provided through class libraries. The result is a bare-bones language that requires very little memory, has easy access to the machine, runs fast, but requires much additional software to make it useful to application programmers.

C++ inherits a minimalist philosophy

Vendors of C++ realize that their customers require more than a bare-bones language. At present, there are several C++ products on the market that provide rich development environments that mimic the functionality of Smalltalk. However, all these extensions are written as separate programs and are closed to the programmer. If a vendor provides a browser, for example, that browser is delivered as a monolithic program that can't be modified or extended.

Vendors supply the additional software

The flip side of the minimalist philosophy behind C++ is that it gives maximum flexibility in the choice of tools to developers. They can choose their own editors; they can buy specialized debuggers; they can use different compilers for different purposes; and they can mix and match class libraries to get the functionality they want. Many programmers prefer this freedom over the convenience of an integrated development environment. Given the popularity of C, there is no shortage of quality tools for C++.

But quality tools are available

Editors

Editors are an excellent case in point. There is a very rich selection of sophisticated programming editors that have benefited from years of refinement in the field. Typically, they offer all the features you'd expect in a good word processor, such as search and replace functions, plus many features specific to C and C++ programming.

There are many good editors

These features include automatic indentation, routines for checking language syntax and program structure, and built-in help facilities that explain the commands of the language and give examples. With some editors, these examples can be cut and pasted directly into a program.

They offer strong programming features

Editing is important in C++

To be fair, the importance of sophisticated editing features is much greater in C++ than in Smalltalk. With Smalltalk, you rarely deal with more than 20 lines at a time, so you don't need a high-powered editing tool. C++ code, on the other hand, is file-based. Depending on the programmer's style, files can run anywhere from 10 to 1,000 lines long. Sophisticated editing tools are essential in this case.

Class Browsers

Class browsers are available

Some vendors who sell C++ development environments include class browsers that are similar to those in Smalltalk. In general, however, these browsers don't offer as much functionality as Smalltalk browsers.

But they are not very interactive

For example, the browser typically relies on the most recently linked version of the program, so it can quickly become out of date if you make many changes between compiles. In some environments, the browser is available in the debugger but not in the editor, making it hard to locate classes for revision. Also, the browser usually lets you view code but not modify it. The only browser I'm aware of that allows direct editing of viewed methods is the one that comes with Objectworks\C++.

Debuggers

Debugging C++ used to be very hard

C++ debuggers have been a sore point with programmers because C++ was originally implemented as a translator, as described in Chapter 7. In order to debug a C++ program, the developer would first run the translator to convert C++ code into C code, compile the C code, link the program, and then run the debugger against the C code. Since the conversion to C stripped all the object-oriented features out of the source code, it was very hard to figure out what was wrong with the original program. The fact that C++ changed all the function and variable names through a process known as *mangling* didn't help matters much.

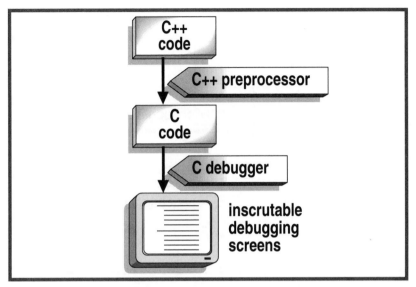

Debugging C++ Using a Preprocessor

Now that C++ is widely available in compiler form, there are several debuggers that work directly from C++ code. This greatly simplifies the debugging process. Errors can be traced to the offending line of source code, breakpoints can be set in the original C++ code, and programs can be single-stepped through C++ commands and messages. Most C++ debuggers also allow programmers to inspect variables at every step, and some allow developers to back up over previously executed lines of code and restart from an earlier point.

Good C++ debuggers are now available

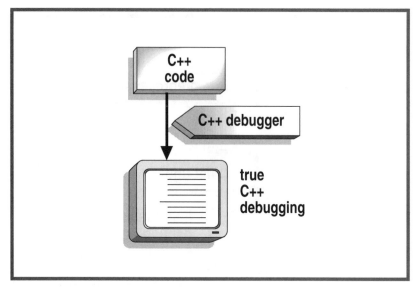

Debugging C++ Directly

But these debuggers aren't fully interactive

However, it's not possible to make changes directly in the debugger with C++. To correct a defect, it's necessary to exit the debugger, reenter whatever editor is being used, make the required change, recompile the modified code, relink the application, then reload the debugger to test the modifications. Integrated C++ environments typically simplify this process by making the transitions easier, but debugging C++ will always be a slower process as long as C++ is implemented as a conventional compiler.

Building Applications

C++ development is very traditional

Application development in C++ is very traditional compared to Smalltalk. Basically, you create and compile all the classes you need, then link them together into an executable file. Of course, the process is highly iterative, but that's the essence of it.

It results in stand-alone programs

The advantage of this traditional style of development is that, done properly, it leads to small, fast executable files. This is in contrast to Smalltalk, which usually requires a run-time engine to accompany every application. So, once completed, C++ programs carry considerably less overhead than do Smalltalk applications.

Integrated Environments for C++

ParcPlace, the vendors of ObjectWorks\Smalltalk, have recently introduced a companion product called ObjectWorks\C++. Their goal was an ambitious one—to duplicate the richness of the integrated Smalltalk development environment for C++. This is hard to do because C++ lacks some features of Smalltalk, such as weak typing and dynamic binding, that make interactive development particularly easy. Nonetheless, early versions of the product, while not yet measuring up to their Smalltalk product, offer much more integrated functionality than most C++ systems.

ParcPlace puts C++ in a Smalltalk environment

Another vendor that provides an integrated environment for C++ is Borland International. Borland C++ comes with a good editor, a fair class browser—unusual in any C++ offering—an excellent debugger, and a fairly extensive class library. For PC-based development, it is one of the best C++ environments available.

Borland also offers an integrated environment

To the extent that the language permits it, vendors of C++ compilers are striving to provide the same kind of integrated environment that Smalltalk users enjoy. The progress to date has been good, and there is always the chance that the C++ language itself will continue to evolve in ways that facilitate progress in the development environment.

C++ environments are improving

CASE AND 4GLs FOR OBJECTS

Many object enthusiasts seem to assume that the arrival of objects means that *Computer Aided Software Engineering* (CASE) tools and *fourth-generation languages* (4GLs) are no longer needed. In fact, just the opposite is true. These tools must be redefined to meet the needs of object technology, but there is much to be gained by applying these proven tools to object-oriented development.

CASE and 4GLs can work fine with objects

They can also smooth the transition

Moreover, object-oriented CASE and 4GL tools can serve as bridge technologies, smoothing the transition to objects by not requiring everyone to master all aspects of object technology right away. Developers who have worked with CASE and 4GL tools in the past can continue to work pretty much as they always have, without fully understanding the object language underneath their tools.

CASE for Objects

Current CASE tools don't work well with objects

Some vendors of traditional CASE tools are now advertising their systems as being compatible with object technology. However, most of these tools are based on the classic entity-relationship model, which is incapable of representing some of the most fundamental concepts of object technology. These concepts include true inheritance, polymorphism, and the encapsulation of data by procedures.

New tools are being developed

Fortunately, a new generation of CASE tools is being developed specifically to meet the needs of object technology. Although some of these tools retain the flavor of entity-relationship models, they are fully equipped to handle all the advanced concepts of object technology.

But functionality is limited

At least one object-based CASE tool can translate designs directly into code, saving programmers from having to make the translation manually. However, like traditional CASE tools, object-based CASE is most useful for defining the overall structure of code and data. The methods these tools generate are generally rather simple, usually having to do with the storage and retrieval of information in variables. Virtually all other methods have to be programmed by hand.

Manual extensions can't be absorbed

Of course, once the output of a CASE tool is modified by hand, it can no longer be processed by the CASE tool. This places a serious limitation on the usefulness of CASE for actual code generation. Its primary use will probably continue to be in the early phases of software development.

The precise role of CASE tools for object-oriented development will depend on the methodology being used. For development teams that stay with the traditional software development life cycle, CASE may prove to be a very useful tool for supporting the early phases of that life cycle.

The role of CASE will vary

For teams that adopt the layered software approach described in Chapter 5, object-oriented CASE tools will be applied in different ways at each level. At the class level, they will help with the design of the class hierarchy. At the model level, they will perform their more traditional role of supporting the analysis and design of complex systems. If they are applied at the application level at all, they will probably be most useful for doing a quick "sketch" of a design to provide a starting point for the rapid prototyping process.

The layered model calls for a different role

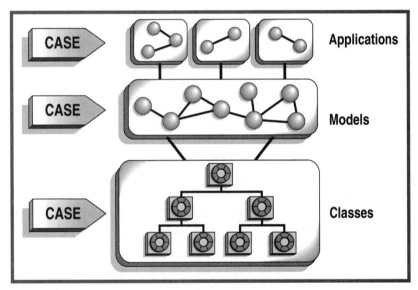

Layered Uses of CASE

Objects and 4GLs

There is a very natural compatibility between object technology and 4GL environments, including screen builders, report writers, and their underlying 4GL languages.

4GLs also work with objects

The match is just now becoming apparent	This match hasn't been very apparent to date because the early applications of object technology were primarily in the scientific and engineering arenas. However, as object technology moves into the mainstream of computing, the need for 4GL services is becoming increasingly apparent. Commercial 4GL products are already available for both Smalltalk and C++, and more are in the works.
Object 4GLs make sense	Object-oriented 4GLs make a great deal of sense. No matter how sophisticated a language you may be using, it isn't very productive to generate data entry screens and reports by programming every screen event by hand. It's much simpler just to paint the forms and reports on the screen and let a 4GL tool generate the actual code.
Object 4GLs are similar to standard 4GLs	Object-based 4GLs differ only slightly from their non-object ancestors. For example, object 4GLs can generate either code or parameters, and the same tradeoffs apply. That is, code generators require recompiling and relinking in order to reflect the effects of a change. By contrast, parameter-based systems allow immediate updates, but they require the use of a run-time system and may execute more slowly than compiled code.
There are some important differences	As with CASE tools, there is a serious temptation for vendors of conventional 4GL tools to label them "object oriented" in hopes of increasing market share. However, to be truly object-oriented, these tools must respect the encapsulation of objects and not create redundant information in screens and reports outside of objects.
Example: Limiting input data	For example, suppose you have an entry screen for filling in customer information. For that matter, you might have several such screens in different departments, each serving a different purpose. With a conventional screen builder, information about the contents of each field would be embedded in the entry screen itself. But in object technology, you want to keep all the information about customers safely tucked away inside the actual customer object. So a true object-oriented screen builder would send a message to a customer object to check input, not duplicate those checks in every screen that referenced that customer object.

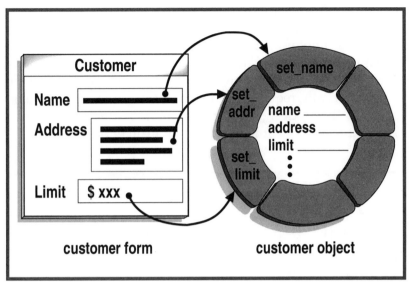

An Object-Orientated Form

Object 4GLs can also provide more analytic power than traditional 4GLs because they can tap the underlying power of the class libraries and the language itself. For example, when deriving a value for a field in a screen, a complex series of object interactions could be triggered to compute a value or to suggest appropriate entries given the information already provided. Ordinary 4GLs can't invoke procedures to this degree, so they are much more limited in the services they can provide.

Object 4GLs can excel in other ways

TOOLS FOR SHARED DEVELOPMENT
Problems with Shared Development

Object-oriented programming has a curious historical bias that has now come back to haunt it. In the 1970s, when the Xerox team was conceiving Smalltalk, part of their zeal came from a rebellion against the prevailing mainframe mentality. It was a truly radical notion on their part, but they imagined that one day the cost of computers would drop to the point where individuals could have their own, personal machines. In fact, Smalltalk was originally viewed as the software for *Dynabook*, a handheld computer conceived by Alan Kay that was little more than an electronic slate.

Smalltalk was way ahead of its time

But it didn't anticipate team development

Twenty years later, the technology has finally caught up with Kay's vision, and lightweight, slate-like computers are now an accepted technology. In another way, however, his vision may have missed the mark. There is no indication that he anticipated the extent to which the software for these "personal" computers would, ironically, require large teams of programmers to develop. So Smalltalk was designed purely as an individual development tool. There was very little provision for team efforts.

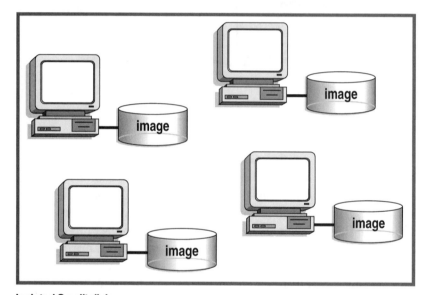

Isolated Smalltalk Images

The problems go beyond code sharing

Shared development in an object-oriented language includes all the standard code-sharing problems, such as keeping track of different versions, making sure that only compatible versions are linked together, and so on. But these problems are further compounded by inheritance, since a change in a high-level class can affect the behavior of all the classes below it in the hierarchy. Do all the subclasses get new versions as well? If so, do all the compatibilities have to be rechecked for these subclasses?

It gets worse from here, but suffice it to say that code management for large teams working with object technology is a much more demanding proposition than it is with traditional languages. To date, object-oriented development teams have tended to be fairly small—say five to ten people—so code management could be handled on an informal basis. As the teams and projects become larger, better tools for shared development work are becoming necessary.

Code management is difficult with objects

Smalltalk Code-Management Systems

Fortunately, progress is being made on this front. The first code management system for Smalltalk was the *Application Manager* for Smalltalk/V. It was originally marketed by a company called SoftPert, which has since been bought by Coopers & Lybrand. The product adds a number of useful project-management features to the basic Smalltalk image. There is now a companion C++ product to go with it.

Application Manager pioneered the field

A more powerful tool for Smalltalk is *ENVY/Developer* from Object Technology International. ENVY supplies complete version control and allows new versions of classes and objects to be quickly loaded into any image. It also provides access control to classes by individual and development group, and it supports cross-platform development. ENVY also assists in the process of configuring compact run-time deliverables.

ENVY adds more power

A more recent entry into the team-tools arena is *Convergence/Team* from Instantiations Inc. Like ENVY, Convergence provides full version control and rapid updating of Smalltalk code. It also provides a range of options for locating classes in the shared repository, helping developers find the classes they need. At present, Convergence is available only for ObjectWorks\Smalltalk.

Convergence is the latest entrant

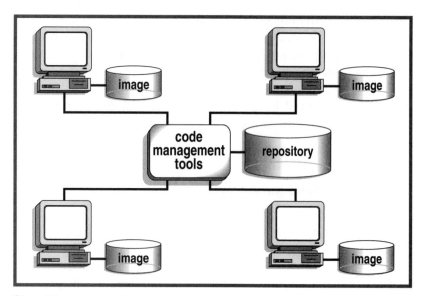

Shared Development Tools

Object databases should help

Logically, object databases should provide the ideal environment for shared development. They provide all the essential controls: versioning, security, check-in and check-out, locking, and other transaction management services. And they provide all these services at the object and class level. However, no one has yet implemented a full code management system on an object-oriented database. It's only a matter of time until the technologies converge.

CONCLUSIONS

Languages come first, tools last

Chapters 7, 8, and 9 have provided an overview of the object-oriented languages, databases, and development tools currently on the market. The ordering of these chapters is significant in two ways. First, it reflects primacy of need: You can't do much of anything without a language; you can't build applications with persistent data without a database; and it's hard to do either of these things well without good tools.

The ordering of these chapters also reflects the maturity of the marketplace. The languages are still evolving, but they are quite stable now, and any changes are bound to be backwardly compatible with earlier versions. The databases are a bit fresher to the market, but some of them have been in commercial use for several years and are definitely ready for serious deployment. Many tools, on the other hand, are still in their formative stages and are changing rapidly.

Languages are the most mature, tools the least

In a sense, this is a positive sign. It means that the industry has reached the point where it has a stable platform on which to build increasingly refined tools. The down side is that companies that adopt object technology today may find themselves dealing more directly with languages and databases than they would like. Alternatively, they may find some high-level tool that serves their purposes today, then have to migrate to more powerful tools as they become available.

The immaturity of tools is a weakness

In the meantime, there are two relatively safe bets. The first is to adopt one of the versions of Smalltalk, which provides nearly everything you need in the way of tools, and augment it with one of the project-management systems. The second is to go with a version of C++ that offers a solid browser and debugger, decide whether you want to use its editor or one of the more powerful stand-alone editors, and rely on a traditional source-code management system for team development work.

But it is safe to make the move now

10

Building Object-Oriented Information Systems

It is clear from the preceding chapters that a variety of languages, databases, tools, and environments is now available to support object-oriented development. In this chapter, we address how to combine these diverse elements to create effective, integrated information systems. For object-oriented languages and tools to work well, they have to work together, and they have to work transparently across a broad spectrum of machines and operating systems.

Object inform ation systems require integration

Before wrestling with the problem of weaving object components into corporate information systems, however, a prior issue must be resolved. Is this, in fact, the right technology for the next generation of information systems?

But we must be sure that the technology is correct

MEETING THE NEEDS OF MANAGEMENT

In Chapter 2, I defined four basic criteria that a technology must meet to support the next generation of information systems: It must handle complexity better, provide more flexibility, be more responsive, and improve the overall quality of information systems. Does object technology satisfy these four requirements?

Does object technology meet the needs of management?

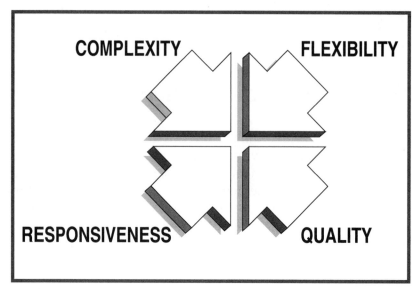

The Four Requirements

There are three ways to answer this question

This question is really the central issue of this book, so we want to arrive at the best answer possible. There are actually three different ways to judge how well object technology meets the requirements established in Chapter 2:

1. Examine the features of the technology and match them against each of the requirements.

2. Put the technology to the test and evaluate its performance in practice.

3. Survey the experiences of companies who have tried object technology and see how well the technology has met their needs.

We will pursue all three paths

The final three chapters of this book pursue each of these approaches to assessing the potential of object technology. The first section of this chapter evaluates the characteristics of object technology to see how well they meet the stated requirements. Chapter 11 provides a set of guidelines for making your own assessment of object technology. Finally, Chapter 12 provides candid, first-hand accounts of the experiences of other companies that have adopted this technology.

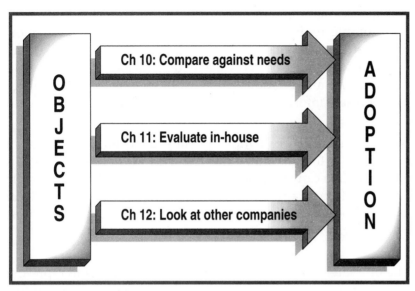

Three Ways to Answer

1. Handling Complexity

The first requirement is to provide better mechanisms for dealing with complex information. Object technology fares pretty well in this regard. It can handle any kind of data that can be digitized, including complex multimedia information. That takes care of complexity at the level of raw data.

Object technology handles complex data types

Object technology not only handles complex data types in a graceful manner, it allows these data types to be defined as new primitives in a system. This makes them available for building still more complex data types, with no requirement for the higher-level data types to be concerned with the structure of the lower-level types. As described in Chapter 4, object technology accommodates complexity by supporting modularization on multiple levels, mimicking the organization of living systems.

These data types may become primitives

Object technology embraces all prior data models

At the information-management level, object technology deals with complexity by providing an all-embracing model for information structures. Again, the object data model is a superset of all the preceding generations of data models, including the hierarchical, network, and relational models. In effect, object technology can represent information structures of any arbitrary complexity.

Encapsulation manages complexity

In addition, the encapsulation of related data and procedures is a very effective tool for hiding complexity, and we've seen how this encapsulation can be carried out on multiple levels in large-scale systems. In effect, any complexity that can be expressed on a local level can be hidden at the next level up, making even the most complex structure easier to understand.

Objects represent complexity naturally

The ultimate backstop in dealing with complexity is to represent it in a natural, understandable form. No matter how much information hiding we do, we can't hide the fact that real-world organizations are highly complex, intricate systems. The best solution for dealing with this "residual" complexity is to represent it in its natural form. Because object technology is based on modeling real-world objects and events, even complex object systems can be relatively easy to understand and maintain.

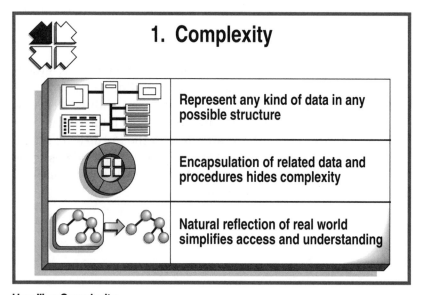

Handling Complexity

2. Providing Flexibility

Object technology also fares well on the flexibility criterion. The most important source of flexibility is the high degree of modularization provided by the technology. So long as the message interfaces are not altered, developers are free to change any aspect of how objects carry out their tasks. They are also free to add new classes of objects to a system, move methods and variables up and down the class hierarchy, or make other kinds of changes without affecting any of the other code in a system.

Flexibility is provided by better modularity

The layered development methodology described in Chapter 5 can extend this flexibility even further because it insulates applications from changes in models and classes. For example, you can change the way you store information about customers or even the way you model your customer interactions, and most of your sales, support, and other customer applications should be unaffected.

Layered development increases flexibility

Inheritance also contributes to flexibility by providing a simple mechanism for creating general procedures and variables, discriminating among special cases, and handling exceptions by overriding procedures at any level. These mechanisms are particularly valuable because they are a natural reflection of human understanding. Building systems that reflect reality as we normally perceive it makes it easier to understand and modify those systems.

Inheritance also adds flexibility

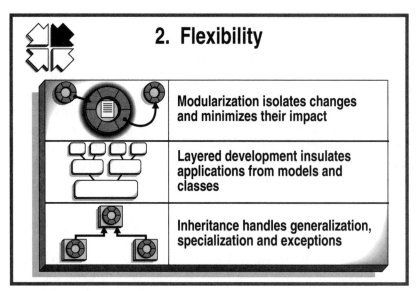

2. Flexibility

	Modularization isolates changes and minimizes their impact
	Layered development insulates applications from models and classes
	Inheritance handles generalization, specialization and exceptions

Providing Flexibility

3. Increasing Responsiveness

Fast retrieval increases responsiveness

Object technology improves the responsiveness of information systems in several ways. First, it allows complex information structures to be stored and retrieved considerably faster than relational technology, as shown in Chapter 8. This not only makes routine operations faster, it also allows managers to ask complex questions about corporate problems and get meaningful responses more quickly.

Active objects also aid responsiveness

Another aspect of object technology that increases its responsiveness is its ability to package procedures with the data they monitor and manage. Given the capacity for active objects, as described in Chapter 7, this feature allows objects to take initiative whenever their internal state calls for some kind of action. Active objects can react to changes in the environment immediately rather than waiting for an application to come along and discover something unusual.

On a larger time scale, object technology improves responsiveness by allowing new applications to be generated up to an order of magnitude faster than with conventional programming methods. This means new solutions can be deployed quickly enough to be of real help in managing a business. Also, because object technology is more amenable to change, it is often possible to modify an existing system rather than build a new application to meet changing needs.

Application development is faster

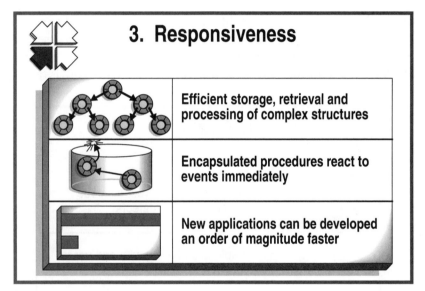

3. Responsiveness

	Efficient storage, retrieval and processing of complex structures
	Encapsulated procedures react to events immediately
	New applications can be developed an order of magnitude faster

Increasing Responsiveness

4. Enhancing Quality

Finally, object technology can provide a significant boost to software quality at each of the levels outlined in Chapter 2: absence of defects, fitness to purpose, and usability.

Object technology can improve quality

With regard to absence of defects, object technology often reduces defects because systems are composed primarily of proven, reliable components. In addition, the improved modularization of object systems allows defects to be isolated and corrected more easily than with monolithic applications.

Reuse of proven components decreases defects

Fast development increases fitness to purpose

With regard to fitness to purpose, two aspects of object technology help to ensure a better fit to users' needs. First, the fact that new applications can be developed faster increases the likelihood that the solutions they provide will still solve the original problem by the time they are actually delivered. More important, the fact that solutions are developed in close cooperation with end users through rapid prototyping helps ensure that users get the solutions they really need.

Usability is also increased

As to the third aspect of quality, usability, the graphical interface of most object systems makes them considerably easier to use. The potential for process animation can be used to further enhance usability by making it easier to understand what a system is doing.

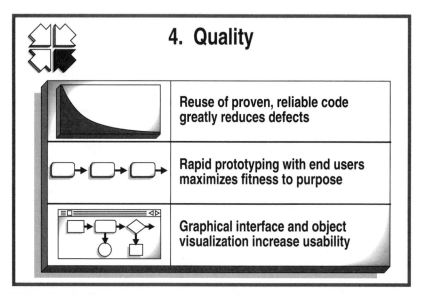

4. Quality

	Reuse of proven, reliable code greatly reduces defects
	Rapid prototyping with end users maximizes fitness to purpose
	Graphical interface and object visualization increase usability

Enhancing Quality

Object Technology Meets the Requirements

It appears to pass the tests

In short, object technology appears to meet the four criteria set out at the beginning of this book. That doesn't mean that it guarantees solutions—improperly used, it can lead to systems that are just as bad, if not worse, than the ones we've lived with in the past. But if the proper methodologies are applied, the technology appears to be better adapted to the new requirements than any other technology available.

STANDARDIZING OBJECT MANAGEMENT

The essence of object technology is to mix and match reusable components to assemble software systems rather than create them from scratch. If objects are to be assembled, however, they must be compatible with one another. This is rarely a problem when writing a single program because all the objects are written in the same language, run on the same machine, and use the same operating system.

Objects must be compatible

But building entire information systems out of objects is quite a different matter. Objects have to interact with each other even if they are written in different languages and run on different hardware and software platforms. For example, imagine trying to get the systems in the accompanying figure to work in harmony.

This is hard with distributed systems

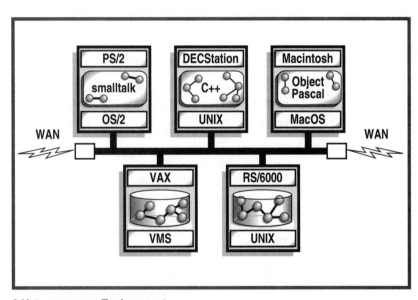

A Heterogeneous Environment

We need standards for objects

Clearly, we will soon need standards for managing objects in heterogeneous environments. Fortunately, this requirement has been anticipated. Unlike many segments of the computer industry, the upcoming need for object standards was recognized several years before the need became acute, and the prospective vendors of object technology launched a collective effort to agree on industry standards in advance of their major product introductions.

The Object Management Group

The OMG was founded to formulate standards

The Object Management Group (OMG) is a nonprofit industry consortium founded in 1989 to address the issues of object standards. The group currently includes more than 200 companies, ranging from such industry giants as IBM, Microsoft, Apple, and AT&T/NCR down to the smallest vendors of services and reusable components. All of these companies have agreed to work together to create a set of standards acceptable to all.

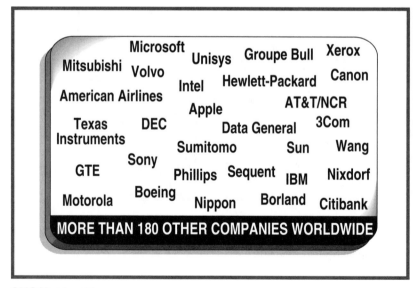

OMG Membership

Essentially, the OMG is striving to define standards in which the location, environment, language, and other characteristics of objects are completely transparent to the other objects that access them. Its mission is to bring about agreement on standards and then promulgate those standards to both vendors and consumers of object technology.

The OMG seeks to make differences transparent

Unlike some other industry consortia, the OMG will not actually distribute products. OMG will, however, certify the compliance of commercial products with the agreed-upon standards so that individual consumers of these products do not have to determine compliance for themselves.

OMG does not distribute products

Moreover, the OMG seeks to define standard object-based facilities for supporting a variety of advanced features:

OMG also defines standard facilities

- **Distributed transactions**, in which interactions among a group of objects either take place as a whole or do not take place at all

- **Concurrent execution**, in which many objects can carry out their methods at the same time, on either the same or different machines

- **Versioning of objects**, in which changes in object structure are tracked and references among objects always point to the appropriate versions

- **Notification of events**, in which objects can ask to be automatically activated and informed whenever certain events take place elsewhere in the system

- **Internationalization**, in which country-specific variations can be handled automatically, allowing applications to operate across international boundaries without modification

The Generalized Object Model

OMG adopted a more general object model

To achieve these objectives, the OMG decided to embrace a more general model of object software than we have been discussing. This model doesn't invalidate the earlier model—it just views it as a special case of a more general approach to building systems out of objects.

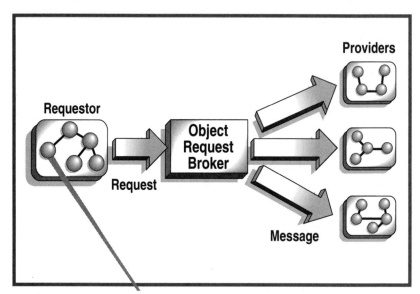

The Generalized Object Model

Requests go through a broker

In the *generalized object model*, requests for object services are sent to an *object request broker*, a program whose job it is to keep track of all the objects in a system and the kinds of services they can provide. Requests to this broker can specify the object that is to provide the services, as in the model we have discussed so far. But requests can also specify a list of alternative providers, or they can give no provider at all and leave the decision entirely up to the broker.

The Object Request Broker (ORB)

The object request broker selects the best available object to satisfy a given request, using criteria it has been given in advance, then the ORB passes the request along as a message to the selected object. The form of this message is automatically adjusted to satisfy the format of the receiving object. The receiving object acts on the message, returns a response to the broker, and the broker translates that response into a form that the initial requestor can understand.

The ORB finds a provider

The use of the generalized object model offers two key advantages over the more specific object model:

The ORB improves communication

1. It **provides a common interface** for objects of different origins to interact with one another. As long as an object can issue a request in the standard format called for by the object request broker, objects can communicate transparently across different languages and platforms.

2. It **improves the modularity** of software. In this model, objects have less knowledge about each other, so they are freer to change. In fact, they don't even have to know about each others' existence—they only have to indicate what they want done and leave the rest up to the broker.

The standard for the object request broker has been finalized, and commercial versions of the ORB are available from a variety of vendors. Standardizing the ORB is a major step forward for object technology because it allows the use of the technology to scale up to the enterprise level without requiring companies to lock themselves into proprietary architectures.

A standard has been defined

Levels of Interaction Between Objects

The ORB focuses on high-level interactions

Although it will play an essential role, the object request broker will not be a clearinghouse for all object interactions. Rather, it will act primarily as the coordinator for interactions among large-scale object components such as screen interfaces and spreadsheet processors. In most cases, the components themselves will be written in a single language using direct communications between objects.

It is best at coupling components

The reason for this division of labor is that sending messages through the ORB necessarily involves a processing overhead in selecting objects, translating formats, and performing other services. In local, tightly coupled application components where the language is fixed and the receivers are known, it will be much more efficient to perform direct message sends. On the other hand, for coupling these components together into larger systems, particularly across a network, the overhead of the ORB should be an insignificant consideration in light of its benefits.

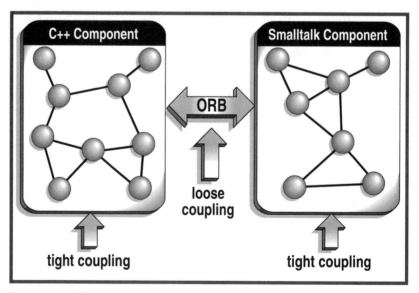

Two Levels of Coupling

The OMG Reference Model

The Object Management Group has invested considerable effort in figuring out not only how object-based software components should interact, but also what sorts of components should be available for application construction. As with the ORB, the goal is to gain agreement among vendors as to the overall architecture of an object-based system so all their components can work together in harmony, giving maximum freedom of choice to the developers and end users. The general architecture they have come up with is called the *OMG Reference Model*.

The OMG also identifies software components

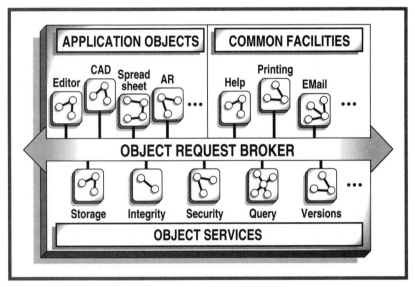

The OMG Reference Model

The backbone of this model is the object request broker. The ORB acts like a software bus, allowing various components to be combined simply by plugging them into the system.

The ORB is the backbone

The lower half of the model, below the ORB, is the system level. This section contains the basic services that all object systems would have to provide. Many of these services are database-orientated oriented, but of course with object technology they apply to procedures as well as data.

The system level contains essential services

The application level meets specific needs

The upper half of the model, above the ORB, is the application level. This level contains components that are optional, depending on the needs of specific applications. These components can be mixed and matched in any desired fashion.

This layer has two parts

The application layer is divided into two halves. On the left are *application objects*, which provide the specific functionality required to perform a business task. Examples include text editors, spreadsheet engines, and accounts-receivable modules. On the right are *common facilities*—tasks that most applications must carry out, but are traditionally duplicated within every application program. In this model, these services are coded only once and placed in a common area where all applications can use them.

These are conceptual distinctions only

The distinctions among the three types of facilities are primarily conceptual in that they are designed to help vendors and consumers think about the different kinds of roles that object components can play. In practice, there is very little distinction—an application component would typically call a service component to carry out some task, but a service component could request services from an application component in turn.

Components are easily recategorized

Similarly, components can be "moved" from one category to another as our understanding of their roles changes. For example, if we find that some of the optional service components are essential in most situations, we can simply redefine them to be core services and place them down in the lower level. The only practical consequence of this change is that all applications could then depend on their presence.

The Impact of Object Components

Components could change the shape of software

It's a big jump from defining an ORB to entering the age of plug-and-play software. It will take a consistent industry effort to develop components that provide the necessary interfaces and functionality to work together smoothly. However, if we can overcome these obstacles, we should be amply rewarded for the effort. This section describes a few examples of how computing might change as a result of moving to component-based software.

One of the most challenging problems in enterprise computing is to get applications to allocate processing across multiple machines. Using techniques called *remote procedures calls* (RPCs), it's possible to execute procedures on other machines. But most RPCs require that all the machines be configured in advance to do their part, which means that the allocation of processing load is fixed.

Computing is hard to distribute

Because ORBs use dynamic binding to pull the pieces of an application together, the location of an object component providing a service can be determined at run time. In fact, that location could be declared to be one of the criteria for how the ORB chooses the component to provide a service. Specifically, the ORB could be programmed to give preference to components that are sitting on idle machines. This technique would allow companies to dynamically allocate processes over their networks, taking maximum advantage of their computing resources.

ORBs could help distribute the load

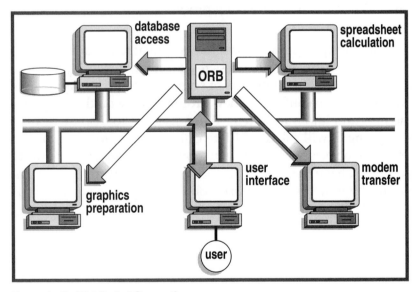

Dynamically Distributed Computing

Software will become more open

Another implication of component-based software is that application software may become more open. Just as PC owners can customize their machines by buying special-purpose PC boards and peripherals, these same end users could modify applications by mixing and matching components. For example, you should be able to choose a single interface component and apply it to all your programs, or get all your software to communicate through the same mail system.

Software development should become simpler

In addition to giving consumers more options, software components should simplify the job of developers. They will no longer have to reinvent the user interface, write a file-management system from scratch, and build drivers for every printer ever made. Instead, they can concentrate on what they do best and simply assume that the supporting components will be available on the target system. So a CAD vendor can concentrate on CAD functionality, and the developer of an inventory tracking system can focus on the actual tracking process.

Installation may become much easier

Software components also have the potential to make the process of installing software much less tedious than it is today. Instead of going through endless lists of screen types, printer types, and other options to configure a new program, we would simply load the program into our system. When it needs to display or print something, it will ask the ORB to call up the appropriate display or printer objects. And when you upgrade your display or printer, you won't have to reinstall all your existing software. You'll just install the new display or print objects, and your software will automatically make use of them.

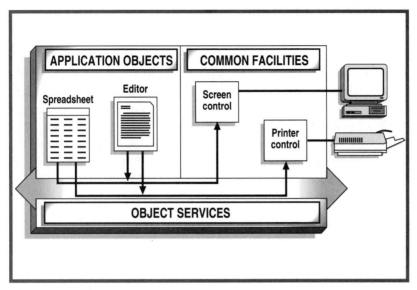

Automatic Connection to Services

Conforming to the Standard

Achieving benefits such as these depends on the industry stabilizing on a single standard for object interactions. Unfortunately, the software industry doesn't have a very good track record at supporting standards. The many variations of "standard" SQL and the battle of the two Unixes reflect the temptation to seek a proprietary edge rather than adhere to a standard.

These benefits require a standard

Despite this track record, there is reasonable cause for optimism with regard to object standards. There are two aspects of the OMG effort that are unique in the history of software. First, the standardization effort was undertaken well before vendors had committed themselves to proprietary solutions. Second, OMG is not one of several rival "standards" bodies. It is *the* standards consortium for object technology, and it includes every major player in the industry.

We have a unique opportunity with OMG

Vendors and consumers both should support OMG

Our best hope is that IBM, Apple, Microsoft, Sun, HP, and all the other big players will stand by their commitments to the OMG consortium and resist the temptation to split the market with proprietary solutions. Consumers of object technology, particularly those with large budgets, can help ensure that we get a real standard by insisting on OMG compliance as a condition of purchase. It's in everyone's interest to make this concordance work. The sooner we have a common framework for object components, the sooner we can begin to realize the benefits of object technology on an enterprise scale.

OBJECT APPLICATION ENVIRONMENTS
Enterprise Object Platforms

Object-oriented platforms are being developed

Although standards are just now being put in place, major software vendors are already gearing up to provide enterprise platforms for object-oriented information systems. AT&T/NCR has released its COOPERATION product; IBM is making its AD/Cycle and Repository products increasingly object oriented; Microsoft continues to provide glimpses of object-oriented operating systems; and Apple has teamed up with IBM to move its forthcoming object-based operating system into the mainstream of corporate computing.

These platforms should accelerate development

The purpose of enterprise platforms is to provide the kinds of services described by the OMG Reference Model. These platforms will allow companies to buy as much generic functionality as possible and focus their efforts on developing applications unique to their own organizations. Compared with starting from scratch, building an object-oriented information system on top of an existing platform will be much more cost effective.

COOPERATION is the furthest along

To illustrate the usefulness of enterprise platforms, consider CO-OPERATION from AT&T/NCR. It provides a comprehensive, open architecture for integrating heterogeneous software and hardware systems across multiple networks. It does this at multiple levels:

- At the operating system, it allows applications to run transparently across DOS, OS/2, and Unix.

- It provides common communication services to span a variety of network architectures, including both local area networks (LANs) and wide area networks (WANs).

- At the other end of the scale, it allows applications to run under a variety of interfaces, including Microsoft Windows, IBM's Presentation Manager, OSF Motif, and HP's New-Wave.

- In between these platform and user interfaces, COOPERATION offers a wide variety of services for scheduling activities, managing the flow of work, accessing databases, communicating over the network, and managing distributed applications.

- . In addition, COOPERATION includes a repository for storing and retrieving reusable software components, providing an essential medium for building a corporate library of reusable object-based software components.

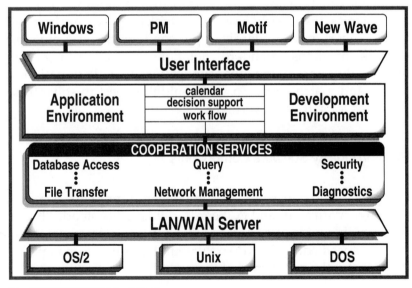

The COOPERATION Architecture

The Software Components Industry

Enterprise platforms support software components

Enterprise platforms should also give a much-needed boost to the fledgling software components industry. With an OMG-based standard to work against, component makers should be able to create products that will sell in sufficient volume to justify their development costs. However, the availability of enterprise platforms won't clear away all the hurdles of the software components industry.

Selecting components won't be easy

Suppose the components market really did take off, and you wound up with a shelf full of catalogs describing the multitude of classes, models, and application components that you could mix and match to assemble new applications. How will components be documented in these catalogs? How will you find the components you need? How can you be sure that a print component from Company A will be fully compatible with a spreadsheet component from Company B?

It will take time to sort this out

These won't be easy problems to solve. But we know that the problems can be solved—the hardware components industry demonstrates that clearly. However, it took the hardware industry years to work out standardized pin configurations, compatible families of chips, standard notations for describing chip functionality, and all the other conventions that allow designers to mix and match chips. So we shouldn't expect to solve these problems for software overnight.

Building Quality Software Components

Quality is a serious problem

Assuring quality in software components represents a special challenge. With chips and PC boards, rigid quality standards provide a high degree of confidence that any given component will work as specified. Defects do occur, but they are rare enough that the industry thrives in spite of them.

By contrast, software quality has a rather poor track record. This will naturally make developers wary of buying software components out of a catalog and plugging them into mission-critical systems. We clearly need to make some changes if commercial components are going to work:

We need new guidelines for software quality

- We must **improve the quality of software** in general and of individually marketed components in particular. As described later in this chapter, we will probably need a "quality first" program comparable to manufacturing efforts to bring about this change.

- We need to **develop quality standards** by which components can be rated. Ideally, these standards would include all the levels of quality described in Chapter 2, not just the absence of defects.

- We may also need some sort of **certification process**, comparable to the Underwriter's Laboratory seal, to assure buyers that software components have met the quality standards described previously.

It isn't clear who will take the lead in these efforts. Certainly OMG has a major role to play in setting standards for quality and perhaps participating in certification programs. But the vendors of software components will have to champion quality and prove they can deliver it if they are to create the kind of trust that the hardware components industry enjoys.

Everyone will play a role

Compensating Component Creators

There's another way in which marketing software components represents a unique challenge. With hardware, the value of a component lies in its physical existence. If you want one, you have to buy one. With software, the value of a component lies in its creation; its actual physical form is only a few thousand bytes of information on a disk, and that can easily be copied at nominal cost.

Compensation is also a problem

This problem is not new

This problem has plagued the software industry for many years, particularly since the advent of the PC with its small, more easily copied software. To date, no solid solution has been found. The industry has given up on copy protection techniques and has turned to legal enforcement to minimize software piracy. But enforcement is difficult, and it will only get harder with tiny, reusable components that are even easier to copy and harder to trace.

Solutions have been proposed

The proposals for addressing this problem break out roughly as follows:

- Use **conventional licensing techniques**, granting either individual or site licenses to use components. This approach relies on the honesty of consumers of these classes and the rather limited enforcement of copyright protections.

- **Charge a one-time fee** for each component and allow buyers to copy the component freely thereafter. This system would probably be the simplest to administer, but it might lead to arbitrarily high prices on components since developers of these components would see a minimum of individual sales.

- **Bill for usage** by embedding counters in each component and adding software to enterprise systems that can read and report these counters. This scheme has the advantages of amortizing costs over the lifetime of components and letting the value of a component be determined by its actual usage. But it could be rather difficult to track and enforce, and companies might well regard it as a major nuisance.

- **Lease components** by the month or year, such that companies could copy them freely as long as the lease was up-to-date. This has some of the advantages of the preceding scheme but would be easier to administer.

Subclassing raises new problems

Regardless of what scheme is adopted, the problem of compensation is complicated by subclassing. Some difficult questions arise if a component is used to derive a subclass, particularly if the subclass changes a lot of the original functionality.

The nesting of components introduces yet another complication. The "food chain" of components could get quite long—one vendor's class is used by another to build a low-level component, which is used by a third vendor to build a high-level component, which a fourth vendor incorporates in an application and sells to a company. How is the compensation for the value added at each step to flow back down this chain until it reaches the original vendor?

So does the nesting of components

Solutions Will Take Time

These problems shed some light on why the software components industry hasn't blossomed as quickly as some people had hoped. On the other hand, it seems likely that all these problems can be solved eventually. The same economic forces that led to the adoption of standard hardware components should ultimately prevail in software as well. The companies that can overcome the obstacles to provide proven, reliable components should have a wide-open market waiting for them.

These problems can probably be solved

To date, the companies that have entered this arena have tended to be smaller companies moving in from other established businesses, such as vendors of traditional subroutine libraries or marketers of object-oriented consulting and courses. In each case, the move into components is a relatively low-risk venture with a correspondingly low profile. Component vendors are beginning to emerge, but it is going to take time before business starts to boom.

Component vendors are emerging slowly

In the meantime, the adoption of object technology shouldn't be tied to the emergence of component vendors. The use of object technology isn't affected by the number of commercial components on the market. The basic strategy remains the same: Buy what you can, build what you must, but start assembling solutions as soon as possible.

Don't wait for this industry to take off

There is plenty to work with right now

In the realms of C++ and Smalltalk, there is an ample supply of reusable components for generic functions such as user interfaces and database access. Those components, possibly combined with the reusable functionality offered by COOPERATION or other enterprise platforms, should be enough to get any company started with object technology.

A NEW MODEL OF CORPORATE COMPUTING

Object technology suggests a new model

If we look beyond the actual construction of information systems, we see that object technology has the potential to change the way companies think about corporate computing. Since corporate computing is in a bit of a muddle at most companies just now, that potential could prove to be important.

This model comes from many sources

This last section includes some of my speculations on how corporate computing might evolve as object technology makes its impact felt. This speculation is grounded in real-world experience in helping companies adapt to object technology. While I am not aware of any one company that has made all the changes I describe, I have seen every aspect of this model in practice in one or more organizations. What follows, then, is an attempt to weave my collected observations into a meaningful pattern that may provide some guidance for organizational change.

Problems with the Current Model

The current model isn't working

The current model of corporate computing isn't working very well. It's creating friction, disarray, and internal competition that is escalating the costs of getting work done through computers. The root of the problem is that there isn't just one model of corporate computing, but two:

1. There's the classic **mainframe model**, in which all information and development are centralized. This model is, of course, the one embraced by the traditional IS organization.

2. Then there's the new **personal-computing model**, in which end users craft their own solutions to their computing needs. This model is embraced by virtually everyone with a PC on his or her desk.

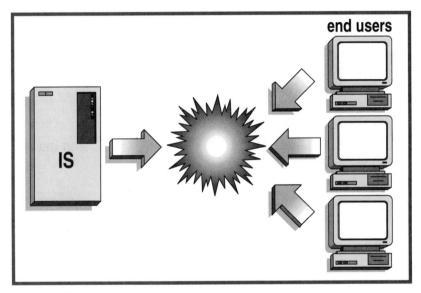

Clashing Models

Despite the friction, both models have valid arguments to support them. IS managers are struggling to maintain order in the face of the PC invasion. They know from hard experience that corporate data isn't safe in the hands of end users, and that solutions developed by end users are impossible to maintain once the developer leaves the company. End users, on the other hand, have had their fill of the 18-month backlog and are determined to generate their own solutions in spite of IS's concerns.

Both models are reasonable

Meanwhile, departments, divisions, and other business units of the organization are caught in the middle of this struggle. On the one hand, they are consumers of information services, and they share the frustrations and the desire for independence of end users. On the other hand, they are providers of information services, and they share the frustrations of MIS when it comes to managing applications and information within their units.

Departments are caught in the middle

The situation is deadlocked

And so it stands. The struggle between these two contradictory models of corporate computing is extracting a high cost both economically and emotionally. We need some way to break out of this deadlock.

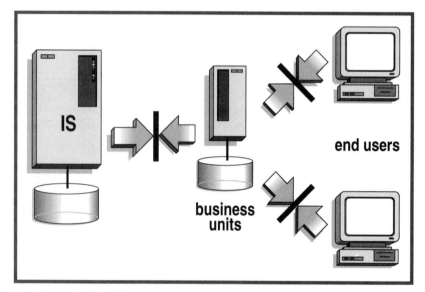

The Computing Deadlock

Layered Development Offers a New Model

Layered development offers a new option

The layered approach to software development described in Chapter 5 suggests a way of merging these conflicting models of computing into a single model that works for everyone. There are no guarantees that this solution will work, and success certainly depends on a general willingness to break out of established patterns and rivalries. But at least it offers a fresh alternative to the current stalemate.

Development is distributed by layers

The basic idea behind this approach is to distribute the development effort across the organization according to the layers in the software. Assuming three layers, it would work like this:

1. **IS is responsible for classes.** Their job is to create, test, and maintain the standard classes that will be used throughout the organization.

2. **Business units are responsible for models.** Working with IS personnel, they design and maintain the business models that describe their particular operations. The models they develop become standards within their units.

3. **End users are responsible for applications.** Working with IS and their business units, they define their business needs and help create application-level solutions using rapid prototyping techniques.

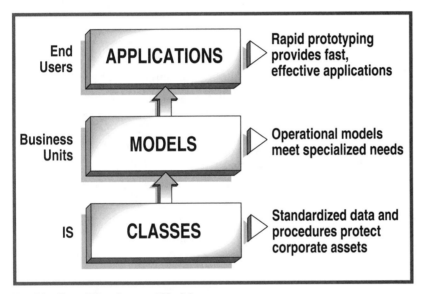

The Distributed Development Model

Since classes handle both procedures and data, IS is still responsible for standardizing both software development and information management. Within the guidelines set by IS, business units are free to standardize both their business operations and information through the models they build. Within the guidelines of each business unit, individual managers can determine how operations and data within their groups are handled.

Standards are also distributed

Here's a simple example of this kind of distributed development effort in practice:

Example: Modeling the sales process

1. **IS builds and distributes reusable classes** that encapsulate procedures and data for dealing with various corporate operations, such as sales and personnel management.

2. The various **departments use these classes to build models of their operations**, such as sales cycles and hiring procedures.

3. Individual **managers use the models to build applications** that solve their immediate business needs, such as tracking leads, monitoring quotas, and developing hiring plans.

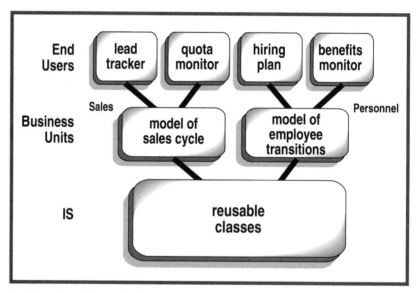

An Example of Distributed Development

The process is not linear

Of course, the process is not as linear as this example suggests, and it probably doesn't even take place in the order listed. The driving force would normally be the business models, which determine the required classes and enable the desired applications.

IS as a Horizontal Operation

In describing this distribution of the computing effort across an organization, I'm not suggesting that end users do the actual programming of their applications. I believe that computer professionals should be used for *all* IS activities within a company, and that they should all belong to the same IS organization.

End users shouldn't program

The way to achieve the distribution of the layered development process while still keeping professionals in the loop at every stage is for IS to become a more horizontal organization. Instead of centralizing its resources, it should deploy the majority of them out to the various business units to do the work of developing models and applications.

IS must become a horizontal organization

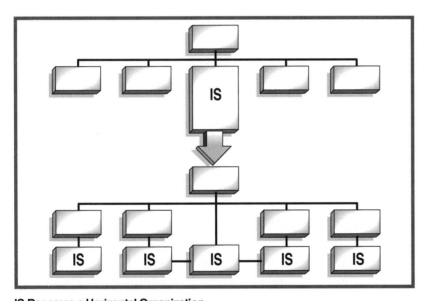

IS Becomes a Horizontal Organization

This is already an established trend

This is not, of course, a radical new concept—it's simply a way to leverage a trend that is already well established in most large organizations. In fact, this trend is so strong that IS managers are now wrestling with the problem of what responsibilities ought to remain within the central core of IS. The model of corporate computing described here may help with that dilemma. In essence, it says that IS should continue to carry out its traditional responsibilities, but it should do so in closer cooperation with the people it serves.

Creative management techniques are required

Managing this arrangement will not be easy. If application programmers report to individual department heads, for example, it will be hard for them to represent the needs of IS when it comes to standardization and other delicate matters. Conversely, if they report to IS, they may not be as responsive to departmental needs as they should be.

Deployed IS personnel have dual evaluations

The best solution may be to have all IS personnel belong to the IS organization, but to have most of them "on loan" to individual departments. If their performance reviews were equally weighted by IS and their assigned departments, they could be rewarded not for serving either group alone but for developing solutions that satisfied both groups. This would not always be easy, but at least it would increase the chances that the required cooperation would take place.

Rethinking Traditional Roles

Job descriptions may change

An important implication of this new model of corporate computing is that we may need to rethink the traditional job descriptions within IS. In the past, people have been categorized in terms of their roles in the standard software life cycle: analysts, designers, programmers, QA personnel, and maintenance staff. If the software life cycle is compressed into the development of every class, model, and prototype in the layered model, it no longer makes sense to define jobs according to the stages of that life cycle.

What makes more sense is to define jobs in terms of the new roles that IS professionals will play—constructing classes, building models, and prototyping applications. These three roles require very different skill sets:

They should be based on new roles

- **Class constructors** need the strongest low-level programming skills because they are creating the robust, general-purpose components that will form the basis of all corporate software.

- **Model builders** need software engineering skills at a higher level. They must be able to understand complex systems and break them down into multiple levels of modules, interacting with class constructors to get the services they require from the lowest-level objects.

- **Application developers** need a mixture of programming, business, and people skills. They must be able to work well with managers to help them analyze problems and design solutions, and they need to understand enough about the business issues to make that interaction a productive one.

There is an obvious precedent for this division of labor. The inspiration for layered software development is the success of this approach in hardware. With hardware, there are no systems analysts who define the requirements of a new computer from its enclosure all the way down to the internal structure of its individual chips. Nor would the same engineer be asked to lay out both a chassis design and a chip design—the skill sets involved are simply too different. In the same way, we shouldn't ask application developers to design and construct new classes for corporate-wide use.

This is the same division as in hardware

On the other hand, none of the old skills should be lost—we still need people who understand analysis, design, programming, testing, and maintenance. The main difference is that developers at every level will need to master these skills, including specialized knowledge of how they apply to their own level.

But the existing skills must be preserved

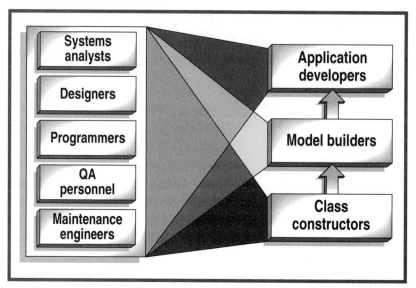

Changing Job Descriptions

Improving the Quality of Software

QA is a special case

One possible danger in this reorganization of job descriptions is that the quality assurance process might be shortchanged. Programmers are notoriously poor at testing their own code, which is why a separate QA department comes in at the end of the process and performs thorough tests on the code.

The concept of QA must change

But this approach to quality needs to change in any case. One reason why the quality of contemporary software is so poor is that QA comes at the end of the line. This approach is taken from an antiquated manufacturing model—as products roll off the assembly line, they are tested to make sure they are okay.

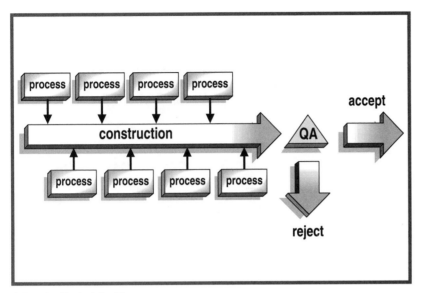

QA at the End of the Line

Manufacturers have learned from hard experience that this back-end approach to quality simply isn't sufficient. Quality must be designed into a product from the very beginning. With JIT ("just-in-time") manufacturing, each person in the line is responsible for the quality of his or her work—and for shutting down the line on the spot if a defective piece comes from upstream. Each person is also responsible for problem-solving with other operators to find the source of the problem, fix it, and get the line running again as soon as possible.

We should learn from manufacturing

Object technology provides an excellent opportunity to adopt the same philosophy in software construction. As with manufacturing, quality should be an explicit design goal of every class, model, and application. Developers at every level should be rewarded for quality; no developer should accept a defective component; and every developer should be responsible for repairing any defects in his or her own creations.

Quality must be designed in

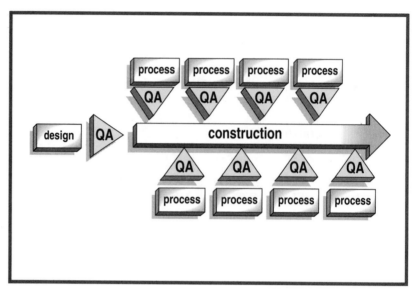

Building in Quality

End Users Also Must Change

End users also must change

These are some of the changes that may take place within IS if companies are to fully leverage the advantages of object technology. But end users will need to change, too. They must move from a competitive relationship with IS to a true partnership, doing what *they* do best and leaving to IS personnel what *they* do best.

We need a new partnership

Here is a rough model of a partnership that should be much more productive than the "demand and disappoint" relationship that prevails in most organizations today:

- End users should be educated in how to **articulate their needs clearly and to give constructive feedback** on successive prototypes.

- **End users and application developers work together to analyze a user's requirements and design a solution.** Having the end user participate in the actual design is crucial, and it's perfectly feasible with object technology.

- **Application developers do the actual prototype construction,** including testing, delivering, and maintaining applications over their life span.

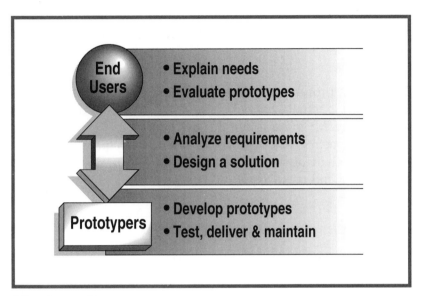

A New Partnership

One of the biggest changes in this proposed partnership is that end users would not code—they would manage, supervise, or do whatever they were paid to do. Many end users would resist this change because it would mean giving up the "joys" of programming.

End users must give up coding

But this is not a bad development. In truth, end users have become spoiled. They've been able to do the fun part of programming, getting an application up and running quickly, without having to deal with any of the drudgery—the careful design, thorough testing, systematic debugging, documentation, and all the other tasks that turn "quickie" applications into corporate assets.

They can't do an adequate job of it

*And it's not what
they get paid for*

Nor should they. A number of studies over the years have shown that end users who program—be it in macros, menus, or database languages—tend to be less productive at their real jobs and, ironically, less likely to be promoted. So it is generally not productive for a company to have its end users building applications, even if permitting this practice appears to take some pressure off the IS organization.

*This may be an
interim solution*

Eventually, prototyping tools may become so intuitive and easy to use that it actually makes sense for end users to do their own prototyping. My guess is that this will take much longer than most people expect. In the meantime, we need a partnership that works—both in the sense of getting solutions running quickly and in allowing end users to get on with their real jobs.

11

Adopting Object Technology

If you've made it this far—even if you took the systems track and skipped Chapters 4 through 9—you're probably sufficiently interested in object technology to at least give it a try. This chapter starts with a practical, proven method of testing the effectiveness of the technology within your own company.

Here's how to get started

Assuming that object technology proves its value in your own evaluation, you will need to address a series of key questions at the corporate level: Should you make the move to objects? If so, where should you start? How much should you invest in the transition, and how should you allocate your resources? How can you preserve your investment in your existing systems?

Adopting this technology raises many issues

This chapter addresses all these questions. My goal is to give you a concrete plan of action for making the move to objects with a minimum of grief and a maximum return on your investment. There are, of course, no guarantees, but these suggestions have all been proven in the field, so they should at least provide some useful guidelines in your own transition to object technology.

This chapter offers proven guidelines

PUTTING OBJECTS TO THE TEST
Choosing the First Model

The first thing you need to do is select some aspect of your business to model using object technology. This is not an easy decision, but it's an important one. Choosing the right area and scale for your first model is a major factor in determining the success of your initial experiences with this technology.

Pick an aspect of your business to model

In general, what you want to do is *demonstrate the power of object technology in a highly visible manner with a minimum of risk and disruption.* Let's break that objective down into its component criteria.

There are three main criteria

1. Demonstrate the power

You can best demonstrate the power of object technology by picking an application that involves complex entities with complex interactions—ones that are best represented by a simulation. This is where object technology really shines, and it's a challenge that traditional methods have trouble meeting. You are likely to get the most spectacular win in this arena.

2. Make it visible

You want the results of your first project to be visible in three different senses:

1. It should **focus on the core business** of the organization so its relevance to corporate competitiveness will be immediately evident.

2. It should have a **graphical user interface** so that it shows well and clearly demonstrates the superior interfaces of object systems.

3. If possible, it should **animate the internal processes of the system** on screen so that observers can appreciate what's happening with the actual business objects behind the interface.

3. Keep it independent

Finally, the first system should be as independent of other systems as possible. There are several reasons for this:

1. You want to **avoid systems integration** as much as possible during the proof-of-concept phase.

2. You want to **minimize corporate politics** until you have a solid demonstration of the technology.

3. You want to **protect the company's operations** from the effects of your initial learning experiences.

Measuring the Benefits

The more carefully you measure the results of your pilot project, the easier it will be to assess the value of object technology. Few companies actually take the time to measure productivity improvements—the benefits are usually so apparent from their early experiences that they don't feel that measurements are necessary. However, promoting a new technology within a large organization is rarely easy. If you become convinced of the value of object technology, measured results may help you convince others in your organization.

Good measures can be very helpful

If you decide to take this route, here are some guidelines to conducting a truly informative test:

Here are some guidelines

1. First, **build a model of a familiar application domain**. Build up a small library of reusable classes as part of this process.

2. Then **prototype three applications** on top of that model. That will help you get the hang of the prototyping process, and it will also force the model into shape.

3. Finally, **measure the development speed and quality** of the third application. Apply all the measures you would normally use in evaluating a software development effort.

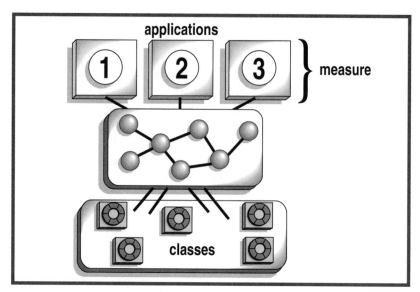

Evaluating Object Technology

Wait for the third application

Doing three applications is important. The first application will almost certainly proceed much slower than you are used to because of the learning curve, the need for changes to the underlying model, and unforeseen surprises. By the time you build the third application, these hurdles will be behind you, and you should find that your productivity has soared.

A controlled comparison is best

If you want a more powerful demonstration of the benefits of object technology, have a different team build the same application using your current methods and compare the results in terms of requirements and performance. Alternatively, you can set it up so that your third application is the same as a previously developed system for which you have the appropriate measures.

Whichever way you go, you ought to see a highly significant advantage at this point. From my experience, a productivity improvement of five-to-one or greater is a reasonable expectation. The accompanying illustration gives the rationale for this advantage in visual terms: The volume of code required for the third prototype is a small fraction of the code required to build the same application from scratch because you are reusing all the foundation work you've already done. This is exactly the point of object-oriented development.

This gives you a good productivity ratio

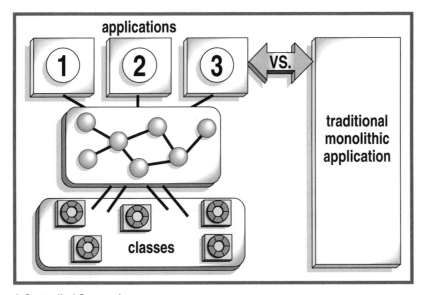

A Controlled Comparison

You can take this demonstration one step further. If you really want to see the full advantage of object technology, try changing the requirements in fairly significant ways and then have both teams modify their code to meet the new requirements. The measured benefits ought to increase dramatically in this further test.

You can also evaluate extensibility

Don't shortcut this evaluation process

The most important point to make here is that you can't measure the benefits of object technology by buying a few copies of C++ and having your existing programmers try building an application with it. First of all, the learning curve will kill them, voiding any possible comparison. More important, they won't realize the biggest advantages of object technology because these advantages accrue from the reuse of past development efforts.

Evaluate the full methodology

In short, you must evaluate the full methodology in order to get an accurate reading of its value. Anything short of that will produce misleading and disappointing results.

A Strategy for Deployment

Stage your first real application

Once you have demonstrated the productivity of object technology to your satisfaction, you are ready to scale up to a true, deployable application. Here is a sequence that generally works well:

1. First, **do a stand-alone demo** system. This forces you to get a model in place and demonstrates the feasibility of the approach. If you followed the procedure outlined previously, you have effectively completed this stage with your third prototype application.

2. Then **develop a working application** that actually draws information from existing systems. This allows you to sort out the integration problems while dealing with any political issues and turf battles that may arise.

3. Finally, **develop a deployable system** and start moving it into the field. At this point, your objective is to demonstrate the value of this technology to the corporate bottom line.

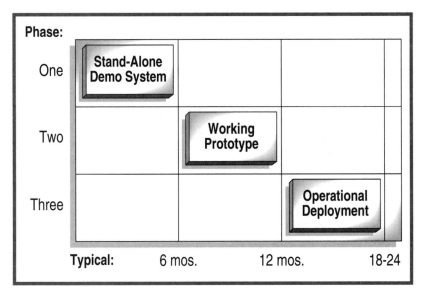

Deploying the First Action

The time line I've shown in the illustration is reasonable given that modest but adequate resources are allocated. Obviously, these times will differ based on many factors, including not only resources but talent, training, leadership, and the use of outside experts.

The time line may vary

An important aspect of this staging is that you have something real to show as quickly as possible. Having been burned by so many empty promises in the past, most managers are highly suspicious of new technologies. The sooner you can show tangible results, the better.

Build on results

Staffing Your Early Efforts

The best way to get results quickly is to bring in an experienced team to smooth your entry into object technology, then work closely with them to learn the new techniques. Here's a reasonable division of labor:

Use an experienced team

1. **Let the hired experts build the original model and code the demo,** using you primarily to give them the required information about your business. Depending on the complexity of your first application, you may have a working demo in as little as a month or two.

2. **When it comes to building the working application, your own people should handle as much of the integration and user interface as they can.** You know your own information systems and user environment better than the consultants do, and this is a good time to start getting your programmers involved.

3. **Have your own programmers deploy and support the application.** By this point, your programmers should understand the code and be ready to assume ownership of it. The outside team should remain available primarily to provide backup.

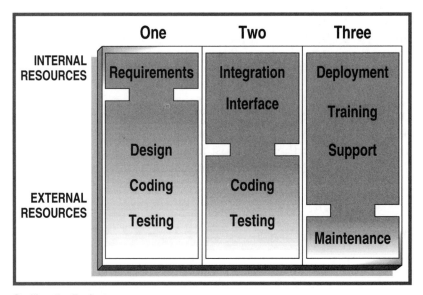

Staffing the Project

This is obviously not the only possible strategy for deploying your first application. You could do the application entirely in-house, or you could farm it out altogether. I recommend this approach because it gets you off to the fastest start while also getting your internal conversion process started as quickly as possible.

This gives you a quick start

MIGRATING TO OBJECT INFORMATION SYSTEMS

If your early experiences with object technology have gone well and you are ready to begin the process of converting to object technology, you can simply continue on as you have begun, building more models of your operations and developing applications on top of them.

You can duplicate your early successes

But sooner or later you will run into a problem. Your new object-oriented systems will start bumping up against your existing systems and the people who manage them, and the resulting conflict of cultures and technologies will create new problems for you to manage. It's important that you anticipate this conflict and have a plan for dealing with it.

But eventually there will be a conflict

This section describes a combination of techniques for migrating your information systems to object technology. This migration will start slowly, and it may not be complete for many years. But with careful planning and persistent effort, you can eventually convert your company to an object-based information system. Better still, you can do it without sacrificing your investment in existing systems.

What follows is a possible migration strategy

The Starting Point

The next illustration shows, in simplified form, the starting point for virtually every large organization. Its information systems consist of an ad hoc mixture of databases, often including every generation of technology we've identified. I've shown three databases in the illustration, but large companies often have as many as three *hundred* separate database systems.

Most companies have many databases

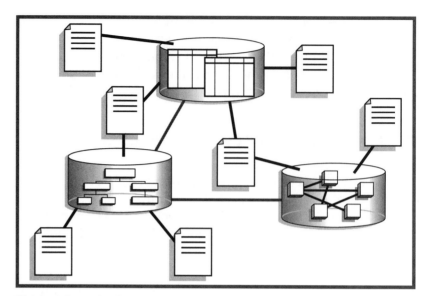

Disjoint Information Systems

These are accessed by hundreds of applications

In addition to these repositories of data, there are usually hundreds or even thousands of applications that have been developed to access these databases and execute corporate procedures. These applications are typically written in many different languages, and in most cases the original developers of the applications have long since left the company.

The coupling of these systems is loose

Finally, there is a very loose coupling among these diverse applications and databases. Some applications are aware of two or more databases, and some databases are aware of each other. In general, however, the connections are very ad hoc, and they are usually made at the application level rather than the database level. Better information integration is a very high priority for most large corporations.

Strategies for Migration

The most obvious way to make the conversion is simply to pull out all the existing systems and rebuild them using object technology. This approach tends to produce rapid but somewhat disappointing results. If you are considering this strategy, my recommendation is that you declare Chapter 7, the solvent form of bankruptcy, instead. It leads to the same end but creates a lot less disillusionment along the way.

You can't do it all at once

Clearly, the only realistic approach is to migrate to a new generation of information systems over time, adding new capabilities without disrupting the old. The two general strategies for doing this I call *divide and conquer* and *unite and conquer*. They can be viewed as alternative approaches, but they are actually complementary. Either one eventually leads to the other.

There are two strategies for migration

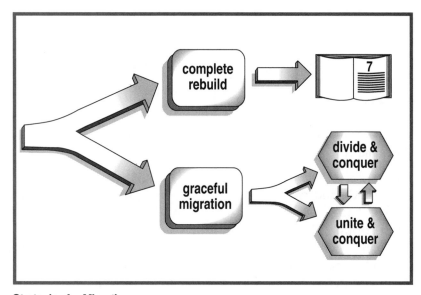

Strategies for Migration

The Divide-and-Conquer Strategy

Solve the hardest problems first

The divide-and-conquer strategy is simple: You examine your existing applications and figure out which ones are (a) not doing the job and (b) well-suited to object technology, based on the criteria described earlier. One by one, you build object-based systems to replace them. Gradually, object technology replaces more and more applications.

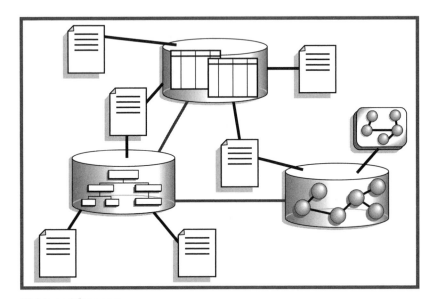

Divide and Conquer

This leaves you with incompatible systems

The divide-and-conquer strategy is a safe, proven approach that will probably get you well into the transition with only a modicum of disruption. The only serious drawback of this approach is that it means your information systems are partially traditional and partially object-based. This can make integration difficult and keep you in an awkward state of transition for years.

The Unite-and-Conquer Strategy

At some point during the migration process, you should consider the unite-and-conquer strategy. The essence of this strategy is to integrate your corporate information systems using an object-oriented framework while still maintaining legacy systems undisturbed.

Eventually, you may want to convert completely

The best way to do this is by building models of corporate processes, as described in this book. Within these models, objects can be programmed to access your existing databases to pull up the required information and translate it into object form.

Use models to integrate information

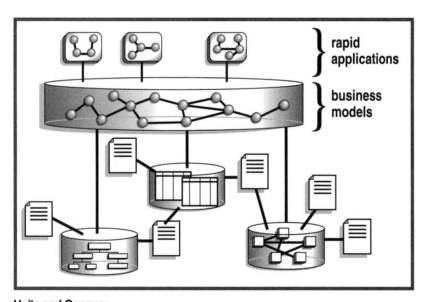

Unite and Conquer

Existing applications run undisturbed

From the point of view of existing applications, nothing has changed—the data stays where it's always been, and the programs continue to function normally. But from another point of view, your new models "contain" (by reference) all the information of the company. When you use these models, it's completely transparent where the information actually resides. This allows new object-based applications to be constructed on top of your models, using rapid prototyping techniques, just as though the company had fully converted to object technology.

Complete integration involves combining models

To achieve complete integration, you need to tie the various models of corporate processes together so that they interact just as they do in the actual corporation. At this point, your combined enterprise model acts as a kind of lens through which you can view all the operations of the company in an object-oriented manner. The fact that most of these operations are still supported by traditional technology does not impair the clarity of this object-based perspective.

Encapsulating Legacy Systems

You can put wrappers around legacy systems

An extension of the unite-and-conquer strategy is to absorb legacy systems by making them appear object oriented. The essence of this technique is to put object-oriented shells, called *wrappers*, around legacy systems to let them interact in an object-oriented environment without having to recode them. The wrapper accepts messages from other objects, calls on the conventional software to perform the requested operations, then returns a result to the calling object.

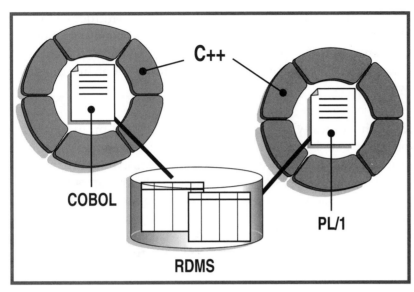

Wrapping Existing Programs

This technique offers a relatively painless path to integration. To the outside world, the legacy system appears to be fully object-oriented. As far as the legacy system itself is concerned, nothing has changed. It continues to receive traditional function calls or user requests, and it generates the same responses it always did.

This form of integration is not hard

The simplest version of this strategy is to place a wrapper around an entire program. If need be, you can translate messages into commands it understands by feeding it simulated keystrokes, then capture its screen output to formulate a response to the message. This is particularly easy to do with mainframe software, which typically has a thin, character-based interface.

You can wrap entire programs if you like

A more ambitious—and effective—version of this technique is to decompose an existing program into its component functions, placing an object wrapper around each. Then you reassemble the components using the message-based interface. The program runs just as before except now it is sending messages back and forth rather than making function calls.

You can also decompose programs

This may seem pointless at first

At first glance, this may not seem like a very productive thing to do. You take a working program apart, add some messaging code to it, and get back a program that does the same thing but is bigger and slower than the original. So far, it doesn't look like much of a win.

But there are real advantages down the line

The win comes when you embed the modified program into an object-oriented environment. All of its functions are now reusable components, so the code they encapsulate is available to all other programs in your system. You also have the option of upgrading the legacy system on a piecemeal basis, replacing only those objects that need repairs and leaving the rest intact. In short, you can bring legacy systems into the object era function by function, without bringing entire applications down for repairs.

This technique works well for COBOL programs

The value of decomposing existing software depends on how well it was modularized in the first place. If the program was developed using functional decomposition, which generally leads to rather poor objects, or makes extensive use of global variables, then it is probably not worth the effort. Experience shows that classic COBOL programs often decompose into very useful objects. If you have a lot of COBOL code on hand, as most large companies do, you should consider using the wrapper technique for upgrading legacy systems.

Completing the Conversion

You will probably use all these techniques

Ultimately, you will probably use a combination of the "divide" and "unite" strategies, together with a certain amount of wrapping to bring legacy systems into the fold. The following illustration shows the kind of system you would have eventually if you used this combination of strategies.

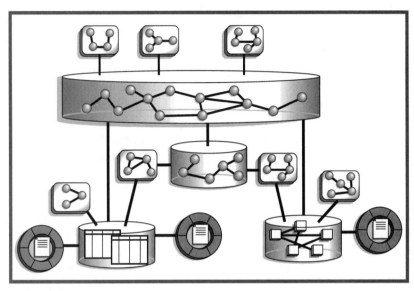

A Reasonable Goal

Functionally, this system is entirely object based, so the conversion is complete from that standpoint. Realistically, however, it is bound to contain legacy systems that you simply don't want to touch, either because they are too fragile or because there is no payoff in bringing them forward. Given the strategies described previously, you can afford to leave these systems alone until they die of old age. You don't have to go in and change every line of code in your company.

This system is effectively object-oriented

The bottom line is that this approach converts you to a consistent, object-based information system in the shortest possible time yet gives you all the time you need to complete the job. That gives you the optimal balance between speed of conversion and conservation of resources.

This is the most cost-effective path

TRANSFORMING THE ORGANIZATION

Object technology affects the entire organization

Making the move to object technology requires much more than just adopting a new language or database. As I emphasized in Chapter 5, it also requires that you change the way you think about software and manage its development. On a larger scale, however, the changes go well beyond the actual software and affect the way you function as a company. To get the maximum benefit from this new technology, you must to be willing to embrace change at every level of your organization.

Information systems can't be transformed in isolation

This may sound like a rather grand claim. After all, we're only talking about a new way of building software. In fact, I'm not exaggerating the situation in the slightest. The quality of your information systems is one of the major factors in determining the competitiveness of your company, and the importance of these systems increases every year. But transforming corporate information systems is of limited value without corresponding changes in they way you gather and use that information.

The JIT of Information Systems

The adoption of JIT illustrates this point

The best way to communicate the full impact of object technology is to compare it with just-in-time (JIT) manufacturing. Conceived primarily by W. Edwards Deming, JIT was largely ignored in the United States but was quickly embraced by the Japanese. Once the Japanese began to threaten our position as the world's leading manufacturer, American manufacturing companies began to take JIT seriously and adopt some of its premises.

Adopting JIT is an all-or-none proposition

But many companies were reluctant to accept the entire philosophy of JIT. After all, they reasoned, we're only talking about a better way to assemble cars. So they restricted their changes to the factory floor, rearranging machines and reallocating responsibilities. And they learned a hard lesson. Adopting JIT is an all-or-none proposition. You don't get any rewards for going a quarter of the way there.

As the following figure illustrates, converting to JIT affects every level of the organization. Manufacturers who embraced change at all these levels have been very successful with JIT and have become much more competitive in the international market. Those who didn't are still trying to figure out why their investment in new equipment didn't pay off.

JIT affects every level of the organization

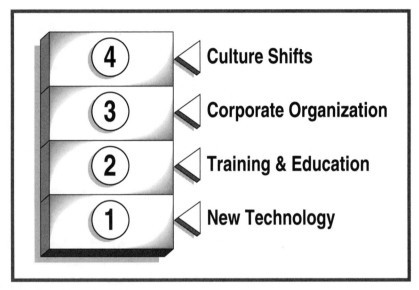

Effects on Every Level

Converting to object technology may not require quite the degree of commitment that converting to JIT calls for. But, like JIT, it eventually affects every level of an organization. Although you can reap considerable rewards simply by changing the way you build software, maximizing corporate competitiveness based on this new technology requires an investment in all four levels.

Object technology also affects every level

1. Upgrading Technology

The technology conversion is not expensive

At the level of new technology, the problems aren't nearly as serious as the ones posed by JIT, which requires rebuilding factories from the ground up. Converting to object technology does require the use of workstations or high-end PCs, but most companies are already making the move into distributed computing anyway. You also need new software development tools, but those are no more expensive than traditional tools for PCs and workstations.

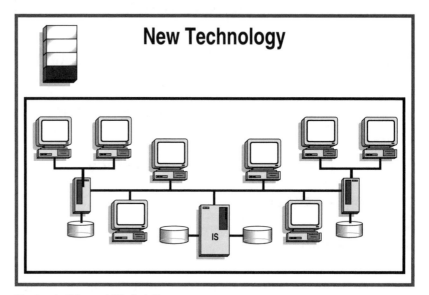

Moving to PCs and Workstations

This is not where the real investment lies

Overall, depending on the size of your company, you can probably make the technical conversion to object technology for less than the cost of a single, traditional mainframe development project. So the technology level requires some investment, but this is not where the real cost lies.

2. Training and Education

A much larger investment is required for training and education. This is money well spent, but it does require an exceptional commitment to education right from the start of the conversion. One of the most common remarks I have heard from companies who have begun the conversion to object technology is that they wished they had invested more in education up front because it would have saved them a lot of grief and expense down the road (see the case studies in the next chapter).

Training requires a larger investment

The primary function of training is to instill new skills. These skills will be required for the new hardware, operating systems, and languages that your people will be using with object technology. It's also important to do cross-training on traditional roles as part of your reorganization. This gives you much more flexibility in the allocation of human resources to systems development projects. It is a lesson learned with JIT that applies particularly well to the adoption of object technology.

Skills acquisition is the bare minimum

In contrast to training, the function of education is to create understanding of new concepts. These include the principles of object technology, the techniques and advantages of programming by assembly, and other subjects all the way up to an understanding of how more responsive information systems increase corporate competitiveness.

Education is even more important

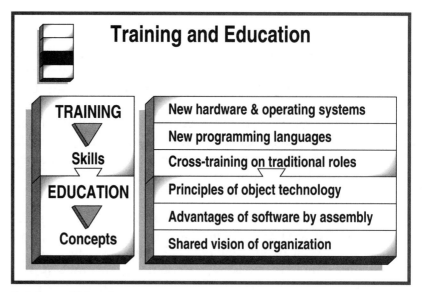

Training and Education

Both are essential   It's important to emphasize that both training and education are essential to making a successful conversion. Specifically, if you try to train without educating, your people will start using the technology without really understanding what they are trying to achieve. That's much more likely to lead to chaos than consistency.

Training pays off   American companies are generally reluctant to spend much money on training. But training pays off; in fact, it has a consistently high return on investment. A study by the American Society for Training and Development covering the 50-year time period between 1935 and 1985 found that American manufacturers invested 15 times as much on capital equipment as they did on training. Yet the return on investment per dollar spent on training was more than twice as great as the return on investment in capital equipment.

By contrast, the Japanese understand the value of training very well, which is one reason they can outperform us in the manufacturing arena. When Nissan opened its first U.S. automobile plant in Tennessee, it spent an average of $25,200 per worker on training and education—a total of $63 million—before it ever opened its doors. That's a phenomenal investment by American standards, but it clearly paid off—the U.S. plant matched the quality and productivity of Nissan's Japanese plants from the day it opened.

The Japanese know this very well

People often want to know how long it takes to get up to speed with object technology. It's hard to give a simple answer because it depends on so many factors, including how much you invest in education and training, whether you use outside experts to "jump start" your efforts, and whether you have people on board who can provide ongoing mentoring. Averaging across all those factors, however, it typically takes programmers about six weeks to become functional in an object-oriented language and about six months to become fully proficient.

The object learning curve

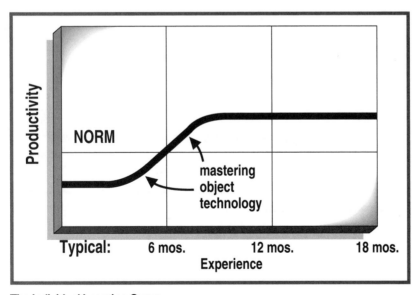

The Individual Learning Curve

There are two costs implied here

Two costs must be borne during this transition period. The first is the cost of the education and training. The second is the reduced productivity during the learning period. Although the programmer will ultimately repay this investment through increased productivity, it could take a while to realize that return on investment.

But the biggest return isn't shown

But the individual learning process is only part of the object experience curve. Viewed as a whole, the entire development organization is learning how to solve problems with reusable classes and is building up a store of those classes. That, in fact, is where the real investment lies, and it is where the biggest return can be realized. Only to the extent that a company is willing to invest in robust, reusable components will object technology really pay off.

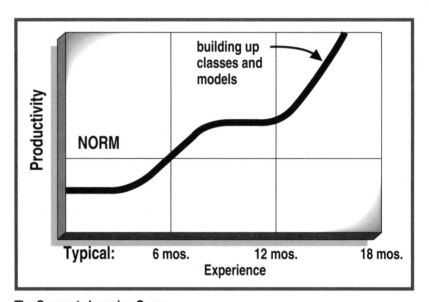

The Corporate Learning Curve

3. Organizing for Maximum Advantage

While you can certainly adopt object technology without changing your corporate organization, you can be much more successful if you make some adaptations. There are actually two different kinds of changes you should consider making: changes that enable the technology, and changes that are enabled *by* the technology.

Adapting the organization can increase success

We have already considered examples of the first kind of change in the preceding chapters. These include:

Some changes enable the technology

- **Realigning IS job descriptions** to fit the new way of building software. This is not a minor change; people are used to the classic distinctions among analysts, coders, and other specialists, and many will no doubt resist being retrained and reclassified.

- **Transforming IS into a horizontal organization** by decentralizing its operations. As noted in the preceding chapter, this is a trend that's already well underway. Object technology simply puts a new twist on it, one that may actually help IS organizations make the shift.

- **Redefining the role of end users** in the systems development process. This change is bound to produce resistance. However, a new partnership between IS and end users that gives end users good business solutions in a timely manner would greatly reduce this resistance.

We are still early in the experience curve of object technology, so it's too soon to list with any certainty what kinds of changes will be enabled by object technology. However, the following are likely candidates:

Other changes are made possible by the technology

- **Flatter organizations.** Virtually every large company is looking for ways to flatten the steep, bureaucratic hierarchies that have evolved since the turn of the century. Object-oriented information systems should support this effort by capturing many of the corporate administrative procedures directly in software, reducing the need for manual paper shuffling.

- **More fluid organizational structures.** Probably the most important effect will be to allow companies to change their structures more quickly in response to market changes. Current information systems lock companies into fixed structures. The dynamic modifiability of object-oriented systems should reverse this effect and actually facilitate organizational change.

- **More dynamic allocation of resources.** Given the reduced resources required for development, it should be possible to assemble temporary teams of managers and prototypers to create solutions to emerging business problems, increasing the responsiveness of the organization.

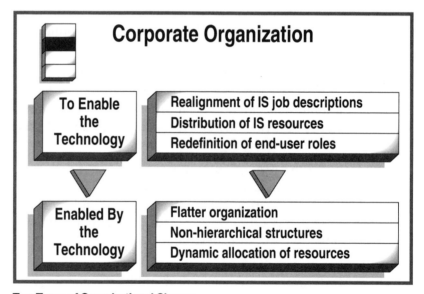

Two Types of Organizational Change

There are certainly more changes to come

I'm sure these suggestions only scratch the surface. Part of the fascination of working with object technology on an enterprise scale is discovering ways in which it can help reorganize corporations to maximize competitiveness.

4. Evolving the Corporate Culture

Gaining the full benefits of object technology will call for some changes in corporate culture that may not come easily. In the short term:

Changes in culture are important

- You need to **introduce new reward structures** to optimize the new development process. For example, application developers should get paid more for generating fewer lines of code, not more.

- You need to **foster new partnerships** where animosity was once the rule. This is particularly true between IS and end users, but many other partnerships also will be required to agree on standard classes and models.

- You need to **build a commitment to reusability**. This means that developers should design for future uses, not just the for the problem at hand.

Cultural changes also will need to take place over the long term. Again, these are a bit harder to characterize until we have more long-term experience with the technology, but here are a few that seem likely:

Long-term changes are also important

- You need to **establish a positive attitude toward change**. Sustained change is going to be a way of life for large companies for the foreseeable future, and object technology is one of the best vehicles for embracing that change. But it can't do the job alone—people have to be willing to change, too.

- You need to **bring formal and informal systems into alignment**. One of the things that enterprise modeling does is clarify the difference between the "official" way of doing things and the way they really get done. If enterprise models are to work, they must be based on reality. Any conflicts between this reality and official policy will lead to tension and confusion as people attempt to satisfy incompatible requirements.

- You have to **instill a positive attitude toward sharing knowledge** and embedding it in corporate information systems. This can be a difficult transition for people who have always been rewarded for the uniqueness of their knowledge. The solution is to reward them for the use of knowledge, not its possession.

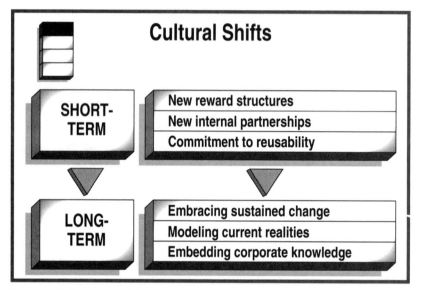

Changes in Corporate Culture

Reversing the Four Wedges

We began with four wedges

In Chapter 2, I described four forces of change that threaten to shatter organizations that fail to cope with them. By examining the nature of these forces, I suggested four ways in which our information systems must improve to help us cope effectively with these threats. The essential theme of this book has been that, properly applied, object technology can satisfy those four requirements.

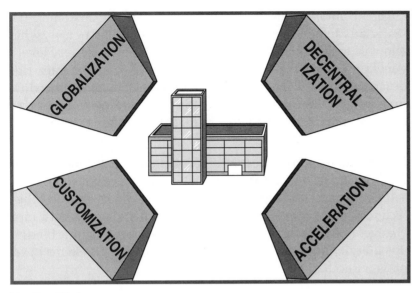

The Four Wedges

By satisfying these requirements, we should be able to meet the needs of management to a degree not possible with traditional technologies. For example, class hierarchies offer a natural way to capture the differences among nations without duplicating information unnecessarily. Similarly, by embedding nation-specific procedures in objects, we can make them smart enough to accommodate the national differences that global organizations must deal with.

Internationalization is made easier

Similarly, the high degree of modularity of object technology should facilitate the development of decentralized information systems, while still allowing these systems to integrate into an overall corporate information structure. In fact, the multilevel modularity of object technology, which mimics the structure of living organisms, provides a natural model for achieving decentralized operations without sacrificing the integrity of the organization.

Decentralization is also facilitated

Customization is facilitated as well

Object technology also helps us get closer to the customer. The major advantage comes from the use of class hierarchies, which allow us to capture information about customers at every level of generality, from the most generic concept of a customer right down to the client. Moreover, we can have dedicated procedures for dealing with each class of customer, including coding exceptions for individual customers to meet their unique needs.

Object technology copes with accelerating change

Finally, the responsiveness of object systems, including the rapid deployment of new applications, should be a major force in offsetting the accelerating pace of business change. Indeed, object technology shows its greatest strength when dealing with rapid change. Particularly with systems that support dynamic binding, it is literally possible to make changes to running systems in seconds without affecting ongoing operations.

Object technology turns the threats into weapons

In short, object technology can not only ward off the threat of the four wedges, it can potentially cope with them so well that they are transformed into competitive weapons. The companies that make the transition first will have a tremendous advantage over their competitors because they will be better equipped to anticipate change, respond to change, and even control change in their markets.

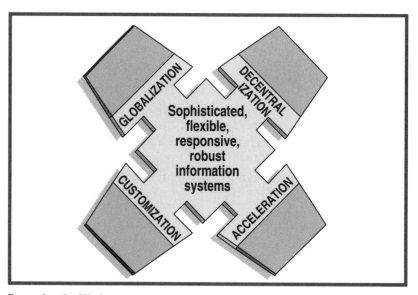

Reversing the Wedges

12

Commercial Applications of Object Technology

This final chapter describes real-world examples of object technology in action. These examples are intended not only to demonstrate the range of applications that are yielding to the object approach, but also to give you an opportunity to learn from the experiences—good and bad—of companies that have already taken the plunge into object technology.

This chapter describes real-world examples

You can read these examples in any order or combination. If you are mostly interested in core business applications, skip ahead to the last three sections of the chapter. If you simply want a summary overview of what other companies have learned, go directly to the final section.

The examples can be read selectively

How the Examples Were Selected

In selecting the examples described below, I used three basic criteria:

I used three selection criteria

1. **The application must be commercial in nature,** in the sense that it is meant to increase organizational effectiveness or provide indirect support for goals. This criterion ruled out many research systems that are excellent examples of object-oriented development but might be of minor interest to the business community.

2. **The application must be completed or well on the way to completion.** This criterion eliminated pilot projects or other efforts that had little corporate commitment. With one or two exceptions, all the examples in this chapter represent significant investments in object technology.

3. **Companies must be willing to identify themselves.** Many companies were comfortable talking about their object applications only on the condition of anonymity. I'm sure they had legitimate reasons for imposing this condition, but anonymous reports don't carry as much credibility as ones from companies that are willing to publicly identify themselves.

The examples provide a cross section

The examples represent only a few of the many commercial applications that are currently deployed or nearing deployment. To provide a reasonable cross section of applications, I selected three projects each from six different areas: engineering, manufacturing, graphical information systems, financial applications, business management, and enterprise modeling.

The areas are reviewed in order of adoption

These six areas are discussed in roughly the order in which they have adopted object technology. The areas span the complete continuum of adoption: Object technology is rapidly becoming the standard platform in engineering applications, whereas it is just now coming into commercial use in enterprise modeling.

ENGINEERING APPLICATIONS

Engineering was the first to benefit

Many of the early applications of object technology come from the engineering arena. The reasons for this are straightforward: Engineering applications deal with complex, highly structured data that is difficult to represent in conventional programming languages. In addition, many engineering applications gain considerable leverage from the modeling and simulation capabilities of object technology.

Mentor Graphics' Falcon Framework

Mentor Graphics makes engineering design systems

Mentor Graphics Corporation, founded in 1981, is one of the leading vendors of engineering design software. Its original package, which was developed in Pascal, had become overstressed by 1984. Demands for new functionality and increased interoperability among tools were becoming increasingly difficult to meet.

In 1985, Mentor Graphics took a major gamble—it decided to replace its first-generation product with an entirely new product based on object-oriented technology. Moreover, it decided to scale up its product to embrace the entire life cycle of engineering design and to encompass concurrent design techniques for the entire spectrum of electronic, mechanical, and software components.

Mentor Graphics shifted to object technology in 1985

This is how *Falcon Framework*, one of the largest applications ever developed using object technology, was originally conceived. In 1990, the first version of the product was introduced to the marketplace. Many lessons were learned in the intervening five years.

It took five years to build Falcon Framework

Mentor Graphics chose to develop Falcon Framework in C++ because of its good portability and its likelihood of being a future standard in the engineering arena. AT&T's C++ was still in the Beta-release stage when Mentor Graphics made its language decision, so the company had to suffer through all the growing pains of a new language. But the company worked closely with Bell Labs to iron out the bugs, and it continues to be the largest user of C++ outside of AT&T.

Mentor Graphics chose C++ for the project

Falcon Framework was an ambitious undertaking. The development team grew from six people in 1986 to more than a hundred in 1990. When the product shipped, it contained about 1,200 classes, more than 10,000 methods, and consisted of more than half a million lines of C++ source code. Moreover, the Falcon Framework itself is only part of the Mentor Graphics product suite, which includes more than 3 million lines of C++ code. Given that object-oriented programs typically provide comparable functionality in a fraction of the traditional code size, the total effort was probably equivalent to a COBOL project with at least 10 to 15 million lines of code.

Falcon Framework is a large system

Agreeing on base classes was hard

Adopting object technology initially created tensions among Mentor Graphics' development teams. In the past, separate teams had developed individual programs, operating independently until it was time to perform final integration. Now these independent teams had to agree on a common set of base classes and develop specialized classes only within their own domains. There was no natural "owner" to take responsibility for these shared classes, and it was hard to reach agreement on their definition.

QA took over the care of classes

Eventually, the quality assurance group stepped in to play that role, approving all design changes to base classes and enforcing the consistent use of these classes. In effect, QA moved itself from the end of the software development cycle to the very beginning. Mentor Graphics had discovered what manufacturers have known for a decade: Putting quality first leads to better products.

Object technology made the project possible

Once the core classes were agreed on, construction of the product accelerated rapidly, and the system took form much faster than it could have using conventional techniques. In fact, looking back, Mentor Graphics has concluded that a project of this scope simply would not have been possible without the advantages of object technology.

NIST's STEP Editor

A standard is required to describe products

One of the most difficult problems in engineering is defining parts and products in a way that can be shared across different computer systems and stored in a common format. Complicating this problem is the tremendous range in the complexity of products—anywhere from a bolt to a battleship. Clearly, a universal standard is required, and the National Institute of Standards and Technology (NIST) is participating in its development.

The emerging international standard is the *Standard for The Exchange of Product (STEP) Model Data*. An earlier attempt at a standard, built using conventional programming and database techniques, proved inadequate for representing complex products. STEP uses object-oriented concepts, languages, and databases to manage the complexity of product descriptions in a fast, effective manner.

The new standard is object-oriented

As STEP is being formulated, tools are being developed to support the system. One tool that is critical to the success of STEP is a dedicated editor for creating and modifying product descriptions. In order to determine what features such an editor would require, NIST developed a prototype editor called *QDES*—a tongue-in-cheek acronym for the *Quick and Dirty Editing System*.

STEP requires an editor to define products

QDES was developed in Smalltalk-80 by one person in two to three months. The editor was packed with advanced functionality and was an impressive achievement for three staff months of work. But, as its name clearly implies, it was just a quick prototype to demonstrate the feasibility of developing a full-featured editor for STEP descriptions.

A prototype was created in three months

The completed prototype was shown to a few end users to get their feedback. Not only did the users like what they saw, they refused to believe it wasn't a working product. They quickly adopted QDES and began using it for their daily work. The prototype has been in production use for over a year and a half and has undergone numerous revisions to meet the increasing demands of its user base.

Users thought it was a production system

In fact, requests for repairs and enhancements to QDES have become so frequent that the original developer has no time to make the underlying changes that would turn the prototype into a genuine production system. In the words of one user, QDES became "the prototype that wouldn't die."

The system has never been rebuilt

*It's important
to manage user
expectations*

There's a clear moral to this story: It's so easy to create the appearance of production-quality systems with object technology that users not only fail to recognize the limitations of a prototype, they expect large chunks of functionality to be added on a moment's notice. It's important to manage user expectations and to help understand that real engineering is still required to create production software systems.

Hewlett-Packard's VISTA

*HP developed a
"faceless instrument"*

Some years ago, Hewlett-Packard conceived of a new type of electronic instrument called a *faceless instrument*. As an alternative to its single-purpose hardware with built-in dials and displays, HP would build software to allow general-purpose workstations to emulate a wide variety of electronic instruments. The user of this system, which became known as *VISTA*, would be able to mix and match instruments in windows on the same screen, providing maximum flexibility in monitoring, measuring, and control.

*They chose Objective
C as their language*

HP developers quickly settled on object technology as the most flexible, extensible platform on which to build this new kind of instrument. The language they chose was Objective C, which provided many of the advantages of Smalltalk while leveraging their existing expertise in C programming.

*There were three
superclasses*

VISTA classes were organized under three major superclasses:

1. **Virtual instrument objects** handled the external data-gathering operations, insulating the rest of the system from all the details of the measurement hardware.

2. **Measurement objects** displayed data in real time in windows on the user's screen. A user could select any mix of measures to view at any time, moving and sizing the windows to create an optimal display.

3. **Result objects** recorded incoming data, made adjustments for calibration, took averages, and performed other statistical tasks. Placing average objects on the screen next to measurement objects was a particularly useful technique.

The designers of VISTA experienced a problem that required a careful work-around. In the system, many different things had to occur at the same time, including recording the measurements, updating the display, and processing user actions. Since Objective C didn't support true concurrency, techniques for performing background tasks during idle moments were developed. The techniques worked well, but built-in concurrency would have provided a simpler solution.

Language concurrency would have helped

VISTA turned out to be a sizable project, involving as many as 30 developers and resulting in more than 300 classes and more than 100,000 lines of code. Given the scale of the project, HP gave careful attention to its methodology. It evaluated a number of different approaches and ultimately adapted the traditional waterfall model to better fit object technology. HP also defined more than 20 software metrics to be applied at each stage of development (see Kraemer, "Product Development Using Object-Oriented Software Technology": *Hewlett-Packard Journal*, August 1989, p. 98).

VISTA was a large project

This attention to methodology and metrics was essential to HP's success in this project. In the words of Tom Kraemer, who led the development effort, "Establishing good software development practices is even more important than object-oriented technology."

Good methodology was essential

MANUFACTURING SYSTEMS

Following engineering, manufacturing is probably the hottest area for the application of object technology. The advantages of object technology in this arena are basically the same as in engineering: Objects can represent complex data structures such as bills of materials and assembly sequences, and the simulation capabilities of object languages provide a major advantage in representing manufacturing operations.

Manufacturing is the next hot area

EDS's Maintenance Management System

EDS employs 20,000 programmers

EDS is the world's largest system integrator. As such, it currently employs more than 20,000 programmers. Like most organizations, EDS wants to grow its business and increase its revenues to a multiple of their present levels. However, these corporate goals raise the specter of managing upwards of a hundred thousand programmers!

The company needs big productivity improvements

EDS has investigated various technologies that promise to enhance productivity and reduce the number of programmers required for any given project. The company has considerable experience with CASE tools, and informal estimates indicate that CASE can shave about 10 to 15 percent off the total development effort. Those are useful reductions, but EDS was intrigued by the order-of-magnitude productivity gains promised by object technology. The search for bigger gains led the company to perform an experiment to assess the potential of object technology.

EDS brought in Servio to run a test

Because it lacked an experienced internal team of object-oriented developers, EDS turned to an outside firm to help with its assessment. At that time, I was the head of a business unit at Servio Corporation that was developing manufacturing applications. Given that we had skilled Smalltalk programmers and a base of reusable classes for building manufacturing applications, we represented a natural choice for carrying out EDS's experiment.

The project was to replicate an existing system

The project selected for the study was a *Maintenance Management System (MMS)* used in General Motors plants to keep machinery in proper working order. The existing MMS scheduled over 10,000 maintenance jobs a month and handled both preventive and corrective maintenance. It also tracked the maintenance history of all machines and managed the inventory of spare parts.

The original system was written in PL/I

The existing MMS was written in PL/I and consisted of 265,000 lines of source code. It required 152 staff months to design, develop, and test, with a total project duration of 19 months. The finished program required 13.6 megabytes of main memory to run.

The object-oriented MMS developed by Servio was written in Smalltalk-80 and was superior to the original by more than an order of magnitude in all of the measures just described. It consisted of 22,000 lines of source code, it took 10.4 staff months to develop, and it was completed in 3.5 months. The finished program required 1.1 megabytes of main memory.

The object-based system was much smaller

Performance of the two systems was roughly comparable, with a slight edge going to the PL/I system in worst-case scenarios. However, the PL/I system had undergone years of tuning, whereas the Smalltalk system was delivered just as it was originally assembled. It is likely that, with proper tuning, the Smalltalk system could have matched or exceeded the performance of the PL/I system in all areas.

Performance was roughly comparable

Perhaps the most remarkable aspect of this comparison was the productivity improvement obtained with the use of object technology. The Servio team that developed the new MMS consisted of four people, two of whom were on the project half time. In fact, all of the actual programming was done by a single programmer—the other members of the team worked on design, built data-input screens, documented the system, and performed other support tasks.

Only a single programmer was required

Even including the support staff, the measured productivity ratio for design, coding, and testing was 14:1. To my knowledge, this number represents the most precise productivity comparison of object technology with conventional approaches available to date. Bear in mind, however, that this ratio was achieved with an experienced team that understood the industry and had a good collection of reusable classes on hand for immediate reuse. Order-of-magnitude benefits are clearly possible, but they don't come automatically.

The productivity ratio was 14:1

EDS is moving to-ward objects

A company the size of EDS does not make changes quickly, but object technology is definitely making inroads within the company. After completing this initial project, EDS and Servio developed a second object-oriented application, and EDS is currently running that application on-line in a GM plant. EDS is now starting to develop object applications internally and has at least five new projects underway.

Texas Instruments' Semiconductor CIM System

TI is building an advanced manufacturing facility

Manufacturing semiconductor components is a slow and painstaking process, requiring high volume runs to achieve reasonable economies of scale. Hoping to make low-volume production more profitable, Texas Instruments has teamed with the Air Force Wright Laboratory and the DARPA Microelectronic Technology Office in an ambitious effort called the *Microelectronics Manufacturing Science and Technology (MMST) Program*. The goal of this effort is to produce order-of-magnitude speed improvements and cost reductions in this critical type of manufacturing.

The software component is a CIM system

A key component of this effort is a *Computer Integrated Manufacturing (CIM)* system that automates the advanced manufacturing facility, reducing human intervention to a minimum. In essence, this system will simulate the operations of the MMST facility in real time, seamlessly integrating all activities from high-level planning to shop-floor control.

TI is committed to object technology for CIM

CIM has proved to be an elusive goal for manufacturers, but TI believes that it can be achieved through the use of object technology. Its rationale is that object technology is a natural platform for a manufacturing system, and that the reuse of standard components could cut maintenance costs dramatically.

TI chose to use two different versions of Smalltalk for the project: Objectworks\Smalltalk from ParcPlace for the management workstations and Smalltalk/V from Digitalk for the machine-control systems. They selected the GemStone database from Servio for object storage, and they purchased both training and tools from Knowledge Systems Corporation and Object Technology Incorporated.

They are working with Smalltalk and GemStone

The MMST CIM project is still in the design phase, but the results to date are encouraging. They have devoted about 23 staff months to the prototype and have produced 393 classes and 45,000 lines of code. This represents a production rate of about 23,300 lines of code per person per year, as compared to accepted industry standards of 3,000 to 4,000 lines using conventional languages.

Prototyping efforts have been highly productive

Curiously, the estimated size of the completed CIM system continues to decrease as the system grows, which is the reverse of what usually happens with large systems. The initial estimate was 500,000 lines of code. That estimate was subsequently reduced by half, and a year later the estimate dropped below 200,000 lines. Clearly, part of the conversion to object technology is learning just how much smaller object-based systems are than conventional systems.

Estimated system size decreases continuously

TI did an extensive analysis of the problem domain before they began their prototyping effort. Once the prototyping was underway, they realized that they could have avoided a great deal of tedium associated with describing object behavior by starting the prototyping effort much sooner. As they have progressed in their project, they have moved away from the traditional waterfall model of development and focused more on an iterative method involving prototyping at each stage. To a large extent, this approach has been made feasible by the productivity of the Smalltalk language and environment.

TI is moving away from the waterfall model

Sequent Computer's Hardware Diagnostics System

Sequent computers have sophisticated diagnostics

Sequent Computer Systems builds highly parallel computers. Like all large computers, Sequent's machines have built-in diagnostics to assure that all components are working properly. In addition to the usual tests, Sequent's diagnostics have to deal with the added complexity of a variable number of processors in a tightly coupled configuration.

Sequent used objects for several reasons

When Sequent decided to enhance its built-in diagnostics system, it decided to use C++ instead of C. It chose an object-oriented language for several reasons:

- **The ability to represent hardware as objects.** Given the sophisticated architecture of Sequent's computers, it was much easier to represent its components as objects than to distribute knowledge of these components across a large number of procedures. Also, using objects to represent hardware components insulated the rest of the diagnostics system from any changes in the underlying hardware.

- **The ability to create special versions through inheritance.** Given the wide range of configurations for Sequent machines, it was wasteful to create unique diagnostics systems for every configuration. Sequent's solution was to create a generic diagnostics system, then subclass this system for different configurations.

- **The ability to extend the system.** New diagnostics are constantly required as new functionality is added to Sequent's line of computers. With C++, new tests can be incorporated into existing suites with little or no change in the existing code.

Sequent achieved significant code reuse

On the whole, Sequent found that C++ met or exceeded its expectations. The kernel diagnostics system consists of 208,000 lines of source code, of which 145,000 lines are shared among two or more subsystems. Specific diagnostics tests add another 366,000 lines, bringing the total to 574,000 lines of source code. This total is considerably smaller than it would be with a comparable implementation in C because of inheritance and reuse.

Sequent's C++ diagnostics system is a finished product that has been shipping with its machines for nearly two years. Over that time, numerous extensions have been made to the system, and they all have been reasonably easy to incorporate. The extensibility Sequent sought from object technology has clearly been realized.

The system is easy to extend

While Sequent is pleased with the results it achieved using C++, it experienced its share of problems in converting to object technology. Some of the lessons learned are:

Sequent learned from its experience

- **Recruit and reward a champion.** The move to objects is not easy. You need someone with a firm commitment to the technology to start the process and keep it moving forward.

- **Plan on the learning curve.** Expect the inevitable drop in productivity as C programmers convert to C++. Don't set unrealistic expectations for the first project or everyone will be disappointed.

- **Put the right tools in place.** The need for good tools may not be apparent until a project is well underway. Identifying the right tools early on will help smooth the conversion.

- **Don't create objects for objects' sake.** Programmers who are new to object technology can easily make simple procedures complex by turning them into objects. What starts out as an object may actually be better represented as a method or variable.

GEOGRAPHIC INFORMATION SYSTEMS

Another vertical market that has been quick to adopt object technology is the development of *geographic information systems (GISs)*. GISs are software systems that provide access to information based on maps or diagrams rather than tables or queries. For example, a GIS might let you view a map of the United States and click a mouse on any city to see a detailed map of that city, locate various categories of restaurants, or see a demographic breakdown of the population.

GISs provide visual access to information

GISs leverage object technology

GISs benefit from object technology in a number of ways. A major benefit, as with engineering and manufacturing, is the ability to manipulate complex information structures as simple objects. Another benefit, which makes the geographical part possible, is the multimedia nature of object technology. The components of composite objects can be maps, charts, routings, sketches, voice annotations, or any other kind of information that can be digitized.

Petroleum Information's Sorcerer's Apprentice

Oil exploration is data intensive

One of the major challenges facing petroleum companies is the continuing need to find new sources of oil. As the reserves in known locations dwindle, the search for new sites becomes increasingly difficult. Explorationists—the geophysicists and geologists who identify new sources of oil and gas—now spend up to 80 percent of their time finding and organizing existing data in order to analyze it. In effect, they have become "data detectives," collating and cross-referencing relevant data in hopes of discovering clues as to where new reserves might be found.

PI provides graphical data and access tools

Petroleum Information (PI) is the standard source of information for the domestic U.S. oil and gas industry. It supplies geologic and geodetic maps, well data, production logs, and other vital information that helps explorationists do their job. It also seeks to provide leading-edge tools to aid explorationists in their search. Given the nature of the problem, the optimal tool is a geographic information system.

Current GISs have some drawbacks

Current GISs tend to be rather expensive, difficult to integrate, and hard to use. A typical system runs on a minicomputer or workstation, costs about $100,000, and requires that a company reformat and load all of its data into the GIS database rather than simply connecting it to the existing systems.

PI saw these drawbacks as opportunities to create a competitive advantage in its market. Accordingly, it set out to create an inexpensive, desktop-based GIS that would give its customers graphical access to the wealth of information in its existing databases. It chose the Macintosh as its development platform, selected Macintosh Common LISP as its development environment, and used CLOS (the object-oriented extension of Common LISP) as its development language.

PI set out to build a map-based data browser

Rather than jumping into building a GIS application, however, PI first constructed a generic application framework it called the *Sorcerer's Apprentice*. The Sorcerer's Apprentice contained all the code for constructing maps, accessing PI's and the customer's data, integrating information across multiple sources, browsing data both visually and textually, and providing many other services.

First it built a generic framework

Building a generic framework proved to be a very productive strategy. PI has now developed three major applications in rapid succession using this framework: a GIS that traces all the natural gas pipeline facilities in North America; an executive information system for gaining daily access to worldwide drilling activities; and a system for performing exploration risk analysis based on historical drilling statistics.

PI can now roll out GIS applications quickly

All of these applications share a common graphical interface, all permit map-based information access, and all support a variety of data browsing and collating facilities. This common functionality is achieved entirely through the reuse of code, which is currently running 80 percent or better. In effect, most of the code for a new application is already completed before PI begins work on it.

They are achieving 80 percent code reuse

Like many other companies that have adopted object technology, PI soon learned that it was more effective to use rapid prototyping to develop its applications than to write extensive specifications. It also learned to involve its end users early in the prototyping process in order to satisfy their needs as closely as possible.

They also adopted rapid prototyping

PI is pushing the application envelope

PI has enjoyed considerable success with its new development strategy, and the company believes it has moved its development efforts into a realm that is unavailable using conventional methods. In the words of Mike Wirth, who headed this project, "Our goal was not to build something in an hour which otherwise would have taken a day, but rather to build applications in three months which simply couldn't have been built at all before."

NOAA's Automated Cartography System

NOAA produces millions of charts a year

The Coast and Geodetic Survey Agency, a part of the National Oceanic and Atmospheric Administration (NOAA), produces and distributes millions of coastal charts each year to private, commercial, and federal customers. It creates these charts from a vast database of information about contours, depths, wrecks, buoys, channels, and countless other terrain features.

Compiling charts is slow and difficult

The most difficult and expensive aspect of this process is chart compilation, in which lines, icons, and text are used to create a map of a specific portion of coastline. Compilation requires highly trained experts to decide which features to include, select appropriate iconic and textual representations, and resolve conflicts in the spacing and drawing of these representations. It is no simple task to produce a chart that is sufficiently comprehensive, informative, and readable to meet the needs of its users.

Automatic compilation has been an elusive goal

One of the long-standing goals at NOAA has been to automate the compilation process, producing charts directly from its database. To date, no technology has proved adequate to the task. Drawing systems can't resolve conflicts, and expert systems can't handle the wide range of expertise required. However, the advent of object technology gave new impetus to NOAA's goal of automated cartography, and NOAA has made considerable progress in making it a reality.

The man who is spearheading this effort is Dave Pendleton, who heads up the artificial intelligence program within NOAA's charting lab. Using the GemStone object DBMS and Smalltalk-80, Pendleton's team built a detailed model of a small portion of the U. S. coastline.

NOAA is now applying object technology

This model contains all the essential features described above, together with their relationships. Each feature has methods for plotting and describing itself in various levels of detail, and inheritance is used liberally to avoid redundancy. For example, a lighted buoy with a bell inherits all the qualities of lighted buoys and of buoys in general, so very little information is required to incorporate this particular type of buoy.

Modeling is central to its approach

To compile a chart, a Smalltalk program sends messages to the objects within a certain region asking them to plot themselves. Depending on the type of chart the cartographer is creating, all the objects in the region may receive messages or certain types of objects will be filtered out by not including them on the "mailing list." If two or more objects attempt to use the same space on the chart, the objects involved are sent a "declutter" message asking them to represent themselves in reduced detail.

Objects in the map area plot themselves

This is a highly simplified account of how automated cartography is being achieved, but it should give you a feel for how making objects responsible for their own behavior can distribute expertise throughout a model and enable applications that might not be possible with conventional technologies.

Expertise resides in the objects

A self-managing cartographic model could be used for other purposes in addition to creating printed maps. For example, charts could be generated in real time and displayed on a computer screen aboard a moving vessel. The map would scroll as the vessel moved along the coast, and a pilot could "query" the map by highlighting selected features or zooming in on a particular region. The system could also provide auditory navigational warnings, helping even the least attentive captain keep his tanker from running aground.

Real-time charting could help vessels navigate

This would have many benefits

This application of object technology is still in its early stages, largely due to a lack of funding. However, it clearly has vast commercial potential for both the federal government and private enterprise. Pressing forward on this application could save lives and protect the ecology as well.

Object technology has proven its value

Summing up his experiences with object technology over the past three years, Pendleton concludes that "within a decade, possibly sooner, almost all new systems will be implemented using object programming techniques, languages, environments, and databases. The dramatic improvements already evident in productivity, quality, and reliability are just too important for U.S. industry to ignore."

Command System's Maestro

Maestro is a command and control system

The last example in this section is not a conventional GIS, but in many ways it provides the same functions and serves the same purposes. Command System Inc. (CSI) is building a graphical command and control system for the U.S. Marine Corps. While the primary application of this system is military, CSI is tackling problems that are critical to all large organizations, and it has recently begun to develop versions of its system for commercial environments.

It is based on the concept of cooperating units

The essential problem the company is grappling with is how to coordinate the combined actions of many independent units and subunits, all of which may be in intermittent communication with each other. While the U.S. military still tends to think in terms of top-down control, CSI is building a system that supports varying degrees of autonomy at lower levels. In essence, it views the high-level commander as a conductor attempting to orchestrate the actions of many players and maintain harmony among them. Which is why its system goes by the code name *Maestro*.

Maestro is programmed in C++ and runs on IBM-compatible PCs. The system is capable of running over a loosely coupled network tied together with any combination of hard wire, telephone, or radio communications. The interface is highly graphical, providing strategic and tactical views of field operations. Operators use mouse controllers to select various terrain features or combat units, requesting or providing further information that is automatically combined into a larger picture.

The system runs on loosely coupled networks

Creating Maestro required CSI to solve some unusual problems. For example, although it operates over a network with heterogeneous communications media connecting units that are constantly changing their locations, it does not require a network administrator. Building self-management into the network was difficult but essential. In combat situations, losing the network administrator to an enemy strike would bring down the entire system.

The network is self-managing

In the spirit of the object approach, all elements of the network are responsible for their own network operations. When a unit logs onto the net, it automatically notifies other units and assumes its place in the chain of command. When it logs off, messages and requests are automatically rerouted to accommodate its absence. Imagine if business networks could reconfigure themselves in this way, automatically adjusting to the availability and current location of key personnel!

The network reconfigures itself dynamically

Like other systems described in this chapter, Maestro depends on maintaining an overall model to make the system work. In fact, Don Willis, the president of CSI, is convinced that getting the basic model right is the critical aspect of object-oriented development. In Maestro's case, the model is a complete simulation of battlefield operations, with unit, terrain, message, command, and report objects all interacting in real time to reflect the developments on the battlefield.

Maestro is based on real-time modeling

Given the vagaries of government funding, the development of CSI's system has consisted of months of boredom punctuated by weeks of terrific programming. The current system, including the self-managing network, consists of 90,000 lines of C++ code. It was created by six people in 90 days.

The system came together very quickly

*It has clear commer-
cial applications*

When I last spoke to Don Willis, the Marine Corps had authorized CSI to take the system to the next stage of development, and all six programmers were frantically coding again. The ultimate fate of Maestro remains to be determined. But if the Marine Corps doesn't adopt it, it would make a fine candidate for a graphical enterprise management system.

FINANCIAL APPLICATIONS

*Financial companies
are adopting objects*

Financial institutions, being somewhat more conservative on average than other kinds of organizations, often lag behind in adopting new technologies. However, object technology has made more than a few inroads into the financial arena, especially in the highly competitive brokerage business.

Wyatt Software's Portfolio Management System

*Wyatt Software
developed a portfolio
manager*

In 1988, Wyatt Software decided to develop an object-oriented system for managing global portfolios of fixed-income investments. The *WyCASH+* product is fairly large, consisting of 600 classes and 2.1 megabytes of executable code. It took two years to develop by a team that started out with two Smalltalk programmers and grew to five programmers and a full-time financial expert.

*Wyatt built its own
Smalltalk tools*

WyCASH+ was developed in Smalltalk/V, with calls to assembly language routines for handling remote communications. Given the poor state of team development tools on the market in 1988, Wyatt developed its own tool for integrating the work of multiple programmers. The tool included a difference browser that could find discrepant definitions of the same class and assist a developer in resolving them. Wyatt also developed an automated testing system that contains over 6,000 tests and is still growing.

Wyatt reports that it didn't encounter any major problems in developing the system, in part because it started with talented, experienced Smalltalk programmers. It did find that solid design work is absolutely essential and that modularization above the object level is crucial to building a robust, modifiable system. Wyatt also found that the best way to develop a module was to put a Smalltalk programmer together with a domain expert and have them craft the system through an ongoing partnership.

Programmers partnered with financial experts

WyCASH+ shipped in 1990 and is now used by money managers and investment bankers in such companies as Ameritech, Kellog, and State Street Bank. Wyatt and its clients regard the system as a success, and the company is now developing a multiuser version that runs on a network and handles variable-income investments in addition to fixed-income instruments.

WyCASH+ is a successful commercial product

Hambrecht & Quist's Phoenix Broker System

The stockbrokers at Hambrecht & Quist (H&Q) must manage a great deal of information in real time in order to serve their clients' needs. In the past, they have done this by surrounding themselves with an array of terminals providing everything from current quotes to wire-service news feeds. Monitoring all that information and making sense of it was not an easy task.

Stockbrokers need a lot of information

Enter *Phoenix*, a Macintosh-based system that integrates all this information under a single interface and presents most of it in graphical form. With Phoenix, brokers can do a much better job of tracking and analyzing the information that will affect their clients' investments.

Phoenix brings that information together

Phoenix was constructed on Macintosh computers using MacApp, Object Pascal, C, and assembly language. The Macintosh Programmer's Workshop was used to combine the work of the various programmers and make the different languages work together. A MIPS minicomputer was used as a central server, communicating with the Macintoshes over AppleTalk on an Ethernet network.

Phoenix runs on a network of Macintoshes

The system was built in six months

Phoenix was constructed by a team of four programmers in six months. The finished product contains about 50 classes and consists of 40,000 lines of source code. The system went on-line in 1989.

It runs on 300 Macintoshes

Phoenix has been in constant use on nearly 300 interconnected Macintoshes for over two years. H&Q are continuing to enhance the system with software monitors and alert features to bring relevant information to their brokers' attention. On the whole, Phoenix has been a successful tool in helping H&Q's brokers serve their clients.

Midland Bank's Windowed Technical Trading Environment

Midland Bank created its own trading system

H&Q is not the only company that is building trading support systems. Midland Bank, based in the United Kingdom, has constructed a system called *WiTTE*, the *Windowed Technical Trading Environment*. WiTTE allows currency, futures, and stock traders to build their own trading systems based on any combination of real-time indicators and historical market data.

WiTTE was constructed in layers

WiTTE was constructed in three layers. The base level provides the communications links and was written in C and assembler. The next layer, also written in C, performs real-time calculations on incoming data. The highest layer was built in Smalltalk/V PM. This layer handles all interactions with the traders, including graphical presentation of incoming data. The three layers communicate via dynamic data exchange (DDE) and can be spread across a network to distribute the processing load.

WiTTE was built by two teams

WiTTE was constructed by two teams. One wrote the communications layer and base systems software, while the second wrote the highest-level Smalltalk layer and the WiTTE tools for real-time calculations, etc. In spite of the great complexity of the Smalltalk layer, the first modules were produced in less than one man year. The system consists of a 3-megabyte Smalltalk image plus 8 megabytes of executable C code.

The biggest problem faced by the Midland team was the absence of network support for change management of Smalltalk code. With such a small team, they were able to coordinate changes informally. With a larger team, formal tools would have been essential.

The lack of tools hurt

WiTTE is a modular system. The first front-end Smalltalk modules were released in the summer of 1990 and are now in use in Midland's United Kingdom Treasury Dealing Room.

WiTTE is a production system

BUSINESS MANAGEMENT APPLICATIONS

One of the most exciting frontiers for object technology is mainstream business applications. It has taken a little longer for object technology to breach the walls of traditional MIS shops, but the major pull for object technology in Fortune 500 companies is now coming from within MIS. The following are just a sample of the kinds of systems we can look forward to in the next few years.

MIS is now adopting object technology

Brooklyn Union Gas's Customer Management System

Brooklyn Union Gas has the distinction of being the first company to use object technology on a large-scale, mainframe project. They turned to object technology because their current customer management system had become so rigid over the years that they could no longer respond to new business opportunities or track changing regulatory constraints. Rather than try to build a new system that would meet their current requirements but soon become obsolete, they opted to build a system that could adapt to meet constantly changing requirements.

Brooklyn Union is a pioneer in object technology

This was no small challenge. The existing system, which had been built 13 years earlier, was used by 80 percent of the company's employees to interact with over a million customers on a daily basis. It spanned an extensive array of information services, including billings, meter readings, cash processing, collections, service orders, and account services.

The existing system was very large

Adopting objects was a bold move	The decision to adopt object technology for its next-generation customer system was a bold move. This decision was made nearly a decade ago, when object technology was just emerging from the research labs. Yet here was a municipal utility—typically the most conservative of organizations—preparing to rebuild a mission-critical business system using this brand-new technology!
There was no object language available	There were numerous obstacles to overcome. The most immediate problem was that there were no object languages for mainframe computers, a problem that continues to plague the technology. To solve this problem, Brooklyn Union teamed up with Andersen Consulting to design an object-oriented preprocessor for its existing language, PL/I. Its new customer system would be written in this new language, converted to standard PL/I code, then compiled and linked like a traditional program.
The system architecture was very advanced	System design began in 1984. The resulting architecture presaged some of the most advanced development work in object technology today. It consisted of three layers: the object layer, the function layer, and the process layer. Although the correspondence is not exact, this architecture is very similar to the layered approach described in Chapter 5.
The object layer contains basic classes	The object layer models the basic business objects, such as customers, meters, and bills. It also contains *policy objects*, which capture generic rules for conducting business together with 500 lookup tables for rates, schedules, calendars, and other tabular data. Another important innovation was *activity objects*, which track the interactions with customers. These activity objects provide a complete audit trail of all customer interactions.
The function layer models the business	The function layer combines these basic objects into a comprehensive model of all customer interactions. In fact, building a working model of these interactions was the central thrust of the design effort. In addition to combining the basic objects into a model of the business, this layer includes workflow-automation objects called *function managers*. These objects contain scripts that allow them to automatically execute such standard procedures as billing a customer or initiating a customer service call.

Implementation of the system began in 1987 and was completed in 1990. The system contains 10,000 program modules, 400 on-line programs, 118 batch programs, 150 on-line dialogs, and 251 reports. In all, it consists of 900,000 lines of source code. Remarkably, it is 40 percent smaller than the system that preceded it, which contained 1.5 million lines of code. This reduction is directly attributable to code reuse.

The system is large

The system was placed in operation in January 1990. Because the new system was so complex, it could not be run in parallel with the old system and had to be brought up all at once. The system came up virtually without a hitch. It was stable after a week, and within two months Andersen Consulting was able to pull out and leave maintenance entirely to Brooklyn Union.

The system came up quickly

The maintenance team for the system now consists of 12 people, which is remarkable given that it contains nearly a million lines of code. What makes this low level of maintenance particularly striking is the high load level of the system. It is accessed by 850 employees every day, and it generates 40,000 bills, 80,000 credit activities, and 250 reports every night. It also manages a database containing more than 100 gigabytes of data.

Maintenance is low despite high loading

This system has also reached the goal of easing revisions. Recently, a change that would have required 40,000 lines of new code was implemented with only 2,000 lines because of reusability, an advantage of 20:1 in extensibility over conventional systems.

Revisions are much easier

In describing its experiences pioneering object technology, Brooklyn Union Gas and Andersen Consulting pass on to other companies the following observations:

Many lessons were learned

- **An object-oriented system is a model of the business.** Thinking in these terms requires a radical shift away from the usual emphasis on functional decomposition and data structuring. Making the shift takes time and effort, but the payoff is big because the resulting system reflects the actual structure and process of the business.

- **Object-based systems rely on active data.** Again, this is a radical shift away from the old model of active processes and passive data. The payoff here is simplification of complex systems. Objects know how to take care of themselves.

- **Object technology requires new methodologies.** Brooklyn Union and Andersen Consulting had to invent their own methodologies because they were pioneering this technology on a grand scale. Many of the techniques they developed, including layered software construction and independent testing at each layer, would still be considered advanced by contemporary standards.

- **Object technology allows systems to change faster than businesses.** Brooklyn Union is no longer locked in place by its information systems. It is literally the case that the systems can change faster than the company can!

Apple's Decision Support System

A DSS lets managers view corporate data

As companies become large and diverse, they need tools for consolidating information about their operations into understandable, graphical charts and diagrams. Such tools are generically called *decision-support systems (DSS)*. Because most large companies keep their operational information on mainframes, DSSs are typically mainframe programs that do collection and analysis on the mainframe and use terminals or PCs to show the results to end users.

Apple wanted a DSS on a desktop

When Apple Computer needed a decision-support system, it decided to take a different approach. Believing that personal computers hold the key to the future of computing, Apple wanted a DSS that ran on the desktop. Mainframes and minicomputers would continue to serve as warehouses for the data, but all the DSS functionality would sit on the desktop. The result was *MacDSS*, the *Macintosh Decision Support System*.

The goals for this system were not modest. Apple not only wanted the full power of a mainframe-based DSS, it wanted additional features not available in most DSSs. The requirements list included: multidimensional spreadsheets with "rotating" views, rule-based data models, full "drill-down" and consolidation features, powerful visualization and charting tools, extensive reporting features, and "hot links" within reports to keep them current at all times.

Apple also wanted extensive functionality

As a major vendor of object technology, Apple had a wealth of object-oriented tools at its disposal. It used MacApp for the interface, Object Pascal for the programming language, and the Macintosh Programmers Workshop for coordinating the efforts of multiple programmers.

All the required tools were available in house

MacDSS was constructed in cooperation with KPMG Peat Marwick, who provided the financial expertise and participated in the actual construction of the system. Between six and eight engineers worked on the system at any given time, often in two separate locations. The resulting system was, by object standards, quite large, consisting of nearly 200,000 lines of source code.

The resulting system was quite substantial

MacDSS was successfully deployed within Apple and has been in daily use for over two years. In 1990, it was packaged as a commercial product, and it is now sold and serviced by KPMG ExIS, a subsidiary of KPMG Peat Marwick.

MacDSS is a success

There is little doubt that objects were essential in placing so much functionality in a small, desktop machine. In the words of James Joaquin, who headed the development effort, "The use of object design and object programming are without question the primary reason for the successful completion of the MacDSS project."

Objects were essential to this project

Guiness Peat's Aircraft Configuration Project

Guiness Peat leases aircraft

Guiness Peat Aviation (GPA) of Shannon, Ireland, is the largest aircraft leasing company in the world. When GPA buys airplanes, it purchases communication gear, galleys, seats, and other components separately from individual manufacturers in large lots at reduced prices. Aircraft manufacturers provide production schedules to GPA, and GPA coordinates the purchase and delivery of all its "buyer-furnished" components to meet those schedules.

It needed to coordinate aircraft configuration

Managing this coordination is an extremely complex process. GPA has hundreds of aircraft on order, and each aircraft has hundreds of buyer-furnished components that must be ordered from companies in many different countries in different currencies at varying exchange rates. GPA needed a system to initiate specifications, generate purchase orders and delivery schedules, monitor shipments and deliveries, and manage invoice receipts and approvals.

BFE is a distributed, PC-based system

The system it built to meet these needs is called the *Buyer Furnished Equipment (BFE)* system. BFE was implemented in Actor running under Windows on DOS-based personal computers. It is supported by the Gupta SQL relational database server, which stores the values contained in persistent objects. The system operates over a Novell network and spans the entire GPA enterprise.

A "spiral" methodology was used

The BFE system was constructed in cooperation with Object Databases, which provided both expertise and hands-on development work. An iterative, "spiral" methodology was used, preserving all the critical stages of the standard waterfall method but allowing the system to evolve rather than be fixed at the outset. This approach also allowed BFE to be integrated with existing systems on a gradual basis rather than placing it on-line all at once.

Because of time constraints, BFE was implemented in three phases. Initially, a relational 4GL system was used to build entry screens to load data directly into the database. Later, object-oriented entry screens were constructed using Actor, embedding SQL statements directly into the Actor code. In the final phase, an Object SQL interface was developed that allowed Actor to deal only with true objects, delegating the task of composing and decomposing those objects for storage to a separate object-management system.

BFE was implemented in phases

In addition to getting a system up and running quickly, this phased approach allowed careful comparisons to be made among three different development modes: a conventional 4GL approach, an object-oriented system with embedded SQL statements, and a fully object-oriented system with a relational object server. Object Databases made the most of this opportunity to measure productivity, reuse, and other benefits of object technology.

This phasing allowed approaches to be compared

For example, at the end of the first phase, the resulting code was examined to determine reusability. Approximately 50 percent of the object code was found to be reusable. By contrast, none of the 4GL code was considered to be reusable because routines had to be constantly rewritten and retested even for minor changes.

Object-oriented code was highly reusable

The object-based portions of the system were also much easier to debug and modify. For example, changes in constraints on date screens caused about *200 times more work* in the 4GL system compared to the object system. In the 4GL system, each routine for each of five dates on 40 screens had to be modified and tested. In the object system, only a single change had to be made to the date class.

The object system was easier to modify

The entire system was constructed in six months by 12 programmers. Much of that time was spent bringing 9 conventional programmers up to speed on object technology. If this training time is factored out, a productivity improvement of 4:1 was obtained using object technology over 4GL tools on this first project. Estimates for future projects indicate that experience and increased code reuse would allow this ratio to grow to 8:1.

Productivity benefits ran as high as 8:1

The system is a
success

The BFE system went on-line in April 1991 and has been fully operational since then. It has eliminated a great deal of manual labor, improved scheduling and coordination, and enjoyed a high degree of user acceptance.

ENTERPRISE MODELING SYSTEMS

Objects are begin-
ning to span the
enterprise

Not only is object technology penetrating mainstream business applications, it is also helping to move business management up to a new level. Because object technology is so well suited to simulating complex systems, it is possible to create business models that span an entire enterprise and capture the essentials of its inner workings.

This will lead to
more competitive
organizations

Applications at the enterprise level are just beginning to emerge, but they hold the promise of transforming the way managers view and operate their businesses. As the Brooklyn Union story makes clear, programming with objects in the large is inherently a model-building process. The better we understand this process, the more we can increase the competitiveness of our enterprises.

HP's Hierarchical Process Modeling System

HP developed a
method for modeling
processes

In the mid-1980's, Hewlett-Packard developed a new notation, called *Hierarchical Process Modeling*, for documenting business processes and tracking the flow of information throughout a company. The system was well conceived and well received, but the time required to produce readable diagrams by hand was prohibitive. The obvious solution was to build a software system that automated the diagramming process and printed the resulting documents. That is how HP's *Hierarchical Process Modeling System (HPMS)* came into being.

HPMS was
implemented in
Smalltalk

HP selected Smalltalk as its language for this project, but it didn't have any Smalltalk programmers available for the project. It solved this problem by contracting with Knowledge Systems Corporation (KSC) to build a proof-of-concept prototype. KSC delivered a working prototype of HPMS a month later.

HP was delighted with the prototype. It not only executed the functions of the process modeling method faithfully, it revealed weaknesses in the method that had not been apparent when diagrams were generated by hand. Rather than develop a new specification on paper and request a revised prototype, HP worked directly with KSC to revise the prototype and incorporate new insights.

The prototype worked very well

In effect, the prototype became its own specification. HP had moved into a rapid prototyping mode, and it found this approach to be much more efficient for developing HPMS functionality. After several months of refinement, the HPMS was released to selected end users for their feedback.

HP shifted to rapid prototyping

The response was totally unanticipated. Users not only liked what they saw, they mistook it for a completed application and immediately put it to use. Of course, they discovered numerous bugs and had many changes they wanted made, so the HPMS team was suddenly swamped with maintenance demands. Like NIST with its Quick and Dirty Editing System, the HP team found that they had created "the prototype that wouldn't die".

End users quickly co-opted the prototype

The salvation for the effort came from HP's Strategic Consulting Group, which found the tool to be an invaluable aid in working with their clients. They helped fund the transformation of the prototype into a true production system and soon began to generate new business solely on the basis of this modeling tool. In the words of one consultant, Wayne Asp, "HPMS enables me to build a model in days that looks like it took weeks." HPMS had found a home.

The Consulting Group sponsored productization

Like NIST, HP learned some important lessons from its experience with a Smalltalk prototype. One of these is to manage users' expectations carefully. Given the power of object technology, it's all too easy to create a quick prototype that looks and feels like a finished product.

HP learned the dangers of showing prototypes

But the technology proved itself

Of course, the flip side of this coin is that new functionality can be incorporated much faster than with conventional techniques. In fact, Larry Marran, who originally conceived the methodology and initiated the project, concluded that, given the constraints they were working under, their accomplishments with HPMS "probably could not have been achieved with other technologies."

Maintenance has been easy

HP has also found that Smalltalk applications are much easier to debug than traditional programs. Over 90 percent of all reported defects in HPMS were removed in less than half a staff day. Defects that required more than two staff days were extremely rare, accounting for less than .05 percent of all defects.

Run-time performance is good

Finally, HP found that, although it had chosen Smalltalk for fast development, achieving good run-time performance was not a problem. The first production release was up to ten times faster than the prototype in many critical areas, and an additional week of tuning improved overall performance by yet another order of magnitude. Their conclusion: Algorithms are much bigger contributors to efficiency than language.

Andersen Consulting's Business Animator

Andersen wanted a business animator

John Davis, the partner from Andersen Consulting who shepherded the Brooklyn Union Gas project through to its spectacular success, has gone on to even more interesting projects. His challenge was to "come up with a way to show an entire business operation, in all its everchanging glory, on a computer screen." The system created in response to this challenge is called the *Animator*.

The system was built using Smalltalk

The programmers on the project selected Objectworks\Smalltalk as their development environment. They began by constructing a basic model of an organization and then adding an information-tracking system. Once the basic model was constructed, they were able to add new business units, information flows, and other elements at will.

The use of inheritance greatly simplified the construction of the model. By creating special cases of a *document* class, for example, they could define different kinds of documents without having to repeat the generic characteristics of documents in each type. Of course, composite objects were also key, allowing divisions to encompass departments, departments to contain people and equipment, and so on.

Inheritance played a major role

Each element in the model has methods for animating itself on the screen. For example, if a department sends a memo to another department, a tiny document icon floats across the screen from the first department to the second. The incorporation of animation as a method within an object is another example of encapsulation; as business elements are added or subtracted, the ability to show them in action on the screen is automatically added or removed. This is much simpler than modifying a separate animation tool every time the business elements change.

Business elements animate themselves

In a spectacular demonstration of rapid prototyping, the Andersen team had the Animator up and running in just one month. When asked how long the project would have taken with conventional technology, they estimated at least six to seven months.

The Animator was built in one month

The Animator has also proved itself to be very amenable to change. At one point, the development team decided to restructure the system to use a single window instead of occupying multiple windows. This change would allow the user to simply "drill down" into the structure of an organization instead of opening new windows to see structural detail. They implemented the entire change in less than four hours.

The system is easy to change

DEC's Enterprise Modeling System

Digital Equipment Corporation (DEC) has been looking for ways to improve the process of designing the structure and operations of businesses and has developed a number of techniques for facilitating that process. One of these techniques involves modeling a real enterprise and allowing managers to explore the effects of changes on this model.

DEC uses enterprise models to train managers

Managers are asked to improve an existing model	In a course taught by Digital Japan, managers are provided with a design for a supply chain business. They are also shown the model in action on a workstation, using an object-oriented simulator equipped with business animation tools. Students are exposed to a number of techniques for improving enterprise design, including DEC's own TOP Mapping approach. In the afternoon, the students are divided into groups of four, and each group is asked to spend the rest of the day redesigning the organization to improve its operations.
Their changes are incorporated overnight	Although the managers in this course clearly like the graphical business simulator, they are not overly impressed because they have seen simulation systems in the past. What they aren't told is that the simulator is object-oriented and can be modified very quickly to accept new design decisions. In fact, after the managers have left for the day, a small team of developers comes in and makes all the design changes requested by each team. On average, it takes about four hours to incorporate each team's changes.
Object technology makes this possible	When the managers return the next day, they are often stunned to find their revised models up and running on their screens, and they are very curious to find out how this was accomplished. The ability to make these changes so quickly is due to the encapsulation provided by object technology. In fact, most changes can be made simply by "rewiring" structural units of the organization. All the processes associated with those units, including their animation on the computer screen, automatically adapt to the new organization.
This is a compelling demonstration of objects at work	Steven Forgey, the leading architect of this modeling system, believes that DEC's enterprise modeling system is one of the most compelling demonstrations yet of the power of object technology. When managers discover that they can not only monitor the operations of a company in real time but also make fundamental changes to its organization literally overnight, they are immediately convinced of the value of this new kind of software.

CONCLUSIONS

Looking back over these 18 applications of object technology, several important themes emerge. Most have already been stressed throughout this book—indeed, they *inspired* this book—so I will only summarize them briefly here. In bringing these conclusions together, I am also drawing on many other case studies not included in this chapter.

Several themes emerge from these examples

Object Technology is Fulfilling Its Promise

The single most important conclusion to emerge from these studies is that object technology really does work. I am aware of a few failures using the technology, and it is clear that success requires much more than just buying a new compiler. But most companies that have invested in the technology have been pleasantly surprised to find that it actually lives up to its promises.

Object technology really works

MIS managers have heard promises of order-of-magnitude benefits so often in the past that making such claims for object technology actually tends to reduce the credibility of the approach. However, it is clear from these examples that improvements on this scale *are* possible with object technology. They don't come automatically, and they aren't likely on the first couple of projects. But they are definitely achievable by any company that is willing to make the required investment in reusability.

Order-of-magnitude benefits are possible

A conclusion that appears throughout this chapter is that the object-oriented replacements for existing systems are invariably smaller than the original systems, even though additional functionality has been added. Object-based systems are typically a fraction of the size of the originals, and order-of-magnitude reductions in code size have been obtained. Systems with a few hundred thousand lines of object-oriented source code are now delivering the same functionality as COBOL and PL/I systems with millions of lines of code.

Object-based systems are smaller

Object technology integrates well

One concern that many companies have is that they don't want to make the conversion to object technology overnight. They have existing systems that may continue to run indefinitely, and they don't want to sacrifice their investment in these systems. The examples in this chapter should put that concern to rest. Very few of these examples relied solely on object technology. The majority of them demonstrated quite clearly that object technology can—and should—be integrated quite smoothly with existing languages, databases, and applications.

Object technology opens new territory

Many companies reported that the systems they developed with object technology simply wouldn't have been possible using conventional approaches. In reaching this conclusion, they weren't speaking theoretically—in principle, any complete programming language can be made to perform any arbitrary task given sufficient time and resources. But time and resources are always at a premium. What these companies found was that object technology allowed them to push the envelope of what is feasible in software given real-world constraints.

Object systems can change faster than your company

Once companies have converted to objects on a large scale, they generally find that their information systems can change at least as fast as their businesses can. This means that the days of being locked into outmoded business practices by obsolete information systems are truly over.

Adopting the Technology Requires Change

New methodologies are required

The waterfall model of software development clearly doesn't work for object technology, and virtually every company that tried to apply it either modified or abandoned it during their first project. Most companies found that rapid prototyping was much more effective than detailed specification in producing usable systems in short time frames. Yet many companies also stressed the importance of solid design. As with the layered approach described in Chapter 5, the trick is to maintain traditional programming disciplines without letting rigid sequential stages cripple the power of object technology.

One of the most common themes to emerge is that building models is the essential process of programming with objects. While it is possible to build small programs directly from classes, large-scale systems require the appropriate use of models. Particularly with mainstream business applications, it is vital to build a solid, working model of your corporate structure and operations. Once you have done that, solutions to specific problems can be generated very rapidly.

Modeling is the essential process

Adopting object technology not only changes the way you view software, it also affects the way you think about your company. The synergy between these two kinds of change has the potential to transform your organization. For example, many companies are moving away from static, hierarchical structures toward more dynamic, flexible teams (Savage, *Fifth-Generation Management*: Digital Press, 1990). In software terms, these companies are switching from static binding of resources to dynamic binding. The capability of object technology to support dynamic binding in a business model directly mirrors and enables that trend.

Object technology changes the way you think

One of the most common observations that companies made was that they wished they had devoted more time and resources to training before they began programming their systems. Many companies also commented on the importance of educating management in the new approach to software so that management and staff do not work at cross purposes. It is clear from these experiences that converting to object technology requires a greater investment in training than previous software development techniques.

Education and training are crucial

The single most common complaint about object technology is the lack of good tools, particularly tools for supporting shared development work. Many companies have had to make do with conventional source-code management systems, build their own code-management tools, or simply do without. This situation is changing fast, and reasonably good tools should be available in 1992. However, these tools will have to mature quickly if they are going to keep up with the requirements of large-scale object programming.

Lack of tools is a major problem

*Expectations must
be carefully managed*

Object technology is good, but it's not magic. Yet end users who see dazzlingly sophisticated systems constructed in a month by one person immediately conclude that anything is possible. To avoid problems such as "the prototype that wouldn't die," end users must be educated as to both the advantages and the limitations of object technology. Developers also need to be aware of the risks of deploying too much functionality too quickly. In particular, the use of preproduction software must be carefully controlled.

Object Technology is Ready Now

*Object technology is
ready for prime time*

There is one final theme that runs through all these case studies: Object technology is ready for prime time. Commercial applications have been successfully developed using the technology, and some of these applications have been in daily use for three or more years. Moreover, the benefits claimed for the technology are observed in virtually every application described in this chapter. Object technology is no longer a promise. It's a reality.

*The time to make the
change is now*

In short, object technology is ready to elevate your company to a new level of productivity and competitiveness. The decision to make that leap is yours. But bear in mind that while you are thinking, your competition may be acting.

Index

ALSO BY MAX HAINES

THE SPITTIN
CHAMPION
OF THE WORL

MEMORIES OF ANTIGONISH

THE SPITTING CHAMPION OF THE WORLD

MEMORIES OF ANTIGONISH

MAX HAINES

VIKING
CANADA

VIKING CANADA

Published by the Penguin Group

Penguin Group (Canada), 90 Eglinton Avenue East, Suite 700, Toronto, Ontario, Canada M4P 2Y3
(a division of Pearson Canada Inc.)

Penguin Group (USA) Inc., 375 Hudson Street, New York, New York 10014, U.S.A.
Penguin Books Ltd, 80 Strand, London WC2R 0RL, England
Penguin Ireland, 25 St Stephen's Green, Dublin 2, Ireland (a division of Penguin Books Ltd)
Penguin Group (Australia), 250 Camberwell Road, Camberwell, Victoria 3124, Australia
(a division of Pearson Australia Group Pty Ltd)
Penguin Books India Pvt Ltd, 11 Community Centre, Panchsheel Park, New Delhi – 110 017, India
Penguin Group (NZ), cnr Airborne and Rosedale Roads, Albany, Auckland 1310, New Zealand
(a division of Pearson New Zealand Ltd)
Penguin Books (South Africa) (Pty) Ltd, 24 Sturdee Avenue, Rosebank, Johannesburg 2196,
South Africa

Penguin Books Ltd, Registered Offices: 80 Strand, London WC2R 0RL, England

First published 2007

1 2 3 4 5 6 7 8 9 10   (RRD)

LIBRARY AND ARCHIVES CANADA CATALOGUING IN PUBLICATION

Haines, Max
The spitting champion of the world : memories of Antigonish / Max Haines.

ISBN-13: 978-0-670-06483-0.
ISBN-10: 0-670-06483-1

1. Haines, Max—Childhood and youth. 2. Antigonish (N.S.)—Biography.
3. Antigonish (N.S.)—History—Humor. I. Title.

FC2349.A58Z49   2007   971.6'1404092   C2006-906402-4

Visit the Penguin Group (Canada) website at **www.penguin.ca**

Special and corporate bulk purchase rates available; please see
www.penguin.ca/corporatesales or call 1-800-810-3104, ext. 477 or 474

To my daughters: Susan, Maureen, and Eleanor

CONTENTS

INTRODUCTION

My three daughters, Susan, Maureen, and Eleanor, were raised in Canada's two largest cities, Toronto and Montreal. Throughout my career as a crime writer, they never seemed to tire of hearing about my escapades growing up in my hometown of Antigonish, Nova Scotia. Each night at bedtime, it was not unusual for one or all three to beg me, "Tell us a little boy story, Daddy." I always obliged.

Sometimes it was difficult to visit a serial killer in prison, fly back home to Toronto, and, a few minutes later, be accosted by three little girls begging to hear "a little boy story."

For over three decades I have filled an entire page in the *Toronto Sun* relating dastardly criminal cases. I've run the gamut from Cain's slaying of Abel to O.J. Simpson's acquittal.

As my three daughters grew to adulthood, they urged me to write a book about my childhood in Antigonish. Their mother willingly joined their campaign.

Recently, I agreed to discuss their proposal with my

publisher, Penguin Canada. To my amazement, editor Diane Turbide thought it a brilliant idea. As I verbally related some of the chapters I planned for the book, she began to laugh. That's the history of how this book came into existence.

Many names in this book have been changed to afford some privacy to the individuals involved. In other instances, authentic names have been used. Some of the stories have been embellished to add humour and/or pathos.

To research the book and refresh my memory, I recently spent some time in Antigonish and informed several members of the community that I was going to write a humorous memoir about the town. Everyone thought it a great idea. I am forever grateful for their assistance and kind words. I am also indebted to Wendy Thomas and Susan Haines for their encouragement and guidance.

Having confessed to embellishing some of the incidents in the book, I must also add that there is a basic truth in every story. Yes, I did pluck chickens. Yes, I was a member of the University Naval Training Division and was there when the *Magnificent* went aground. And yes, Mother St. Regina did firmly believe that I stuck my tongue out at the statue of the Virgin Mary.

And so, after twenty-six books solely devoted to real-life murder and its ugly ramifications, I have finally acquiesced to my family's wishes and have written about what it was like to grow up in the finest small town in Canada.

THE SPITTING CHAMPION OF THE WORLD

MEMORIES OF ANTIGONISH

ANTIGONISH

My family consisted of my father, who stood five feet five inches tall, and my mother, who was somewhat shorter, together with my older sisters, Shirley and Lucille, better known as Lukey. We lived on Court Street. I would love to give you the number on Court Street, but in the years we will be reviewing, there was no such thing in our town.

Now that you've met my immediate family, come along with me to my hometown, the way it used to be in the late thirties, forties, and fifties. In those days, in order to travel from the mainland of Nova Scotia to Cape Breton Island, it was necessary to go smack dab through Antigonish.

No one driving through town would have any idea that the strangest and, at the same time, most lovable characters in all of Canada lived in this tiny speck of a town situated a few miles from the Atlantic Ocean.

There were no traffic lights, no mail delivery, and no numbers on doors—no need for any of those modern encumbrances. Every one of the 2500 souls who called Antigonish home knew one another, if not by their given names, by their nicknames. They all had some distinguishing feature that was incorporated into their nicknames. This was necessary because of the preponderance of MacDonalds, Chisholms, Frasers, and MacGillivrays. Oh, sure, there were a few oddballs like the Wong and Haines families, but generally speaking most everyone had a nickname.

There was "Huey the Drag," so-called because Huey was born with one leg shorter than the other. As a result he dragged one leg behind him. Archie "Spruce Beer" came from a family that manufactured the best illegal beer in the county. "Long John" MacDonald simply was too lean and too tall. Charlie "Up Yours" Chisholm was thus named because he responded with the not-too-discreet "Up yours" to almost anything you said to him. "Big Arse" Carmen MacDonald's nickname is self-explanatory.

Let's go up Main Street from our house on Court Street. Right on the corner was Angus Fraser's smoke shop attached to Dan Joe MacDonald's shoe repair shop. In an emergency a person could urinate behind Dan Joe's shop without being seen by anyone unless someone happened to be in our kitchen looking out the window at the time the emergency occurred.

Right beside Fraser's smoke shop was an old house occupied by two elderly ladies from the New York area. No one knew why they had settled in Antigonish, but throughout my youth that house was occupied by Old Bea and Old Annie. The two ladies didn't go out at all, but spent most of their time peering from their front window watching the world go by. Actually, it wasn't the world, it was the snail's-pace activities of us locals. Of course, if they looked out their back window, they would witness the men urinating behind Dan Joe's.

Next door was Veronica's Variety Store, which featured penny goods. You could purchase seven licorice babies at Veronica's for a penny. Chocolate bars were a nickel. Her display case was chock full of such favourites as Cherry Blossom and Jersey Milk, as well as Moir's bagged chocolates. To this day, the thought of that display case causes me to salivate.

Forgive me if I skip over stores and structures that held little fascination for me. I well remember the white Protestant church on the corner of Main and Church Streets. Its graveyard adjoined our backyard. The graveyard was often used as a shortcut from Church Street to my house. At night it could be a scary place. Rumour had it that anyone using the well-worn footpath after dark disturbed the dead who, if you tarried, could lure you into their graves. I always raced through the graveyard.

Barker's grocery store was just across Church Street and was the largest grocery store in town if you dismissed MacDonald Brothers and those upstart Sobeys from Stellarton. If you wanted to purchase two pounds of sugar, it was scooped into a paper bag and weighed on a scale on the counter. If you wanted a can of Heinz beans, you indicated your preference to "Blind Francis" Foley, who would fetch it for you. Blind Francis knew his way around Barker's and never made a mistake despite being blind as a bat. He added up your purchases in longhand on a sales slip. Here too he never made a mistake and was as fast as a calculator, which no one had ever heard of in those pre-supermarket days.

Barker's had strange items for sale. They had on display every conceivable mousetrap ever invented. Barker's also featured freshly snared rabbits hanging by their hind legs outside the entrance, a rather disgusting sight to behold. Blind Francis said that the rabbits were a good seller. He didn't find them disgusting at all, seeing as how he never actually saw one.

Next door to Barker's was Goodman's junior department store, which had a special feature like no other in Antigonish. Outside the main door was a glassed-in display area, which you could walk completely around. Anyone behind the display area could not be seen from the street. In winter, the sheltered area was a relief from the cold as well as a good place to sneak a drink out of your rum bottle without being observed. In both summer and winter the front of Goodman's store was an ideal place to neck with your girlfriend.

When Father Danny MacDonald caught Joe "Snooker" Fraser and Charlene "J.J." MacDonald doing more than necking, he threatened to tell their parents, which kept the town buzzing for the better part of a week.

Proceeding up the street, it was necessary to pass Kerton's hardware store, owned by our MP, Roger Kerton, who was never in the store. Instead there were several clerks who were perpetually in a state of intoxication from early afternoon until closing time. Everyone in town knew if anything was required from the hardware store, it had best be purchased in the morning. Tommy "Toothless" Charles, Billy "Little Cock" MacDonald, and Francis "Fritz" Hanson were useless in the afternoon, but knew their entire stock inside out if approached before noon. Little Cock was the manager and captain of the good ship Kerton Hardware. Ask him about anything from fans to pipes to hose nozzles, and he could pick it off a shelf or procure it from the back warehouse. At 1 P.M. he was as useless as his nickname.

Fritz Hanson had only been in town for nineteen years and was still considered to be an outsider. Fritz got his name during World War I in France when he and his buddies were gainfully employed in trench warfare. According to witnesses, one night a Canadian soldier shouted, "Francis!" A German soldier, only a few feet away, shouted back, *"Ich bin Fritz,"* whereupon Francis Hanson shot him dead. Receiving some acclaim from his buddies, the story goes that Francis went up and down the line shouting, *"Wo ist Fritz?"* Whoever answered was shot dead by Hanson. Francis Hanson was mentioned in dispatches for that little exercise. Besides, he gained a nickname that endured for the rest of his life.

If you were really unlucky, you could have Tommy "Toothless" Charles wait on you in the afternoon. Due to his affliction, Toothless could not be understood clearly. Anyone who knew him avoided entering into a conversation with him. One day Toothless, who had teeth up to that time, pointed to Little Cock's member and commenced laughing hysterically, whereupon Little Cock picked up a piece of pipe and struck Tommy across the mouth. From that day on he was known as Toothless. Needless to say, he never laughed at Little Cock again.

Further up the street, Brennan's Store stood majestically kitty-corner across from the post office. Mr. Brennan was unique in that he was always sober and always in his store. His claim to fame involved a bit of Antigonish folklore. Apparently, during the war years, a stranger in town, a dwarf with a hump-back, walked into his store and asked for two pounds of sugar. When told the price, the dwarf indicated surprise at the increase in price. Mr. Brennan explained that sugar was up due to the war. When he asked for a pound of tea, he was again surprised at the increase. Mr. Brennan gave his stock answer. The price of tea had gone up since the war. The dwarf asked for a jar of Schwartz peanut butter. Again, he was amazed at the cost. Again, Mr. Brennan explained that peanut butter had gone up since the war.

At about this point, more to change the subject than anything else, Mr. Brennan inquired, "What is that on your back?"

Without batting an eye, the dwarf replied, "That's my ass. It's gone up since the war."

The post office was the place of employment for anyone out of a job who had voted Liberal during the war years. It really wasn't work. Everything took place indoors and there was no heavy lifting. An employee simply had to place the incoming mail in mailboxes, which were limited in number. Our box was number 73.

Outgoing mail required a three-cent stamp, which was an easy request to fill, unless the customer happened to be

George Wong. George was forever writing to Canton, China. Bill "That's three cents" Coughlin would hide in the post office bathroom when he saw George walking in with a letter. China didn't come under the three-cent column. There were customs declarations and weighing to be done and calculations to be made. No, George was not popular in the post office, but he was the most popular man in town when he was behind the counter of Wong's Café. He served the best chop suey in town, which one could argue was not much of an accomplishment, seeing as his was the only restaurant serving chop suey.

Right across from the post office stood the Oak Manor Men's Wear, under the management of "Drools" MacDonald. No one knew why, but Mr. MacDonald drooled all the time. Over the years, he had become an expert at catching the drool in a handkerchief as it left his mouth. It became a sort of game watching how adroitly he picked off that drool before it hit the counter.

When it was prom time at St. Francis Xavier University, you could get measured for a tuxedo at the Oak Manor. Drools would do the measuring, after which it took a whole week for the tux to be delivered from Halifax. This led to complications. Many a lad was stuck for the sixteen-dollar rental fee after his girlfriend refused to attend the prom with him. Drools was adamant. There were no refunds if you attempted to cancel. He also inspected each tux returned to the Oak Manor after prom night. If you had too much to drink and vomited over your tux or even if a friend brought up on your tux, Drools made you pay for the dry cleaning. The Oak Manor Men's

Wear was the only establishment in town that rented tuxedos, so Drools's rules were the law.

Gordon "P.G." MacIsaac's nickname was unique. Many a local called him P.G. without ever knowing his real name. You see, P.G. passed gas. Not the type you can hear, but the silent, odorous type that reminded victims of the odour around large paper mills. The fact that P.G. was a taxi driver did nothing to alleviate matters. When P.G. let one go, realizing the distress he caused his passengers, he immediately pulled over. His fares scrambled from the cab. Around town this became known as the "Passed Gas Evacuation Routine." It was later shortened to the "P.G. Evacuation Routine," and so another Antigonish nickname was born.

Right around the corner from the Oak Manor on College Street was the *Casket* office. To this day, outsiders get a chuckle hearing of a newspaper called *The Casket*. It is supposed to represent a casket of jewels, depicted by a line drawing of a chest overflowing with jewels on page one.

If you kept walking up College Street and made a right on St. Ninian Street you would come to St. Francis Xavier University, the pride of the entire town. Since Antigonish had no industry of any kind, the university was the largest employer in town. Years later, St. F.X. was recognized as the finest undergraduate school in the entire country.

By far the most popular nicknames applied to MacDonalds, Chisholms, and Frasers, which were the most common surnames in town. It was useless to call anyone Joe MacDonald. There were far too many, which necessitated inserting his father's name. Sometimes that wasn't enough and Joe's grand-father's name had to be added. Hence, Joe was known as Joe "Jack Will" MacDonald.

Outsiders couldn't understand what was meant when a local said, "Up Yours got measured for a new pair of pants by Drools. He is going over to Archie Spruce Beer's place to play Auction Forty Fives with Joe Jack Will, Little Cock, and Toothless. P.G. will drive them over, unless there is an evacuation."

These were some of the characters who lived and loved in my hometown when I was growing up. Here are some of their stories.

MARY ELLEN THE SPOOK

I wasn't born when it happened, but this tale has been indelibly imprinted in my memory since I was a youngster. Maybe Mary Ellen sparked my interest in intrigue, which has fascinated me throughout my life.

One cold day in January of 1922, the MacDonald family of Caledonia Mills, which consisted of a few scattered farms and little else, woke up to the smell of smoke in their farmhouse. The MacDonalds had one daughter, Mary Ellen, an adopted sixteen-year-old who wasn't the sharpest tool in the shed.

Alexander MacDonald asked his wife, Grace, if she detected the strange odour. She said she wasn't sure, but thought she smelled something different. Alex then asked Mary Ellen if she smelled anything. Mary Ellen, with her straight black hair, piercing eyes, and pasty complexion, swore that she smelled smoke. Alex went about his daily chores, as did the women, and no more thought was given to the odd odour, especially since no sign of anything burned was found.

That night, after the farm animals were bedded down, Alex

looked in on his daughter. She was sleeping soundly. He banked the fire in the kitchen stove and set aside kindling for the morning. By the time he turned in, his wife was also asleep, no doubt exhausted from another day of household chores and farm work, which seemed to never end.

Next morning, when Alex woke up, there was no mistaking the smoky odour or the haze that seemed to permeate the entire house. Alex roused his wife and daughter. Initially, he thought of evacuating his home, but after investigating he could see no flames, nor indeed any evidence that a fire was the cause of the smoke. Since no harm appeared to have taken place and the haze cleared after Mary opened all the windows, Alex didn't give the matter much notice. When he met his neighbour, Frank Sommers, at the end of his woodlot, he leaned against the fence separating the two properties and idly mentioned the incident of the smoke to Frank.

Frank had once spent a year and a half in Boston before deciding that the marginal farm his family owned in Caledonia Mills was the life for him. He considered himself the most worldly of all the farmers in the area.

"Did you ever consider spontaneous combustion?" Frank inquired.

Since Alex MacDonald had never heard the words "spontaneous combustion" before in his life, he immediately responded, "Can't say I have, Frank."

"I tell you what, Alex, after I'm through cutting wood I'll take a look through your place and see if I can't come up with some reason for the smoke."

"Sounds fine to me, Frank. See you around suppertime."

That evening, promptly at six-thirty, Frank showed up at the MacDonald farm. After a cup of tea accompanied by tea biscuits liberally spread with homemade strawberry jam, Alex escorted Frank through the farmhouse. The upstairs was as neat as a pin, except for the master bedroom, which Grace embarrassedly explained away by saying, "I'm cleaning our quilt and that's the reason it's not on the bed." Downstairs, Alex, Grace, Frank, and Mary Ellen traipsed from room to room.

Frank checked the damper in the kitchen stove. Nothing there that would cause smoke. In fact, there was no evidence of anything amiss until Frank happened to look up. There, about eight inches from the ceiling, was a six-inch patch of wallpaper burned away. Frank, now taking on the manner of Fabian of Scotland Yard, barked out an order. "Get me a chair, Alex."

Once the chair was in place, Frank stood on it and examined the charred wallpaper. Like most farmhouses, the walls had been papered over many times. In the MacDonalds' case, there were six layers of wallpaper, which had been glued one on top of the other. "Here's the origin of your smoke, Alex, but don't ask me how that patch of wallpaper ignited."

The two men then had another cup of tea and talked about the unusual occurrence. "Tell you what, Alex, I'm going into town tomorrow and I'll speak to Tom McCann about it."

Tom McCann was chief of the Volunteer Fire Department in Antigonish. He shook his head when Frank Sommers told him of the strange event at the MacDonald farm, but he took the entire matter seriously. "I'll go out there tomorrow. Those poor people could be burned to death in their sleep."

Bright and early next morning, before Tom had a chance to drive anywhere, Alex MacDonald was already in town, telling everyone that his herd of Holstein cows, which were always secured in their stalls each night, had been found out in the snow-covered pasture that morning. Something strange was going on at his farm. Grace and Mary Ellen had slept soundly all night and hadn't heard a thing. Alex was frantic. First the smoke, now the cows—something had to be done.

I don't know how the *Casket* got wind of the haunted house at Caledonia Mills. At first it wasn't much of a story—it was just some obscure fire out in the country. Will Smith, a young reporter at the paper who had worked his way up by first selling ads to local stores and then mounting a successful subscription campaign, was assigned to look into the haunted house rumour. He quickly learned that fire chief Tom McCann was going out to Caledonia Mills that day. Smith decided to get a lift with Tom, who explained that since the fire had taken place at night, he was planning to arrive at dusk. Will told his boss, Archie MacGillivray, of his plan. Archie knew a story when one stared him in the face. A story headlined "Casket Reporter to Spend Night in Haunted House" appeared on the local news page the very next Tuesday. The *Casket* was a weekly parish paper that published on Tuesdays, for reasons known only to Archie and God.

As soon as the *Casket* hit the street that Tuesday, the news spread like wildfire. There wasn't that much to do on a bitter cold January day in 1922 in small-town Nova Scotia. Certainly, Tommy Swift's shoplifting episode didn't carry the weight of a haunted house. After all, what's a few boxes of licorice pipes compared to a bona fide ghost just outside of town?

When Will and Tom arrived at the MacDonald farm, they found that they were not alone. Neighbouring farmers had surrounded the house as soon as the sun set. It wasn't clear whether they were attempting to keep evil spirits from leaving or entering the house. Big Len Simpson appeared to be their leader. Len stood over six feet tall. He was broad shouldered and fully bearded, and for all the world looked like a statue of Paul Bunyan.

Tom approached Big Len carefully. "Looks like you fellows have things pretty well under control," said the fire chief.

"Yep, no one's going to set fire to a neighbour's house while us boys draw breath."

"That's what I'm here for, Len. I'm the fire chief and I've come to inspect the house in case arson was the cause of the fire. You never know, someone might be trying to burn the place down and just by luck the fire went out. Young Will here is planning on staying in the house all night."

"Makes sense to me, Tom. I'll tell the boys to go home, that the situation is in good hands." With that, Big Len ordered his troop of vigilantes to disperse. It wasn't a tough job. It was so bitterly cold outside that they welcomed the chance to go home to their pot-bellied stoves.

Inside Tom and Will made themselves known to the MacDonalds. Tom noted that the patch of burned wallpaper was nowhere near the stove in the kitchen. He looked at it and figured that it would have taken a great deal of heat to produce a fire that would ignite that patch. Craziest thing he had ever come across in his six years as fire chief if you discount the raccoon that got into the MacIntyres' closet. While chewing up matchsticks, the raccoon had ignited the entire contents of the closet, including itself. The animal ran through the house, setting fires that eventually burned the structure to the ground.

Tom kept his thoughts to himself. He made sure young Will would be comfortable for the night and left the premises. Grace put the kettle on the stove and made Will a cup of tea. It was time for bed. Mary Ellen was the first to retire for the night. She kissed her mother and father, said goodnight to Will, and went to her bedroom. Grace showed Will his bed, which was actually a cot in the kitchen, where he could observe and apprehend any arsonists, ghosts, or other mischief makers during the course of the night.

Will stayed awake for a good two hours. He could hear Alex snoring, but finally, exhausted after the trip and the anticipation of encountering a ghost, he drifted off to sleep. At about three in the morning, a noise awakened him from his sleep. There, staring at him through the kitchen window, was a Holstein cow. The cow's mooing had woken him. Will also quickly realized that a patch of wallpaper on the kitchen wall was on fire. He instinctively picked up a damp rag lying nearby and rubbed it over the blazing patch. Instead of putting out the fire, rubbing it made it worse.

Will hurriedly pulled up his pants over his long johns, put on his gumshoes, and awakened the family. He scampered out of the house, running all the way to a neighbouring farm, a distance of some three-quarters of a mile.

Next Tuesday's *Casket* featured a new story about the mysterious goings-on: "Reporter Will Smith Forced by Ghost out of Haunted House." The story was spreading beyond the local area, though. The main newspaper in Nova Scotia, the *Halifax Herald,* contacted its stringer in Antigonish to go to Caledonia Mills to cover the ever-expanding haunted house story. A.E. Williams hitched his horse and sleigh for the trip to Caledonia Mills. Upon his arrival he discovered that the ghost had been busy. No fewer than thirty individual fires had been started in the house and no one knew how so much heat had been applied to the wallpaper to produce those fires. Williams was in the house when Alex shouted, "There's another one in the parlour!" Williams ran to the parlour, and there, not very far from the organ Alex's father had brought from Scotland, was a patch of wallpaper ablaze in the middle of the wall.

Williams made his way back to Antigonish and reported to his paper that this was no small story. There really was a ghost setting fires in Caledonia Mills. The next day, the *Halifax Herald* featured the story under the headline "Unexplained Fires Fuel Suspicion of Spiritual Occurrences" by A.E. Williams.

The entire town was talking of little else but the mysterious fires, particularly after the American Society for Psychical Research was reported to be sending an investigator all the way from New York.

A few days later, Mr. Frederick Tirips stepped off the train. He was a slender, good-looking man with a handlebar moustache, but it wasn't his good looks that drew the attention of the locals. Under his overcoat, Mr. Tirips wore a grey striped suit, a white shirt, and a red polka-dotted necktie. He was an imposing sight for Antigonish. Out he travelled to the MacDonald farm. By this time Grace's tea biscuits and strawberry jam were becoming famous. She offered several to her guest, pointing out that she had picked every one of the strawberries herself.

Mr. Tirips had investigated psychic phenomena all over the world. He went about his task like a general planning an invasion. Did anyone know what had happened to the damp rag Will Smith had used while attempting to put out the fire? Grace quickly located it outside on the rubbish heap. She explained that her daughter, Mary Ellen, had thrown away the rag immediately after the fire was finally extinguished. Tirips smelled the rag and muttered, "Just as I thought."

Alex asked, "What do you mean, 'just as I thought'?"

"There is still a smell of gasoline on the rag. That's why it not only failed to extinguish the fire, it was instrumental in accelerating the flames."

"Oh" was all Alex could say, but he thought to himself, "This Tirips guy is one smart cookie."

Tirips looked at the location of each fire. Then he asked the three members of the MacDonald family to take up the exact positions they had occupied when the fires had started. In each case, Tirips found that Mary Ellen was always closest to the flaming wallpaper. Next, Tirips had a meeting with Alex and

Grace. He told them that in similar cases he had investigated, most of the time the youngest member of the family had been instrumental in setting fires and moving objects. He had no idea how Mary Ellen had generated enough heat to set the fires, but he was sure she was the villain of the piece. He did put forth one theory, however. He observed that wallpaper often formed bubbles or bumps, which, if covered over with glue, could be ignited at the bubble locations without the application of intense heat.

Tirips went back to New York and made out his report, the results of which found their way to Nova Scotia. He strongly suspected Mary Ellen, who was immediately christened Mary Ellen the Spook. There was even a rumour that Sir Arthur Conan Doyle, the famed author of the Sherlock Holmes books, was coming to our county to investigate the strange happenings at Caledonia Mills, but nothing ever materialized from this rumour.

In less than a year, the MacDonald farmhouse caught fire and burned to the ground. A few months later, my mother placed an ad in the *Casket* for domestic help. Within a day, a quiet young girl with a pasty complexion and straight black hair knocked on our door. The girl, whose name was Mary MacDonald, probably the most common name in Antigonish County, was applying for the job. She said she could clean dishes, scrub floors, and prepare meals. In general, she gave a good impression.

Mother hired her on the spot and showed her to her room. Next morning, my father thought he detected the faint odour of smoke in the house, but on investigating could find nothing amiss. Later that day, Mary was putting the wash out on the line when two neighbours dropped by. "Mrs. Haines, did you know you have Mary Ellen the Spook working for you?"

Just as the women had seen Mary Ellen, so had Mary Ellen spotted them arriving at the house. Well aware of her reputation, and realizing that the neighbours had identified her, Mary Ellen quietly went upstairs to her room, packed her belongings into a cardboard box, and left our home and our town, never to be seen or heard from again.

THE SMELT BABIES

January 1, 1931, was a stormy day to start the new year. It was also the day when my mother experienced some slight discomfort in the region of her tummy. She had good reason, too. She was nine months pregnant. My father, in a state of excitement, called the doctor, who strongly suggested that he take my mother to the hospital right away. Back in those ancient times, giving birth to a baby was an activity that could consume a lengthy period of time. At the first sign of discomfort, the doctors would send the expectant mother to hospital, where she could cool her heels for up to a week awaiting the blessed event. The usual period of time spent in hospital after giving birth was approximately a week, making the entire exercise a possible two-week event.

My mother had already been a victim of such situations, having given birth previously to my sisters, Shirley and Lukey. I grew up hearing rumours that I was an accident, but as I didn't know what that meant, I paid scant attention.

Away my parents went in my father's sporty blue Ford pickup truck with my mother's already packed suitcase. The storm made the trip a slow, hazardous one. Snowbanks were piled high on each side of Main Street. Instead of the usual five minutes, it took a good twenty minutes to travel the half-mile from Court Street to St. Martha's Hospital, including the time spent making three attempts before Dad and the pickup conquered the hill to St. Martha's.

Once in hospital, Mother met the other pregnant ladies, all of whom she knew well. There was tiny Mrs. Wong, hefty Mrs. MacDonald, and chubby Mrs. Chisholm. The ladies spent their first day gossiping about other women in town, particularly Joan J. Fraser, who was expecting a baby without the benefit of a husband.

Back in 1931, the sin of becoming pregnant without a husband was akin to bloody murder. Most girls went to Boston, where they had the nasty tumour removed before it spread. This bogus excuse was believed by absolutely no one, but served the purpose of removing the pregnant girl from the area. Usually the girl's mother adopted the child and brought it up as a sister or brother to its own mother. In Antigonish County, a whole slew of young mothers were sisters to their offspring.

At the conclusion of day one of my mother's confinement, my father happened to be at the Royal George Hotel smoking Sweet Caporal cigarettes and telling tales of the bad old days in Lithuania, when who should walk in but Big John MacDonald, whose wife, Lottie, was at St. Martha's anticipating the same blessed event as my mother. Lottie was spending her second day in hospital and was sorely missed by Big John.

He proclaimed in the lobby of the Royal George, loudly enough for everyone to hear, "Alex, if us men had anything to do with it, those babies would be born in a few hours." He went on to announce that he missed his tea in the afternoon. My father and Big John bonded that day. They conversed, covering such diverse topics as Bennett's government, which was throwing the country to the devil; the Toronto Maple Leafs; and speculation on the identity of the impregnator of Joan J. Fraser.

My father and Big John decided to stroll down to Wong's Café to speak to George Wong, whose wife was in St. Martha's with Lottie and my mother. George welcomed the two men, who made a strange-looking pair. Big John towered six feet three inches over my father's five feet five inches. They had no sooner entered the café than George said, "Glad to see you. I miss my wife something terrible. There's not a waitress who can take her place. You just missed Willie Chisholm. His wife's expecting, too. Been at St. Martha's for two days so far."

In walked Willie, dragging on a Buckingham cigarette and inhaling the total volume of smoke produced by that powerful product. "I just took a walk up to the post office to calm my nerves. My Helen has been in St. Martha's for two days and not a thing has happened. Our two dogs miss her, too."

Four men about town, with a total of thirteen children among them, missed their wives. Big John went on to say that he hoped his wife didn't for a moment think he was going to bring up the kindling from the cellar each evening after she came home from the hospital with their sixth child.

My father, who was the youngest of the four men, said, "Shirley's only ten and Lukey's seven. I can't expect them to cook and clean. The place has turned into a mess in a little over a day. George, if this goes on any longer, we're coming here to eat."

Willie said, "There ought to be a law. Two days in the hospital is the maximum that should be allowed to have a baby. Once the women knew there was a deadline, those babies would pop out like mushrooms."

By January 4, my mother had spent three nights in the hospital when my father visited St. Martha's and explained his revolutionary idea to Sister Mary Joseph. He had purchased a huge mess of smelts at Barker's and wanted to take all four pregnant ladies to our house for a feed of smelts. Sister Mary Joseph's response was swift: "Alex, I never heard of such a preposterous idea."

Undeterred, he explained that he would fry up the smelts himself. The women wouldn't have to lift a finger. In an hour and a half, they would be back in the hospital. What could be the harm?

Sister Mary Joseph replied, "I'll tell you the harm. What if one or all of those women went into labour at your house?"

"I'd call Dr. Murphy, just like you'd do if they went into labour at the hospital."

Ever so gradually, Sister Mary Joseph relented. The four women, with tummies the size of basketballs, prepared to leave the hospital. The cab of my father's blue pickup truck had limited space, so he used the tier method to fit all four into the cab. Lottie, by far the largest, sort of spread out and took up all the space of tier one. On top of her perched Helen Chisholm, with tiny Mrs. Wong and my mother squeezed into the area between Helen and the roof of the cab. My mother swears that it was necessary to lower the window to allow her stomach to hang out.

The Model A Ford pickup with its chrome bumper, mounted headlights, and running board, complete with four ultra-pregnant women stuffed into the cab, made quite a sight that afternoon. All four moaned loudly when the Ford crossed the railroad tracks, which caught the attention of Donald Jones, who was shovelling snow off his driveway at the time. Correctly assuming my mother's stomach was indicative of the condition of the other ladies in the Ford, Donald shouted, "Alex, you're going the wrong way. St. Martha's is that way!" pointing frantically toward the hospital.

Right in front of Angus Fraser's smoke shop, while making the turn into Court Street, my father miscalculated—and the truck skidded into a snowbank. My dad tried to rock the car free, but succeeded only in spinning the Model A's wheels. Besides, he had a great deal of difficulty finding the gear shift, as it was enveloped by various parts of Lottie MacDonald's body.

Inside Fraser's, the assorted men in the backroom smoking cigarettes attempted to ignore the load of pregnant ladies stuck in the snowbank just outside their window. Finally, it was Angus Fraser himself who suggested that they "give Alex a push." Reluctantly, Roger Kerton, MP, rose from his chair and extended his arms, all the while yawning loudly. Slowly, he put on his overcoat. Seeing this display of bravado, the other men in the room grudgingly left the comfort of the hot, smoke-filled room and made their way into the cold winter day. As they pushed, Norm Phee happened to be going into Fraser's for a pack of cigarettes. When Norm saw the predicament the men were in, he suggested the passengers get out, lightening the load. This suggestion was made out of ignorance of the passengers' condition. In unison the men shouted, "We'll never get them back in."

Norm's suggestion was so extreme that the men seemed to find added strength. During the very next concerted effort, the truck sprang out of the snowbank. Once at our house, the ladies disembarked. Actually, they fell out of the truck after much jostling. Lottie MacDonald complained of having no feeling whatsoever in her legs. My mother waddled hurriedly up the steps and flung open the door without so much as a word, so anxious was she to use the bathroom.

My father assisted the women into the house. He immediately set about lighting the kindling in the Enterprise stove. Once the kindling was burning, he carefully placed coals on the flames until he had a roaring fire. The women settled in nicely with cups of hot tea.

The smelts were extracted from the icebox. They had already been cleaned and rolled in Robin Hood flour and most of the heads had been removed. A block of fresh butter was placed in the frying pan. Just when the butter was turning slightly brown and sizzling like the devil, the first smelt was dropped into the pan. Helen Chisholm inquired, "Alex, did you leave a few heads on for me?"

"Sure thing, Helen, I know you love them."

My father had thought of everything. The women gathered around the kitchen table over the objections of my mother, who thought they should be seated in the dining room. She acquiesced to her companions' wishes that they eat in the kitchen, much to the relief of my father.

No one kept a record of how many dozen smelts those four women consumed that day. There are those who say that my father had to run to Barker's to procure more smelts while the meal was in progress. What is known for a fact is that all four women refused the rice pudding he had laboriously prepared for dessert.

When they finished eating, the women were placed back in the cab of the Ford. Mrs. T.A. MacLean, looking out her dining room window, observed the order of placement in the cab. She has verified that Lottie took her place on the bottom of the pile, but could not be exact as to the positioning of the other three. In later years my father would claim that he actually pushed my mother's bottom to squeeze her into the cab.

Off they went to St. Martha's, travelling particularly slowly as they turned the corner in front of Angus Fraser's smoke shop. Sister Mary Joseph was waiting at the front door of St. Martha's, relieved that her charges were being returned to her in good condition. All the ladies, including my mother, thanked my father profusely for the delicious smelts.

Within twelve hours of their return to the hospital, all four women gave birth to four healthy offspring. For years, the children were known around town as "the smelt babies." Sister Mary Joseph put it in a nutshell when she told my father, "It was the smelts that did it."

The babies did well.

Willie Chisholm Jr. went on to become a successful lawyer practising in Montreal.

Jenny Wong became a beloved registered nurse in her hometown of Antigonish.

Francis MacDonald received several university degrees and was elevated to the position of vice-president of a large multinational financial institution.

As for me, I wrote books.

PUBLIC SPEAKING

In my career as a crime writer I have done quite a bit of public speaking. At the conclusion of my talks people come up to me and say, "You looked so natural," or "These speeches must be old hat to you." When I hear these remarks, my mind goes back to my hometown and my very first public speaking engagement.

When I was a kid, the population of Antigonish was 2500. There were no gymnasiums, swimming pools, or other facilities for children. The youngsters of the town made their own fun.

My two older sisters, Shirley and Lukey, and the other kids in town put on two plays each year. When I was five years old, my sisters approached me with the great idea that it would be just wonderful if I introduced the Spring Follies. Not knowing what they were talking about and never having attended a play in my short life, I replied, "Yes, I'll do it."

Lukey said to Shirley, "He's so cute."

Shirley replied, "We'll have to dress him up. He can't wear those dungarees and smelly sneakers."

Shirley was referring to what later would become known as jeans and running shoes. Looking back at my old dungarees, I must admit that they were full of holes and faded to streaky shades of blue. Little did anyone realize back then that manufacturers would spend fortunes attempting to capture that very look. My sneakers were brown and made basically of cloth and rubber. The cloth portion was ripped and torn and the rubber soles were worn thin. They sweated like blazes. Since I didn't wear socks, Shirley's warning about distasteful odours was well founded.

I overheard my sisters explaining the situation to my parents at one of our formal Friday-night meals. I refer to the formal aspects of the meal because we dined in the dining room as opposed to the kitchen, where we usually ate. Our dining room consisted of an entire set of heavy black furniture, which my mother referred to as ebony. It was the most hideous I have ever seen. The picture of King George VI did nothing to break up the drabness of that room.

"Daddy, he can't introduce a play in his regular clothes," Lukey implored.

Shirley said, "I don't care how many baths he takes; those sneakers have got to go."

My father argued, "But he never wears socks. He might throw one of his tantrums. Why don't you get Donnie Kennedy to introduce the play?"

Lukey interjected, "But, Daddy, we want our own brother to introduce the play."

My father finally consented. "It's okay with me if it's okay with Maxie and your mother."

At that precise moment Mother was in the kitchen extracting a brisket from the oven of our Enterprise stove. She walked into our hideous dining room and immediately agreed that little Maxie would introduce the Spring Follies.

The Board of Directors of our household had sealed my fate. That's how, at the age of five, I got my very first gig as a public speaker.

There were details that had to be addressed. My sisters took me to the Antigonish Co-op to pick up my new duds. I objected strenuously, but finally consented to the ordeal. The shopping trip was an abject failure. The Co-op had only stocked two colours of jackets, pants, and suits, and these were black and brown. Shirley said, "It's not a funeral, it's a play. The whole town will be there. I don't want my little brother in mourning clothes." She and Lukey dragged me out of the store. My sisters arrived home almost in tears. They agreed that there was no way I would take the stage in Fraser's barn in my everyday clothing. There was even talk of giving up on having me introduce the play. I snapped to attention. This was great. I would never go shopping with my sisters again. This uplifting thought was immediately terminated when Shirley and Lukey explained their predicament to my mother. Everyone but me became instantly happy. Mother performed this transformation with just two words, and those two words were "Eaton's catalogue."

I was well acquainted with Eaton's catalogue. When we boys played road hockey we often used the catalogue as shin pads. It was by far the fatter of the two catalogues found in every house in town. The other was Simpson's, which was used on the other leg. Back in the era when I was five years old, a few homes in town still didn't have indoor plumbing. Invariably, Eaton's catalogue was used as toilet paper in their outhouses. Naturally, if it was a two-holer, there would be Eaton's on one side and Simpson's on the other. Later on, as we grew older, Eaton's catalogue also provided us with our introduction to pornography, or what we thought was pornography. My favourite page featured brassieres, while other boys in town were partial to the corset section.

A flurry of activity occupied the three women in my life. They probed and measured my body from every angle. Forms that came with the catalogue were filled out.

Much discussion ensued about the colour of my suit. Finally, the details were completed and the pre-addressed envelope was mailed.

We didn't have mail delivery, so my sisters went to the post office every day hoping to find a notice in mailbox number 73 that a parcel was waiting for us at the wicket. Finally it arrived, and they ran home to show my new clothes to my mother. Unfortunately, I was uptown buying penny candies at the time with Donnie Kennedy and wasn't available for the try-on.

A few moments later I walked into a hornet's nest. There, on the kitchen table, was a grey suit complete with short pants. My new shoes were basic black and sported a red, white, and blue Union Jack on the tops. Shirley insisted that I take a bath before I touched any of the new garments. The Board of Directors unanimously seconded this suggestion. All present agreed that

I looked great in my new duds. I found the grey socks confining. I felt as if my toes couldn't breathe.

It was Lukey who took me aside and introduced me to my lines, which were all typed out. Since I couldn't read, it didn't matter much to me. Lukey explained that she and Shirley would read it over and over until I memorized every line. Here is how it went: "WELCOME TO THE SPRING FOLLIES. (Applause. Max, you wait until it dies down.) WE REALLY HOPE YOU ENJOY THE SHOW. (Applause. Max, bow and then leave the stage.)"

Several activities occupied the kids of Antigonish for the next two months. Angus Fraser donated crepe paper to help decorate his barn. No one seemed to mind that the crepe was interspersed with signs that urged you to smoke Sweet Caps or to chew Wrigley's Gum. My mother would ante up the sandwiches and lemonade that she and Mrs. Cameron would serve at intermission. Old Man Boyd contributed benches and chairs. It was agreed by all involved that admission would be three cents per person, under ten years only one cent, babies free.

Isabelle MacEachern, who had once acted in the *Pirates of Penzance* at St. Francis Xavier University, was our producer/director/instructor and all-round play putter-onner. That woman had the patience of Job. She conducted our first rehearsal in Fraser's barn. Of course, there was no audience. I performed extremely well. Who wouldn't, with the two wicked sisters directly out of Cinderella bugging me every minute: "WELCOME TO THE SPRING FOLLIES (Applause. Max, you wait until it dies down.) WE REALLY HOPE YOU ENJOY THE SHOW. (Applause. Max, bow and then leave the stage.)"

Of course, there was no applause because at rehearsals the barn was empty. Miss MacEachern said I had the whole thing down cold and that I was the new Mickey Rooney.

She didn't have as much luck with Jason MacDonnell, a thirteen-year-old who had been singing "Danny Boy" since before he could say "Mama." It didn't matter how many times he tried the line "The pipes, the pipes are calling." It came out "The pipes, the pipes are falling." I thought Miss MacEachern would explode, her face became so red. Joe Fraser did his tap-dance routine without a flaw at every rehearsal, which was somewhat of a bore. How many times could you stand there watching Joe jump up and down like he did at the last Fall Follies and the Spring Follies before that. Margaret MacDonald, sixteen, did her Highland fling. Many thought she was big-headed wearing all those medals she had won at the Highland Games, but Miss MacEachern said she added a degree of class to the show. I didn't know what class meant. John MacPherson, thirteen, had great bird calls, but he felt that his Guysborough County wood swallow wasn't perfect. He kept repeating that swallow until I heard it in my sleep. To this day, I can't get that annoying sound out of my mind. Miss MacEachern repeatedly told him that she thought it was wonderful, but John, a perfectionist, insisted on doing his stupid wood swallow over and over again.

Shirley and Lukey sang a cappella a song that went, "I'm forever blowing bubbles, pretty bubbles in the air. They fly so high they reach the sky." My mother always cried when they sang that song in our house. I thought it was a silly song. I was the only member of our family who blew bubbles, and as any five-year-old knows, not one of the bubbles ever reached the sky.

The day of the play arrived. My sisters took me into our hideous dining room for a last run-through. I said my lines perfectly. "WELCOME TO THE SPRING FOLLIES. (Applause. Max, you wait until it dies down.) WE REALLY HOPE YOU ENJOY THE SHOW. (Applause. Max, bow and then leave the stage.)"

I watched through our dining room window. At first, a few people strolled down Court Street. Then it appeared that most of the women in town were walking by our house and into Fraser's barn. There were even a few men accompanying their wives. The parents of the main participants in the play had front-row seats. Miss MacEachern explained that this practice was normal. She even had Bobby Boudreau print out Reserved signs for the front row.

I donned my new clothing. Lukey said, "He looks cute."

Shirley said, "Did he wash his feet?"

Both agreed that this was the best I had ever looked in my life. The new shoes pinched my toes.

My sisters took me to the back door of Fraser's barn. As they explained, performers have to remain unseen until the curtain goes up. In reality, it wasn't a curtain, but two sheets with attached strings that Mrs. Forbes had sewn together. By pulling on the strings, the sheets would part nicely, revealing the background of crepe paper accented by coloured balloons.

The sheets parted. There I stood, in front of friends and neighbours. This was not like rehearsal at all. The barn was chock full of people and they were all staring at me. There was Mrs. Forbes and Mrs. Cameron and Mrs. Fraser and Mrs. MacPherson and my mother.

I blinked.

My lines, my lines, I must remember my lines.

I started, "Welcome to the Spring Follies. Applause. Max, you wait until it dies down."

Everyone started to laugh and I couldn't figure out why. I continued, "We really hope you enjoy the show. Applause. Max, bow and then leave the stage."

By now, everyone was roaring with laughter. They say Old Man Boyd had to hold his stomach. Mrs. Forbes laughed so much her glasses fell to the floor. James Jessup dropped his cane. Something had gone wrong. I became nervous. I bowed. That's when I urinated in my new suit. As I walked off the stage, the urine had run down my leg and was squishing inside my new shoes with the Union Jacks on top.

To this day, when I do any public speaking, I insist on a podium. Just in case.

MOTHER ST. REGINA
AND THE PEANUT BOLSTER

I was not what you would call a big fan of Mother St. Regina. She was my Grade One teacher. Soon after my unfortunate experience introducing the Spring Follies, I was thrust into the world of academia.

Mother St. Regina had a chalky complexion, which set off her jet-black habit. Truth to tell, she resembled a ghost. Somewhere in the folds of her habit she kept a pocket watch hidden, which she checked every ten minutes. I don't know why, because heaven knows she wasn't going anywhere.

To get to Morrison School, I had to walk up Main Street, turn left at Church Street, right at St. Ninian Street, and past Mount Saint Bernard College, where the girls went to school and where nuns taught them not to associate with boys. A left turn at the hill brought me to Morrison School, so named for Bishop Morrison, who lived in what was referred to as "The Bishop's Palace," located beyond the school.

We were released from school at noon and had to be back

at 1:30 P.M. This left plenty of time to eat, run errands, play road hockey, pick up treats from Angus Fraser's store, and still be back in school on time.

On this particular day, which has been embedded forever in my memory, I picked up a peanut bolster at Fraser's store. Now I should explain that a peanut bolster was good value for a penny. It was a hard caramel candy, shaped like a cigarette and filled with peanut butter. The outside was covered with deep, dark, delicious chocolate. The idea was to lick away the chocolate, bite through the brittle caramel, and finally get to the peanut butter. If you discount jawbreakers, my favourite noonday treat was a peanut bolster.

Equipped with my customary feast, I proceeded up Main Street past Holy Kate's store. She was called Holy Kate because as a young girl she once visited Rome. Legend has it that she actually saw the Pope. The story of Holy Kate's visit has been greatly exaggerated over the years. Sometimes it was said that she had a private audience with the Holy Father. At other times, he supposedly blessed our Kate. She returned to town and opened a store specializing in bibles, crucifixes, and the like. Forever after, she was known as Holy Kate.

Up the street I walked. I threw a couple of stones off the bridge into the river and watched the resulting expanding circles. By now, the chocolate part of my peanut bolster had been licked clean. I loved to pretend the barrel of caramel was a cigarette just like my father smoked. I kept the candy in my mouth like a cigarette, occasionally extracting it to flick off imaginary ashes. I turned right and walked up St. Ninian

Street, past the convent with its array of religious statues displayed on the raised lawn.

I sauntered up the school hill, stopping just before entering to bite into my peanut bolster. I bit. The caramel gave way to spill a generous portion of peanut butter into the far reaches of my mouth.

I entered my classroom. There stood Mother St. Regina. Despite my tender years, I realized in an instant that there stood one infuriated nun. For starters, the chalky pale complexion was gone. In its place were fire-engine-red blotches on both cheeks. Shaking with anger, she addressed the class: "I have just witnessed the actions of a boy who has committed the foulest, most disgusting act ever perpetrated by a pupil of this school. What's more, I know the identity of this despicable boy."

I figured it was Richie Benoit, who was known to masturbate behind the school pretty well every Thursday at recess. I thought Regina had finally nailed him. I was wrong.

"Max Haines, you bad boy, come up here in front of your classmates. Tell the class what you did, you bad, bad boy."

I remained silent as a church mouse. I had no idea what the rosy-cheeked Regina was talking about. Maybe she had finally flipped.

"Well, there you have it, class, this despicable boy hasn't got the decency to confess his sin and beg for forgiveness. I'll tell you what he did, may the good Lord forgive him. While walking up St. Ninian Street, he stuck his tongue out at the blessed Virgin Mary. I saw it with my own eyes from a convent window."

At this juncture I attempted to interrupt, for I realized that a terrible injustice was taking place. Regina had mistaken my chocolate-free peanut bolster for my tongue. I suppose the caramel barrel could be mistaken for a tongue. All I was doing was emulating grown-ups smoking cigarettes.

"Please, Mother, it was a peanut bolster."

My protestations fell on deaf ears. Mother St. Regina knew as much about a peanut bolster as she did about the back seat of a Chevy.

I squirmed, I wiggled, but Regina was not to be denied. "The idea that any student of mine would behave in such a manner is unthinkable. But, class, this boy did the unthinkable by disrespecting the blessed Virgin Mary."

I attempted to break in before she passed the death sentence: "Please, Mother, it was a peanut bolster."

It was no use. Regina was on a roll and would not relinquish her summation. Finally she got to the sentencing phase. "What punishment is severe enough so that this bad boy will show some remorse for his frightful sin?"

After what I thought was a minimal deliberation period, she announced that I was to stay in after school for one hour cleaning blackboards, emptying wastebaskets, and cleaning chalk brushes. The sentence was to run for a full month.

Regina wasn't through. "You vile little boy, you will bow to the statue of the Virgin Mary every day on your way to school."

That was it. No road hockey. No stealing pears from Mrs. Copeland's tree. From 3:30 to 4:30, when all my friends were gainfully employed in these pursuits, I would be acting as janitor back in our classroom.

The first morning of my sentence dawned bright and sunny. I walked up St. Ninian Street and bowed low in front of the statue of the Virgin Mary. This would be the easy portion of my sentence. After all, who would know if I passed by without bowing?

Then I saw her. Regina was glaring down at me from a convent window. At precisely 8:45 every morning, I bowed to the statue. Out of the corner of my eye, I could see Regina monitoring my bow. She never missed.

It occurred to me to purchase a peanut bolster, lick off all the chocolate, and walk by the convent. I thought better of the idea. There was no messing around with Regina. For a solid month, I cleaned those blackboards and each morning bowed as I walked by the statue of the Virgin Mary.

I don't know what happened to Mother St. Regina. She probably has long forgotten the peanut bolster incident, but I just thought I would set the record straight. Mother St. Regina, I never stuck my tongue out at the statue of the Virgin Mary. Honest.

I'm the one who sent you the dirty Christmas card.

OUR VERY OWN FIREBUG

We didn't have what you would call crime in our town. We did have Red Archie, the one and only town cop, whose main duty consisted of walking up Main Street at about 10 P.M. to see that all the stores were locked. As far as I know, he never discovered one open in the history of the town.

Occasionally, Red Archie would find a citizen totally inebriated. He would accompany the drunk to the jail, where he came under the jurisdiction of Willie MacIsaac. Willie ran a loose ship. Being incarcerated in Antigonish didn't mean that you were under lock and key. You could stroll out and chop wood on Court Street for Mrs. Haines, who lived just a stone's throw from the jail. Or you could go uptown and shoot a game of pool at the Celtic Hall Pool Room.

Keep in mind that our town had the highest liquor sales per capita in Canada. I realize that there were no actual statistics to prove such a statement, but in the 1950s the townsfolk talked proudly of that fact, which I'm sure was nothing more than a rumour. I have witnessed a fist fight when someone from

Sudbury claimed that unique distinction. We Antigonishers were proud of our ability to consume alcohol in large quantities.

Red Archie was kept busy hauling drunks to jail. On cold winter nights, the jail was one of the more comfortable refuges in town. Regulars got to know Willie really well. Whenever the intoxicated individual sobered up, he would face Judge MacLean, who would usually sentence him to ten days in jail. A thirty-day sentence was only applied when the drunk gave Red Archie a hard time, such as swinging at his head instead of being taken into custody in a more peaceful manner.

Generally speaking, our town was peaceful. That's why we all enjoyed a good fire. When the volunteer fire department bell rang, every able-bodied person over the age of nine ran to the fire station on Sydney Street to find out the location of the conflagration. Fires were a major diversion. They were particularly enjoyed if the house or barn was owned by a rich person.

Every house or barn in town was insured because Harold Power was the best insurance salesman in the world. Harold resembled a stuffed whale. He had a big pot belly that protruded between his suspenders. He talked a lot, but it was a rare individual who understood what he was saying since he kept a pipe in his mouth as he explained the advantages of purchasing insurance from him.

"It's MacDonald's barn," someone would shout, "you know, Joe Jack Will's place on Hawthorne."

The crowd around Sydney Street waited for the bell to stop ringing and for the lone fire truck to take off for Hawthorne Street. As nothing was more than a mile and a half away, you could either run or catch a ride to the fire. To this day, I have a tremendous urge to follow fire trucks.

Once at the scene, the crowd reacted in two distinct fashions, depending on the quality of the fire. If the fire was mostly smoke pouring out windows with no flames evident, you could cut the disappointment with a knife. "Not worth our time. Not like the old days when fires had a chance to heat up." Then there was the reaction to the good fires. "Let her rip, boys, she's a dandy." To get such a reaction, flames had to be shooting out the roof. Red Archie would ask the crowd to move back. Now, that's a fire.

No one thought it unusual when Whidden's barn caught fire on a Tuesday night at around 9 P.M. We ran up to Sydney Street and heard the news. "It's up Main past the interval. You know, Whidden's barn. They say she's a doozie." We caught a ride in Augie's taxi. He didn't charge for fires—he was going there anyway.

Flames lit up the star-sprinkled summer night. Our volunteer fire department did what they could. Chief Fred Landry shook his head. "She's a beauty," he said. It was a well-known fact that Fred enjoyed a good fire as well as the next fellow.

No one thought much about Whidden's barn. Next day Harold Power let everyone know that Mr. Whidden had fully insured the barn, right down to the contents. It had been a routine fire, which only held the town's interest for a day. Two days later, a skunk was run over on Church Street, making a dreadful smell. Mrs. Brady wrote about the skunk in the *Casket*. She had a column called "Around Town and County." In it, she criticized the reckless drivers on Church Street and referred to the skunk as "one of God's little creatures."

The fire was forgotten until the following Tuesday evening. Son of a gun, but around 9 P.M. the fire bell on Sydney Street rang in its distinctive manner. We all raced up to see the fire engine take off, with Fred Landry in the rear putting on his fire helmet. He waved and shouted, "It's a boxcar down at the station!" We took off for the station. Once there, we saw Fred and the boys pouring water into what appeared to be a half-full boxcar. As far as we could see, there were no flames, but lots of smoke. Finally, Fred and his men turned off their hoses. Water gushed out the open boxcar door.

I don't know who picked up the label off the ground, but there was no mistaking it. The label was from a bottle of Oland's beer. Word spread quickly. Len MacDonald shouted, "This boxcar is half-full of beer." The gushing water pouring out of the boxcar slowed to a trickle. Despite the lack of flames, no one was leaving the scene of this fire.

It was left to Fred to make the decision. It took him all of thirty seconds. "Boys, we'll have to unload her to investigate the origin of the fire." With that announcement, Fred hopped in the boxcar. Joe Cameron followed quickly. So did Colin Ferguson. In no time flat there was a human chain unloading cases of Oland's beer.

A wild time was had in Antigonish that night. Tom MacIntosh fell out of Mrs. Copeland's pear tree and broke his leg. Tom himself could offer no explanation as to why he was up in that tree. The best he could come up with was "I guess I just wanted to eat a pear."

The Sharp brothers tore the sign off Sergeant Vic Staples's office door. It read RCMP Detachment. As a result of the brothers' indiscretion, Red Archie took them into custody and marched them down to Willie's jail.

Then there were myriad drunk and disorderly characters who kept disrupting the peace of the town into the wee hours of the morning. This became particularly annoying to those not partaking of Oland's beer, especially when Huey Lloyd Ferguson insisted on marching up and down Main Street playing his bagpipes. It turned out to be the busiest night of Red Archie's life.

Next day, John Franks, while picking up his mail at the post office, said in front of Holy Kate, "Quite a coincidence, a fire on the same day at the same time exactly a week apart."

Tommy Chisholm replied, "That boxcar was no fire. Fred said it was the rim of the roof of the boxcar that somehow caught fire and made all that smoke. Now, Whidden's barn, that was a fire."

Bill MacGillivray, whose most outstanding feature was his three distinct chins, butted in: "I'll tell you what, if there's another fire next Tuesday, that would be something."

All day the following Tuesday the good folks of the town talked of little else than the two fires at the same time exactly a week apart. There was tension in the air. Crispo and MacIntosh's hardware store sold its entire stock of four fire extinguishers. No one actually said the words firebug, but the thought was on everyone's mind. Even Father Gallivan stated right in Ross's Tobacco Store that the two fires were quite a coincidence.

That night, at precisely 9 P.M., the fire bell rang. Fred and his crew of volunteer firefighters were playing cards in the fire station when the call came in. Evidently they were anticipating a fire. Allison Carruthers, the Maritime Telephone and Telegraph switchboard operator, called Fred excitedly to tell him that the entire salt ponds were on fire. People on Church Street felt threatened. The fire could spread from the bone-dry grass on the field through some dry woods to their properties. The entire town attended the fire, which was quickly extinguished by Fred and his boys.

This was serious. Red Archie was stumped. He asked Sergeant Vic Staples for assistance. Vic went down to the field and noted that, at the edge of the grass fire, someone had recently cut dry alders. There were a few wood chips on the ground below the bushes. From these clues, Vic deduced that someone had cut the alders in order to whittle chips to start the grass fire. No question about it. The town had a bona fide firebug in its midst.

On Thursday, just two days later, Red Archie picked up a hobo whom he saw loitering—and whittling on a stick—near the station. The poor man spent the night in jail until the next day, when Vic Staples received word from Truro that the hobo had spent all day Tuesday and Tuesday night in the Truro jail. When last seen, that hobo was hopping a freight out of town.

Talk of the firebug dominated all conversation in our community. On Tuesday night, my sister Lukey and I sat in our dining room with its heavy, black, hideous furniture, waiting for the fire bell to ring. My mother and father thought us both silly, sitting there waiting for a fire bell. After all, we were living in a crime-free community, or so my father thought, until the bell rang. We both took off like scalded rabbits to Sydney Street. The fire engine, with Fred in command, had obviously been waiting for the call. He was already on his way to the scene of the fire. This time, it was a vacant house on Bay Street in the East End. By the time my sister and I got there, flames were shooting out the windows.

Charlie the Painter said, "The old place was falling down anyway."

Bits MacDonald chimed in, "She was an eyesore."

Johnny MacPherson put the whole town's thoughts into focus when he exclaimed, "I wonder who's setting these fires?"

There was some talk of bringing in real detectives from Halifax, but a local faction nixed the idea, expressing confidence in Red Archie and Sergeant Vic Staples. The Antigonish firebug received some publicity. The *Casket* moved Bishop Morrison's bout of pneumonia off the front page for the more dramatic headline "Antigonish Arsonist Stymies Authorities." The story went on to describe the four fires in detail, noting that they all occurred around 9 P.M. on Tuesday nights. Mrs. Brady noted in "Around Town and County" that the firebug lit fires that did not endanger citizens. The fires had taken place in a barn, a boxcar, a field, and a vacant house.

Some readers of the *Casket* disagreed. What if that wild field fire had spread through the woods to houses on Church

Street? Local men sometimes used the vacant house on Bay Street to consume a few quarts of Oland's. What would have happened if they had been drinking in the cellar when the whole thing caved in? It was just the town's good fortune that a tragedy had been averted. The *Halifax Herald* ran a piece under the caption "Antigonish Arsonist Still at Large." It featured a photograph of Sergeant Vic Staples studying wood chips on the ground. Everyone agreed the photo was a good likeness.

By the time the fifth Tuesday rolled around, the entire town was on edge. Maybe the arsonist was a stranger who had arrived in the community only a month or so previously. That's how Reuben Gunn's nephew Philip came under suspicion. He had come to town to bury old Reuben, who had made his living selling vegetables that he grew himself and peddled door to door. Philip came all the way from Springhill to attend the funeral and was pleasantly surprised to learn that he had inherited Reuben's run-down home on Church Street. The property wasn't much, but it was big and had potential as a commercial site.

It was on a Monday morning that Bill MacGillivray spotted Philip whittling away beside his house. To add credence to Bill's suspicions, Philip had cleaned up the property of old tires, broken boxes, and just plain trash. He was burning the entire kit and caboodle in the backyard. Bill knew a firebug when he saw one. They say he ran all the way to Red Archie's office and told the town cop of his suspicions. Cool as a cucumber, Red Archie made discreet inquiries. Sure enough, Philip Gunn had arrived in town just before the first fire. He was seen to light a fire in his backyard and, above all, he was seen whittling, an activity that all God-fearing local men had the good sense to abstain from.

Red Archie was sure he had his man. He picked up Philip Gunn, advising him that he would be staying with Sergeant Staples of the RCMP from 5 P.M. on Tuesday until 8 A.M. on Wednesday. Philip Gunn, who apparently was operating one pint short of a six pack, was totally enamoured of staying with a real live Royal Canadian Mounted Policeman. There are those around town who say that he asked Vic for permission to try on Vic's scarlet formal dress jacket, which Vic himself wore only during Highland Games week.

My sister Lukey and I sat in the dining room waiting for 9 P.M. to roll around. Whistling Bill, humming "Swanee River," walked by our open front door, stuck his head in, and said, "Aren't you going to the fire station?" We had never thought of such a move, but it made a lot of sense. We joined Whistling Bill, who then enlightened us: "There may not be a fire tonight."

"Why not?" my sister piped up. "There's always a fire on Tuesday night."

"Didn't you hear? Reuben Gunn's nephew Philip set the fires. Vic Staples is sticking with him like glue all night. He won't be able to set a fire."

When we approached Sydney Street, we realized that Whistling Bill wasn't alone in condemning Philip Gunn. The town was split. There were those who were convinced that Philip Gunn was the arsonist. Conversely, others claimed that the poor guy had no motive for setting the fires. He had no way of knowing old Reuben would have a heart attack and drop dead in his tomato patch.

While these somewhat heated arguments were taking place, we were all startled and perversely pleased to hear the fire bell peal out its message of smoke and flames. Fred roared past the crowd, shouting, "Another vacant house, just out the Harbour road past Bay Street."

Lukey and I got a lift from Buddy Kelly and roared down Main Street, past St. Martha's Hospital, and up the hill. There was a blaze in the summer sky. That old house, with flames shooting out the roof, was a sight to see. Using an economy of words, Whistling Bill summed it up nicely. "Best yet," he said.

Everyone was in a festive mood. Lenny MacDonald thought Whidden's barn was just as good. With brow furrowed, he ventured, "Got to wait until the contents go. There wasn't much in that old house. Remember, Whidden's barn was full of hay. Now that was a fire."

Bad Ronnie Reynolds strolled by, eyes opened wide, enjoying the fire. When sparks flew out the window, he seemed to give off a sort of shudder. Reynolds had earned his nickname for fist fighting up in Sudbury. They say Bad Ronnie worked the mines and each payday would get drunk as a skunk. Most paydays, he would land in jail for fighting. The fact is, Bad Ronnie had only two months before gotten into a fight at the Celtic Hall dance that almost cost Bernie MacDonald his eye. Guys who witnessed the drunken brawl said that if Red Archie hadn't broken up the fight, Bernie could have been seriously injured or worse.

Judge MacLean had made quick work of Bad Ronnie, sentencing him to ninety days in Willie's jail. He was often let out to cut kindling wood for my mother and others. That's how I got to know him. We talked back and forth. Mostly he talked about the good times he had had in Sudbury, where there was plenty of excitement—not like this one-horse town.

It was Whistling Bill who mentioned that he was surprised to see Bad Ronnie out and about at night. Wasn't he supposed to be serving that ninety-day sentence in Willie's jail? Just then Red Archie, practising crowd control, walked by. Whistling Bill said to him, "I thought Bad Ronnie was serving a jail sentence. It's 9:30 P.M. and he was here enjoying the fire a few minutes ago."

Red Archie's eyes lit up like a Christmas tree. "You're right, Bill. I'll speak to Willie about this."

Next morning, Red Archie had a tête-à-tête with Willie. He attempted to be diplomatic. After all, Willie had been jailer for as long as anyone could remember. His wife, Ruthie, was reputed to make "the best damn jail food in Nova Scotia." Now, Red Archie knew very well that Willie let his prisoners go uptown to break the monotony during the day. He also knew Willie had an iron rule that all his charges had to be back in jail by 8:30 P.M. In fact, Willie is supposed to have uttered the most inane statement ever made by a jailer. When some of his prisoners abused their privileges, he scolded, "If you guys aren't back here by 8:30 P.M. sharp, I'm locking you out."

Willie sheepishly admitted to Red Archie that some of his boys stayed out well after 8:30. "Aha," barked Red Archie. "So

Bad Ronnie could have set those fires and returned to his cell late."

"Yes," confessed Willie, "it is possible. What's more," he went on, "that pile of empty cardboard boxes in the back shed seems to have gone down lately."

Red Archie almost flipped. What would be better to start a fire than dry cardboard boxes? How had they gone off base thinking that the arsonist had started the fires by whittling shavings off a stick?

Red Archie contacted Sergeant Vic and told him of his new suspect. Next day, the sergeant went down to the jail to interrogate Bad Ronnie. Unfortunately, he wasn't in, but was easily located feeding cattle at Vince MacDonald's farm. Bad Ronnie weakly defended himself, saying, "I couldn't have set those fires. I was in jail." Sergeant Vic told Bad Ronnie that he would convince Judge MacLean to go easy on him if he pleaded guilty. Bad Ronnie agreed. At a five-minute trial, he was sentenced to three years in Dorchester Penitentiary.

When Sergeant Vic asked him why he had set the fires, he replied seriously, "This town needed some excitement and I gave it to them."

I'll say this for Bad Ronnie. Those Tuesday-night fires were the most exciting nights of my life. To this day, Lukey and I often talk of the thrill of hearing that fire bell.

Reuben Gunn's nephew Philip sold the old Gunn residence within a week. I can only assume he never practised whittling again.

JACKIE AND CONNIE

You can imagine my surprise and horror when I moved from Grade Two into Grade Three and into another classroom shared with Grade Four. There stood my old nemesis, Mother St. Regina. As was her custom, Regina ran a tight ship. School started promptly at 9 A.M. If you were late, the door to the classroom was locked and you had to knock to get in. Regina then had you stand in front of the class and give your reasons for being late. It was embarrassing, but it had the desired effect on everyone, with the exception of Jackie and Connie MacNeil.

Jackie proved to be the greatest storyteller in the entire world. Although there was only one year difference in their ages, Jackie towered over his brother. Together, they were better than Bud Abbott and Lou Costello. Jackie sported a regular haircut, while Connie had a mop of disarrayed brownish red hair, which gave him a comical air without his even saying a word.

The MacNeils lived on a farm a few miles from town. From the very first day, their storytelling abilities came to the fore.

On the first day of school, a knock broke the silence of the classroom. Mother St. Regina opened the door. "Now, young gentlemen, can you tell the class why you are late?"

Jackie responded, "Please, Mother, we got up bright and early to do our chores, but when we went to the barn one of the calves was lying down heaving something awful. Isn't that right, Connie?"

"That's right, Jackie."

Jackie continued, "I went into the house and told Mum. She said, 'Run and get the vet.' Isn't that right, Connie?"

"That's right, Jackie."

"Please, Mother, Connie and me ran and fetched Dr. MacLellan, who started off right away in his car. He was just past McInnises' field when a tire went flat. Isn't that right, Connie?"

"That's right, Jackie."

"Please, Mother, by the time we got back to the farm, that calf was up and about as if nothing had happened. Dr. MacLellan said he would drive us to school, but he stopped at the Eastern Auto to have his flat tire fixed. Isn't that right, Connie?"

"That's right, Jackie," came the usual instant reply.

Tiny veins stuck out on Mother St. Regina's neck as her patience reached the breaking point. Exasperated, she said, "Take your seats!" Little did she know that as often as two or three times a week she would have to endure Jackie and Connie arriving at school any time between 9:05 and 9:15, always with a terrific yarn to tell.

A few days later, a knock was heard once more on the classroom door. In time, Jackie's knock would become familiar to us kids. It was a distinctive rat-a-tat-tat. Mother St. Regina opened the door. There stood Jackie and Connie.

"Well, now, young gentlemen, can you tell the class why you are late?"

You bet your life Jackie could. "Please, Mother, we were flooding the rink behind the barn when the hose sprang a leak. I had to go into the house to get some tape to repair the leak. Isn't that right, Connie?"

"That's right, Jackie."

"I repaired the leak and went back into the house. Mum took one look at my feet and said there was no way I was going to school with wet feet, so I had to change my socks and shoes. Isn't that right, Connie?"

"That's right, Jackie."

"Please, Mother, while walking to school, I realized I only had one overshoe on, so I had to go back home to get the other overshoe. Isn't that right, Connie?"

"That's right, Jackie."

Mother St. Regina's face turned as red as a cherry. I think she realized for the first time that she was fated to tolerate these two boys for a full school year. As the term progressed, we all waited expectantly for the distinctive rat-a-tat-tat on the classroom door. Old Regina grew to dread the encounter judging by the look that came over her face when she heard the knock.

Probably the highlight of Jackie and Connie's storytelling career came when they brought bogus physical proof of their escapades to their teacher. "Please, Mother, last night I forgot to clean out the barn. Early this morning my mum said, 'You boys have to take your responsibilities seriously. Now you go out there and clean out that barn.' Isn't that right, Connie?"

The ever-faithful Connie replied, "That's right, Jackie."

"Please, Mother, you know how cold it was last night. I tried to clean the barn as best I could, but some of the cow dung was frozen to the floor and we had a hard time prying it loose. Isn't that right, Connie?"

"That's right, Jackie."

"Please, Mother, here is a piece of frozen cow dung for you."

Mother St. Regina's face was on fire. I thought her cry of "Take your seats!" had a louder and more authoritative ring to it than usual.

But there was no escaping the Jackie and Connie show. Poor old Regina realized that although her system was working for the rest of the class, it was a dismal failure with Jackie and Connie. She was one stubborn nun, though, and wouldn't back down and change her rules. Two little farm boys were not going to dictate how she ran her class.

Rat-a-tat-tat. Mother St. Regina glared as she opened the door for Jackie and Connie. "Please, Mother, me and Connie left our house in plenty of time to get to school when the colt got out of the barn somehow and we had to find him. Isn't that right, Connie?"

"That's right, Jackie."

"Please, Mother, all of a sudden, we saw the colt in Pelly's field. He had his neck stuck in a wire fence and was pulling his head something awful. We couldn't let that colt choke to death so we got his neck out of the wire fence and led him back to the barn. Isn't that right, Connie?"

"That's right, Jackie."

"Please, Mother, when we got home, Mum said we were two fine sons for having rescued the colt. She said, 'You boys sit right down and have some hot chocolate. You must be very cold after such an ordeal.' Isn't that right, Connie?"

"That's right, Jackie."

And so it went for the entire school year. Mother St. Regina survived the ordeal. I learned later that she normally taught summer school, but after her encounter with Jackie and Connie she simply rested for the summer in a place where nuns go to rest.

We all graduated from Grade Three to Grade Four, which really meant that we attended a classroom across the hall. That's when we met our new teacher. Mother St. Brigitta was an altogether different kettle of fish from Mother St. Regina. She was shorter than our previous tormentor and can best be described as roly-poly.

On that very first day she laid down the ground rules. We all stifled a chuckle when she warned us that the classroom door would be locked at 9 A.M. sharp. Any boy coming to class after that time would have to knock. Once inside, he would have to stand in front of the class and explain why he was late.

Next day, at 9:10 A.M., we heard the familiar rat-a-tat-tat. There stood Jackie and Connie.

"Please, Mother, our mum was cooking some home-fried potatoes to go with our bacon and eggs when some fat splashed into the fire. Isn't that right, Connie?"

Connie was prompt to reply, "That's right, Jackie."

Jackie went on, "We both dashed to a closet where we found an old piece of canvas. We put the canvas over the fire and put it out. Isn't that right, Connie?"

"That's right, Jackie."

Mother St. Brigitta's face grew serious. "You poor darlings, it's a good thing you weren't hurt."

Jackie couldn't resist, "Please, Mother, in the rush to get the canvas on top of the fire, Connie turned his ankle. It was so painful that Mum soaked it in cold water until the swelling went down. Isn't that right, Connie?"

"That's right, Jackie."

Next day, when 9:15 rolled around, we all waited for the familiar rat-a-tat-tat. Jackie didn't disappoint.

"Please, Mother, Connie fell right off the foot log into the river. It was ice cold. Isn't that right, Connie?"

"That's right, Jackie."

"I found a branch and passed it to Connie and that's how I pulled him out. His clothes were soaked so I had to take him home. Isn't that right, Connie?"

"That's right, Jackie."

Mother St. Brigitta was never quite the same after that. She realized that for a solid school year she would have to endure the Jackie/Connie stories, as they came to be known around the school. Sometimes as she stood there anticipating the knock on the door, we could see her clenching her hands.

Somehow, Mother St. Brigitta survived the sick calves, the runaway horses, the leaking hoses, the dog that needed burying, the cat stuck in the tree, and other nonsense that Jackie would make up on the spur of the moment. Connie always verified every word. Like her colleague before her, Mother St. Brigitta retired to the home where nuns go to rest.

We all moved to Grade Five. Because it was the first day of school, we had a guest, parish priest Father Gallivan. Our regular teacher was a civilian, Robert Rogers. He announced that, as was the custom in the school, the classroom door would be locked at 9 A.M. His little speech was interrupted by a rat-a-tat-tat. There stood Jackie with his faithful companion and brother at his side.

From force of habit Jackie started, "Please, Mother, er, Sir, Connie and me started off in plenty of time to get to school by nine, but when Connie jumped McInnis's fence, he ripped his pants bad. We had to go home. Mum said she would sew up the pants, but she couldn't find the brown thread so she sent us over to Mrs. Cameron's to borrow thread. Isn't that right, Connie?"

"That's right, Jackie."

Mr. Rogers had veins along his neck, which none of us had noticed before. Now they seemed to materialize out of nowhere and were much more visible than those of Mother St. Regina. He sort of growled, "Sit down."

Father Gallivan and Mr. Rogers had a meeting. It took place right beside my desk. Mr. Rogers let Father Gallivan know that he was aware of the experiences of Mother St. Regina and Mother St. Brigitta with these two boys. Because they spoke so low, I couldn't make out the whole conversation, but I did catch certain words like "lies" and "wrong." Father Gallivan told the two MacNeil boys to stay after school. He wanted to have a chat with them.

Next morning, we all giggled when we heard the trademark rat-a-tat-tat.

Mr. Rogers took a rather victorious authoritative stance when he asked, "Well, why are you boys late for school?"

Head bowed, Jackie said, "We slept in. Isn't that right, Connie?"

"Please take your seats," interjected Mr. Roberts politely. He had won. He would not require a rest home that summer. He would teach summer school as planned. Jackie and Connie arrived at school punctually after that day. On the odd day when they were late, Jackie answered in a one-sentence, straightforward way. It was the end of an era. From that time on we started class each morning with things like arithmetic and spelling.

As I grew older, I never forgot Jackie MacNeil and his brother, Connie, who for years made the start of each day a joy rather than the usual drudgery.

When it came time for me to leave my hometown, my curiosity got the better of me. I had to ask Jackie what Father Gallivan had said to him so many years before. Jackie told me, "Father Gallivan didn't mince words. He said, 'If you two punks don't stop lying, your tongues will rot away and your heads will fall off.'"

Jackie shrugged. "I was only a kid. I couldn't take the chance."

MORTON THE BOYFRIEND

You would think enemy aircraft had been sighted over our home on Court Street. I soon learned it wasn't enemy aircraft. It was worse, much worse. My eldest sister, Shirley, was bringing her boyfriend home from Halifax for the weekend.

As a nine-year-old, I lacked experience in the boyfriend department. Shirley was a cool older woman of nineteen when she fell in love with a Dalhousie University dental student. Shirley was employed with the Nova Scotia government. No one really knew what she did, and in my opinion she was totally ill-equipped to work at anything other than combing her hair. All she talked about was this particular student attending Dal.

I hated Morty even before I met him. All dentists, even potential ones, were not to be trusted by a nine-year-old. Evidently Shirley had been dating this Morty for some months. I overheard my mother say to my father that this was serious. She said she could feel it in her bones. Shirley was going to marry this boy.

As a result of this pronouncement, it was imperative that the Haines family make a good impression. I apparently brought down the standard my mother believed we should strive to attain. For example, my smelly sneakers with the holes in the little toe area were not to be seen while Morty was visiting.

"But Ma," I implored, "they're so comfortable and besides, they're the only pair of shoes I own."

She stared at me in that reproachful manner mothers have of looking at nine-year-olds and said, "We'll buy you a new pair."

My father, who had exhibited no interest in our conversation, now sat upright, declaring, "Don't you think you're going too far?"

Mother looked him straight in the eye. "And you, your suspenders, or braces as you call them, have got to go."

Mother made plans, complicated, intricate plans. She insisted that Morty sleep in the spare room, which we jokingly referred to as the rough room. It had been thus named because anything that didn't fit in the rest of the house was unceremoniously tossed into the rough room.

Mother declared that everything would be moved to the cellar to make way for the new paint job that would transform that rough room into a fit place for a Dalhousie student. When Lukey inquired who would move all that junk, my mother replied, "Maxie will help your father and you."

That's how I came to lug Gus Barbera's trumpet out of the rough room together with a copy of A Tale of Two Cities, the pages turned yellow with age. The trumpet was in our rough room because Gus had required eight dollars for two bottles of rum and had given the trumpet to my father as collateral nine years earlier. As for *A Tale of Two Cities*, I don't know how it got there. Day after day, we carried, pushed, and dragged useless material out of that room into the cellar.

My mother got her way, as she usually did. By the time Denny the Painter showed up, that room was empty. Denny took one look and declared, "I'll have to put a coat of primer on her to seal up those water stains. You see here, Mrs. Haines, beside the window where the water dripped in? She'll take a coat of primer, all right." Following Denny's gnarled finger, Mother had to admit there was an unsightly stain in the plaster. Anticipating her next question, Denny said, "I can have her done by the weekend if all goes well." That did not sit well with my mother. The last time Denny made a promise to have a paint job done, he had walked out the door and hadn't been seen for three weeks.

When Mother brought this distasteful detail to the fore, Denny replied, "That was different, Mrs. Haines. Medical emergency."

Mother knew all about his medical emergency. Denny had been beaten up by Casey Fowler when Casey caught him peeking into his wife Rosie's bedroom window while she was disrobing. Denny, who obviously had an overwhelming urge to observe women in various stages of undress, took a bad beating from Casey—bad enough to necessitate his jaw being wired at St. Martha's. The entire unsavoury incident laid up Denny for the better part of three weeks.

"Denny, this is serious, the room has got to be completed by Friday. The new bedroom set is being delivered on Saturday morning. Morton and Shirley are arriving on the noon train."

My parents had discussed what they would call this stranger: the friendly "Morty" or the more formal "Morton." When asked for my opinion, I made the mistake of responding, "I couldn't care less." That little remark was instrumental in having me sent to my room.

Denny showed up as promised, and primed and painted that old room until it looked and smelled like a room at the Royal George Hotel. One wall was deep blue, while the other three were powder blue. A stark white bedroom set complemented the room so it looked like heaven. You would swear you were floating in the clouds, a fit lair for God.

Gregor Myette pulled up at the train station in the Royal George Hotel's station wagon and met Shirley and her boyfriend, God. Gregor had a pot belly, spoke with a decidedly French accent, and was perpetually cheerful. The station wagon was painted dull grey with black letters across the side displaying for all the world to see that it belonged to the Royal George Hotel.

Once Gregor had delivered them to our home, Mother instructed me, "Maxie, run and fetch Morton's suitcase." Apparently the decision on the potential dentist's name had been made. To my parents, he would be forever Morton, and/or God, if you like. God shook my hand and said he was glad to meet me. I looked up and for the first time noticed that God had a suggestion of a moustache above his upper lip. I disliked him at first sight.

I lugged that suitcase up to heaven. He must be planning on doing a lot of exercising, I thought. The suitcase was so heavy I figured he had barbells in there. My sister Lukey curtseyed in front of Morton, much as people do when they meet the queen. As they walked into the house, I noticed out of the corner of my eye that Shirley held God's hand. This was indeed serious. I had consistently attempted to extricate myself from holding my sisters' hands and deeply resented their hugs. God seemed to like holding Shirley's hand just fine.

That evening at dinner, we had soup and chicken, with tomatoes and cucumbers from our own garden. My father spilled a bit of the juice of a tomato on his new shirt, provoking a kick under the table from my mother.

There were other indiscretions that served to keep my mother on edge. My father blew on his chicken soup, which would have been forgiven had he not slurped as he ate. I didn't think the sound was too obvious, but later at the meal postmortem Mother claimed it sounded like thunder.

Shirley, the sneak, held God's hand under the table. Conversely, God kept pushing my sister's hand away, proving that he wasn't rotten through and through.

At last our meal was completed, which led to another dilemma. What to do with God for the rest of the evening? I thought my mother might drop dead right then and there when my father suggested that they could go down to the CNR cattle pens and look at the fine shipment of calves that he was sending off to Canada Packers the next day. God, who had little choice in the matter, readily agreed that he could think of nothing he would rather do on his first night in his girlfriend's hometown than look at fifty bellowing calves before they were shipped away to be slaughtered. Even I felt a pang of sympathy for God as he climbed into that smelly cattle truck with me and my father.

During the ten-minute drive, God brought up a strange experience that had happened to him upon his arrival in town. He had attempted to pay Gregor Myette and, at the same time, give him a tip, as he exited the Royal George Hotel's station wagon. Gregor had insisted that Alex's daughter didn't need to pay anything. With that, God had responded, "Here, take this as a token of my appreciation."

"No way," Gregor had replied. According to God, Gregor had become downright indignant and had appeared to hurry away in a bit of a huff. My father explained to God that no one had ever even thought of tipping Gregor in all the years he had been driving the station wagon for the Royal George. Gregor had probably never thought of such a thing himself. Locals simply didn't pay Gregor when they were driven home from the station. God shouldn't take offence; it was a local custom.

There were several local customs that God would be introduced to in the weekend he spent at our house. He actually refused to give Dinny Stewart a cigarette when Dinny, as was his custom, approached him in the confidential manner of an undercover FBI agent and muttered those fateful words that every Antigonisher had heard for thirty years: "Got a ciggie?"

Poor God thought Dinny was a bum, never realizing that he was the son of one of the wealthiest men in town. He refused

to part with a cigarette, and soon the whole town was gossiping that Shirley Haines had brought an uppity Dalhousie
student home to meet her parents.

On Day Two of his visit, God remarked that Whistling
Willie's incessant humming was annoying. He simply had no
way of knowing that old Willie had been sitting on that rocking
chair on Fraser's veranda for a quarter of a century, humming
and rocking. It was sort of Willie's job to hum and rock. Like
birds chirping, no one gave it a second thought.

On Saturday night Shirley made the mistake of taking God
to the dance at Celtic Hall. He should have been warned that a
fight usually broke out around 9 P.M. You could pretty well set
your watch by fight time. The reasons for fights breaking out
were varied and interesting. On one particular night, Joe Jack
Will's daughter Vickie was dancing with a McIntyre from
Lanark. Joe Jack Will thought that McIntyre was holding his
daughter too close. He approached McIntyre and said, "Son,
you're holding Vickie too close. That's not how we dance at the
Celtic."

Instead of exhibiting respect, McIntyre, who had once won
a trophy in Halifax for placing second in the foxtrot competition, took exception to the remark. "I'll hold Vickie any damn
way I please" was his diplomatic response. Joe Jack Will swung,
striking McIntyre just below the right temple. The blow sent
him reeling, but did not knock him off his feet.

Before McIntyre could lunge at Joe Jack Will, cooler heads
prevailed. Several suggested that they settle matters outside in
the parking lot of Cyril Reddy's garage. Friends, onlookers, and

other interested parties retired to the parking lot to take in the fisticuffs. While Big Fred Thompson was explaining the rules of the fight, Joe Jack Will hauled off and hit McIntyre flush in the nose, breaking it upon contact. Blood gushed from his busted beak as he lay prone on the asphalt.

The fight between Joe Jack Will and McIntyre was exceptionally brief, but that wasn't always the case. Some fights lasted the better part of an hour, particularly when the participants forgot why they were about to fight. From opening skirmish on the dance floor to the parking lot of Cyril Reddy's garage, ten minutes had elapsed. What with the excitement and all, the pugilists couldn't remember why they were furious with each other. They would raise their arms and dance like Nureyev without ever striking a blow. When the crowd started to boo and disperse, the warriors invariably shook hands and returned to the hall. On those occasions, you couldn't help but overhear remarks such as "Lousy fight" and "Chicken fight."

Unfortunately, God witnessed a horrific battle between Roy MacDonald and Billy Campbell, both of whom were a bloody mess when the battle was halted through the intervention of Red Archie. Evidently, it had started over a longstanding dispute concerning a property line between the two farmers, whose farms were located near Arisaig.

God was heard to say, "Uncivilized."

On Sunday, Shirley and God took off for Halifax. Within a year, they married.

A few years later, I was shocked and, at the same time, displeased when my parents informed me that Lukey was bringing her boyfriend, Sammy, from Halifax to spend a weekend with us. Lightning had struck twice.

The junk was moved to the basement. Denny painted the rough room. Lukey and God the Second were arriving by train. Not to worry, Gregor Myette would pick them up at the station. I overheard my mother lecturing to my father, "We will not call him Sammy. The more dignified Samuel will be used at all times."

Lightning had indeed struck twice.

HERE, HOPPY, TAKE MINE

When I was eleven years old, our town had virtually no recreational facilities of any kind. We did have the Capitol Theatre, which played three different movies a week. The same film played on Monday and Tuesday, then there was a change for Wednesday and Thursday and another change for Friday and Saturday.

On Saturday afternoon there was a matinee, which all the kids in town attended. The most popular by far were the Tarzan movies. A close second would be cowboy movies, particularly those featuring Hopalong Cassidy.

It cost eighteen cents to take in the movie. Most parents gave their kids a quarter, which doesn't sound like much today, but twenty-five cents provided us kids with everything we needed for an outstanding afternoon. We could buy seven licorice babies for one penny and two honeymoons for an additional penny. For those not initiated into the world of honeymoons, this delicacy consisted of a generous portion of caramel covered with a layer of deep, dark, delicious chocolate. An ice cream cost five cents.

Around two o'clock I would enter Alcoin's Variety Store, flash my quarter, and spend two cents on seven licorice babies and two honeymoons. Then it was up to Sam Thompson's store for my five-cent ice cream. Thus equipped, I made my way to the theatre to be met by my friends Ronnie Len MacDonald, Fred "Squinty" Simpson, and Billy MacLean. There was expectation in the air when I placed my remaining eighteen cents on the counter and received my ticket.

Resplendent in his bright blue uniform with yellow stripes, Old Man MacPherson, who doubled as ticket taker and janitor, stood beside a metal canister with a slot in the top. He sighed as he ripped my ticket in two, dropping one half in the canister and returning the other half to me. Old Man MacPherson was about forty-five years old, but looked ancient to me. He had a craggy face and a slight suggestion of grey on his balding head. He knew that my chocolate ice cream would melt and drip to the floor, making it disgustingly sticky. He also knew that the paper bag that held my penny goods would find its way to the floor as well. Multiply my mess by a hundred kids and Old Man MacPherson realized that he would be cleaning up that theatre well into Saturday night.

Back then, no one seemed to realize that children playing with guns was a bad thing. Most of us owned cap guns, and the more fortunate few had bows and arrows. The bow and arrow owners became Indians by virtue of their weapons, while cap gun owners became cowboys for roughly the same reason. We didn't know that the word Indian was politically incorrect, and we certainly never thought of calling Ronnie Len MacDonald a native.

Without exception we all carried jackknives. As a result we spent hours whittling and playing games with our knives. "Spank the Baby" was a favourite of mine, while "Double Over the Shoulder" was a close second. To my knowledge not one boy was ever accidentally or intentionally cut by a jackknife. Equipped with ice cream, candy, cap guns, and jackknives, we kids entered the theatre.

Gene Autry was not our favourite cowboy. He sang too much. Roy Rogers sang a lot too, and besides he messed around with Dale Evans all the time. True, his horse Trigger was cool, but you can't watch a movie for an hour waiting to see Roy jump off a cliff onto Trigger's back just as he is about to be captured by marauding Indians.

Hopalong Cassidy was our man. Hoppy could get out of more jams than either Gene or Roy. At the last second, Hoppy would swim the rapids, jump off a cliff, discover a cave, and escape with his white hat intact. That man was unstoppable. In hand-to-hand combat with a tomahawk-wielding Indian, Hoppy always won out. He rolled in the dust with that Indian and always managed to get the upper hand. His horse, Topper, was at his side, sensing trouble. Topper could anticipate that outlaws who had just robbed a bank and had taken a lovely young blond customer hostage were hiding out in yonder cave. Don't ask me how Topper would know everything that would happen in the next five minutes. That horse never failed Hoppy, although you would swear that from time to time both

Hoppy and Topper were in such a jam that Divine Providence couldn't rescue them.

That's where Billy MacLean came in.

You see, Billy would never even think of attending a Hopalong Cassidy film without a box of Cracker Jack and his trusty cap gun. Billy stood out from the rest of us because he opted for a five-cent box of Cracker Jack rather than the standard ice cream.

There was Hoppy tied to a stake. His faithful horse, Topper, was secure in a nearby corral. It was pitiful to hear the horse whine in frustration. Topper was distraught at the sight of Hoppy about to be scalped, have his heart eaten, and what was left of him set on fire. Hoppy, in obvious discomfort, mumbled, "If only I had my gun."

Billy MacLean sprang into action. No ruthless band of Indians was going to treat his hero in such a shoddy manner. Billy tossed his box of popcorn in the air and exclaimed, "Here Hoppy, take mine!" With that startling exclamation, Billy threw his cap gun to Hoppy on the screen. The force of the gun made a slight dent in the vicinity of Hoppy's nose before clattering to the floor.

Hoppy was saved when the chief's daughter pleaded for his life. Billy wasn't as fortunate. Old Man MacPherson was sweeping out the front vestibule when projectionist Charles Archer ran down from the projection room with the startling news: "Some crazy kid is throwing things at the screen."

Cool as a cucumber, Old Man MacPherson put on his bright blue jacket and rushed to the seats occupied by us

Hoppy fans. "Okay, boys, who threw the gun?" he wanted to know.

His question was met by complete silence. Any cowboy worth his salt knows that you never squeal on a buddy. Old Man MacPherson declared in a no-nonsense voice, "Until I know who threw the gun, not one of you will be allowed in this theatre when a cowboy movie is playing. I swear to God, I really mean it. Now, who threw the gun?"

About fifteen boys answered in unison, "Billy MacLean." So much for the cowboy code of silence. Old Man MacPherson took Billy by the ear and escorted him out the front door of the theatre.

From that day on, Old Man MacPherson did a cursory search of every boy entering the theatre when a cowboy movie was playing. His astute action put a stop to all horseplay in the front rows, but it never had a chance of erasing the memory of Billy MacLean's immortal words, "Here, Hoppy, take mine!"

THE SPITTING CHAMPION
OF THE WORLD

It is a rare phenomenon when a man is remembered fifty years after his fifteen seconds of fame for having manufactured and delivered the most colossal spit of all time.

GoGo Green had a local reputation in town as the all-time world champion spitter. If spitting had been an Olympic event, GoGo would have stood front and centre on the podium. Legend has it that when GoGo was five years old, his father discovered his son's unique talent when they visited Angus Fraser's tobacco and confectionery store where several men of the town sat around smoking and telling lies to each other to pass the long winter days.

In the backroom sat Angus Fraser, tall, skinny as a rail, puffing on his pipe, king of all he surveyed. Angus reluctantly rose only when someone honked their horn for gas at the lone gas pump situated in front of his shop or when a customer strolled in looking for cigarettes or candy, which wasn't often. Most of the assorted men lounging about in the backroom, realizing Angus's aversion to motion of any kind, would get up from their chairs and serve themselves, as they knew the tobacco and cigarette stock better than the owner.

My father had a regular seat beside the single window, where he could spot a farmer coming down Court Street with a cowhide for sale. He would break the existing world record for the hundred-yard dash and beat the farmer to our house, which was the next building on the street. My father was the main cowhide buyer in town. He did a brisk business because he had a secret. As he weighed the farmer's cowhide, he would gently inquire if his customer would fancy a wee swig of rum. In forty years of cowhide buying, no one ever refused his invitation. From above a wooden board under the ceiling of the old barn, a bottle was produced. No one ever argued about price per pound or anything else. The deal was consummated in under three minutes, allowing my father to return to Angus's shop in time to hear how every Progressive Conservative in Canada should be drawn and quartered.

Duncan Chisholm, between coughs, discussed only one topic, and that was politics. He would stare blankly out the window as the other men discussed crops, sex, and the latest exploits of hockey star Rocket Richard. But let the conversation turn to politics and Duncan's eyes would light up. He would bellow like a moose in heat, "Mackenzie King is the greatest man on earth since Jesus." That was quite a statement, considering that Jesus had many fans in the backroom of Angus Fraser's store.

Al MacIsaac, the undertaker, didn't say much. He mostly listened, with occasional glances at the phone, which was mounted on the wall. When it rang, Al would spring into action. Another call from St. Martha's Hospital required his services.

All the men stiffened in their chairs, waiting for Al to identify the deceased. The men, ever the optimists, upon hearing the name of the dearly departed, would exclaim, "Oh, the newcomer. Only been in town six years. Hardly got to know him." Or another might declare, "Poor bugger, had to be at least ninety-six, his time was up." The men returned to the topic under discussion before the phone rang. All except Al. He had to attend to business.

Old Man Boyd was an exception. He had no first name and was known only as Old Man Boyd. Besides, he was a relative newcomer, having arrived in town from God knows where only fifteen years before. With no visible means of support, it was rumoured that he was retired and received a healthy pension from some company in Toronto. A few years after he arrived in town, the men in Fraser's shop, reluctant to accept a new member into their unofficial club, checked out his mail by asking the postmaster, Tom Norton, to let them know if a large company in Toronto was sending cheques to Old Man Boyd. They were somewhat disappointed to learn that, other than the *Farmer's Almanac,* Old Man Boyd received no mail whatsoever. No one ever inquired as to his source of income again.

Roger Kerton, MP, sat on an empty wooden Coke crate. He didn't rate a chair because for a good portion of the year he was in Ottawa. Roger didn't say much, which is an understatement.

He didn't say anything. When John Diefenbaker swept the Liberals out of power, it was discovered that Roger had delivered his maiden speech some twenty-six years before. Not one word since that time. His lack of speaking in Parliament received some novelty notice in newspapers. The men in the backroom of Angus Fraser's shop could have told the press of the country, if anyone had asked them, that Roger hadn't said a word in Fraser's shop for well over thirty years.

Hughie MacDonald, who stood an even five feet tall and was a charter member of Fraser's backroom, was devoid of any hands whatsoever. No one in town really knew how Hughie lost his hands. There were those who claimed that while he was visiting Montreal as a young man, he lost his balance and fell under a streetcar. Then there were those gossipers who would swear up and down that Hughie had been intoxicated when he fell under that streetcar in Montreal so many years before. Truth to tell, Hughie had no hands and that was that.

It was to this illustrious group that little GoGo first displayed his spitting prowess. Without a word of warning, GoGo, one hand clasped in that of his father, decided to spit. The lad made a direct hit into a tin can that sat precariously on a radiator. The water-filled can, which once held Turret tobacco, alleviated the humidity problem in the back shop. No one had the foggiest idea that they had stumbled upon what would later be known as a humidifier. At Fraser's shop, the men simply knew that if you filled an empty Turret tobacco can with water and placed it on the radiator, Duncan Chisholm would stop coughing.

Some say it was my own father who broke the astonished silence by asking GoGo to repeat his unusual feat. That's when Handless Hughie rose from his chair, extended himself to his full five feet, and declared that a measurement should be taken. A tape was produced. Naturally enough, Hughie couldn't do the measuring himself.

The men measured the distance of GoGo's spit. The blob had travelled from in front of the confectionery counter where GoGo had been attempting to make up his mind whether to spend his one cent on an old-fashioned chocolate or a licorice pipe, through an open doorway to the back shop and smack dab into that Turret tobacco can. It was a good ten feet. Al MacIsaac was the first to suggest that since the lad was only five his unusual talent would undoubtedly develop as the years went by. Certainly GoGo was a town treasure. Could he duplicate the feat?

GoGo's father, justifiably proud, asked his son to stand in front of the confectionery counter and let one go toward the can. GoGo just stood there with his nose running. After much cajoling by those present, he pointed to a licorice pipe in the display case. Hughie stood up waving his handless arms and exclaimed, "The little bugger won't do it until we buy him a licorice pipe." GoGo was given the pipe. He chewed for a while until he had a mouthful of black saliva. Then, taking a stance that later was to become famous, he thrust his head forward. Those present on that day of discovery said that his eyes glistened like bright embers crackling in a fireplace. With his head thrust forward, his back arched, eyes aglow, he let her go.

Kerplunk! The men applauded. It was Angus himself who voiced his suspicions: "Plain luck. He could never do it again." You could hear a pin drop.

Undaunted by this outright challenge to his God-given talent, GoGo pointed to the licorice pipes in the display case for the second time. Angus, displaying a degree of generosity and agility never witnessed by his colleagues before or since, produced a licorice pipe without even an inkling of who was to pay for the confectionery.

GoGo shoved the pipe into his mouth and chewed vigorously. He wiped away assorted matter emanating from his nose with his sleeve. As the men gazed, he stepped back a few feet. Someone remarked, "We are looking at a good twelve-footer." GoGo thrust his head forward and arched his back. With eyes glistening, he let her go. That blob of black saliva floated in a high arc, just making it from the store proper through the doorway and into the back shop. Kerplunk!

From that moment on, GoGo had a place in the history and folklore of Antigonish. Initially his talent was the private domain of the men in the backroom of Fraser's store. If he happened to be passing by and was sighted by the men, he would be called inside. Once bribed with a licorice pipe, he would perform. As the months turned into years, the distance of GoGo's spitting prowess increased dramatically. It got so that he could score direct hits from a distance of fifteen feet. It was a sight to see—the thrust of the head, the arched back, the glowing eyes, and the actual flight of blackness into that Turret can, since christened GoGo's can.

A feat of such magnitude could not stay a secret for long. As time passed, rumours drifted up Main Street. In the Rex Café, the conversation often centred on GoGo's talent. Billy MacCrimmon thought a move should be instituted to have spitting become an Olympic event. Others wanted to see GoGo perform in the flesh. Overheard in front of Zena Cameron's jewellery store was the remark, "I hear that GoGo Green is some spitter."

In time, GoGo's father received requests for his son to perform in public. That's when the good citizens of the community discovered that they had a reluctant hero on their hands. Most times, when his father produced his trademark licorice pipe and gave the command, "Let her go," our hero would just stand there, nose running, but no sign of that head thrust forward, that arched back, those glowing eyes.

As if measuring his audience, there were other occasions when GoGo would perform magnificently. There was the time in MacInnis's barber shop when GoGo is said to have planted a twenty-footer, which many felt might be a world record. Another time, in the Celtic Hall Pool Room, before several St. Francis Xavier students, they say GoGo, after obtaining his licorice pipe, sank a twenty-footer into a smaller tin than his trademark Turret can, which by this time was lugged about by his proud father.

As a teenager, GoGo didn't display his talent that often. For one thing, the novelty gradually wore off. For another, the town produced other heroes. There was the two-headed calf born on Mount Cameron Farm that captured the imagination of the locals and achieved regional fame when it was displayed at the Antigonish Fall Fair. Alas, the calf died of natural causes shortly after the fair. There were rumours that Donny MacDonnell fed the calf candy, which hastened its demise. We can only assume he gave equal amounts to each of the two heads.

It was around this time that Bull Eyes moved into town. He was a large boy with broad shoulders, arms like lampposts, and legs that looked like the trunks of trees. He was simply big all over and stood a foot taller than the rest of us twelve-year-old boys. Bull Eyes had the distasteful habit of bending his index finger while making a fist and striking any passing boy between the elbow and shoulder. It hurt like hell and had kind of a paralyzing effect on the entire arm for a good fifteen minutes. We avoided Bull Eyes as much as possible, crossing the street when we saw him coming. We would place grown-ups between us and Bull Eyes at every opportunity. Still, the cunning devil would sneak up on you, deliver the wicked blow to your arm, and be gone in a flash.

Once, he hit Johnny MacDonald so hard that there was talk around town that Johnny's mother was going to contact Bull Eyes' parents and complain that her son couldn't move his arm for three days.

I would be remiss not to point out Bull Eyes' most outstanding feature—his eyes. No one in Antigonish had ever witnessed eyes like that in the long history of our town. For starters, they protruded at least three-quarters of the way outside his eye sockets. The irises were so grey as to be black. To add to the horror of the sight, tiny red veins were scattered hither and yon throughout the whites of his eyes. Without a doubt, Bull Eyes was the most hated and, at the same time, most feared kid in town.

The main street in Antigonish was about a mile long. It had a sunny side and a shady side. During the dog days of summer, we boys hung out on the sunny side. There was enough room on the steps of the Royal Bank of Canada not only to sit down but also to lean back on the wide abutments on each side of the steps and survey all who passed on both the shady and sunny sides of Main Street.

On one such fine day in summer, Bull Eyes was walking down the sidewalk on the sunny side of the street. Surely, he wouldn't mess with us in a group but would walk on by.

Then it happened. As he approached the bank, he yawned. Not a quick catch of his breath, but a long, relaxed yawn, the kind where you stretch out both arms. That was the exact pose Bull Eyes assumed as he drew near. From out of nowhere, there was a loud, guttural sound, a rasping clearing of the throat. GoGo repeated the excavation of materials from deep in his throat. His running nose added to the blob forming in his mouth. There was no licorice pipe as in months and years past. There was no Turret tobacco can in sight. This was to be an impromptu performance.

GoGo stuck out his head and arched his back, eyes glistening. He paused, as if studying the velocity of the slight breeze. He let her go. It was a thing of beauty. As the sun caught the projectile in mid-flight, it gave off a yellow-greenish glow. Trajectory perfect. Velocity exact. Distance excellent. The blob floated like a dove, up, up into the air, as if propelled on invisible wings until finally it commenced its descent, slowly at first. Gradually it gained speed, covering a good twenty-two feet before it landed smack dab in Bull Eyes' yawning mouth.

A cheer went up from the assorted group of boys. It was as if the scores of times Bull Eyes had made our arms go numb had been vindicated. He stopped in his tracks, dumbfounded. A glance at the boys slapping GoGo on the back made it perfectly clear what had transpired. Not knowing what to do, the object of GoGo's spectacular talent ran away.

Bull Eyes never hit another arm from that day on.

THE SAILOR'S GRAVE

In his dictionary, Mr. Webster defines fear as "a distressing emotion aroused by impending pain, danger, or evil, either real or imagined."

When I was twelve years old, I endured the most frightening incident of my entire life. Having been born in close proximity to the sea, I naturally enough grew up hearing stories of high adventure and tragedy that took place on the Atlantic Ocean.

Of all the stories, one tale came alive because there was concrete evidence that it had actually taken place. Near the shore stood an old, dilapidated house bearing all the signs of close to a century of wind, salt air, and high tides, which tended to erode everything around the spooky structure. The house was painted dark brown, but the elements had taken their toll on the paint, which in many places had entirely chipped away.

Old Mrs. Springer lived alone in the run-down house. She had chalk-white, matted hair. Her face can best be described as being one great wrinkle, with more lines than a road map of the Maritime provinces. Mrs. Springer hated company of any kind and vocally, sometimes with a broom in hand, would chase annoying boys away from her front stoop. The more she chased us away, the more schemes we thought up to annoy her.

The most outstanding feature on the Springer property was a small gravestone that stood forlornly in the eroded earth some distance from the house. The inscription read "Unknown Sailor." Decades earlier, a decomposed body had washed ashore. With no means of identifying the body, it was buried in the closest isolated piece of earth available. Later, Mrs. Springer's father bought the property and built the house, an imposing structure at that time. Now, it was a spooky old house occupied by an eccentric old lady who wanted nothing more than to be left alone with her dog, a mutt of no known breed. That dog was as nasty as Mrs. Springer herself.

We preteen boys had other ideas. We were forever inventing ways to aggravate Mrs. Springer, often knocking on her door and running away. Hidden in nearby bushes, we would take perverted pleasure in seeing her, accompanied by her yapping little dog, open the door and scream at her adversaries. All the while the nasty little dog would bark its heart out.

It was Sam Brady who came up with the brilliant idea. He told Frenchie Benoit and Frenchie told me. We figured it was the best idea since Robin Hood became buddies with Friar Tuck. We would write spooky notes to Mrs. Springer in blood, wrap the notes around rocks, and send them flying toward her door. The noise would bring her on the run. She would read the notes and be scared stiff. Anyway, that was the scheme in theory. It didn't exactly work out that way.

All three of us conspirators had scabs on our knees from falling out of trees, falling off bikes, and just plain falling. We decided to pick off our scabs and use the ensuing gushing blood to write the notes.

"Frenchie's scab is the biggest. His goes first," Sam suggested.

"Yours is practically falling off," Frenchie said, pointing to my left knee.

"Why not Sam's?" I countered.

"No, Max is the smallest, his scab should be the first to be picked."

I cringed and closed my eyes as Frenchie jerked that scab from my knee. It hurt like blazes. Instead of a stream of blood, a tiny speck appeared, certainly not enough for our evil purposes.

"The idea is too good to give up on. We've got to think of something else," Sam declared.

A day passed. Despite the conspirators meeting on two separate occasions, no blood substitute was forthcoming. That evening, at the Brady household, Mrs. Brady served meat loaf. Sam picked up the Heinz ketchup bottle and shouted, "I found it!" He ran to the phone and told Allison Carruthers of the Maritime Tel and Tel to connect him to number nine. I answered the phone. Sam said only three words, "I've got it!"

With that information tucked away in my brain, I called Frenchie and the three of us met that very evening. In his exuberance, Sam brought along the ketchup bottle. We all agreed the substitute was brilliant in its simplicity. Next day we formulated the execution of our diabolical plot, but first the notes had to be written. Frenchie wrote the first Heinz ketchup note. It was simple and to the point: "You will die tonight." Sam wrote: "They are coming to get you now." I thought "Death to All Unbelievers" had a nice ring to it because I had heard it once in a movie.

The notes were meticulously tied to rocks with string. We planned to strike after supper that very night. It was dark when we gathered in the bushes on the perimeter of the Springer yard. I had never been there at night before and couldn't help thinking about the unknown sailor buried only a few feet away from our hiding place, between us and the house. Supposedly, on windy nights, the sailor could be heard wailing eerily from the grave, "Let meee ooouut!" Some related that he cried out, "I'm drowning, won't someone save me!"

These thoughts had never entered my mind during daytime visits to the Springer property, but in the pitch blackness of a moonless night my mind played tricks on me, especially with the rhythmic beating of the waves pounding on the shore a short distance away. As I crouched there, I could swear I heard the sailor's voice saying, "Leave old Mrs. Springer alone!" It was a whining, whimpering voice that seemed to be timed between waves. I didn't want to admit it to Sam and Frenchie, but I was frightened. I turned to my two partners in crime. Frenchie's hands seemed to be trembling; Sam's face was as white as a ... well, a ghost.

The question at hand was which one of us would carry the rocks to within throwing distance of Mrs. Springer's door. I suggested Sam. He suggested Frenchie and Frenchie suggested me. This was cause for discussion. I put forward what I thought was a strong argument. We all knew Sam, a pitcher on the softball team, had the best throwing arm. Sam felt that Frenchie should be the rock thrower because he was the fastest runner, which I thought was a valid argument.

In the end, I was chosen as the rock thrower because I was the smallest. This decision made no sense whatever to me, but I was accustomed to performing distasteful acts because I was the smallest. Every time we stole apples, who had to climb the tree and shake the branches? Me, that's who. Reluctantly I took on my task as being an inevitable fact of life.

Like a kamikaze pilot, I accepted the rocks and my companions' good wishes as I left the relative safety of the bushes and made my way across no man's land. I managed to get close enough to Mrs. Springer's door to throw the message-clad rocks. They made a loud sound as they hit her door and an even louder noise as they fell on her front porch and rolled around.

All hell broke loose. The door flew open. There was Mrs. Springer in her nightgown, equipped with a broom and accompanied by her barking, rotten dog. She should have stopped and read our notes. After all, that was our plan. Instead, she hopped down those steps, displaying little evidence of her advanced years. Waving her broom, she shouted out orders to her mutt, "Go get 'em, boy, go get 'em."

Thank God the deranged woman stopped advancing at the bottom of her steps. I can't say the same for man's best friend. Obeying his mistress's orders, that growling, barking beast made a beeline for me. I took off like a bat out of hell. My foot caught on something. I sailed through the air, coming down spread-eagled, flat as a pancake, on my stomach. I opened my eyes. There, not more than six inches from my head, was the grave marker. Although there was no moon, I could make out the words "Unknown Sailor."

Somewhere in the far recesses of my mind, I was sure the sailor was beckoning me into his grave. Before I could formulate a plan to outwit the dead sailor, that stupid dog caught up to me and was making concerted attempts to bite my legs. With the sailor seeking my body and the dog attempting to have lunch on my extremities, I was in big trouble. In desperation I managed to adjust my body so I could use both arms and legs. I crawled to the bushes, which I thought concealed my fellow conspirators. Once there, I realized they had retreated at the first sight of Mrs. Springer. Deserted by my friends, I found a stick and was able to ward off the crazed dog and make good my retreat.

So, Mr. Webster, I want to point out to you that the moment that I was lying on the sailor's grave with the dog barking at my legs and Mrs. Springer in her nightgown waving her broom could be used as the very definition of fear.

MY CHICKEN-PLUCKING CAREER

It was Donnie Kennedy who told me that the Antigonish Co-op was hiring boys to pluck chickens during the summer vacation. The pay was five cents per chicken, which seemed fair enough to me. The Co-op building, where the plucking would take place, was right beside the jail. As both Donnie and I lived on Court Street, it was also a very convenient place to work. Travel time by slow walk was three minutes, as opposed to those delivery jobs uptown that would take a good ten minutes' travel time.

Donnie and I were introduced to our fellow pluckers on our first day at work. All three were serving time in Willie MacIsaac's jail for various petty crimes. All three were Mi'kmaq Indians. Joe Steamboat had stolen a mantle radio from a house near Heatherton when a Mrs. Chestnut had left it blaring near an open window. Joe claimed that she had it playing so loud that he couldn't concentrate on his blueberry picking. He had picked blueberries for so many seasons that the area was unofficially considered to be his blueberry patch. Joe explained before Judge MacLean, "I stole it so it would shut up." Of course, Joe was referring to the radio. Dismissing the noise pollution defence, the judge threw the book at Joe, sentencing him to thirty days in jail.

Thomas Bigfoot got into a fight at the Dingle Dance Hall over a girl from Mulgrave, whose boyfriend retaliated by saying that all Indians should be locked up on their reservations. Thomas broke a Demerara Black Diamond rum bottle over the boyfriend's head, knocking that unfortunate gentleman out cold. Thomas would have done more harm had it not been for the intervention of Red Archie, who just happened to be attending the dance himself. One witness to the event, Big Nose Phil McPhee, said that Thomas showed a great deal of restraint by only swinging that rum bottle once instead of pouncing on his fallen victim and giving him a proper trouncing. Judge MacLean felt that Thomas had been provoked to strike out after the insult to his race. The good judge sentenced Thomas to only fifteen days. In summing up, the judge pointed out that we couldn't have people hitting other people over the head with rum bottles for any reason.

Francis Frogs Voice had been apprehended making moonshine in the woods near his home at Doctor's Brook. The RCMP officer who made the arrest claimed that the moonshine was the best he had ever tasted. Judge MacLean sentenced Francis to thirty days.

These, then, were my fellow workers in the chicken-plucking business. In my short time in the poultry industry, I grew to like all three.

Our boss, who turned out to be none other than jailer Willie MacIsaac, gave us a little speech on our first day. The birds would be dunked into a steam bath. Willie would personally handle the machine, which plucked about ninety percent of all the feathers off the unfortunate fowl. As soon as the series of suction hoses pulled out the feathers, it was our job to pluck the remaining nasty little feathers from the legs, wings, and necks of the chickens. Every time we completed a bird, we were to put an X under our name on the sheet of white paper that had been placed on the wall. At the end of the day, Willie would add up the number of X's under our respective names and pay us accordingly.

We hung the chickens by their feet, heads down, so that they were exposed for plucking. All five of us pluckers stood in a precise row. On either side of me were Thomas Bigfoot and Francis Frogs Voice.

It was not easy work. If you were unlucky, you could get a stubborn chicken with an inbred urge to hold on to its pinfeathers. Since piecework was the name of the game, that bird could take three times as long to pluck as its relatives. Do the math. That reluctant rascal could cost me fifteen cents.

With the steam permeating the air and the scalded chickens giving off an ungodly odour, the small room was like a scene from Dante's Inferno. Francis Frogs Voice had the disagreeable habit of talking to his dead chickens, particularly those that were hard to pluck. He interspersed his rasping words with screams and shouts in the Mi'kmaq tongue, which I didn't understand. Fortunately, Thomas Bigfoot acted as my interpreter. When

Frogs Voice let out a scream, Thomas would whisper to me, "He just said 'You goddam bird, I hope I eat you at Wong's Café in the chicken chow mein.'" At other times Frogs Voice would cast disparaging remarks on the chicken's lineage.

Thomas whispered confidential information to me about his two fellow pluckers, such as the reason for Francis's last name. "Frogs Voice comes from a long line of frogs who once inhabited Doctor's Brook. They were really frogs, who gradually over the centuries developed into men and women. The only thing left from their ancient days was their harsh voice. In this way the entire family tree became the Frogs Voice tribe."

As soon as Thomas had finished explaining his personal Darwinian theory, Francis commenced hitting his chicken with a series of judo chops to its back while yelling at the lifeless creature.

"What's he saying now?" I innocently inquired.

Thomas whispered, "He told the bird that its rotten feathers were so tough to get out he was putting three X's under his name."

That was the first hint of the skulduggery that was about to take place in the Co-op chicken-plucking room. At the end of the day Willie added up everyone's tally. Joe Steamboat, 70. Thomas Bigfoot, 64. Francis Frogs Voice, 82. Max Haines, 40. Donnie Kennedy, 43. The total came to 299. Willie then added up the number of birds sitting in rows, big as life, all plucked and pretty as a picture. The total came to 194. There were 105 birds unaccounted for.

Obviously the honour system wasn't working. Willie had a solution. He took the difference of 105 chickens and divided by five, which came to 21. That was the amount he would take off each of his five employees. That left Joe with 49; Thomas, 43; Francis, 61; Max, 19; and Donnie, 22. I received ninety-five cents for my day's work, Donnie $1.10. Something was rotten in the state of Denmark.

After work that first day, I went home to be greeted by an irate mother. There were tiny feathers in my hair; my clothing was drenched from the steam and other foreign material that had originated from the chickens. My mother took one look and said, "You smell like a dead chicken." She went on to insist that I take off all my clothes and soak in the bathtub for a good half-hour. Only then was I allowed to join the rest of my family for dinner.

Donnie and I met that evening. We realized our fellow pluckers were indiscriminately putting X's under their names. If they wanted X's, they would get X's. Next day Donnie and I entered Dante's Inferno for another day of chicken plucking. My first bird received three X's, and so it went all day. Donnie and Max chalked up big numbers. The final tally stood at Joe, 72; Thomas, 68; Francis, 90; Max, 121; Donnie, 119, for a whopping total of 470 chickens. Willie shook his head and told us there were exactly 205 fully plucked chickens on the rack. He was short 265 birds. Using his system of dividing by five, he simply took 53 birds off each name. I ended up with 68 chickens at five cents a chicken for a take-home pay of $3.40. Donnie made $3.30. Who says crime doesn't pay?

That evening when I went home, my mother took one look at me and said, "That does it. Your chicken-plucking days are over." She explained that after day one, my shirt had been thrown out because it was unwearable. She mentioned something about never being able to get the smell out. Now, with day two under my belt, my sneakers had to go as well. Mother said my voice was changing, I was beginning to sound like a frog.

Donnie's mother must have had roughly the same idea, because later he knocked on our door and told me his mother had forbidden him to go back to work plucking chickens.

Next day, we both sheepishly told Willie that we were resigning our positions as chicken pluckers. He didn't seem to mind. Apparently, Red Archie had apprehended two hoboes stealing corn from the Camerons' farm. They had been lodged in jail and were more than happy to accept a temporary career as chicken pluckers at the Co-op.

To this day, I can't look a chicken wing in the face.

ARCHIE SPRUCE BEER'S DIVE

While many memories that pass through my head about my hometown are of events that generally took place in the summer, winter also held its share of strange and unusual incidents.

The citizens of Antigonish were deeply involved in hockey, more specifically with the home team, the Antigonish Bulldogs. The Bulldogs were a senior team in an era when every team in Canada could vie for the Allan Cup, awarded to the best team in the country outside of the National Hockey League. Our Bulldogs played in Memorial Rink, which was devoid of artificial ice. As a result, the building was freezing cold in the winter. No one seemed to mind. The rink was full every night the Bulldogs played.

There were three ways for kids to gain entrance to the Bulldogs' games. One was to pay the entrance fee, which was by far the most unpopular. The second was to carry in the duffle bag and skates for one of the players and be allowed in for free. To accomplish this feat, you had to know one of the players and meet him for the long walk to Memorial Rink.

I knew Neil MacKenna and usually met him at his father's drugstore for the trek up Main Street and then through the university campus to the rink. Neil was one of the stars of the team and rarely let me down, but on occasion I would show up at the drugstore only to be told that Neil had had to leave for the rink early or couldn't meet me for some other reason. That's when I became a member of group three, by far the most popular group of kids around town attempting to take in a game of our beloved Bulldogs.

Because Memorial Rink was still years away from artificial ice, the windows were left open to let the frigid air enter the brick building. To prevent rotten kids like me from sneaking in, bars had been placed across the windows at intervals that would allow only the skinniest of youngsters to squeeze through. Kids who could have been contortionists managed to wiggle through the bars. The more desperate among us succeeded in bending the bars, making just enough room to push through. Sometimes adults already in the building assisted us kids by pulling arms and legs.

Once, before the game started, Toby MacInnis got caught between the bars. When the game commenced, the adults who were helping him gain entrance abandoned their task to watch the game. By the time the first period was over, the grown-ups returning to their task found that Toby had almost frozen to death. Between the first and second periods they succeeded in extricating him from the cold grip of the bars. The Bulldogs went on to win that game in the third period and Toby is rumoured to have said, "It was worth the wait."

There was one particular game that gained a degree of notoriety, not because of anything that was done by the players on the ice, but rather the near-death experience of Archie Spruce Beer. The game was a playoff between the Bulldogs and the hated New Glasgow Bombers. There had been intense rivalry all season long between the two teams. Certain local businessmen refused to do business with New Glasgow. A bottling firm in New Glasgow, while making its rounds of Antigonish stores, found that its soft drinks had suddenly gone out of favour. Conversely, restaurants in Antigonish learned that residents of New Glasgow travelling to and from Cape Breton were boycotting their establishments. Feelings ran high. Local children chanted, "Fee, fie, fo, fum, I smell the blood of a New Glasgow bum." In New Glasgow, their counterparts vocalized, "Antigonish, Antigonish, rotten potatoes and stinking fish."

The rink was jammed, so that every normal vantage point was occupied. Because it was freezing cold both outside and inside the rink, fans didn't mind being squashed together like sardines. More resourceful fans brought along liquid refreshments to protect them from the bitter cold.

Since it was the fifth game of the best-of-five series, the rink not only was packed to capacity, but was actually overflowing. Braver souls, many fortified by the devil rum, crawled out onto supporting beams high above the ice surface. These individuals sneaked drinks out of their rum bottles without difficulty while the game was in progress. All wore heavy winter garments, so it was not a trick to hide the bottle inside a windbreaker or over-coat while everyone was glued to the action on the ice. Between periods, they would crawl down from their perches to stretch cramped legs and to take a swig in more comfortable surroundings.

At the end of the third period, the score was tied 3–3. One goal would decide who would go on to play the winner of the Cape Breton series that was taking place between Glace Bay and Sydney. The mood was electric. The rafter crowd crawled down to stoke their collective furnaces with rum. The game was well into overtime when the talented and hated Boots Baird got a breakaway. He roared down left wing and shot wide, missing the net by inches.

At that precise moment, Archie Spruce Beer fell twenty-five feet from the beam he was perched on to the natural ice below. He didn't move a muscle. A hush came over the crowd. Dr. T.B. MacDonald clambered over the boards and rushed to Archie's stretched-out form on the ice. The Bulldogs' trainer was there with the doctor, as were several players from both teams.

They carried Archie off the ice on a stretcher. The game resumed, but the starch seemed to be out of the Bulldogs. Boots Baird cemented his title as the most hated man in Antigonish by scoring the winning goal and ending the Bulldogs' season.

After the game the crowd at Wong's Café could talk of little else but the condition of Archie Spruce Beer. Rumour had it that he was at St. Martha's Hospital with multiple injuries, but nothing of a more concrete nature was forthcoming. Next day, more definitive reports circulated through town. Dr. MacDonald announced that Archie had suffered a broken maxilla, broken mandible, broken right scapula, broken humerus, broken ulna, broken radius, assorted broken carpal bones, broken metacarpal, assorted broken phalanges, broken pelvic bones, broken femur, broken tibia, broken patella, broken tarsal bones, as well as metatarsal bones. His total recovery took several months.

In the meantime, the exact injuries were summed up rather succinctly: "Archie broke every bone in his body." In time, this synopsis was more or less borne out by hospital officials. An addendum was tacked on to the rumour: "He broke every bone in his body, but a mickey of Demerara Black Diamond rum was found intact in his back pocket."

And so ended the hockey season in Antigonish.

About the only other item of interest that happened that year had nothing to do with hockey or winter. It was a beautiful spring day when the Crystal Cleaners incident, as it came to be known, took place.

Our town had only one bona fide dry cleaning establishment, namely Crystal Cleaners. It was a family-owned business with but one competitor, an outfit from New Glasgow, whose van picked up cleaning from individual customers once a week. This service wasn't that satisfactory as it took a full week for your cleaning to be returned. The van, with the name Rain or Shine Laundry written in big letters on the side, was driven by an undersized man with a big nose. When he picked up or delivered laundry, he was invariably intoxicated. When too drunk to drive, he brought along his brother Fred, who was the same size but had a regular nose. Fred's main claim to fame was that he had never touched a drop of alcohol in his life. Usually he would remark, "My brother Alf makes up for both of us." This statement was accompanied by a great deal of laughter.

The two brothers often had trouble locating finished items in their van. On several occasions they had neglected to place the dry cleaning in the van in New Glasgow. When that happened, customers had to wait an additional week for their dry cleaning.

No wonder Crystal Cleaners, run by owner Cyril Swales, did so well. Located on Church Street, right across from St. James United Church, it was central to everyone in town. Besides, Cyril was a pleasant man who would see to it that missing buttons were replaced or pockets were patched. Mostly everyone in town patronized Crystal Cleaners.

Phil MacDougall, who witnessed the following incident, has told the story hundreds of times. Phil, who did odd jobs around the CNR station in exchange for living quarters, gained a degree of notoriety for being present when the incident occurred. According to Phil, he was standing at the counter of Crystal Cleaners waiting to take delivery of his CNR shirt, the one with the little CNR logo embroidered on the pocket, when Cyril, who was loading something into the boiler, turned to give him his shirt. There was a loud swishing noise. Cyril spun around. The boiler was gone. It travelled straight up, slashing through the roof like a knife through butter, continuing in flight across the street and over St. James United Church. The boiler came down with a thud, glancing off the roof of Alcorn's

Confectionery Store and coming to rest in the alley between Alcorn's and the Co-op Store.

No one was hurt. No one could believe a huge boiler could possibly travel through the air like a rocket and up over the church. I joined the crowd gawking at the boiler. It was a miracle. Townsfolk talked of little else, except of course Archie Spruce Beer's near-death experience.

Anyone who says living in a small town is boring should have lived in Antigonish the year Archie took his dive and Cyril's boiler became airborne.

MY FATHER
THE AIR RAID WARDEN

During World War II, my father was the air raid warden for Court Street. The position carried with it some minor responsibilities, which he took very seriously.

In retrospect, it is difficult to fathom why we would be concerned about a German air raid since Antigonish wasn't strategically located, nor did it produce anything that could remotely be called militarily significant. The fact is, we didn't have a single factory producing anything at all. Some greater authority must have believed we were in imminent danger and decided to institute air raid drills.

My father was issued a steel helmet, an armband, a stirrup pump, and a whistle. When the town's siren went off, all lights in town had to be extinguished. Barring that, a black cloth had to be placed over windows so that no light escaped.

Not one enemy aircraft was ever spotted in all of Nova Scotia, a situation that seems to have been lost on those responsible for national security. There were some scares that did not involve aircraft. A fisherman from Williams Point, a few miles from town, reported seeing an enemy submarine, but it turned out to be an empty metal oil drum. The sighting caused great excitement for a few days, but as quickly as the potential invasion was anticipated, the scare died down.

Then there were the three men who were arrested by Red Archie because they had foreign accents. The three strangers suddenly appeared in town one day. Since they didn't speak English, it was assumed they were German spies. As soon as they made themselves understood, it was learned that they were three Danish students sent over by their government to study at St. Francis Xavier University.

The first evening the air raid siren went off, the town went into a tizzy. My father quickly slipped his armband on and just as quickly noted that the light on the porch just off the kitchen was glowing brightly at our immediate neighbour's house. With me in tow, he knocked on the door of Mrs. T.A. MacLean, whose husband was a major in the army.

"Mrs. MacLean, you'll have to turn off your porch light. This is an air raid drill," my father said in his thick Eastern European accent. Dad was from Lithuania and had landed in this country as A. Hans. My mother, born in Chatham, New Brunswick, thought it would be classier to one day simply add the "i" and "e." That's how we became the Haines family of Antigonish.

"I'm sorry, Alex, I can't do that. I'm in the middle of pickling cucumbers," she replied.

This was a genuine dilemma. Our family had for years been the recipients of Mrs. MacLean's pickles, sometimes as many as three jars.

"But it's right here in my manual. There are no exceptions. All lights have to be turned off or covered with a black cloth."

"Well, now, why didn't you say that, Alex? I have an old black coat of the Major's. We could tie it around the lampshade so I'll be able to see on the porch to finish my pickling, but there will no light shining outside. Will you give me a hand?"

"Sure, Mrs. MacLean."

With the agreement in principle now in place, my father proceeded, with the help of a chair, to secure the Major's coat around the bulb. It glowed inside the porch, but nary a beam could be seen from outside. I placed my hand in my father's hand. We left Mrs. MacLean to her pickling and made our way next door to Collie MacDonald's house. No question about it, there was a tiny beam of light shining through the front window.

My father knocked on the door. "There's a tiny bit of light shining through your front window. Can you cover it up?"

"Alex, you come in for a cup of tea—there's no German planes about tonight," said Mrs. MacDonald.

"I know there are no German planes, but we must be prepared. Can't you just cover the tiny opening?" my father pleaded.

"Oh, all right, Alex, you're such a fusspot!" With that, she covered the opening with a navy blue scarf. "There, it's fixed. Are you satisfied now?"

After a cup of tea for my father and a cup of cocoa for me, we continued down the street. At the MacGillivray residence we saw a light shining in the garage behind the house. My father knocked on the front door, which elicited a loud bark from King, Mr. MacGillivray's dog. Mr. MacGillivray lived alone with King, his wife Gloria having passed away years earlier from a severe case of botulism. She was such a disagreeable woman that there was some talk that her husband, Don James Joseph, or D.J.J. as he was called, might have poisoned her. There was even the rumour that the contents of Gloria's stomach had been sent to Halifax for analysis, but I have never been able to confirm this rather distressing tale. Some of the men in town were heard to whisper among each other that it required a special boxcar to ship poor Gloria's stomach to the province's capital. No doubt this comment was an obvious reference to the late Mrs. MacGillivray's girth, which by any standard was substantial.

"Let's go around in back to the garage," my father said, as he clasped my hand and led me down the darkened driveway. D.J.J. appeared in the doorway. He was holding a bottle of Bacardi dark rum in his hand. Big Collie was there, as well as Whistling Bill.

"Come in, Alex, have a wee nip of rum."

"D.J.J., you have to put out the lights."

Big Collie agreed, remarking, "Makes no difference to me."

With the initial salutations out of the way, my father held the bottle to his lips and took a deep drag. "Don't tell your mother, Maxie," he said, referring to the gulp of rum he had just consumed.

The bottle made the rounds from my father to D.J.J. to Big Collie and back to my father. Sticking strictly to the job at hand, my father said, "D.J.J., you still have to put out the light. Is there anything you can wrap around the bulb?"

"There's an old Union Jack around here someplace. Will that do?"

"Let's give it a try, boys," laughed Big Collie.

In due course, the lampshade was wrapped with the old flag. My father went outside to test it. No light shone through. Inside there was just enough illumination to pass around that bottle of Bacardi rum.

We proceeded down the street, but encountered no further light of any kind. Just as we were about to enter our house, though, my father noticed that Bea New York's lights were ablaze on the corner of Main and Court Streets. This posed a problem. Main Street was not his jurisdiction. Dan Joe MacEachran covered that section of town, but it didn't seem right that the entire town was in pitch blackness while one house was glowing like a full moon.

After some deliberation, my father decided to knock on Bea New York's door and tell her to put out her lights. Now, Bea New York was not a local. About ten years earlier she had moved from New York when an aunt died and left her the house at Main and Court. No one bothered with her last name, but quickly noted the New York accent. From the first week in town she was known as Bea New York.

At five feet ten inches tall, Bea was the tallest woman in town. She was all skin and bones, had a tiny nose and two eyes that appeared too big for the rest of her face. You could tell that Bea had been a rare beauty in her day. Now on the wrong side of sixty, she had sort of dried up. Huey Dunphy said that once when he was delivering groceries from Sobeys he was in Bea New York's house. There were pictures of her behind a big bubble. She appeared to be dancing with hardly any clothes on at all, just that annoying bubble. In addition, he observed a framed poster in the living room featuring Bea Bubbles, Exotic Dancer.

Together we approached Bea New York's front door. There was no answer. My father appeared perplexed. "I hope Bea isn't ill," he said to no one in particular. He gingerly tried the front door. It swung open by itself. The whole place was lit up like Times Square. I looked at the pictures on the walls. Some were faded with age, but there was no mistaking Bea New York. Some forty years earlier, she *had* been an exotic dancer known as Bea Bubbles. There was a provocative framed poster proclaiming "Beautiful Sexy Bea Takes It All Off—Almost!"

"Let's check the kitchen," suggested my father. No sign of Bea in the kitchen. "Maybe we should speak to your mother," my father said, as he most often did when faced with any type of decision. As if answering himself, he said, "I'm going upstairs to look around."

When we reached the top of the stairs, I thought I heard a noise emanating from what I took to be the bathroom. My father pushed the door and it swung open. There sat Bea New York in her bathtub. Tiny bubbles covered her entire body except for her head. Embarrassed, my father said, "Bea, the whole house is lit up like a Christmas tree. Don't you know there's an official air raid drill on right now?"

For my part, I turned to leave, having learned years earlier that little boys shouldn't gaze at women who are not fully clothed. Evidently my father never subscribed to this philosophy. Maybe because of her earlier association with bubbles, Bea didn't seem to mind talking to a neighbour from her rather suggestive position in the bathtub.

"Oh, Alex, I never gave that stupid notice in the *Casket* another thought. Simply forgot about the whole thing. Why don't you just turn out all the lights in the house as you leave?"

"Good idea, Bea, but how will you see to get out of the tub?"

"You're right, Alex. You'll find some candles in the drawer. Would you kindly light them for me? I'll put a cloth over the bathroom window after you leave."

"It's a deal, Bea. Remember, no lights."

With those words, we made our way out of the house, turning out lights as we went. My father and I glanced up at Bea's bathroom and, sure enough, that last vestige of light disappeared.

We returned to our house to be greeted by Mother, who said, "You were gone an awfully long time. Anything go wrong?"

Now a veteran of the air raid warden game, my father replied, "Strictly routine."

I LOST MY HEAD

I'm not sure who had the brilliant idea. Maybe it was my buddy Sam Brady. Then again, it may have been me. Sam and I knew that the little bridge leading to Danny Christopher's shack had many loose boards in the centre. This in no way impeded vehicles from crossing the rickety old bridge.

The bridge was only about twenty-five feet long and spanned a small stream between a pond and St. George's Bay. During high tide the pond filled with sea water. At low tide it emptied so that you could actually walk on the mud flats.

Sam and I often crawled out on support pillars under the tiny bridge to fish when the tide was turning. While I don't remember who came up with the idea, I do recall that we both agreed that it was original and clever and had to be implemented without delay.

It is a rare occurrence when an idea so devious, but at the same time so brilliant in its originality, creeps into the minds of two boys with absolutely nothing to do during the long hot summer vacation.

We loosened two boards in the centre of the bridge and found that we could stick our heads up through the opening. I went first. Sam surveyed the effect from a short distance in front of the bridge. "Perfect," he shouted. Anyone driving around the turn and approaching the bridge would believe that there was a head lying on the centre of the bridge.

We decided that we should pull our stunt at night. The approaching vehicle would pick up the decapitated head in its high beams. The driver would be scared out of his wits, slam on his brakes, and investigate. Sam and I would be long gone by the time the traumatized driver was able to reach the spot where he had been pretty sure he had seen the head. The driver would find absolutely nothing because we would have had time to replace the missing boards before making good our escape.

That very night we sneaked under the bridge just as it was getting dark. We waited and waited. The awkward position was beginning to tell on our joints. Besides, it was a dreary, lonesome place to be in complete darkness under a bridge with the ever-present trickle of water flowing beneath us. We stayed there until we could stand it no longer. Not one car visited Danny at his shack that night.

Undeterred, we decided to give it another try the very next night. At dusk we crawled into position. When night fell, I wanted to leave. Just then we heard the muted sound of a car approaching. Sam said, "You go." I stuck my head through the opening in the centre of the bridge.

Fred Cutler and his wife, Sheila, approached in their Chevy. Sheila shouted, "Oh my God! A head!"

Fred slammed on his brakes. Both jumped out of their car and slowly advanced toward the bridge. I ducked down and replaced the boards. Sam and I crawled along the bank of the stream without being seen, but we stayed within hearing range.

"Are you satisfied? You almost caused an accident. There's no head here. Really, Sheila, you're an alarmist," Fred admonished his wife.

Sheila, now rather defensive, replied, "I could have sworn I saw a head."

"Don't be silly," Fred interjected sharply. "There's no head. What you saw was a reflection, nothing more. Now let's get in the car and visit Danny."

Sam and I almost split a gut laughing. Our scheme had worked perfectly. All next day we talked of little else but how we could embellish and smooth out our epic scene of horror, although we agreed that it had worked better than we had imagined.

The drawback that had to be overcome was that we were known by everyone who came over that bridge. Despite the fact that the head was in plain view for only a split second, there was the small chance that we might be recognized. Sam solved that little problem by borrowing a wig that had been hanging around his house. I was the one who thought of the lipstick, but I must admit it was Sam who suggested that rather than applying it to the lips, we should draw a jagged line from the forehead to the neck.

That night we crawled into our perch under the bridge. Soon we heard the engine of an approaching car. It was sheer bad luck for the Cutlers that Sheila had left her sunglasses in Danny's shack the night before. Sam stuck his head through the opening in the boards. Sheila yelled, "The head is back!"

Fred slammed on his brakes. "I didn't see a thing," he declared.

"This time I'm sure, Fred. There was a horrible cut right across its face. I saw the blood and everything."

The Cutlers walked toward the bridge. We had already replaced the boards, but so sure were we that the Cutlers would only do a surface search that we stayed in our perches directly below the loose boards.

"See, Sheila, there's no head here. You're imagining things."

"I'm not an idiot, I saw a bloody head right here on this bridge," Sheila replied.

"Look, honey, you've been working too hard at the store. What with the kids and everything, you're overtired. Why don't we just go home and you can lie down. I'll pick up your sunglasses tomorrow."

Sheila gave in. "Maybe you're right, but I could have sworn I saw a head right here in the middle of this bridge."

The Cutlers returned to their car and drove away. Sam and I couldn't believe our good fortune, having hit the same couple on two successive nights.

The very next night Sam and I were in our customary position under the bridge. In the distance we could hear a car approaching. It was my turn. I stuck my head through the hole. Tommy Delorme and his girlfriend, Helen, were in the car. Tommy, who had a few Cokes laced with Demerara rum under his belt, was thinking of only one thing, and that was parking on the sand dunes on the other side of the bridge.

It was he who shouted, "Jesus, Mary, and Joseph, there's a head on the bridge," as he slammed on his brakes. Now sober as a judge, Tommy made his way to the bridge. Sam and I, who had become expert at replacing the loose boards, were underneath the bridge awaiting their reaction. Tommy said, "Helen, I could have sworn I saw a head right there," as he pointed to the loose boards.

"Well, I didn't see a thing. Tommy, are you sure you're not seeing things? I want to go home."

With his chances of a sexual encounter slowly slipping away, Tommy acquiesced. "Maybe I was mistaken. Let's park right over there."

"No, Tommy, I'm not in the mood. I want to go home."

Totally defeated, Tommy swung the car around and drove away. Next day, while having a slice of cream pie and cold milk at Wong's Café, Tommy told George Wong about seeing the head on the bridge. Never one to keep a secret for long, George told "Toothless" Charles, who told the town cop, Red Archie, who told John "Newsie" Cameron, who just happened to work at the Antigonish *Casket*.

Because it was a quiet news week, as it was most weeks in Antigonish, Newsie decided to run a small piece about the mysterious head that had been seen by several citizens on the rickety old bridge leading to Danny Christopher's shack on the gravel road just off the Jimtown road.

A day later, Mr. and Mrs. James McKay, Willie Cameron, and Toothless Charles separately drove out to the bridge to take a look. Naturally, they didn't find a head, nor did they find anything amiss.

On that very day, old Danny Christopher was in town and heard that the bridge leading to his shack was the subject of some attention. Old Danny, living alone in his shack, only a stone's throw from the bay, thought it was wonderful that his falling-down, ancient bridge was receiving some degree of fame. When the locals asked, he admitted that he had never actually seen the head himself, but the old codger couldn't resist.

According to Danny, on windy nights he had heard strange noises around his shack. He had investigated the source of the weird sounds, but had never witnessed anything unusual. With a twinkle in his watery old eyes, he elaborated, "When I was a wee lad, the body of a sailor washed up on shore. The body had no head. Maybe the noises I heard was the sailor at long last returning to look for his head."

When George Wong got hold of that one, the news spread like wildfire. There was a ghost looking for its lost head down by St. George's Bay. The town was abuzz. Folks were driving down to the bridge to see the head, but of course the head never appeared in daylight.

Relishing our new-found, if secret, fame, Sam and I climbed into our perch the following night. Sure enough, Alice and Mary MacGillivray, who had debunked the crazy story of the sailor looking for his head, drove down to the bridge after dark to see for themselves. We didn't disappoint them. It was my turn. I thought it would be a nice touch if my tongue lolled out to add to the gruesomeness of the scene.

Alice, who was driving, wet her pants. Both sisters were too frightened to get out of their car. They made a turn in an adjoining field and took off without looking into the matter further. Next morning, back in town, the two girls related their frightening experience. Old Danny added to the ghost story when he swore that, on a recent windy night, he thought he had heard the voice of the sailor shouting, "Where is my head?"

Newsie Cameron decided to write a more definitive piece on the "Jimtown Ghost." He drove down to the bridge, but could find absolutely nothing of a suspicious nature. Of course, he took his trip in the light of day when there was nothing to be found. In his article he did mention that, in order to allay the fears of the citizens of the rural area around the bridge, and indeed the entire town of Antigonish, local authorities should investigate thoroughly.

Red Archie read Newsie's piece and decided to look into the crazy goings-on at the bridge on a road that led nowhere except Danny's shack. He astutely decided to drive down to the bridge after dark.

There we were, Sam and I, in our perch under the bridge when we heard a vehicle approaching. Sam stuck his head through the opening. In the light of Red Archie's high beams, he must have been quite a sight with the wig, a jagged cut crafted out of lipstick, and his lolling tongue, the recent addition to our ever-improving head.

Displaying the instincts of Fabian of Scotland Yard, Red Archie got out of his car, saw the loose boards, removed them, and shone his flashlight directly at Sam and me. It was the brightest light I had ever seen in my entire life.

Red Archie shouted, "You two boys get out of there right now."

He marched us to our parents' homes and made us confess to them that we were the originators of the "Jimtown Ghost." I thought I detected a slight smile on Mr. Brady's face, but I couldn't be sure. Red Archie made us swear up and down that we would never attempt any crazy schemes ever again. The Bradys and my parents gave their assurance that we two ghost inventors would retire as of that moment. To put the entire episode to rest, Red Archie gave a statement to Newsie Cameron, which ran in the *Casket*.

It read: "Two local youths have been apprehended as being responsible for the rash of bogus 'head' sightings just off Jimtown Road. Be assured that there was nothing supernatural about the sightings. They were perpetrated by two youths as a prank. Charges are pending."

They still are.

HANDSOME BO

It was a hot summer day in July when a knock on our door on Court Street summoned my mother, who was in the midst of preparing codfish and boiled potatoes for dinner. There stood a young man who, for all the world, bore a striking resemblance to movie star Tyrone Power.

"Ma'am, is there anything around the house that needs fixing, anything outside that needs cleaning up?"

"Well, son, yes there is. I could use some kindling for the kitchen stove."

That's how the stranger in town began his career in Antigonish. Being a curious preteen, I watched as the man cut kindling wood for my mother. He didn't just cut the wood; he stacked it neatly in a pile. No one had ever done that before. I sat idly by as the stranger, now perspiring in the midday heat, cut and piled my mother's kindling.

"What's your name?" I asked.

"You don't want to know my name, boy. I'm a hobo. You can call me Bo if you like."

"Where're you from, Bo?"

"From all over. You sure are a curious one, boy."

Just then my mother came out with a plate of sandwiches and lemonade for my new friend.

"Ma, I want to sit on the steps and eat sandwiches with Bo."

Rosie Cameron walked by. She paused when she saw tall, handsome Bo, perspiring, his shirt neatly folded beside the pile of kindling. It was then that I noticed the tattoo high up on his right arm. In bold blue letters it read: Life Is for Living.

"Hey, Rosie," I said, "this is my new friend Bo. Bo, this is Rosie Cameron." Rosie acknowledged the introduction, blushed, and walked on down the street. I couldn't help but notice her looking over her shoulder at Bo eating those sandwiches. Later, I found out that she stopped at Monie MacDonald's house to tell her that there's a guy chopping wood for Mrs. Haines who's the spitting image of Tyrone Power.

Mother came out of the house and gave Bo two dollars for cutting the kindling. When I asked Bo if I could go uptown with him, he insisted that I get permission from my mother. She said, "Sure." After all, Bo was the handsomest, most polite, best worker she had ever run across.

I walked up Main Street with Bo. All the young girls in town took a second look. Bo said that he wanted to show me the intricacies of shooting pool. At the poolroom I told him I couldn't go in because you had to be sixteen years old. Bo said, "Never you mind. I'll handle it."

Billy MacPherson, who ran the pool hall for Mr. R.K. MacDonald, met us at the door. "I'm sorry, sir, no children allowed."

Bo explained that he was a stranger in town and wanted to show young Maxie a few pointers at the table. MacPherson relented: "I suppose it's okay if he's accompanied by an adult."

Bo racked up the balls and broke. The fourteen ball went into a corner pocket. Bo said in a quiet voice, "The cue is an extension of your arm. Your brain will tell your eyes to focus on the object ball and your eyes and brain will tell you when to stroke." Bo potted the one ball. Then the two. He continued, talking to me in a low voice, "Maxie, that wasn't a good shot. It left me with a difficult shot on the three. Remember, it's the position you leave yourself in that's important."

The three ball disappeared in the left side pocket. "I didn't like the sound of my cue striking the cue ball. Always chalk your cue before every shot. That's what the chalk is there for."

The number four ball followed the three in the left side pocket. By now there were a few men watching and listening to my new friend. By association I was being noticed. "He's the Haines kid's friend," I heard one man whisper.

More men gathered around the table. One offered Bo a Coke. He graciously refused as he continued to clean off the table.

MacPherson came over to Bo. "That doesn't happen around here very often. We could use a man with your talent giving exhibitions. Maybe giving lessons, that sort of thing."

"Thanks for the opportunity, but I have to refuse your kind offer," Bo answered.

On the way back to my house, Bo got the bright idea that he should bring my mother a present. "I know just the thing," he said. "A chocolate bar. Everyone likes chocolate. It'll cheer up her day."

Bo was right. When we arrived home, he presented my mother with a Cadbury's Burnt Almond chocolate bar. She was delighted. Imagine a hobo bringing her a present. It was time for dinner. My mother asked Bo if he would like to join us. He politely refused. Later, I heard that he had cleaned the windows at Wong's Café and had eaten dinner there. I figured George Wong had paid my friend by serving him a meal. As a matter of fact, the few people who were there said that my new friend Bo had thanked George in Cantonese.

Next morning, I went uptown and there was Bo sitting on the steps of the Bluebell Inn. He had mowed the lawn and Tilly MacCarthy had given him a room for the night.

Antigonish was a small town. Reputations were made quickly. Here was a stranger who looked like a Greek god. Who else brought a chocolate bar to my mother? Who else cleared the table down at the pool hall and on the same day spoke Cantonese to George Wong? People were talking about this unusual stranger.

I had to find out what made Bo tick. With the frankness of youth I asked him, "Bo, how come you do everything so well and don't accept job offers? As far as I can tell, you can do anything."

"Well now, Maxie, not exactly anything, but gathering up things like money or cars doesn't interest me one bit. I don't want to be tied down. It's just as easy to be polite as it is to be bad-tempered."

I persisted, "Bo, why don't you stay in town? You could get a job easy."

"No, I'll be moving on this evening, hopping a freight train. After all, I'm a hobo."

True to his word, Bo moved on. As far as I know, he didn't say goodbye to anyone. As quietly as he had entered town, he left. He did promise to write me, but I didn't believe he ever would.

I had a hard time getting Bo out of my mind. Who was he? Where did he come from? More importantly, where did he go? My last question was answered that winter by Bo himself. He wrote me a long letter from Fort Lauderdale, Florida. In it, Bo explained that his father had been an engineer employed in China building a railroad. Bo had been born there and had spent the first nine years of his life in China. He went on to say that his reason for being in Fort Lauderdale was simple enough. Why stay in Canada during the winter? He always headed south when the cold weather came.

Bo went on to say that he had just finished negotiating with the town council of Fort Lauderdale to provide running water at the edge of the beach so that the men sleeping on the beach, like himself, could wash and shampoo their hair. Evidently, he was successful in having the city install a pipe at the edge of the beach. He also had a service club pull up each morning with soap and shampoo samples. Bo assured me that he would see me in Antigonish next July when he would cut my mother's kindling for the winter.

I read the letter over and over again. Bo, the man who looked like Tyrone Power, was an enigma. He had the ability to negotiate with officials of a major city, yet he apparently wanted nothing for himself.

It was difficult for me to get Bo out of my mind. What makes a man who was obviously intelligent and, in his own way, accomplished choose the life of a hobo? I found myself anxiously waiting for July to roll around.

During the first week in July the undertaker's son, Vince MacIsaac, was the first to spread the news that there had been a train wreck just outside of town. This was about the most unusual thing that had happened in town since our famous poltergeist, Mary Ellen the Spook, had made headlines years earlier. Vince reported that he had seen the wreck, which was a mass of twisted metal. Because it had been a freight train, there were no casualties other than a hobo who had been crushed under tons of metal. Vince said you could only see the poor hobo's arm if you looked straight down. The rest of the body was covered by the wreckage.

Everyone in town went to view the derailed train. Most peered straight down to see the arm of the lone casualty. I didn't want to look at any part of a dead body, but as we passed the spot where the hobo had been crushed, my friends all looked down. I did too. There, in small letters on the arm of the pinned man, were the words "Life Is for Living."

ROCKET RICHARD
AND TOE BLAKE

All us boys in town worshipped the players who performed in the National Hockey League. We carried their pictures in our pockets, firmly bound with an elastic band. A Gordie Howe was worth five or six lesser players. He was so big and strong in his bright red Detroit sweater. Then there was Ted Lindsay, who played on the same line as Howe. He was smaller, feisty, and simply wonderful.

We waited until Saturday night to hear Foster Hewitt broadcast the Leaf games from Toronto. Syl Apps was as well known in Antigonish as he was in Toronto. Naturally enough, his linemate, Gordie Drillon, held a special place in our hearts seeing as how he was a Maritime boy from Moncton, the lone NHL player from the Maritime provinces.

My mother didn't know anything about hockey but was in love with Syl Apps. She had his framed picture hanging in our kitchen. Each Sunday she would ask, "Did my Syl score last night?"

There were only six teams in the league and all the players were well-known personalities. We knew what they ate, all about their family lives, and what they did off the ice. Red Horner was the most loved and, at the same time, the most hated player in the league, depending on which side of the fence you frequented. In Toronto he was loved for his rough and ready style of play. Fans sent him gifts. In Chicago he received death threats. Before one game rumours circulated that he would be killed if he started a fight with a Chicago player. Instead, fans emptied a barrel of salted herring over his head as he lingered on the blue line to take a practice shot.

This was the environment a rookie named Maurice Richard entered when he joined the league. He displayed a passion and desire to score goals never witnessed before and rarely since. We didn't have television, but the pictures in the newspapers and magazines spoke volumes. There was fire in his eyes. From the blue line to the goal mouth he was unstoppable. I remember retiring my worn-out Leaf sweater for a special Montreal Canadiens number nine jersey. Montreal fans quickly christened him Rocket. If ever an athlete was aptly named, it was Maurice "Rocket" Richard.

That's why it was such a shock when James MacIntosh called me that scorching hot day in July and said, "Rocket Richard is at the Eastern Auto filling up on gas."

"Yeah, sure," I replied, "and my mother plays the outfield for the New York Yankees."

"I'm not kidding, Max, I'm telling you—the Rocket has stopped for gas at the Eastern Auto. Tom MacAdam is doing everything to stall him; you know, checking the oil, checking the tires, that sort of thing, so I can call the guys. If you want to see him, you better hurry. Tom is running out of things to check."

I took a deep breath and attempted to gather my senses. James had once called me and told me that Gregory Peck had just checked in to his mother's rooming house. I ran all the way over to the MacIntoshes', only to find James, his mother, and his sisters laughing their heads off.

"Imagine Gregory Peck not staying at the Royal George," James's mother managed to say in the midst of her loud, cackling laughter.

I wasn't going to be fooled again. There was no way Rocket Richard was in Antigonish filling his car up with gas. Next thing I'll hear was that Toe Blake was with him. Once bitten, twice shy. I wouldn't fall for James's prank for a second time.

Later that same day I strolled up Main Street. The news had spread like wildfire. Rocket Richard had stopped at the Eastern Auto for gas. Miracle of miracles, his linemate Toe Blake was with him. Tom MacAdam had produced a hockey stick from somewhere and both stars had signed the stick for him.

I was shocked—no, dumbfounded. These were not mere mortals. These were the stars Foster Hewitt described on Saturday nights while the entire country listened to his every word. Blake to Lach to Richard—he shoots, he scores!

I sighted Tom MacAdam serving gas at the Eastern Auto. "Where were you? James says he got you on the phone but you wouldn't come over."

"Never mind me, what did they say?"

Tom went on, "Rocket pulled up and said, 'Fill 'er up.' I recognized him right away. Then he turned and said, 'Care for a Coke, Toe?' That's when I knew the guy sitting in the passenger seat was Toe Blake."

"Then what?" I urged.

"They both got out of the car and took two Cokes out of the case and drank them in silence."

I glanced over at the case of Cokes. There were only two empty bottles, no doubt the ones that had been drained by the Rocket and Toe. "Can I see the stick, Tom?"

"Sure thing. Mr. Sears is showing it to the office staff right now but I'll get it in a few minutes."

Mr. Sears came out to the pumps carrying the hockey stick. There, big as life along the shaft were the names Rocket Richard and Toe Blake. I rubbed my hand over the signatures and closed my eyes. I could hear Foster Hewitt—"Blake to Lach to Richard. The Rocket shoots, he scores!"

Mr. Sears broke my reverie. "If it's all right with you, I'd like to hang this stick in the showroom." Tom agreed it was a great idea. That way everyone in town could drop in and see it.

I glanced at the two empty Coke bottles, the contents of which had been consumed by the Rocket and Toe. I blurted out, "As part of the deal, Mr. Sears, can I have those two empty Coke bottles?"

"Sure thing, Max, why don't you and Tom have a couple of full bottles on me? Call it rent for the use of the hockey stick."

"No thanks," I said, "I'll just take the empties."

Mr. Sears shrugged, figuring I just wanted to take the two empties to Pete Poirier's to get two cents apiece for them.

I had other ideas, which weren't lost for a minute on Tom MacAdam. "I'll end up with the stick and you'll get the empty Coke bottles, Max," he whispered.

Of course I had no idea which hockey star drank out of which bottle. Never mind, I had a fifty-fifty chance of being correct when I labelled the bottles.

That's why, over sixty years later, among old plaques and trophies, sit two empty Coke bottles. The one on the left is labelled Rocket Richard and the one on the right is labelled Toe Blake.

MISS DIXON

Recently, a Tampa, Florida, married schoolteacher, twenty-four-year-old Debra Lafave, was charged with having sex with a fourteen-year-old student.

When I was fourteen years old in Antigonish, my friends and I knew all about the sex act, but never thought it would actually happen to us. We made do with staring at the corset section of Eaton's catalogue, where the ladies had no heads, but had everything else intact. Our catalogue became so dog-eared that when my mother ordered anything from Eaton's, the catalogue popped open at the corset section. It was my understanding that Richie Neima was a brassiere man.

On rare but spectacular occasions, word would be spread around town by the younger male set that Mr. Gray was changing the female mannequin in the front window of Goodman's store. We went up and down Main Street pretending not to stare, so embarrassed were we to be seen looking at a nude mannequin. Daniel Francis broke his bike on purpose in front of Goodman's so that he could get a good view.

Sex was on our minds, no question about that. On Saturday afternoons we couldn't wait to see the latest Tarzan movie playing at the Capitol Theatre. I don't mean those sissy Tarzans who became popular years later. I mean Johnny Weissmuller and Maureen O'Sullivan. Weissmuller could give the Tarzan yell like no other actor before or since. Many of us boys imitated Tarzan. Some got the yell down cold. It wasn't unusual to see Hughie Martin MacDonald walking down Main Street beating his chest while giving the Tarzan yell, as if to gather around him his band of gorillas. Antigonish had many strange characters, but was singularly devoid of gorillas.

Johnny MacGillivray almost drowned killing an imaginary alligator in St. George's Bay. When rescued by some older boys, he explained, "The alligator attacked me. I didn't have my dagger with me, so I tried to put a piece of driftwood in his mouth like Tarzan does in the movies." Since alligators were not known to frequent the waters off Nova Scotia, the older boys shook their heads, admonished Johnny not to kill any more alligators, and left the dazed boy on the beach.

Ah, but it was Tarzan's companion, Jane, who was the main attraction for us fourteen-year-olds. Where else could you find a scantily clad beautiful woman swinging through the jungle on a vine? Certainly not in Antigonish, although we did have a rope hanging from a tree in the graveyard behind Cyril Reddy's garage.

In school Friday afternoons was storytime, when each student told a story of something of interest that had happened to him during the past week. After a Tarzan movie had played, a discussion of the movie occupied the entire afternoon. Jane was the focus of most boys' stories and conversation. Richie Neima asked our teacher, Rita Dixon, if Jane wore a brassiere. Miss Dixon, who often expressed the opinion that sex was a vile, despicable act put on earth to increase the population of animals and should not be practised by humans, replied, "Richie, did you get a feeling of Africa when you saw the movie?"

Our Richie, who would have loved to tell Miss Dixon exactly what he would like to feel, instead inquired for the second time, "Does Jane wear a brassiere?"

"We will have no more talk of Jane in this classroom," Miss Dixon declared.

"Does Eaton's deliver to Africa?" Richie wanted to know.

"That will be enough of that."

"Where did their son Boy come from?" Richie pursued.

"Boy came from Heaven, where all God's children come from."

Ever persistent, Richie continued, "Didn't Tarzan use a French safe?"

Miss Dixon turned red as a beet and attempted to change the subject: "Does anyone know the name of the largest river in Africa?"

Hughie MacDonald piped up, "You would never see Jane in a corset."

"Really, boys, is sex all you think of?" an exasperated Miss Dixon inquired.

Bobby Steele, a rather wimpy boy who had only been in town two years and was considered a rank outsider, answered,

"Pretty well all, except in the winter we think of hockey." This statement endeared him forever to his classmates.

Miss Dixon clung to hockey. "Exercise is an admirable recreation, one to be encouraged."

Billy Bennett popped up, "I don't think she wears a brassiere or anything else under that skimpy dress."

Jim MacIsaac volunteered, "Miss Dixon, does Jane have a change of clothing? It gets awfully hot and sweaty in the jungle. When does she change? I agree with Billy. I don't think she wears any underwear."

I should explain that the teller of the best, most interesting story on a Friday received a Jersey Milk chocolate bar. Usually Jackie MacNeil won the chocolate bar relating some animal story that took place on his parents' farm.

"Miss Dixon, you would have been surprised yourself if you had seen the cardinal crash against our kitchen window. Mother said the poor thing was badly injured, but could be brought back to perfect health with tender loving care. My father said it would be best to put the poor bird out of its misery. Mother won the argument, as she usually does, so we kept the bird for a few weeks. Finally, it was well enough to fly, so Mother decided just this past week to release it from its cage. You won't believe this, Miss Dixon, but that cardinal grew so fond of my mother that it refused to leave our yard. Mother tried shooing it away, but it always returned to her. That cardinal was in love with my mother and is there in our yard to this day."

"Jackie, that is a lovely story. You get the Jersey Milk chocolate bar this week."

Now everyone in the classroom except Miss Dixon knew that every word of Jackie's story was a barefaced lie. The teacher made quite a ceremony out of presenting the chocolate bar to Jackie, again remarking what a beautiful story he had told. "It related love, compassion, gratitude, all admirable qualities between a bird and a caring human being."

Just as she was winding down the presentation, Jackie inquired, "Do you think Tarzan and Jane do it in the jungle all the time when no one's looking?"

At 3:30 the bell rang, releasing us from our bondage. Miss Dixon's expression can only be compared to that of the Israelites when the Red Sea parted.

One thing's for sure—our Miss Dixon was no Debra Lafave of Tampa, Florida.

ALLISON KNEW ALL

You would have to call Allison Carruthers the best informed individual in Antigonish. You see, Allison was employed with the Maritime Telephone and Telegraph Company as a telephone operator. She listened in on every phone call in Antigonish while she was on duty. What's more, everyone in town knew that Allison listened to every word.

Allison had an understanding with her customers. She realized that they all attempted to cheat the Maritime Tel and Tel out of long-distance charges. After all, it was a large, impersonal monopoly. No one knew or cared who owned the telephone company, but everyone in town knew Allison. It must be remembered that in the fifties there were no cell phones, no answering machines, and no push-button phones. There were no fancy seven-digit numbers in those days. For example, our telephone number was simply 9. No glamour, but easy as all get-out to remember. In Antigonish, pretty well everyone spoke into a contraption that stuck out of the wall. They held a receiver to their ear. The tendency was to shout.

Allison had auxiliary duties in addition to attending to the switchboard. If you required the time of day, you had only to pick up the receiver and ask Allison. If daylight saving time clicked in, Allison would call several senior citizens to make sure they changed their clocks. She also was an earlier version of the weather person: "It's not raining right now, but it's pretty overcast. I wouldn't be a bit surprised to see rain by noon."

She also had the hockey scores when the Antigonish Bulldogs were playing out of town. You just had to pick up the phone to be brought up to date. "The Bulldogs are ahead of the Bearcats 3–1 midway through the third period. Charlie the Painter got two of our goals."

During the evening, Allison would become the tracer of lost persons, the telephone office being strategically located on the corner of Main and College Streets.

"Allison, my little Jimmy left a good twenty minutes ago to fetch the mail from the post office. He isn't home yet and I'm worried."

"Don't you worry, Mrs. Cameron. I can see him through the window heading down Main Street. He'll be home in a few minutes."

"You're an angel, Allison. What would we do without you?"

Allison was the source of all information: "Sobeys have a special on lamb chops, but they're going fast. Just thought I'd let you know."

Over and above her good works, Allison was a born gossip and there was plenty of gossip to go around in our town.

"Don't kid yourself, Dorothy MacDonald is not going to Boston to have a tumour removed. She is knocked up higher than a kite and is going to Boston to have her baby." Or "Fred Wells was on such a bender, he ended up in St. Martha's Hospital to dry out."

Allison knew everything that was going on in town. At night, when the switchboard wasn't busy, people dropped in on Allison to pass the time. Red Archie, the town cop who had to stay up late anyway, would drop in for a cup of Lipton tea each night at ten when he was through checking all the shop doors on Main Street. He and Allison spent many nights talking about the latest scandal circulating through town. If there wasn't one, they would invent one.

Allison started the great rumour that Wong's Café was serving cat meat in their chop suey. George Wong wondered why orders of other dishes remained brisk, but he was hardly serving any chop suey at all. When George discovered that Allison had made up the rumour, he spoke to her about his predicament. Allison, in her winsome way, admitted that she had made up the story to give everyone in town something to talk about. She told George not to worry, she would fix things up. Next thing he knew, he couldn't keep up with orders of chop suey. In fact, he was selling more than he had before Allison started her rumour. Curious, he asked Allison, "How did you fix the chop suey problem?"

"Easy," replied Allison. "I started the rumour that the government inspector had checked out your restaurant, particularly the chop suey, and found that you were using only the finest ingredients. The inspector himself said, 'Wong's chop suey is the finest to be found in all of Nova Scotia.'"

No question, Allison had a way about her. That's why it was such a shock when she was fired.

Jack Barton, one of the leading businessmen of the town, had attempted to make a long-distance call to Halifax at the ungodly hour of 1 A.M. Try as he might, he couldn't put his call through. He simply couldn't raise Allison. There are those who say he tried every ten minutes for an hour. Totally exasperated, he realized that Allison had fallen asleep at the switchboard. Normally quiet and placid, Jack Barton went down to his basement and emerged with an axe.

He drove the few minutes to the telephone office and knocked as loudly as he could on the door. He had no way of knowing that Allison had come directly to work from a dance in St. Andrew's. She was dog-tired, having danced every set played by Henry Snook and the Happy Go Luckies. She might have been a wee bit hungover as well.

Allison's personal life was of no importance to Jack. He knew only that if he wanted to make a long-distance call, he should be able to accomplish the task without travelling to the telephone office in his pyjamas.

Infuriated, Jack Barton took his axe to the telephone office door. Splinters flew off the old wooden door. Panels popped out, waking up Allison. She figured a suitor she had refused to dance with had gone berserk. Imagine her surprise when she saw Jack Barton sweating profusely in his pyjamas as he swung that axe.

Once the initial trauma of the situation had subsided, Jack explained that a shipment of salmon had gone bad in transit. He had an ad in the *Casket* featuring the salmon and had to have it in his store the next morning. The call to Halifax was important to him. It was to his supplier's home. If a new shipment of salmon could be dispatched immediately, it would reach Antigonish before his store opened. Allison sympathized with Mr. Barton, but could offer no excuses. She had simply fallen asleep.

Next morning, a crowd gathered to gaze at the splintered door. It was quite a sight. Because of its news value, word spread quickly that Allison had been asleep on the job. Somehow, this information got back to an official of Maritime Tel and Tel, who immediately fired Allison.

Everyone in town noticed the change immediately. When you called for the time of day, the new girl imported from Halifax responded in a most unAllisonlike way: "I'm sorry, that's not included in your telephone service."

"Any good specials in the *Casket* this week?"

"I'm sorry, that's not included in your telephone service."

"What time does the dance start in Malignant Cove this Saturday?"

"I'm sorry, that's not included in your telephone service."

Bill McGraw wanted to know how the Bulldogs were doing in Pictou. The Halifax import gave her stock answer, "I'm sorry, that's not included in your telephone service."

Bill told the Halifax import what she could do with her telephone service. When he completed his tirade, he added,

"What's more, I don't want your service. Come on over and take out the bloody phone."

Word spread that Bill had actually had his phone disconnected. Phil Jenson told everyone who would listen that he too was fed up and had his phone disconnected. So did Sam Dobbs. So did Huntley MacDonald.

The straw that broke the camel's back was the half-page ad that appeared in the *Casket*. The infuriated citizens didn't consult an advertising agency. They didn't confer with experts. They didn't hire a focus group. Nevertheless, their ad had the desired effect. It read in bold black letters, "WE WANT ALLISON BACK." To make the cheese more binding, it was signed by most of the leading citizens of the town. The first name on the ad was that of Jack Barton.

Evidently, an executive in an ivory tower at Maritime Tel and Tel heard that the good folks in the small town of Antigonish were having their phones disconnected. He looked into the matter and immediately solved the problem. He rehired Allison.

In no time the town returned to normal. Allison located missing children, gave the correct time, issued her weather forecasts, advised of the specials at Sobeys, and above all let some customers cheat the telephone company out of long-distance calls.

I must admit my mother was one of the chief cheaters. My sister Shirley lived in New Glasgow some forty miles away. She and her husband, Morty, visited my parents in Antigonish every weekend. Mother and Shirley had their own signals. If

Mother wanted Shirley to bring her a loaf of special brown bread unavailable in Antigonish, she would place a person-to-person long-distance call through Allison to a Mr. Brown at my sister's number in New Glasgow. Allison would say to Shirley, "I have a person-to-person call for a Mr. Brown." Shirley would reply, "I'm sorry, Mr. Brown has left for the day." That was the signal to bring a loaf of brown bread when she visited home that weekend.

Every week for years, the swindlers plied their trade. Allison used to wait for Mrs. Haines to place her person-to-person call. She knew very well it was a signal. All that changed when my mother got flustered and blurted out, "Allison, I want to speak to a Mr. Brown Bread at my daughter's house in New Glasgow."

Allison couldn't resist butting in, "Mrs. Haines, hold on please, Mr. Bread will be with you in a moment."

All was right with the world. Allison was back.

UNDER B 10

My mother was not a social butterfly. She and her lady friends had one main diversion, and that was to sit on our veranda on Court Street and watch the world go by. Well, not exactly the world. She could see Whistling Bill rise from his rocking chair and go uptown for cigarettes or Mr. Gunn might drop by selling his vegetables door to door.

Antigonish was a sleepy, peaceful town back in the forties and fifties. As a young boy, it appeared to me that my mother worked from dawn to dusk raising three children and keeping a husband in line.

On Sundays, it was a big deal when we all jumped into the cab of our filthy cattle truck for the five-mile drive to the Dingle for ice cream. It wasn't just a drive; it was an adventure. We stopped at Kell's farm, where my father would ask Mr. Kell, "How's Mackenzie King treating you, Angus?" The answer was always the same: "Can't complain, Alex."

Mr. Kell gave us kids apples, which grew in his own orchard. After patting the calves and watching the border collie rounding up the sheep, we all piled back into the cattle truck to continue our trip.

Once at the Dingle, we had decisions to make. Les Cummings, the owner, had three flavours of ice cream—strawberry, vanilla, and chocolate. We never knew about Rocky Road or any of those fancy flavours, nor did Les. My sisters always picked strawberry. I was a longtime chocolate man. My mother and father invariably chose vanilla.

Although we were a normal family on weekends, Monday morning changed all that. My mother did have one other diversion; call it an addiction if you will. She loved playing bingo.

She began preparing for Wednesday night's game first thing Monday morning. It didn't help matters when my father walked into the kitchen and shouted, "Under B, breakfast!"

Mother scurried about making breakfast for the five of us, all the while muttering, "Where did I put my cardboard markers?" She was, of course, referring to her little cut-out pieces of cardboard, which covered the elusive numbers on her bingo card. In those days Mother had graduated from using beans to cardboard, but had not yet been introduced to plastic disks or newfangled liquid markers.

To get the week off on the right foot, my father often hid my mother's cardboard markers. Around lunchtime they would miraculously appear on her plate as she sat down to eat. All she would say was, "Oh, you, you think you're funny." My father certainly did think he was funny. His little Monday morning caper threw him into a laughing jag, which we all thought might induce a heart attack.

Monday evening, Mother insisted that this coming Wednesday night she was going to study the bingo cards in advance. She knew very well that certain numbers were called all the time. My mother was a B 10 woman of long standing. She simply wouldn't accept a card unless it contained B 10. Another of Mother's favourites was I 19, but she wasn't nearly as adamant about I 19 as she was about B 10.

On Tuesday, our phone never stopped ringing. It was Check with the Ladies Day. What will I wear? My mother normally wasn't that meticulous about her appearance. She wore a simple housedress all week, held together with a safety pin situated between her breasts. Most times she was attired in an apron that had seen better days.

On Tuesdays Mother had a standing appointment to get her hair done at Anna's beauty parlour. Adorned with a blue rinse job, she paraded in front of my father and her three offspring looking for compliments. The three of us always said, "You look great, Mum." My father said, "It's very blue." My mother replied, "Oh, you, you think you're funny."

My mother commenced trying on different outfits on Wednesday morning. The phone rang all day. Other women in town were going through the same procedure. In the afternoon, my mother organized the attack on Celtic Hall.

Mrs. Wheton, Mrs. Fraser, and Mrs. Cameron congregated at our house for the ten-minute walk to the Celtic Hall. "Will that nasty Art Dunphy let me examine the cards? I'm definitely not playing unless I get one with B 10."

"I'm sure he will, Mrs. Haines," piped up Mrs. Cameron.

These women had been friends for over thirty years, but always called each other Mrs., never using first names. It has always been a puzzle to me as to why they would continue to address each other in this manner.

"If I don't get B 10, I'm complaining to the Knights of Columbus. They should know better than to stop us from picking our cards."

"I feel the same way, Mrs. Haines," Mrs. Fraser said, "only in my case it's G 52."

Art Dunphy, who donated his time on Wednesday nights to run the bingo game for the Knights of Columbus, saw the Court Street gang approaching. He whispered to Al MacDonald, "Here comes trouble."

Mrs. Fraser's opening volley: "I don't want to cause a fuss, but I want a card that has G 52 on it. Mrs. Haines wants B 10, Mrs. Wheton wants O 68, and Mrs. Cameron wants B 12." There was a line forming behind the Court Street gang. Big Al MacDonald said, "Ladies, could you stand aside for a moment so I can take care of these customers. Maybe Art can take care of you."

Art Dunphy's head snapped around. It wasn't fair. He got stuck with the Court Street gang last Wednesday. It was Al's turn. Resigning himself to the task at hand, Art figured he might as well start looking for the crazy dolls' favourite numbers.

"Here, Mrs. Haines, here's a nice clean card with B 10 on it."

"Thank you, Art." Mother whispered to Mrs. Wheton, "I told you Art is better than Al. Next week we'll request Art wait on us."

Next up Mrs. Fraser. It took a lot longer to locate G 52, but Art, displaying a great deal of patience, found it. He located O 68 for Mrs. Wheton as well. Mrs. Cameron's B 12 proved to be a stickler. Tiny beads of perspiration appeared on Art's forehead, until finally he practically screamed in elation when he came across a card containing the elusive B 12.

Equipped with their lucky cards, the Court Street gang got down to serious business. Seating was discussed at some length. Because this was the early-bird portion of the festivities there were many seats available. The ladies sat down at what they felt were the choicest seats in the hall. After settling in nicely, Mrs. Wheton thought she felt a slight draft and requested, in the sweetest tone possible, that they all move to a more moderate clime. Clutching their purses, cards, and cardboard markers, they transferred to another location. My mother thought they were now positioned too close to the main entrance. People coming in late would break their concentration and, God forbid, someone might accidentally brush against their cards, dislodging their markers. This latter remark sent a collective shiver through the Court Street gang. They moved for the third time to more secure seats.

Art Dunphy spun the metal cage until a number fell out. He called the number on a microphone, which had a distinct hum. The first number, B 8, drew a four-pronged sigh from the Court Street gang. For the first three games, not one of the gang came close to getting five in a row, as Art explained— vertical, horizontal, or diagonal. A rookie from Briely Brook shouted, "Can we put our marker on the free space now?"

Art, who would have liked to tell the lady just where she could put her marker, replied pleasantly enough, "You can place your marker on the free space at any time."

As an afterthought, Art switched from "vertical, horizontal, and diagonal" to "up and down, across, and from corner to corner."

The games proceeded nicely, but it was obvious by their facial expressions that, with every shout of "Bingo!" the Court Street gang would have gladly murdered the winners, who had pocketed a cool ten dollars each.

The more sophisticated games proved to be even more taxing on poor Art Dunphy. A straight T was the fourth game of the night. Art explained that the first row across the top and the N line had to be completed to make a straight T. It sounded simple enough, but not to the Briely Brook rookie. She inquired, "Does the free space count?"

"Yes," replied Art, suppressing an urge to kill, "it's a good idea to put your marker on the free space right now." That seemed to satisfy the Briely Brook rookie.

A lady from St. Andrews inquired about bathroom facilities, which the Court Street gang thought rather brazen, if not downright crude. Veterans that they were, they had all taken the necessary precautions before leaving our house.

The games proceeded until the highlight of the night—a full card for a cool one hundred dollars. Art called out the numbers. Depending on the luck of the players, he received comments such as "God bless you, Art Dunphy," or conversely, "It's fixed." The Court Street gang was in deep concentration, having purchased extra cards for the big game. My mother could handle eight cards with a certain degree of dexterity if no one spoke a word at her table. Her only comment came when Art shouted, "Under B 10." Mother exclaimed, "You see."

As the Court Street gang started filling their cards, they commenced to whisper to each other, "Mrs. Wheton has only three to go."

"Shush," said my mother.

"Under O 68!" Mrs. Wheton had only two to go. It didn't matter to the ladies from Court Street that almost everyone in the hall had only two or three spaces left to fill. Finally, Art called, "O 66." Someone shouted, "Bingo!" The voice was familiar. That rookie from Briely Brook had bingo, which infuriated the Court Street gang. Mrs. Cameron was the first to comment indignantly, "She won and she didn't even know how to play."

"Beginner's luck," my mother contributed.

The ladies of Antigonish had fun. They had just attended what to them was the equivalent of opening night of *My Fair Lady* on Broadway.

MY GREATEST DAY

I was in Grade Eight when I enjoyed the greatest thrill of my life.

When I was growing up in Antigonish, we had an outdoor rink at one end of Main Street right opposite Chisholm's Shoe Store. That's where Morrison High School played hockey against schools from nearby communities. As a Grade Eighter I worshipped the big boys who attended classes upstairs. Sometimes I would place my foot in the well-worn steps where Sandy Bray and James MacDonald had stepped. Don't get me wrong, these boys didn't have any particular scholastic abilities, but they were terrific hockey players. They consistently beat Mulgrave, New Glasgow, Pictou, and other schools within driving distance.

Our school colours were black and white. How I longed for the day when I would wear that jet-black jersey with the huge white M on the front. Actually, I used to dream about that day, possibly a couple of years in the future, and then only if I was good enough to make the team. Meanwhile, I attended every game our high school played. This was not exceptional, as every student in the school and many grown-ups attended every game.

There were no seats around our outdoor rink, but snow was piled up along the boards and that's where you stood for the entire game. As I remember, no one ever complained, although some games were played in below-zero temperatures.

J.P. MacInnis, who had the reddest face in the world, was the principal of the school. He was also the high school hockey coach. We called him Mr. MacInnis to his face, but he was known as J.P. throughout the school. I don't know if J.P. was a good coach or not, but everyone liked him because he had a quality that is currently out of fashion. He believed that hockey was a game that should be fun.

I was getting ready to go to the rink to play a pickup game on Saturday morning. We had to be off the ice by 11:30, allowing time to flood the rink for the high school game that was to take place at 12 noon. I was all set with my kit bag stuffed with hockey equipment. I carried my bag, stick, and skates up to the rink, where we played against each other for a couple of hours. At 11:30 we went into the clubhouse while the rink was being flooded. I took off my old Antigonish Bulldog sweater, which Terry MacGibbon had once given me, and was looking forward to watching the high school game.

Noon came and went without a sign of the Mulgrave team. At one o'clock J.P. made an announcement that due to a heavy snowstorm between Mulgrave and Antigonish, the Mulgrave team couldn't make it. The game was cancelled. Sandy Bray took off his uniform, as did some of the other high school players, and left the rink. J.P. said the rink would be devoted to public skating. At 1:45, he made a further announcement. The coach of the Mulgrave team had just phoned him from South River. They had somehow gotten through the storm and would be arriving in fifteen minutes.

J.P. looked around the clubhouse. He was short three of his very best players. They had changed and gone who knows where. As he scanned the room, he extracted three black-and-white high school sweaters from an equipment bag. He tossed one to Onnie MacDonald. With a growl, J.P. said, "Onnie, you'll play left wing on the third line." Another toss. "Chisholm, you'll be on the right wing with Onnie." Leo caught the sweater. "Haines," he said, as he threw me that sweater, "you'll centre the third line with Onnie and Leo."

I couldn't believe my ears. I felt the big white M on the black background. It felt smooth to the touch, smoother than fuzz on a peach. My fingers traced the M all the way around the edges. The thought hit me, crashing through my head like a throbbing pain. I was dreaming. My mother would soon shout that it was time to get up. When no one was looking, I pinched myself. No, this was real. I continued to trace the large white M with my fingers. It felt so good.

I could hear the Mulgrave team approaching the clubhouse. A few minutes later, I saw them through the open doorway as they walked from the clubhouse to the rink. God, they were big.

The game started. Onnie, Leo, and I sat on the bench. No

disappointment there. After all, we were the third line. The first period ended with the game scoreless. We filed into the clubhouse. J.P. gave us a pep talk. "You're doing fine. They are big boys, but you guys are better skaters. Hang in there, you're doing just fine."

I thought to myself, "Okay for you to say." Onnie, Leo, and I hadn't stepped on the ice for the whole period.

The second period started. Still our line sat on the bench. By now, there was quite a crowd, about two deep, surrounding the rink. About midway through the period, J.P. shouted, "Haines, third line, get out there!"

My heart flipped. I faced off in their end. The Mulgrave centreman looked like a giant. He towered over me. I looked up at his face. In those days we didn't wear helmets, so I could clearly see the wry grin as he noted my size. The ref dropped the puck, and the Mulgrave giant pushed me aside like a bulldozer getting rid of a tiny mud hill. Onnie looked at me and shrugged. So much for that faceoff. Leo got the puck once, but was bowled over before he could make a move. God, they were big! Our defence held them scoreless until about three-quarters of the way through the period, but their size took its toll. One of their forwards potted one. Thank you, Lord, for not having them score while our line was on the ice.

A few minutes later, we had a faceoff in their end. Onnie skated over to me. "Looks like you got the giant again," he said. "This time, just before he comes charging into you, slip the puck between his legs. I'll get it; he'll come after me and you'll be clear. I'll get the puck over to you somehow."

That's exactly the way it happened. The giant wasn't quick enough. I anticipated the drop and slipped the puck between his legs. Onnie pounced on the loose puck. The giant turned to take him out. Onnie flipped the puck to me. I'll never forget it. There was absolutely nothing between me and the goaltender. I raised my stick and slammed the puck with all my might. It was my first shot on net. It rose like a rocket into the top right-hand side of the net.

The memory of the ecstasy I felt at that precise moment has not left me in over half a century. Leo and Onnie skated over and gave me gentle taps on the backside with their sticks. So did other members of our team. I gave Onnie a tap with my stick. Our line skated off. J.P. said in a gruff voice, "Nice going, guys."

They say your life flashes before you just before you die. I thought that there could never be another moment like this. Not ever.

The second period ended 1–1. I couldn't help but notice that in the third period J.P. gave our line equal time. It got to be routine. As soon as the second line went off, we went on.

Disaster struck when Mulgrave scored, going ahead 2 to 1. Again, I thanked my lucky stars that our line wasn't on the ice.

With about ten minutes to go in the game, we had a faceoff in their end. Onnie skated over. "Let's do it again," he said.

"Onnie, there's no way the giant will let me pull the same thing."

"Give it a try. He's awkward, you can beat him to the draw."

I watched the ref's hand as he dropped the puck. This time the giant didn't hesitate. He ran into me before the puck hit the ice. He won the draw and Onnie was left looking for a puck that wasn't there.

The game was winding down, but we tied it up when our first line scored on a breakaway.

With about two minutes to go in the game, I had another faceoff in the opposing end, this time on the right-hand side of the rink. Leo skated over to me. "Onnie says to do the same thing that didn't work last time. The giant will figure that you won't try to outfox him with something that didn't work. I'll get the puck and feed it to you."

The giant glared. I watched the ref's hand. Just before the giant barrelled into me, I managed to squeeze the puck between his skates. Like a flash, Leo was on the puck. He flipped it to me. I looked up. There was only the goaltender to beat. I shot with every ounce of strength in my body. My heart and soul went into that shot. It travelled between the goalie's left arm and the goalpost. My line mates tapped me on the fanny with their sticks. I hugged them both.

With the score 3–2 in our favour, and the game winding down, Mulgrave pulled its goaltender for an extra forward. Leo promptly shot the puck into the empty net. We won 4–2.

I sat down in the clubhouse between Leo and Onnie. J.P. MacInnis walked over to us. "You boys hold on to those sweaters. You'll need them for the next game."

It was the happiest day of my life.

TRIAL OF THE CENTURY

The Scopes Trial of 1925, when William Jennings Bryan and Clarence Darrow argued about the validity of evolution, was said to be the trial of the century. In recent years, we endured the O.J. Simpson trial, wherein a famous ex-football player stood accused of murdering his wife and her friend. It too was deemed to be the trial of the century.

While these trials were certainly noteworthy, none ever caused as much excitement in Antigonish as my father's trial for purchasing raw wool illegally. Right off the top, I should explain that my father had moved to Antigonish in 1920. As I mentioned earlier, he retained a thick Eastern European accent from his native Lithuania. As the only Jew in a predominantly Roman Catholic community, he remained a bit of a novelty while gradually gaining the respect of his neighbours and the community in general.

For three months during the wool-shearing season, my father purchased wool from local farmers throughout several neighbouring counties in Nova Scotia. He sold the wool to Stanfield's Ltd., some eighty miles away in Truro, Nova Scotia.

For those three months of the year, his business was a simple one. He drove up to the farmer's yard, weighed the wool on a balance scale, and paid the farmer in cash. Everyone was happy. When he accumulated a truckload of wool in Antigonish, he would drive to Truro and sell the wool to Stanfield's.

One fine day my father received an official-looking letter from the province of Nova Scotia. It stated that there was a new agency called the Nova Scotia Wool Marketing Board. It was making an attempt to introduce orderly marketing, at the same time ensuring that the wool-growing farmer would receive a fair and equitable price for his wool. In essence, the letter stated that it would be illegal for my father to purchase wool.

Alex Haines had been buying wool for over twenty-five years, and now he was being told he had thirty days to "cease and desist" from purchasing wool. My father didn't take the directive well. He squashed out his Sweet Caporal cigarette in an ashtray given to him by Roger Kerton, MP, during the previous federal election. Over the objections of my mother, he went out to the barn, loaded the Fargo with wool, and drove it up Main Street to the post office. There he parked for all the world to see that he was still in the business of buying wool. When Len MacDonald strolled by, he was called over to the truck. My father explained what had happened. Len thought the government should be ashamed of itself for depriving a citizen of making a living. Dinny Stewart stuck his head in the Fargo, bummed a Sweet Cap, and agreed wholeheartedly with my father. It appeared that most of the town figured my father had received a raw deal.

Two weeks later, Sergeant Vic Staples of the RCMP called at our house on Court Street. He was accompanied by Constable Will MacGraw. These two officers made up the entire RCMP detachment in our town. Vic, who knew my father well, sheepishly advised him that he was causing a disturbance by parking his Fargo loaded with wool in front of the post office each day. At the same time, Vic advised my father that in a matter of two weeks he would be breaking the law if he continued to purchase wool.

My mother put on the tea kettle and made a few of her famous sandwiches, which consisted of tomatoes from the garden, lettuce from the garden, and cucumbers from the garden, all swimming in Kraft mayonnaise between two slices of Ben's bread. She knew Sergeant Vic could never resist her sandwiches. My mother attempted to sweet-talk Sergeant Vic into relenting, but the officer was adamant. Alex had to stop buying wool and had only two weeks to comply with the law. My father excused himself from the table, explaining that he had to load the Fargo with wool and park it in front of the post office.

At the end of the month, Sergeant Vic Staples knocked on our door. Mother asked Vic if he would care for a sandwich, maybe a cup of tea. Staples was as humble as an RCMP officer could be. He refused the sandwich and explained that my father's thirty-day grace period was up. If he didn't stop buying wool, he would be served with a subpoena, which would necessitate him standing trial. My father excused himself. He had to load the Fargo and park it in front of the post office.

Two weeks passed. My father appeared in front of Judge Neil MacLean, who was a close personal friend. The judge explained that there would be a delay. It seems that the two local Crown prosecutors, Will MacPherson and Donald MacDonald, had refused to prosecute. Two years earlier, Will had purchased my father's old truck and felt that there would be a conflict of interest. Donald, fresh out of Dalhousie University's law school, received a measure of fame when his pregnant mother had been rushed to St. Martha's Hospital by none other than Alex Haines when she gave birth to him. No way these two prosecutors would act against a man who had lived in town since before they were born. Judge MacLean informed the few people present in the courthouse that he would be importing an able prosecutor from New Glasgow, forty miles away.

That evening, Judge MacLean visited us at home. Mother asked if he would care for a sandwich, maybe a spot of tea. The judge smiled gently and confessed that he would appreciate one, but to please go easy on the Kraft mayonnaise. The judge, whose brother in Cape Breton had sold wool to my father for over two decades, was visibly embarrassed. There wasn't that much crime in Antigonish. Oh sure, when intoxicated, the Sharp brothers would tear off the RCMP sign from the door of the Somers Building, where Vic Staples had his office. The lone municipal cop, Red Archie MacGillivray, from time to time would take Lauchie Cheddar Cheese to jail to sleep it off.

Lauchie, whose last name was MacDonald, had the peculiar nickname of Cheddar Cheese because his family made a precarious living producing and selling barley cheddar cheese. There were many Lauchie MacDonalds in town, each with a distinctive nickname, usually derived from the family's occupation or a physical oddity. For example, there was Lauchie the Painter, so named because his entire family were house painters. Hughie the Rooster was easy to figure out once you saw his neck bobbing up and down. Charlie One Leg's nickname is so obvious it doesn't require explanation.

Judge MacLean sat at our kitchen table. The grey-haired, immaculately dressed jurist broached the subject of my father's trial. As he munched on a sandwich, he said in an apologetic voice, "You know, Alex, you can't win. The law is the law." My father replied, "Judge, would it be too late to load the truck with wool and park it outside the post office with the lights on?" Judge MacLean's eyes lit up as he replied, "I don't think it's too late. That would show the bastards."

On the way to the truck my father suggested they take a slight detour to the old barn at the back of the property. "The wool is all stored there," my father explained. Once in the old dilapidated barn, my father reached up to the ceiling and extracted a bottle of Demerara Black Diamond rum from the overhead shelf. "Here, Judge, you take the first swig."

Judge MacLean took a healthy gulp, wiped the neck of the bottle clean with his hand, and passed it back to my father, who duplicated the judge's feat. I don't know how long that bottle was passed back and forth, but legend has it that next morning the empty bottle was found lying on a bed of spread-out salted cowhides.

My father, assisted by the judge, loaded the Fargo with wool. Feeling that my father had had too much to drink, the judge elicited the aid of Whistling Bill Fraser to drive the truck up to the post office. For as long as anyone could remember, Whistling Bill had spent his time sitting in a rocking chair on his brother-in-law Angus Fraser's veranda, rocking and whistling. That's all he did, all day long.

Alex and the judge went into the post office and stared out the window at the curious crowd gathering around my father's truck. The judge chuckled. "That will show the bastards," he said.

Next day, Alex Haines's trial began. Judge Neil MacLean presided. Both judge and defendant appeared a bit peaked. It was a hot day. The old courthouse, with its pillared exterior, looked great from the outside. Inside, it left quite a bit to be desired. The floors squeaked so badly that any movement sounded like a horse and wagon going up a gravel road. The balcony circling the interior of the courtroom was usually empty. There simply was no interest in hearing how the Sharp brothers had torn down the RCMP sign for the umpteenth time. Judge MacLean, in his wisdom, always ruled that the boys had to purchase and install a new sign. Since everyone knew the outcome of every case well in advance, there didn't seem any point in spending a hot day in the old courthouse.

My father's trial was different right from the beginning. A well-founded rumour had spread throughout town that an outsider with a strange-sounding name had checked into the Royal George Hotel. Would you believe Alphonse Dornhoffer? Who ever heard of such a name? He told people that he was a lawyer and had come to rake some hick named Alex Haines over the coals. The whole thing should take no more than an afternoon.

Alphonse Dornhoffer was wrong.

Gregor Myette's brother in nearby Tracadie had sold his wool to my father for as long as he had raised sheep. Gregor, who was driver, handyman, and bellboy at the Royal George, called his brother Fred and told him about the impending trial. Fred expressed the opinion that no one needed any more government interference in their daily lives. He had always been satisfied selling wool to Alex. In fact, it was far better to get cash on the barrelhead rather than wait for a government cheque from some agency no one had ever heard about. Fred told other farmers. All agreed they would attend the trial.

The old courthouse was packed. We lived kitty-corner from the courthouse. Adjoining our house was a field, which my mother called our lawn. That's where she set up a card table to serve her sandwiches and homemade ice-cold lemonade. Everyone going into the courthouse was urged to try a sandwich and a swig of mother's lemonade. Many accepted her generosity. While they wolfed down a sandwich, she emphasized that the tomatoes, lettuce, and cucumbers were from her own garden. The only "boughten" items that found their way into the sandwiches were the Kraft mayonnaise and Ben's bread. Those who didn't gulp down a sandwich on the way into the courthouse assured her that they would drop by on the way out.

The necessary formalities were dispensed with rather speedily by Judge MacLean. Dornhoffer rose from the prosecutor's chair. Whispers spread throughout the courtroom. He was wearing cufflinks that shone like jewels. Right away, no one liked Dornhoffer. He called my father to take the stand. Unlike Dornhoffer with his midnight-blue fancy Samuelsohn suit and shiny cufflinks, my father was dressed in baggy pants set off by a Nova Scotia plaid shirt. He wore his maroon braces outside his shirt, as always.

Dornhoffer asked, "How much did you pay the farmers this season for their wool?"

My father replied, "Ninety-five cents a pound."

Dornhoffer smiled as he asked, "And how much does Stanfield's pay you for the wool for which you paid ninety-five cents a pound?"

"A dollar and ten cents a pound."

You would think Dornhoffer had just received a guilty verdict in the Leopold and Loeb case. He sort of bounded toward the witness stand. "Mr. Haines, don't you think that's an exorbitant profit? After all, you didn't improve the wool. Fact is, you didn't do anything to the wool."

My father, who was acting as his own counsel, listened attentively before replying in broken English, "Young man from New Glasgow, how did you get here?"

Dornhoffer looked at Judge MacLean in a pleading sort of way. The judge said rather briskly, "Answer Alex's question."

Dornhoffer replied, "I drove here."

"And what did you put in your gas tank?"

Dornhoffer, realizing he had stepped into a hornet's nest, responded, "Gas."

"Now, young fellow from New Glasgow, that's called expenses. When you submit your bill for prosecuting outside your county, you'll put in for travel expenses, which will include your stay at the Royal George Hotel. I happen to know that you didn't stay at the Bluebell Inn. So you see, when I pay ninety-five cents and receive a dollar ten, I'm paying a fair price, taking into account my gas, my time, and other expenses, just like you do."

At this point, a slight cheer went up from the gallery. Judge MacLean brought down his gavel, which caused a small cloud of dust to rise from his desk. He shouted, "Order!"

The judge felt that it was a good time to bring proceedings to a close for the day. It was stifling hot in the old courthouse. Besides, he wanted to stop off at our lawn and sample a few of my mother's sandwiches. By now, mother's bleeding hearts had been trampled into oblivion, so popular were her sandwiches. Selected guests, such as Judge MacLean and RCMP Officer Vic Staples, were sneaked into the barn, where they partook of somewhat more substantial liquid refreshment than lemonade.

That night we received a long-distance phone call from my sister Shirley, who lived in New Glasgow. Apparently, Shirley and her husband, Morty, were close friends of Alphonse Dornhoffer and his wife, Cynthia. Besides, the Dornhoffers were patients of Morty's, who was a dentist. Over and above socializing with each other, Shirley and Cynthia worked together at the hospital auxiliary. She emphasized, "Cynthia and I sell peanuts each year for the Rotary Club. She is a dear friend. Daddy, what are you doing making a fool of Alphonse down there in Antigonish? Please cut it out. Obey the law. Just stop buying wool and the whole thing will go away. Hold on a minute, Daddy, Morty wants to speak to you."

Before my father could utter a word, Dr. Star was on the phone. "Alex," he said. He always called my father Alex. "You don't know what trouble you've caused me. Dornhoffer called me this evening. He's staying at the Royal George. They told him there was something wrong in the kitchen and he could grab a bite downtown at Wong's Café. He even suspects he's got the only room in the hotel without a window. Please stop buying wool."

My father's face and bald head turned cherry red. He shouted into the wall phone that Morty should stick to pulling teeth and that Shirley should find a new partner in her peanut-selling fundraising efforts for the Rotary Club. As sure as God made little green apples, he was going to buy wool. He had to excuse himself. It was time to load the Fargo and park it in front of the post office.

Next day, my mother talked my father into wearing a white shirt. Her attempt to replace his suspenders with a belt failed miserably. Besides, she was a busy woman in her own right. Realizing that the demand for her sandwiches outstripped her ability to keep up, she precut the tomatoes, cucumbers, and lettuce. Two card tables were set up well in advance of the crowd, who now knew from experience that they could have sandwiches and lemonade both before and after the proceedings at the courthouse. Our next door neighbour, Mrs. Cameron, added a classy touch when she donated a package of serviettes.

Judge MacLean brought the proceedings to order. Dornhoffer didn't look quite as spiffy as he had the previous day. Conversely, my father looked rather suave in his white shirt if you overlooked the baggy pants and maroon suspenders. Dornhoffer questioned Phil MacDoubie, who had sold his wool to my father for at least a dozen years. Dornhoffer felt this to be a wise move because he had heard that Phil and my father had had words. Evidently, my father had attempted to turn his truck in Phil's driveway and had ended up in a ditch. When he was asked for help in extracting the Fargo from the ditch, Phil explained that a heifer had taken seriously sick and he couldn't leave the animal's side. Phil had been quick to add that as soon as he was through attending to the heifer he would give my father a hand. This didn't sit well with my father and the two men had words. Dornhoffer had heard of the dispute and figured if anyone would say a derogatory word about my father, it would be Phil MacDoubie.

Dornhoffer asked Phil, "Did you ever sell wool to the defendant?"

Phil replied, "Yes, sir, for over fifteen years."

"Did you usually get a fair price?"

"More than fair," came the reply.

Dornhoffer figured he could get a rise if he homed in on the day Phil and Alex had argued. "Did you not refuse to give

Mr. Haines a helping hand when his truck became stuck in your yard?"

"Yes, sir, my heifer was sick and my wife and I were rubbing him down in the barn when Alex asked me to help him out. I refused and we had words, but later Alex showed up with the vet, Archie Campbell. He apologized to me for his outburst. If Alex and the vet hadn't shown, we would have lost that heifer. Why, Alex even brought along a jar of chicken soup that his wife made. Salt of the earth, that Alex Haines."

Dornhoffer shook his head. So much for farmers. He recalled my father to the stand. In an attempt to be aggressive, he asked, "Do you know that buying wool is not legal?"

The question proved to be a mistake. In his heavy accent, Alex replied, "Young man from New Glasgow, I left Lithuania in 1913 in order not to be killed by the Czar of Russia, who was carrying out pogroms against people of my faith."

Dornhoffer interrupted, "Mr. Haines, keep in mind you are the defendant. I am the prosecutor."

Judge MacLean intervened, "Don't talk to Alex like that."

Alex was on a roll. He continued, "I married a Canadian girl from Chatham, New Brunswick, and settled in this town. I raised three children, worked hard at anything that would provide me with a living. I paid my taxes and became a member of this community. Above all, I love this country for allowing me to make a living and now, after all these years, a letter in the mail tells me I can no longer buy wool from farmers who want to sell their wool to me. Tell me, young man from New Glasgow, is that fair?"

Dornhoffer could only cough.

At that precise moment, a half-full bottle of Demerara rum, which had been passed around the balcony, fell to the floor of the old courthouse. It rolled across the floor as its contents poured out. There was a hushed silence in the courtroom. Later, a rumour spread around town that Archie MacDonald had thrown the bottle at Dornhoffer's head, but that wasn't true. Anyone who knew Archie was well aware that he would never sacrifice a half-bottle of rum if his life depended on it. The rum incident, as it came to be known, was a pure and simple accident. However, it did serve a purpose. The judge thought it would be a good time to adjourn for the day.

Next day, Dornhoffer took off his suit jacket. A buzz went through the courtroom. He wasn't wearing his fancy cufflinks. The judge, assuming that my father would take the stand to resume his lecture on economics as well as the Czarist regime of Russia, assumed wrong. Dornhoffer was having nothing to do with Alex Haines. Instead, he summed up by reiterating that the government was attempting to institute orderly marketing to the wool industry much as it had done with the dairy industry.

Alex rested his case with the statement that he could go on all day giving reasons why it wasn't fair to him or the farmers for him not to be able to purchase their wool.

Judge MacLean suggested that the defendant, Dornhoffer, and Sergeant Vic Staples retire to his chambers. Once behind closed doors, the judge told Alex that he was plainly and simply guilty as hell. Did everyone agree that a ten-dollar fine or ten days in jail would be a fair sentence? Dornhoffer, who by this time felt that he had died and gone straight to hell, readily agreed. Vic Staples said, "Fair enough." The judge explained that Alex should pay the fine.

None of the gathering anticipated my father's response. "I'll take the ten days in jail, Judge." Vic Staples coughed. Dornhoffer rolled his eyes.

"Now, Alex, don't be stubborn. Pay the ten dollars and that's the end of this whole messy business."

"I won't pay one cent and that's final. I didn't come to this country to pay fines. All I want is the right to make a living."

Everyone in Judge MacLean's chambers was frustrated. Here was an established member of the community willing to go to jail to prove a point rather than pay ten lousy dollars.

Exasperated, the judge said in no more than a whisper, "Alex, if I pay the fine, would that suit you?"

To which my father replied, "What you do with your money, Judge, is your own business."

And that's how my father's trial ended. Judge MacLean announced his guilty verdict in court, adding that Alex Haines had been fined ten dollars. Most of the assorted spectators, as well as the judge and Sergeant Vic, made their way to Mother's lawn, where they had sandwiches and lemonade.

For a while my father basked in the congratulations of his friends and neighbours. Then he excused himself. He had to load his Fargo with wool and park it in front of the post office.

MY LITTLE NIECE PHYLLIS

In the summer of 1947 there were those of us who followed big league baseball with a passion. The favourite teams in Antigonish were the Brooklyn Dodgers and, for those poor souls who were fans of the American League, the Boston Red Sox. Then, as now, everyone hated the Yankees.

My four-year-old niece, Phyllis, was not particularly interested in baseball, but all that was to change during the dog days of that long, hot summer.

Although I was twelve years older than Phyllis, she and I became fast friends. That kid loved ice cream. I played a game with her. If I asked her who was the handsomest, most charming boy in town, she would look up at me, smile, and say without hesitation, "Uncle Max." I rewarded her with a nickel and we both went uptown to Sam Thompson's store for a scoop of ice cream.

Sam, who knew the score, would greet Phyllis with a degree of fanfare. "Have a seat, Phyllis," he would say as she shimmied up a barstool. "I see you brought the handsomest, most charming boy in town along with you today."

"I'll take chocolate, please," Phyllis replied, as she always did.

"For you, a scoop of crushed nuts on the top," responded Sam, as he always did.

Phyllis and I watched as Sam, with a practised eye, scooped up a heaping portion of chocolate ice cream in slow motion. He then took an elongated spoon and dipped it into a deep canister of crushed nuts. Extracting the overflowing spoon of nuts, he ceremoniously sprinkled them on top of Phyllis's ice cream. He repeated the entire procedure for me, but with far less flourish.

We would walk down Main Street devouring our ice cream before it melted in the cone. I never tired of asking Phyllis the question and treating her to that ice cream. She loved it so.

Back at our house on Court Street, I began to think of Phyllis's capacity to remember facts and repeat them on command. After all, if she could remember who was the handsomest, most charming boy in town she could remember anything.

I decided to feed Phyllis a few facts and see if she could repeat them. The only question I could think of on the spur of the moment was "Who plays shortstop for the Brooklyn Dodgers?" I gave her the answer—Pee Wee Reese. After several rehearsals, Phyllis could tell me not only that Pee Wee Reese played shortstop, but also that Spider Jorgensen played third base.

I thought it was quite remarkable that, when asked the question "Who plays shortstop and who plays third base for Brooklyn?" this four-year-old girl could rattle off their names. Phyllis even became adept at reversing the procedure. "What positions do Pee Wee Reese and Spider Jorgensen play for the Brooklyn Dodgers?" elicited the immediate response, "Shortstop and third base."

I tried out Phyllis's rare talent for my sister Lukey. Phyllis gave the correct answers. Then she embarrassed me by blurting out, "Can I have a nickel for an ice cream?" Right then and there I learned that Phyllis would perform only if she was paid off. Secretly, I was very proud of my little niece, but there was more to come.

Lukey went uptown and told her buddy, Mary Oicle, that she had a remarkable little niece who knew all there was to know about big league baseball. Mary insisted on seeing the performance for herself. She returned to our house, where Phyllis and I were playing marbles. Mary sidled up to Phyllis and asked, "Who plays second base for the Brooklyn Dodgers?" Phyllis looked at me before replying, "I don't know." Then, cute as a button in the sunsuit my mother had purchased from Eaton's catalogue, she returned to our game of marbles. Mary muttered, "Some genius."

I resolved that Phyllis would never let me down again. Constantly I repeated the entire lineup of that season's Brooklyn Dodgers. It's a wonder Phyllis didn't go into ice cream coma. Each session was interrupted by a trip to Sam Thompson's for ice cream. Over and over I drilled her on the names and positions of each player. It took weeks. Finally Phyllis could rattle off the Brooklyn roster: first base, Jackie Robinson; second base, Eddie Stankey; shortstop, Pee Wee

Reese; third base, Spider Jorgensen; catcher, Bruce Edwards; outfielders, Carl Furillo, Pete Reiser, Dixie Walker. Star pitchers were Ralph Branka and Joe Hatten. Main reliever was Hugh Casey.

In frustration, Phyllis sometimes squealed on me to my mother. "Uncle Max won't leave me alone until I recite all the players on the Brooklyn Dodgers," she whined. On those occasions my mother would admonish me, pointing out that baseball was for sissies. "Why don't you teach Phyllis the names of the Toronto Maple Leafs?" She would point to the framed picture of Syl Apps on our kitchen wall and say, "Now there's a player."

Despite our trials and tribulations, as the summer wore on Phyllis managed to memorize every player on the team and his position. To add a little colour to her recitation I cajoled interrogators to inquire, "What's Pete Reiser's nickname?" Phyllis would pipe up, "Pistol Pete." To add even more entertainment value to Phyllis's God-given talent, she was force-fed vignettes of information about the players. Phyllis knew that Pistol Pete Reiser had the unfortunate habit of running into the outfield wall at Ebbets Field.

Sometimes when members of our immediate family quizzed Phyllis, she would interrupt the proceedings by tugging on my leg and whispering, "Do I get another ice cream cone if I answer another one?" In time I convinced her that her sessions were all-inclusive. It was one session, one ice cream cone; no more, no less. Later this rule became flexible in that for certain non-family members she would insist on a second ice cream cone, and, on two separate occasions that I can distinctly recall, she insisted on a third cone before proceeding with answers. All of this took place before Phyllis turned professional and I became her official business manager.

Phyllis's fame as an expert on the Brooklyn Dodgers spread after I took her to the Celtic Hall Pool Room. The boys were half-listening to a game on the radio as they shot pool. Tom MacAdam piped up, "That Hugh Casey is one of the finest starters on the Brooklyn team." Phyllis corrected him with a terse response that could just be heard over Red Barber describing the game: "Hugh Casey is a relief pitcher."

Tom glared. "Little girl, are you trying to tell me that I don't know the Brooklyn Dodgers?"

"Hugh Casey is a relief pitcher," was the only reply.

"Well, now, little girl, I'll give you a shiny new quarter if you can prove to me that Hugh Casey is a relief pitcher." Just then Red Barber intoned, direct from Ebbets Field, "Manager Stoten is bringing in his ace relief pitcher, Hugh Casey."

I'll say this for Tom; he was a good loser. He picked up Phyllis and sat her upright on a pool table, and with much fanfare presented her with a quarter. "Little girl, can you tell me the name of a starting pitcher with the Dodgers?" Phyllis said, "Ralph Branka."

The boys stopped shooting pool. Phyllis was the centre of attention. I told Tom to stop calling her "little girl"; her name was Phyllis.

"I'll give you a dollar if you can name the entire infield of the Dodgers."

Phyllis waited until Tom produced the dollar bill and tossed it on the table. My niece, whom I was learning was a born ham, didn't hesitate. "Jackie Robinson, Eddie Stankey, Pee Wee Reese, and Spider Jorgensen. Do you want the catcher, too?" she inquired, as she scooped up that dollar bill, which in Phyllis's mind represented an abundance of ice cream cones at Sam Thompson's.

Tom and the boys were astounded. All of them considered themselves baseball experts. To have a child, and a girl at that, correct them about their favourite team was akin to the miracle of the loaves and fishes.

I had a hard time dragging Phyllis out of the pool hall. Everyone wanted to question her about the Dodgers. When Johnny "Big Nose" Cameron declared that it was worth five dollars to him if she could tell him the entire starting lineup of the Dodgers, I knew my little niece and I were on to something big.

We left the pool hall and returned home. There was much studying and memorizing to be done. I grilled Phyllis for weeks. It wasn't enough for her to know the names and positions. She required auxiliary information.

Up to the poolroom we traipsed. Phyllis gave my hand a tug as we passed Sam Thompson's. "There'll be plenty of time for ice cream on the way home," I explained.

Phyllis could sense what was to come. I felt she secretly enjoyed every minute of being the centre of attention. In particular, I knew she liked the ice cream part.

As soon as we entered the pool hall the players stopped in mid-game. Phyllis had become more interesting than shooting pool. Tom MacAdam lifted Phyllis up onto her table and started firing questions. She wouldn't open her mouth until someone threw a nickel on the table. Her uncle had taught her well. As soon as that nickel hit the green felt, Phyllis rhymed off the correct answers to every question.

As the summer came to a close, it was not unusual for me to receive a phone call from the pool hall. Invariably, the caller inquired, "What time is Phyllis coming over?" To add excitement to what had become a local phenomenon, the Dodgers won the National League pennant and were scheduled to play the despised New York Yankees in the World Series.

This turn of events gave rise to more work for me and Phyllis. After the Dodgers won the pennant, she and I practically hibernated to study every conceivable question she might be asked. Good thing, too. The guys had taken it upon themselves to dredge up oddball questions to ask my little genius niece. "What was Hugh Casey's record this season?" "Casey won ten, lost four, and had eighteen saves." The boys shook their heads. One said, "Phyllis, you know more about the Dodgers than Red Barber." I knew very well who Red Barber was, but Phyllis didn't know or care about him. She was enduring all the studying, as well as the smoke-shrouded poolroom, strictly for the cash, which we had agreed in advance would go toward one thing and one thing only—ice cream.

The men in the pool hall loved Phyllis. As soon as they saw her, they would throw questions at her about the Dodgers before she could scoop up those nickels. "Hey, Phyllis, what's Branka's ERA?" "2.67." "Hey, Phyllis, what was the Dodgers' record this year?" "Ninety-four wins, sixty losses." For such rapid-fire questions, Phyllis gathered up the nickels, fully realizing that in her haste to answer questions she might be out an ice cream or two.

It was Tom MacAdam who started it that rainy fall afternoon by side-betting Phyllis's talent. He plunked down a five-dollar bill on the pool table with the boisterous claim, "I've got a Dodger question that will stump Phyllis. Have I any takers?" Bill "Shaky" Fraser piped up, "You're covered," as he tossed a fiver onto the table.

"Anyone else want to bet?" Tom asked. "I'll take all bets that I can stump Phyllis." A few guys threw dollar bills on the table. Tom said, "I'll cover them all." He threw a nickel on the table for Phyllis. "Okay, Phyllis, how old is Ralph Branka?" My niece smiled. We had gone over Branka's age because he was so very young to have won twenty-one games. Phyllis practically shouted, "Twenty-one years old!"

Tom looked crestfallen, but he wasn't through. He tossed a twenty-dollar bill on the table with the exclamation that he thought he could still stump Phyllis. Shaky, who had just picked up two fives off the table, quickly said, "You're covered," as he placed his twenty on the table. Several other men put down fives or ones. Tom covered all the bets. There must have been seventy-five dollars on that pool table, which was the equivalent of a few weeks' pay for several of the men in the poolroom that day.

I was only a kid, but I realized what Tom was up to. He knew very well Phyllis would know Branka's age. It was in all the papers and was featured on the radio. He was setting up his friends for a bigger score. Tom was ready to strike. "Now, Phyllis, what is the date of Ralph Branka's birthday?" Phyllis did the best she could. "Nineteen twenty-six," she replied. "No, I want the month and day," Tom responded. Big Nose bellowed, "That's not fair. How could the kid know the birthday of every guy on the Dodger team?" Someone else said, "It's a set-up. Tom's a crook." Meanwhile, Tom gathered up all the bills from the table and tossed Phyllis a shiny quarter as he left the poolroom to a chorus of catcalls.

What happened to all the characters in that Brooklyn Dodgers' summer?

Jackie Robinson, the team's first baseman, is one of the most famous of all baseball players. He broke the colour barrier, paving the way for black ballplayers to perform in the big leagues. Robinson passed away in 1972.

Tom MacAdam later became a successful businessman in New York City.

Ralph Branka went on to have an outstanding career in baseball. Unfortunately he is best remembered for one pitch, which he served up to Bobby Thompson in the ninth inning of a playoff game in 1951. Thompson hit a home run, which gave the New York Giants the National League pennant.

The Brooklyn Dodgers moved to Los Angeles in 1958 to become the Los Angeles Dodgers, which they are to this day.

My niece Phyllis went on to become a registered nurse. She lives in Montreal and has two adult children and three grand-children. I see her every time I'm in that city. Invariably, she brings up the summer of 1947: "Uncle Max, remember when you taught me all about the Brooklyn Dodgers?"

A PLEASANT DRIVE
TO MONCTON

When I was sixteen I received my driver's licence, which wasn't much of a feat in the Antigonish of the 1940s. Charlie Chisholm merely said, "I've seen you driving for years. Here's your licence." I drove away from his office in my father's Fargo truck with the filthy cattle rack on the back.

My father's main means of making a living was buying calves from farmers and selling them to either Canada Packers in Montreal or Swifts of Canada in Moncton, New Brunswick. When he shipped to Montreal, the calves were transported by rail, about fifty to a boxcar. When he sold to Swifts, he would transport seven calves at a time by truck. For years he had driven the calves to Moncton himself, sometimes with me along for company.

Now that I had a driver's licence, my father broached the idea of my driving the calves to Moncton, some two hundred miles away, all by myself. I knew the roads like the back of my hand. His helpers would load the calves onto the truck. At the other end, Swifts employees would unload the truck and herd the calves onto a commercial scale. I would then go to the office and pick up a cheque. It sounded so simple. I accepted the responsibility with a certain amount of satisfaction. My father was treating me like a grown-up.

The day of the trip arrived. My father's men loaded the calves onto the truck. No problem. This was a piece of cake. Joe Findlay pointed out that there was a bull on board. He was tied to the rack with rope so he wouldn't disturb the other calves en route. The bull was somewhat larger than the rest of the animals. Joe showed me that the bull could move his head up and down and sideways, yet was confined to his space. He would not interfere whatsoever with the rest of the animals.

My parents made a big deal at the start of my routine trip. I had enough money for gas. I was told to stop at the Open Kitchen in Truro for something to eat. I figured Christopher Columbus hadn't received as many instructions before setting sail for the New World.

I started off. There was a feeling of importance and independence about the entire undertaking. I was helping my dad by doing a man's work. I rolled down the truck window, letting the invigorating fresh air sweep through the cab of the truck. This was truly the life. All was well with the world.

About forty miles into my trip, I thought the truck felt a little bumpy. I extricated myself from the cab to take a look. The right rear tire was almost as flat as a pancake. I had never changed a tire in my life, but I was a man now and I would change this one.

After hunting for about fifteen minutes, I located the jack and spare tire. It was hard work, but at last I had the flat tire off the truck and was just tightening the nuts of the spare when one of the calves decided to relieve itself. The calf's feces hit the rack with a splatter and plummeted down on my head. I reached for the freshly ironed handkerchief my mother had insisted I take with me and rubbed the excrement out of my hair, ears, and eyes. Nothing seemed to do much good. I smelled to high heaven.

It is difficult to admit even now that I was close to tears when I noticed the stream close by the road. I ran to it and stuck my head in. Blessed relief. After taking off my shirt and letting it soak in the stream, I laid it on a rock to dry out. I still thought there was a distinct odour about my person as a result of my ordeal, but felt that it was a vast improvement from my initial encounter with the calf's deposit.

All's well that ends well. I would soldier on. No one would ever know the particular problem I had encountered. In Truro, I entered the Open Kitchen and, as my father had done for so many years, ordered a piece of apple pie and a glass of milk. The waitress didn't mince words: "You smell terrible. The washrooms are over there," she said, pointing to a sign, which clearly stated "WASHROOMS."

Once there, I noticed that other men shied away from me. After scrubbing as best I could, I felt that I smelled like a bar of Lux soap. On the way back to the dining area, I spotted a gift shop with a rack of shirts, most of which were imprinted with the words "Truro, Home of the Bearcats," but I saw several simply inscribed "Canada." Without hesitation, I purchased one, made my way back to the washroom and changed into my new Canada shirt. After a short period of deliberation I decided to dispense with my odorous shirt in a garbage can. When I returned to my table, the waitress took a deep breath and sighed, "That's better."

I jumped in the Fargo, noting that the mooing calves were causing some concern to motorists in the parking lot. As I approached the New Brunswick border, the skies darkened. Within minutes I was driving through a torrential rainstorm. It soon became clear that the driver's windshield wiper was defective. I rolled down the window, resulting in a torrent of rain cascading directly into my face. Believing that discretion is the better part of valour, I pulled over to wait out the storm.

In a few minutes the rain subsided and I continued on. As if on cue, the heavens opened and once again I found myself in a driving rainstorm. This time the rain was accompanied by thunder and lightning. I wasn't the only one concerned. The calves were mooing in unison. The bull in particular could be heard above the pounding, incessant rain. I drove on, barely able to see the white line on the highway through the intervals when the windshield wiper was sporadically doing its job.

There I was, driving a load of calves for the first time in a thunder and lightning storm with a defective windshield wiper, having just experienced a flat tire, not to mention that a calf had relieved itself on my head. I glanced over my shoulder to look at my now frantic cargo. The bull's head seemed to be upside down, staring at me through eyes that had somehow rolled back in his head so that only the whites showed. He had managed to wind the rope around his neck and was in effect strangling himself.

This called for drastic action. As I pulled over to the side of the road, I knew I had to find some way to get at that rope. I stood on the dung-spattered rack and attempted to reach the rope, but I couldn't do it. With calf manure over my new shirt and assorted blobs over my entire body, I decided that there was only one thing to do. I would have to get six calves out of the truck in order to get at the bull and release him from his predicament. It was obvious to me that as soon as I lowered that tailgate to lead out calf number one by a rope, the other calves would scamper down the open tailgate. I could just hear myself explaining to my father, "Dad, I lost all the calves except one and he's dead."

While these disagreeable thoughts were dancing through my head, I heard an approaching vehicle. I waved it down and was thrilled when the driver pulled over right behind the Fargo. I figured it was a local farmer, but I figured wrong. He rolled down his window and peered out at me through the pouring rain. I must have been quite a sight with my soaking manure-spattered clothing sticking to my body. I thought I heard the woman in the passenger seat saying, "He's some kind of lunatic. Let's get the hell out of here." A cute little blond-haired girl in the back seat said, "He smells like shit."

I attempted to explain that I had a dying bull in my truck and that I had to unload six calves, maybe fewer, to get at the bull and untie the rope around his neck in order to save his life.

All I required of him was to close the tailgate of the truck after each calf was taken out. The driver looked at the manure-spattered tailgate and said, "Don't know anything about cattle. I'm from New York." With that abrupt explanation, he stepped on the gas and drove away.

All was not lost. Another car was approaching. As I waved it down, my heart sank when I saw that the occupants were two elderly ladies whom I would estimate had seen seventy-five glorious summers come and go. The driver, I later found out, was Mrs. Emily Forrester, whose husband had passed away tragically two years earlier when he had fallen off his tractor. She told me she couldn't handle the tailgate. After much consultation with her companion, she suggested that I hop in her car and she would drive me to nearby Amherst, where her son, Bert Jr., would be only too happy to give me a hand.

I looked at the bull. I thought I detected minuscule red veins running through the whites of his eyes, but I might have been imagining that. The bull's breathing was laboured, but basically steady. He might survive if only I could get that rope away from his neck.

I bid goodbye to the mooing calves and barely alive bull and took off with Emily and her companion. The first words spoken by this venerable lady, who in the course of conversation I learned was Helen Hutchinson, were, "He smells terrible." Helen had never married, but was quick to point out that that was not due to any lack of suitors.

We drove to Emily's farmhouse where we met Bert Jr., who I would estimate was thirty years old, but looked older. Bert Jr.

came complete with overalls, the kind with the bib in front. He was holding a half-full quart bottle of Oland's beer in his hand. Upon seeing his mother and her friend Helen, he let out a loud burp.

The old seaman's saying "Any port in a storm" came to mind. His mother explained my predicament to Bert Jr., who seemed to grasp the situation. I know this for a fact because Bert Jr. said, "We'll need some rope and a knife just in case we need to cut that bull loose."

Good thinking, I thought to myself. I altered my opinion when Bert Jr. said he'd just finish his Oland's and we'd be on our way in a few minutes. I didn't want to press but I did suggest that, since the bull was dying, time was of the essence. Bert Jr. grudgingly agreed to leave immediately. I directed him to the location of the Fargo while he took periodic swigs out of his quart of Oland's, all the while explaining how he had slaughtered many a pig with the very knife he was carrying.

We arrived at the Fargo and I was greatly relieved to find that the bull, although in bad shape, was still breathing. Bert Jr. was a great help in removing the calves from the truck. Truth to tell, he did all the work while I was relegated to the job of opening and closing the tailgate.

When it came to the bull, Bert Jr., displaying a degree of professionalism, flashed his knife and in an instant that bull had pupils in his eyes, was standing upright, and was even acting fractious. The bull was retied, and the calves were retrieved from the trees where they had been secured and were returned to the Fargo.

I attempted to pay Bert Jr. for the superlative service he had performed. He reluctantly accepted ten dollars for his trouble, but only after he insisted that we stop off at the liquor store so that he could pick up some Oland's. He also advised that his mother and Helen would be furious with me if I didn't return to their house for a bite to eat.

I followed Bert Jr. in the Fargo. A bite to eat consisted of venison with gravy, the recipe for which Emily said was a family secret. The venison was accompanied by mashed squash dripping with Tatamagouche butter. The meal was rounded off by rhubarb crumble washed down with Lipton tea. It was the best meal I had ever tasted.

Finally, after my acceptance of one of Bert Jr.'s old shirts, which I insisted I would return to him, I was allowed to take my leave.

I made my way to the Swifts' plant in Moncton without further incident, checking on that bull every fifteen minutes. His composure didn't waver. His eyes were wide open and I firmly believe he was grateful for all that I had done for him.

My return trip to Antigonish was uneventful. As I pulled into our yard on Court Street, my father and mother greeted me in much the same manner as Balboa's parents must have welcomed him home after he discovered the Pacific Ocean.

Dad said, "How did it go?"

"Routine," was my answer.

"Where did you get that vile-looking shirt?" Mum inquired.

"You don't want to know," I replied.

THE MYSTERY BOTTLE

With my chicken-plucking career nothing more than an unpleasant interlude in my distant past, my father's political connections procured for me the position of assistant surveyor for the Nova Scotia government. To be more precise, my buddy Hughie MacFadden and I had summer jobs holding a rod and fetching nails and pieces of red ribbon for an engineer who, under the auspices of the provincial government, was intent on rebuilding the road from the town of Antigonish to Antigonish Harbour.

The winding, snaky road had originally been constructed taking the path of least resistance. This involved going around rock outcroppings, circling ponds, and generally making the six-mile dirt road an obstacle course.

Our crew consisted of an engineer and his authentic assistant, wiry Joe Brewer, who basically did all the work. Engineer Bill MacCarthy, a huge man, had only one lung. This affliction caused him to cough and breathe laboriously if he exerted himself in any way. Joe, in turn, had Hughie and me do all the menial tasks, which were below his position in life.

The first day on the job, Bill told us that we would in some cases be traversing private property where the road had to be widened. In these instances we were to knock on the farmhouse door and explain that an assessor would show up sometime in the future to inform them how much money they would receive for their appropriated land. There was one price per yard for cultivated land and another price for uncultivated land. Of course, if the government already owned the few yards on each side of the road, the farmer would receive absolutely nothing. We were not to enter into any discussions concerning money. The assessor would show up in a month or a year, since no one knew when the road would actually be built. All we were attempting to do was to survey the road for future construction.

The first house we approached belonged to Alfonse Hanifan. It was a well-known fact that Alfonse had been left a comfortable income some years earlier when a maiden aunt had been hit by a train in Boston after attending a Bruins hockey game. Alfonse had inherited the income from her estate, which enabled him to have a taxi pick him up at his home each Friday and drive him to the Nova Scotia Liquor Commission store located at the far end of town between Poirier's Canteen and Chisholm's Shoe Store.

Alfonse would buy two bottles of Bacardi rum and a case of Oland's beer. I should point out that Alfonse was one of the few people in town who could afford Bacardi rum, considered to be the Cadillac of rums at that time. It cost appreciably more than Demerara Black Diamond, the people's choice. Also worthy of note was that the case of Oland's beer consisted of quarts, not pints. From the day he received official word from Boston that dear Aunt Bessie had gone to her great reward and had left him with an income, Alfonse put down his pitchfork and never lifted a finger again except to raise a drink to his lips.

Hughie and I approached the farmhouse. Although it was morning, Alfonse was sitting on his front steps sucking on his first Oland's of the day. Hughie said, "Mr. Hanifan, we've got wonderful news for you. The government is going to pave and widen the road going right by your farm."

"I've been working that land all my life and I'll tell you boys, no one is touching one inch of my property," Alfonse replied.

Somewhat taken aback, Hughie attempted to explain. "You don't understand, Mr. Hanifan, it will only be widened by a yard or so, really just expanding the ditch."

Alfonse rose from his step. "Show me," he said.

"Well, we don't know yet exactly. An assessor will be around and he'll tell you precisely."

"Show me," Alfonse insisted.

Together we walked down to the area in front of the Hanifan farm. The old road was as straight as an arrow as it passed in front of his property.

"Show me where the new road is going."

Since Hughie and I had only been in our new position for about an hour, we had no idea, but it didn't take a genius to see that there was nothing but a wide ditch running from one end of the Hanifan property to the other.

We both gingerly pointed to the dried-up ditch. Hughie kicked an old empty Moir's Pot of Gold chocolate box out of the ditch as Alfonse went on to emphasize that he had worked that area for a good many years.

"The government will have to pay me a pretty penny before they go digging on my property. You tell that to your fancy engineer friends."

We said goodbye to Mr. Hanifan and moved on to the next farm, a distance of a half-mile. As we opened the front gate, a huge dog of unknown ancestry came bounding toward us, growling and barking. Hughie stepped back and slammed the gate shut. We would talk to Lauchie Hector MacDonald some other time. As we made up our minds to save our lives, Lauchie came strolling down the driveway.

"That's no way to treat strangers, Max," he said.

As I had never met Mr. MacDonald in my life, I thought it strange that he would address me in such a manner.

"There, there, Max," Lauchie intoned, as he patted the monster, quieting him down appreciably.

I whispered to Hughie, "I get it, his dog's name is Max."

Hughie started off, "Mr. MacDonald, we've got great news for you—the government is going to widen and pave the entire road going down to the harbour. They will be taking quite a bit of that turn here in order to straighten out the road. It will probably take a chunk out of your hayfield, but an assessor will be around to tell you how much a yard you will be getting for the bit of your property that will be affected."

I thought to myself that Hughie was getting his patter down cold when Lauchie interjected, "You boys come with me."

We followed Lauchie, who walked with a slight limp, the result of having been kicked by a horse during a weight-pulling competition at the Antigonish Fall Fair some years previously.

As we approached the road, the hayfield gave way to a tiny graveyard. The two markers were surrounded by an eighteen-inch-high black wrought iron fence. I looked at Hughie, who had his head bowed out of respect. The two markers read "Faithful Companion R.I.P. Maxwell" and "Faithful Companion R.I.P. Maxine."

Lauchie was deeply moved. I thought I detected a tiny rivulet rolling down his weathered cheek as he fought back tears.

"Maxine had given birth to a litter of puppies. I gave them all away except for Max, whom you boys met at the gate. I figured I would have the mother, father, and offspring as company for the rest of my days. For a few months the three dogs were the joy of my life. Then, one day a Hoyt's transfer truck ran over both Maxwell and Maxine, killing them instantly. The driver was a most compassionate man and helped me dig the graves."

I thought Lauchie might stop talking when Max lifted his hind leg and urinated on his mother's grave marker, but nothing could stop him once he was rolling. He ignored Max's indiscretion. "After my Agnes passed away, I thought the three dogs would help fill the void, but suddenly I was left with only Max, who has been a wonderful help to me. I often come down here to visit Maxwell and Maxine. Now, where did you say that new road would be cutting through?"

Hughie, who had become the official spokesperson for the engineering staff of the Nova Scotia government, diplomatically said, "It may not be for years, Mr. MacDonald. The assessor will be around to discuss it with you."

We last saw Lauchie Hector MacDonald limping back to his home with his dog, Max, at his side.

Hughie and I made our way to Bill MacCarthy's car. "Did you tell those two farmers that the road would be coming through in a few years?"

"Yeah, we told them," Hughie said.

For the rest of the day I held the rod while Joe took his sightings through his transit.

As the days turned to weeks, our surveying positions never contained the drama of our very first day until the day Bill said to me, "Max, you and Hughie know the drill. Tell the rest of the farmers along the road that an assessor will be around in a year or two to evaluate any incursions we make into their property."

"Sure thing, Bill," I said, in the familiar way we had of addressing each other.

Hughie and I approached an old weather-beaten farmhouse. There was a huge hole in the screen door, which was hooked closed from the inside. When I knocked, it made a racket. I looked at the name Bill MacCarthy had scratched on a piece of paper and waited for Willie Carruthers to answer his door.

A woman of about sixty years of age peered out from behind the screen door. "Is Willie Carruthers at home?" I inquired.

"I'm Willie Carruthers," the lady said, chuckling and exposing even white teeth behind lips that were full and sensuous, even for a lady of her years. "My name is really Wilhelmina, but everyone calls me Willie and strangers expect me to be a man."

"Is your husband home?"

"No, dear, Charlie has long since gone to heaven to be with our Lord."

"Oh, I'm sorry to hear that, Mrs. Carruthers. We do have some good news for you. We're with the surveying crew and the government is about to pave and widen the road just below your driveway. An assessor will be around to meet with you and decide how much compensation you will receive if it is necessary to encroach on your property."

"Well, now, boys, you shouldn't be talking to me. You should be talking to Charlie's only surviving relative, his sister Mary."

"You are Charlie's wife, are you not?" Hughie inquired rather aggressively, I thought.

"You boys are embarrassing me," she replied. "What's the use, the government will find out in time. You see, I don't own the farm. Mary does. You'll have to speak to her about money. She lives in Mountain View, California. Would you boys care for a spot of tea?"

"What the hell," Hughie whispered to me, as Willie opened the useless hook on the screen door and we entered her home.

Willie had asked us into her house to explain how Charlie's sister Mary happened to own the farm. "Boys, I'm telling you this because I want to let you know that the government has got to get in touch with Mary in Mountain View, California, not me. It all happened a good forty years ago. Yes, it would be just forty. I was nineteen at the time. Charlie was the handsomest thing around these parts. Played the bagpipes like a charm.

"Well, one night at a dance in the Malignant Cove school-house, when the band was taking a break, C.C. (we used to call him C.C. in those days) asked me to go outside with him for a breath of fresh air. C.C., who could have any girl in the county, was inviting me, Wilhelmina MacDonald, to go outside for a breath of fresh air. Boys, I was a looker in those days, no question about it. Before it turned grey, my hair was blond as straw and my complexion as smooth as a baby's ... well, it was smooth. Anyway, instead of fresh air, C.C. thought we should take a rest in a little shed behind the school. That's where we did it, standing up.

"About two months later, I knew I was pregnant, so I talked to C.C. He suggested I go to Boston to have the baby and that he would be waiting for me and the baby upon my return. We would get married, tell everyone we had adopted a baby, and live on the farm which had been left to him by his father. It didn't work out that way. C.C., although in the prime of his life, was making hay one day when he keeled over right there and then. The doctor said it was a massive heart attack. I returned with the baby and was met by Mary. She said no one must ever know that her brother sired a bastard. She took my baby and travelled to Mountain View, California. I've never seen the child since Mary took him from me at the Antigonish station forty years ago.

"Later, Mary wrote me and told me that C.C. had left the farm to her but that I could live on it for the rest of my life. Everyone just assumed that C.C. and I were married. I took his last name and lived here on the farm ever since."

Hughie and I thanked Willie for the tea, which was accompanied by piping hot tea biscuits with rhubarb jam, and took our leave. When we returned to Bill's car, he inquired, "Did you tell a couple more about the process?"

"Yeah," Hughie replied, "but I think any inquiries about the Carruthers should go to a Miss Mary Carruthers in Mountain View, California."

Hughie took some time to explain the Carruthers situation to Bill, who from time to time shook his head.

The rest of our summer went rather routinely, if you discount the bottle incident. In the course of our surveying, we came across a small but deep pond. The plan for the new road called for it to go right through the pond, which measured about fifty feet across. While scampering about the shore, I tripped over what turned out to be a chain. I screamed, "Hughie," as I always did when anything unusual took place. Upon investigating, we found one end of the rusty old chain tied around the trunk of a large spruce tree. We followed the chain to the pond, where it disappeared into the water. By now, Bill and Joe had joined us in pulling the chain up to the surface. We all theorized as to what could be on the other end. Bill jokingly said, "Pirates' buried treasure."

Joe volunteered, "Captain Kidd was up the coast only a hundred and fifty miles away on Oak Island."

At last the treasure broke the surface. It was a bottle containing some kind of liquid. Whatever label might have been on the bottle had long since washed off. The top of the bottle was a ball of decayed matter mixed with rust that had formed from the metal chain that had held it so securely for what we assumed was years.

Joe said, "Let's break the top off and see what's inside."

Hughie interrupted, "No, it could be set to explode."

I added, "It could be poisonous."

We set the bottle aside. It sat there all day, but each one of us, in his own way, couldn't help but wonder what the bottle contained that would make someone take all the trouble to hide it so well that it would be found only by accident.

I thought of a solution. A neighbour, Dr. Will Farrell, was head of the chemistry department at St. Francis Xavier University. He would know what to do. All three of my fellow adventurers agreed that I had come up with a brilliant idea. Bill said, "Let's jump in the car and go right now. It looks like rain anyway."

As the summer had progressed, I had learned that there is a strict code in the engineer's handbook that states you absolutely mustn't survey if it rains. Some engineers believe that it reads you mustn't survey if there is a threat of rain. Our Bill MacCarthy belonged to this latter school of engineering.

We drove to St. F.X. All four of us marched into the chemistry building and accosted Dr. Farrell. We explained our mission and produced the mystery bottle. Dr. Farrell frowned and gazed intently at the bottle, an expression thousands of students had learned to respect. "Let's see now, men. Hot water should do the trick for the neck. I'll boil some right now."

The material on the top of the bottle disintegrated under the hot water. Now that the liquid was exposed, Hughie said, "Stand back in case the fumes are toxic."

Bill said, "There's no treasure in that bottle."

Like a parrot, Joe declared, "There's nothing of value in that bottle."

I asked, "Doctor, how will we find out what that liquid is?"

With that inquiry, Will Farrell, Ph.D. in Chemistry, who had worked summers at Elliot Lake for the Atomic Energy Commission, lifted the bottle to his lips and said, "Only one way to find out, men," as he took a huge gulp from the bottle. All four of us watched, dumbfounded. Dr. Farrell didn't turn blue. He didn't slump to the floor. Instead he said, "Best damn rum I've ever tasted."

We gave the good professor a standing ovation before passing the bottle around and consuming every last ounce.

We never did find out who put that bottle in the pond. Someone later suggested that rum runners would tie up to twenty bottles at a time, spaced about a foot apart, to a chain and submerge them in lakes and ponds to escape being caught with rum in their possession.

As time passed, Bill, Joe, Hughie, Alfonse, Lauchie, and Wilhelmina became memories of a summer long ago. Sometimes, in the dead of night, when I can't sleep, I wonder what became of Wilhelmina's baby and who put that damn bottle down in the pond.

MARY TEASDALE

Mary Teasdale was the ugliest woman in town. She bore a distinct resemblance to Popeye's girlfriend, Olive Oyl, and was so skinny she could hide behind a broom handle. She had an Ichabod Crane–like head, accentuated by two tiny, beady eyes. Her straight black hair did nothing to enhance her appearance, nor did her nose, which had the distressing propensity to be constantly running.

As an unattractive young girl in a small town, Mary was the brunt of cruel teasing. Because she was somewhat of an outcast, she dropped out of school at age fourteen and obtained employment as a laundry helper at St. Francis Xavier University, the town's largest institution.

Summer and winter, you could set your clock by Mary. Six days a week she would trudge up Main Street to the university at precisely 8:30 A.M. After a day of back-breaking work, she would make the return trip home at 5:30 P.M. On Sunday she would attend mass at St. Ninian's Cathedral and spend the rest of the day cleaning her parents' home.

Mary's one diversion was the Antigonish Bulldogs' senior hockey team. She never missed a home game and often took the train to see their "away" games. In those days, the Bulldogs played in the APC League, which stood for Antigonish, Pictou, and Colchester counties. Other than the Bulldogs, there were teams in New Glasgow, Pictou, and Truro. The furthest town from Antigonish was eighty miles away, so it was relatively easy to attend the games that were played outside of town. Mary took in most road games.

One bitterly cold night in the dead of winter I was travelling by train from Halifax to Antigonish. It was one of those nights on which the train seemed to crackle, as if to complain about the permeating cold. The windows of the train were frosted, making it impossible to see outside. The train wasn't crowded, yet I felt claustrophobic sitting there, listening to the steel wheels making their distinctive rhythmic sound as mile after mile drew me closer to home.

At Truro, we ground to a stop while some passengers disembarked and others entered. All were dressed with layers of clothing to guard against the freezing weather.

In walked Mary Teasdale, runny nose and all. She headed straight for the vacant seat beside me. It didn't take an Einstein to figure out that the Bulldogs must have been playing against the Truro Bearcats that night. Mary sat down beside me, because I obviously was the only person she recognized. No doubt I was in for two hours of hockey talk.

"We took the Bearcats 5–2 tonight," Mary volunteered.

"That's terrific," I replied, realizing that in our entire lives not one word had passed between Mary and me until now. She had always been one of those people whom you don't really see. Like the air you breathe, it's always there, but you don't notice it. Mary was visible now. She took out a soiled handkerchief and blew her nose. She kept it crumpled up in her fist in preparation for the running that was soon to follow.

"Shorty MacDougall was terrific in nets. Kept one of those Dorrington brothers from scoring against us on a breakaway in the third." With that morsel of information, Mary and I had run out of common ground. Simply put, we had nothing to talk about. Mary's world consisted of working all week with an occasional hockey game as her only diversion. I presumed that, at thirty-eight years of age, she had long since given up the idea of love, marriage, and children. There was an awkward fifteen minutes when not a word passed between us.

Mary blew her nose. Maybe it was because of the fact that we had no history together that she decided to relate her innermost thoughts to me. Whatever the reason, this non-person began to talk and didn't stop until we pulled into Antigonish.

"It was a night just like tonight, freezing cold, that it happened. Last year I was watching the game in Truro from the cheap end section where you stand for the whole game. I never could figure out why they call them seats."

"Yes, I know what you mean," I replied. It appeared to me we were going to continue to talk hockey, but I was wrong.

"It was between the second and third period when a young sailor started talking to me. I could smell the liquor off his breath."

This wasn't going to be a hockey story after all. Mary blew her nose, rubbed it thoroughly with her curled-up hankie, and continued, "No one had ever paid that much attention to me. He was actually flirting with me."

"Mary, you don't have to tell me this," I said, now fully sympathetic toward this woman. I could picture in my mind's eye an inebriated sailor, his mind fogged over with alcohol, thinking that our Mary was attractive.

She interrupted my thoughts, continuing, "As we got to know each other, he propositioned me."

"Really, Mary, are you sure you want to tell all this to me?"

"Yes, I'm sure."

Mary went on to tell me that she knew exactly who she was and how she looked. Why shouldn't she know the touch of a man? Why shouldn't she experience what it was like to be loved, if only for the briefest of moments? She knew deep down in her heart that it would be most unlikely she would ever be propositioned again. She was a thirty-eight-year-old unattractive virgin, and if she let this opportunity slip away, she would die a virgin.

Together, she and the sailor walked out to his rented Pontiac. The snow crackled under their feet as they made their way across the parking lot. The interior of the car was ice cold. The sailor turned on the heater and opened a bottle of Moosehead beer. They passed the bottle back and forth. Mary didn't like the taste of the beer, but didn't want to offend her new friend. She forced herself to swallow a mouthful every time he passed her the bottle. It was the first time in her life that

Mary had had an alcoholic beverage of any kind. The Pontiac heated up. She and the sailor kissed. He roughly removed her underclothing and they had intercourse.

The sailor suggested that there was no need for them to miss the third period. Mary slowly put on her clothing. In minutes, they were trudging across the parking lot to the rink.

Together they watched the game for a while. The sailor then offered to fetch them both a cup of coffee. He said he would be back in a few minutes, but Mary knew she would never see him again.

Mary went on to tell me that Gregor Myette had met the train and had given her a lift to her home in the east end. Next morning she made her way uptown to the university, but somehow things were different. As Mary's familiar figure passed their stores, merchants waved to her as they had most days for years. Little did they know that this was not the old Mary, this was not the virginal Mary; this was someone who had experienced affection, no matter how crude. In time, Mary put the crudeness out of her mind. For the shortest time, that sailor had really cared for her.

"You can imagine my surprise, Max, when three months later I was sure I was pregnant. Not even my mother noticed, not to mention anyone else. That's how much old skinny Mary was taken for granted. Around the fifth month my tummy protruded noticeably and I knew I had to do something about my condition."

Mary continued, "I spoke to my boss at the university and convinced her that I was rundown and needed some time off.

In all the years at the laundry I had never taken a vacation. Imagine that, Max, vacations had never interested me. I had nowhere to go and no one to go with. Now my boss added up my vacation time, which turned out to be months. Somewhat exasperated, she told me to take as much time as I wanted. When I suggested four months, she did a double take, but agreed.

"I travelled to Boston and contacted a home for unwed women. I was surprised to see how many girls were single and pregnant. This place took care of all the details. When my time came, it was a tough birth, but as God is my witness, I enjoyed every minute of it. My little boy was born in Boston. I got to hold him for a half-hour before he was put out for adoption. One of the nuns told me, as I was leaving for home, that I shouldn't worry—the folks who had adopted my baby would give him a good home."

Mary went on to tell me that the entire experience had given her a new perspective on life. Now, when the townspeople saw the skinny, unattractive woman going to and from the university laundry, it was no longer the old Mary on a one-way journey to nowhere. She knew something that none of them would ever know. Somewhere, there was a child who was brought into this world by a laundry worker from Antigonish.

"I am not a non-person; I am someone," she said.

The train chugged into the Antigonish station. Mary made me swear that I would never tell anyone her secret and I never have, until now. It's been over fifty years. It doesn't matter any more. This past month a friend sent me the Antigonish *Casket*.

There, on a back page, was an obituary. Mary Teasdale, at age eighty-eight, had passed away quietly at St. Martha's Hospital after a lengthy illness. Before her retirement, she had been employed at St. Francis Xavier University for over five decades.

RELOCATING THE
NURSES' RESIDENCE

The long hot summer hung heavily on us town boys. We called ourselves town boys as distinguished from the St. Francis Xavier University students from all over the world.

We did have a few advantages. When the out-of-town students left Antigonish for their summer break, we ten or so town boys were the only remaining eligible males. Other than the local belles, there was one other source of female companionship, and that was the student nurses at St. Martha's Hospital. The student nurses, in their own way, appreciated us.

About the biggest activity in town in the summer was swimming. The girls didn't have transportation, but we did. I had my father's red Fargo cattle truck and my buddy Sam Brady had his father's Pontiac.

It was not an uncommon sight to see two, three, or four girls at the bottom of the hill leading from the hospital waiting for a lift to Mahoney's Beach, some five miles down the road. It got so we knew the girls' shifts and when they would be waiting at the foot of the hill for either Sam or me to pick them up for the drive to the beach.

There was Dot Harris, cute as a button, with her peasant blouse bursting forth with barely concealed treasures. That girl filled out a bathing suit better than Sophia Loren. Sometimes she was accompanied by Helen MacDonald, who had a figure that would stop Big Ben. Rosemarie Fraser was simply beautiful. When you think of a wholesome, virginal milkmaid, picture Rosemarie. These girls were not interested in us town boys in a romantic sense, but we all realized that, with the university in summer session, we were the only act in town. The girls worked hard and they played hard.

Without exception, they loved to party. My friends and I were only too willing to oblige. There was a sort of unwritten agreement between us that we would party all summer and disappear when the university opened and the students poured into town.

Most days we would load up Sam's father's Pontiac with beer and head for the beach. The girls rarely disappointed. There they were at the bottom of the hill waiting for us. We usually stopped off at a fisherman's wharf to pick up lobsters. A pot borrowed from the Bradys' cottage was filled with salt water and brought to a boil. In twenty minutes we were gulping Oland's beer and eating lobsters beside a roaring fire on the beach. The partying went on for hours, interrupted only by refreshing dips in the ocean. I couldn't think beyond those student nurses, Oland's beer, and lobsters.

We had to be careful. The girls were required to be back at the hospital in time to go on duty. That was a bit of a rub. As the time drew near for our return trip to town, everyone was obliged to take a dip in the ocean. This was a sobering-up process that was strictly adhered to. Most days or evenings, it worked perfectly, but the system did have flaws.

On occasion, after their last swim, the girls would insist on one, two, or even three beers before calling it a day. As a result of this last-minute imbibing, the girls would sometimes go on duty slightly inebriated. As St. Martha's was a teaching hospital run by nuns, this behaviour was not appreciated by the staff.

Mary McCarthy was accused of bringing lobsters to a favourite patient, one Joan Cleary, who, at eighty-six, developed severe stomach cramps after consuming two large lobsters. Legend has it that Mary advised Joan to eat the green tamale, which was said to have the effect of increasing one's libido. Evidently, Joan had felt the need to enhance her sexual urges and had eaten up every morsel of tamale in those two lobsters.

Asked to make up a bed by one of the nuns, Dot Harris is reported to have replied without hesitation, "Make it up yourself." This display of insubordination precipitated a formal inquiry. Dot came within an ace of being tossed out of St. Martha's.

The bending of the rules didn't go unnoticed by the nuns. When Rosemarie Fraser appeared on duty wearing one white stocking and one black, the nuns felt it was time to act.

The hierarchy formed an investigative committee reminiscent of the Vatican Council, headed by a nasty piece of work, Sister St. Helene. Displaying abilities made famous by Sherlock Holmes, she soon discovered that her charges were accepting lifts to the beach on a daily basis and, heaven forbid, were imbibing that devilish product manufactured by a company called Oland's from far-off Halifax.

Sister Hell, as we called her, left no stone unturned. She delved deeply into the entire affair. Time was of the essence, particularly after Helen MacDonald dropped a bedpan, spilling its contents all over the floor.

As a result of her investigation, Sister Hell obtained the names of the boys responsible for her student nurses' unorthodox behaviour. She forbade the girls to go out with the boys listed on a special notice tacked up on the bulletin board of the student nurses' residence. The first two names on the list were Sam Brady and Max Haines.

We initially suspected that something was drastically amiss when we cruised to the base of the hill leading from the hospital. The girls were not there. This was the first time such a phenomenon had taken place. Sam figured the student residence must have burned to the ground. He insisted on looking into this matter immediately. There had been no fire. "Possibly an epidemic," Sam surmised, "the place is quarantined."

Sam suggested that we take the bull by the horns and call on the girls just like those fancy out-of-town students would do when the long, hot summer was over. We drove to the front door. Sister Winnifred, whom we called "Winnie the Watchdog," greeted us at the reception area. With a gesture made infamous by German guards in prisoner of war camps, she said nothing, but pointed to the bulletin board. There were our names in black and white, with the warning that any student nurses seen in the company of the boys listed would be dismissed from the hospital.

To say that Sam didn't take the news well would be the understatement of the year. He was furious. Sam marched out of the residence, his face crimson, his hands shaking. He shoved the key into his father's Pontiac and roared down the hill. I implored him to settle down, but he would have none of it. Sam was on a mission. We pulled into Smith's Machine Shop on Church Street. Sam left me cooling my heels in the car. When he came out of the shop, he was carrying a long heavy-duty chain. Without a word, he threw the chain into the trunk of his father's vehicle. We sped back toward the nurses' residence.

I had witnessed Sam's behavioural patterns since childhood, and understanding hit me like a sledgehammer. I knew very well what he planned to do.

With a singleness of purpose, Sam pulled up to the nurses' residence, extracted the chain from the trunk, and wound one end around two pillars holding up the balcony from which Sister Hell observed the world. Sam wound the other end of the chain around the rear bumper of his father's car.

By now, Sam's unorthodox behaviour had attracted the attention of several student nurses, who were cheering him on from their second-storey bedroom windows. Many were shouting slogans. I distinctly heard "Sam's our man!" "We want to swim." "Lobsters forever!"

Sam turned to me, his face red as a beet. "If the nurses can't hitchhike, we'll take the whole damn residence to the beach."

With that proclamation, he stepped on the gas. The nurses' residence didn't budge, but a cloud of gravel and dust flew from the wheels of the car. The Pontiac's bumper popped like a wine cork and lay rattling on the gravel road. Someone called the police.

Within ten minutes, Sergeant Vic Staples of the RCMP showed up. He shook his head, as he had done so many times when confronting Sam and me in similar situations in the past. The first thing Vic said was, "Sam, your father is going to kill you." Then he waved at the nurses, who had begun to applaud. Sam got out of the vehicle and bowed in an exaggerated fashion.

Sergeant Vic then did three things that reinforced our belief that he was the finest RCMP officer in the entire country. He went into the residence and talked Sister Hell into not pressing charges. Other than a slight scar on one of the pillars of the residence, no harm had been done. The second thing he did was call Joe MacVicar at Eastern Auto, who assured Vic that a new bumper would be on Sam's father's car in two hours. Then that wonderful public servant arranged for Sam to pay Eastern Auto so much a month until the new bumper was totally paid for.

With the chain returned, the new bumper in place, and Sister Hell placated, we drove up to Sam's house. His mother met us at the door. She said, "Did you and Maxie have a pleasant swim, dear?"

SAM AND THE LOBSTER

It was a beautiful summer day in May about two weeks into the lobster season when my buddy Sam Brady suggested that a dip in the icy cold waters of St. George's Bay would get the cobwebs out. I concurred, and after a brief discussion it was agreed that the best time for our swim would be around three that afternoon.

The timing wasn't a haphazard decision. This was before the unfortunate incident that led to our becoming *personae non gratae* at the student nurses' residence. The nurses would be at the bottom of the hill below St. Martha's Hospital looking for a lift down to Mahoney's Beach. Our regulars were Mary Foley and Dot Harris. Among us boys, Mary was known as Big Jugs, or in her presence, simply B.J. Dot was nicknamed Polka Dot.

The cab of the cattle truck exuded an unpleasant odour, but B.J. and Polka Dot didn't seem to mind being squeezed into the cab. As for Sam and me, we enjoyed the close quarters. Today would prove to be no different from any other day. There were B.J. and Polka Dot waiting at the bottom of the hill. B.J.

appeared a bit peaked. After they jumped into the cab, Polka Dot explained that her friend had been accosted by an elderly patient who had insisted on chocolate ice cream instead of the regular vanilla that came with his meal. He had clutched B.J. by the hair and wouldn't let go. Mother Mary Joseph used all her strength to extricate B.J.'s hair from the enraged man's grasp. Polka Dot went on to explain that the angry patient had over-turned his bedpan, making quite a mess. After that experience, the cab of the cattle truck smelled like the interior of a Chanel perfume factory.

Away we drove toward the beach. Sam, attempting to emulate the pose of a perfect gentleman, listened attentively to the tale of the enraged patient and, in a sympathetic voice, inquired, "B.J., is there something you want now more than anything else?" Without hesitation, she replied, "A lobster." As if on cue, Sam responded, "You shall have your lobster."

The lobster season was in full swing and we both knew we had carte blanche in pulling up a few lobster traps belonging to our fisherman friend, Billy Mahoney. There was one minor problem: We didn't have a boat. We also knew that Billy was in New Glasgow having extensive dental work performed by Dr. Milne. Billy had been in a brawl in Heatherton, which necessitated his visit to Dr. Milne's office. Rumour had it that his adversary would require plastic surgery. Besides, his boat was tied up in Arisaig for repairs.

Although we were good friends with the student nurses, we never considered them in a romantic sort of way, if you get my drift. After all, we knew that when the summer was over, two thousand virile university students would sweep the student nurses off their feet. It was an unspoken agreement that we were their buddies, companions, and drinking partners during the summer months. When the fall term began, they would attend movies and dances with the university students.

B.J. and Polka Dot didn't want to hear details. For the entire drive to the beach they talked of little else but lobsters. They discussed sucking on the claws, extracting the tail, dipping it in melted butter, and washing it all down with a cool Oland's.

"Sam, your parents' cottage is open. Your folks are in town. We could hunker down in front of the fireplace and eat lobsters and drink beer," B.J. declared.

Polka Dot smiled a wry smile when she said, "The tamale is my favourite part of the lobster."

I became a little apprehensive at this sly insinuation. Everyone knew that the tamale was an aphrodisiac. I replied, "That's nice."

I thought Polka Dot was moving a bit closer to me. She didn't seem to mind the gearshift on the floor between her knees at all. Up to this day, the floor gearshift had been an embarrassment. The nurses had always made sure that both their legs were to the right of the gearshift. Today was different. Polka had one leg on one side and one leg on the other. When I shifted gears I came dangerously close to grabbing her…. well, never mind, you get the idea.

B.J. was also displaying a distinct absence of inhibitions. She was snuggling far too close to Sam. Let's face it, both girls were decidedly horny.

Could this be the day that all unwritten rules were to be tossed aside? The girls were acting strangely. All the while, B.J. talked of eating a fresh lobster. She went into great detail describing how she was adept at removing the claw meat intact, a feat only perfected by seasoned lobster consumers. Polka Dot kept emphasizing tamale, with all the inferences that part of the lobster's anatomy implied.

Finally, we pulled up in front of Sam's parents' cottage. B.J. insisted that Sam produce a lobster. In desperation, Sam declared, "I'll get a lobster. Max and I will find a boat and pull up a few of Billy's traps."

I couldn't believe my ears. You didn't just find a boat at Mahoney's Beach. Half the cottages were not even open for the summer. Certainly, there were no motorized boats just waiting for Sam and me to joyride out into the bay to pick up a stupid lobster for Big Jugs and her faithful companion Polka Dot.

Sam and I saw it at the same time. There, hanging up on the Stewarts' garage, was an old scow that had been there all winter. I figured it was more of a decoration than a seagoing vessel. Sam pointed at it and said, "We could go out in that old scow."

I thought my buddy had lost his marbles. "No way, Sam. Besides, we haven't any oars."

"No problem," Sam said as he pulled a few boards off the Stewarts' rotting deck. "We can use these."

"Sam, you're crazy, there's no way we can make it out to Billy's traps and back in that old scow."

Just then B.J. and Polka Dot came around the corner. B.J. exclaimed, "It's a miracle." She turned to Polka Dot and said, "I knew Sam would never let me down. We'll light the fire in the fireplace and wait for you boys to bring back the lobsters. Sam, your dad won't mind if we help ourselves to a couple of Olands' while we wait."

"No, go ahead," was the generous reply.

We took down the scow and lugged it to the shore. Along the way, I picked up an old tin can that had once held Turret tobacco and tossed it into the scow. Using the old boards from the Stewarts' deck, we managed to row out into the bay. The trip wasn't without difficulty. The seams of the boat, having been exposed to the elements all winter, were far from waterproof. Slowly, water seeped in and sloshed around our feet.

"Take off your shoes," I instructed.

Sam slipped off his sneakers and tied them together before placing them around his neck. "I once saw William Bendix do that in a movie," he shouted.

If it was good enough for William Bendix, it was good enough for me. I followed Sam's lead and placed my sneakers around my neck. By this time it had become difficult to keep up bailing the water out of the scow. Besides, I didn't know if it was my imagination or not, but the bay seemed to be growing angry. Waves were hitting the side of the scow, sending spray over us and adding to the water, which was outpacing my futile attempts at bailing. Sam, an adept rower under normal circumstances, kept flailing away with those two old boards. I have to give him credit. We reached Billy's distinctive red-and-white buoys and pulled up a few traps. It was hard work with a swell in full progress, the boat slowly filling with water, and Sam pulling on ropes while emptying the traps of lobsters. After we extracted half a dozen lobsters, we decided it would be pressing our luck to stay out there any longer.

I looked back at the shore for the first time. Until now, our chief aim had been to make it out to Billy's traps. It looked like an awfully long way to shore. They say it is difficult to judge distance over water. Whomever they are, they are right. I don't know how far we had rowed out into the bay, but the cottages now looked like little matchboxes and the shore nothing but a thin brown line of sand.

Sam was rowing furiously. I was bailing like mad, but it was no use. We weren't moving at all. Despite my efforts, there was too much water in the boat. We were sinking.

"Sam," I shouted, "we're sinking!"

"Keep bailing," he shouted back.

"It's no use, we're sinking!"

By now the freezing-cold salt water was halfway up to our knees and was pouring into the boat. Like us, the old scow was giving up. I jumped overboard. Sam followed. Fully clothed except for our sneakers, we started swimming for shore. Sam was a terrific swimmer. I was only so-so, but despite lack of finesse I figured I could stay afloat for a long time.

The water was cold. I mean Cold with a capital C. While unpleasant thoughts of possibly drowning were dancing through my head, I heard a voice, almost down to a whisper, "I can't breathe." I turned and saw that Sam's sneakers were wound around his neck and were cutting off his air supply.

"Get rid of the sneakers," I shouted.

"I can't," came the weak reply.

I couldn't wait for an explanation but swam to my friend's side. With much effort, I managed to untangle the laces of his sneakers so that finally they fell away. Sam said, "Thanks."

I got rid of my sneakers and we both continued swimming for shore. Don't ever attempt to swim fully clothed. Every stroke requires a mammoth effort. I paced myself and made some slight progress. That's when I noticed that Sam wasn't ahead of me or beside me. I looked back. Sam, who was twice the swimmer I was, was flailing away with his left hand, but wasn't making any headway. Around now I figured we were both as good as dead. If we were going to go under we would go together. I returned to Sam's side and begged him to use both hands. He didn't reply, so I urged him to swim harder. Just a few more yards to go before we would be able to touch the bottom.

I took a sighting, trying to gauge whether we could possibly make it. There they were on shore, cheering us on. B.J. and Polka Dot had grown impatient sitting before that warm fireplace and had ventured out to the shore to see what was delaying us in our quest for lobsters.

Forget about all those fancy moves you see in movies where lifeguards clasp the drowning man and gracefully swim away with him to safety. I got behind Sam and pushed like hell. Finally we touched the wonderful, glorious sand at the bottom of St. George's Bay.

The girls were waiting for us on shore, holding blankets. Both Sam and I were exhausted. He held up his right hand and showed B.J. a squirming live lobster. Now I knew why he hadn't been able to use his right hand to swim. The silly bugger had gone through our traumatic experience holding a lobster in his right hand.

"Here's your lobster, B.J., just as I promised," he said.

B.J. bent over and kissed Sam on the cheek. The girls took good care of us. After all, they were student nurses. They wrapped us in blankets and dried our clothing in front of the fireplace. B.J. even boiled up a pot of seawater and cooked the lone lobster. We dipped the meat in melted butter. Accompanied by Oland's, it was a welcome treat.

All was back to normal when we dropped the girls off at the hospital's student residence. It was the next day that I ran into Sam's father at Wong's Café. He was scanning the *Halifax Herald*. There on page three, in bold black type, was the heading, "Antigonish Youths Near Drowned."

"Have your parents seen this?" he inquired.

"They will kill me," I said over my shoulder as I ran down Main Street to our house on Court Street.

I hadn't told my parents anything about our harrowing experience, not wanting to cause them any concern. The incident was over, although my mother did mention that she couldn't lay her hands on my sneakers. "They were falling apart anyway. You need a new pair," she said.

Out of breath, I entered the house in time to pick up the ringing phone. It was our telephone operator, Allison Carruthers. "You're going to catch hell," she said. "Your sister Lukey is on the line from Halifax and wants to know if you are in the hospital. What the hell were you and Sam doing out in the bay, anyway?"

I coughed and passed the phone to my mother.

"Is Max all right?" Lukey wanted to know.

"He's fine, he's right here beside the phone."

Not satisfied, she insisted on hearing my voice. "Are you sure you're all right?" she asked.

"I'm perfect," I replied modestly.

At last she seemed convinced. I turned and thought it best to 'fess up, since Sam and I had escaped the angry bay and no real harm had been done.

How in the world had our escapade ended up in the newspaper? The answer was simple enough. Sam's mother was a stringer for the *Halifax Herald*. When he told her about our adventure, she thought the incident interesting enough to phone it in.

I sat my parents down and told them the whole story. The impact of the tale was somewhat ameliorated with me sitting there in front of them. My parents admonished me about going out in the bay without a life jacket and that was that.

Years later, when airline stewardesses with Trans-Canada Airlines had to be attractive nurses, I was travelling from Halifax to Montreal. Serving me dinner was none other than B.J. herself. Upon seeing me, her first words were, "God, we had fun when I was in training. Remember the time you and Sam almost drowned getting me a lobster?"

JOIN THE NAVY
AND SEE THE WORLD

On our first day at St. Francis Xavier University, a friend of mine known far and wide as Sneaky B heard that you could join the Navy and go on a free summer cruise. What's more, the government paid you for taking the cruise. As Sneaky said, "Beats working." It took us the usual thirty seconds to join up. The organization wasn't exactly the Navy, it was the University Naval Training Division, better known as the UNTD.

The day we signed up, we met Chief Harry Miller. The chief let us know, in no uncertain terms, that we were to meet once a week in the university gymnasium. He put it rather succinctly, "You bastards be there at 1900 clicks or I'll have your ass." The chief had a way about him. Everyone showed up on time.

I learned a lot about chiefs in the Canadian Navy. They usually have several years' experience so that, all things being equal, they should have been promoted in rank. For some reason or other they were passed over. When not at sea, they were given special assignments. In Chief Miller's case, he was assigned to St. F.X. to make sailors out of us by training once a week in the gym.

That very first Wednesday night, I knew Sneaky B and I were in trouble. There were about twenty-five aspiring sailors in the gym when Chief Miller held court. "I hear that there are two boys from the metropolis of Antigonish who have graced us with their presence. I understand you boys think the world owes you a living. Get that thought out of your heads right now."

Sneaky B made the mistake of interjecting, "Chief Miller, me and Max don't feel the world owes us a living."

"Call me Sir, you scum, and speak only when I ask you a question. Sneaky, why did you join the UNTD?"

"That's an easy one, chief. To go on the cruise in the summer."

"Stand still, you scum!"

The command "Stand still" reverberated throughout the gym and into our very souls. It was a phrase we would hear shouted at us continually every Wednesday night for eight long months.

"I'm sir to you and don't ever forget it. Robert, why did you join the UNTD?"

Robert Robinson was a transfer student from Acadia University and had been briefed by a friend to anticipate such a question. Robert replied, "Sir, I joined so that I could become acquainted with the Canadian Navy. Upon graduating as an engineer I will be able to join the regular Navy and have a satisfying and fulfilling career while honourably serving my country."

Chief Miller smiled. "So you scum are not all dummies. Ten laps around the gym for starters. Gentlemen, we will conclude with rope climbing."

For the first time I noticed the sea of ropes hanging from the ceiling. I couldn't believe it. This demented sailor boy expected us seekers of knowledge to climb ropes.

Chief Miller smiled widely as one boy, Will MacIntosh from Port Hood, Cape Breton, scampered up the rope like a monkey. I didn't know where Will learned how to rope climb and I didn't want to know. The rest of us got a few feet off the ground before slumping to the floor. The chief, who must have been forty-five years old, scampered up his rope in full uniform to show us how it's done.

"It's a long season, men, but I guarantee you before next summer you will all be able to climb those ropes like Officer Cadet MacIntosh and myself."

That's the way it went throughout that fall and winter. We all learned how to climb ropes, march, salute, run laps, and, in general, become a credit to the Canadian Navy. Toward the end of our series of Wednesday night miseries, we were sent to Halifax to take a three-day crash course in navigation. Our instructor, a little man with protruding ears, gave up on us at the conclusion of day two. If we were attempting to find the location of a small island or another ship at sea and came within a mile or two, Ears would shake his head and mumble in a low voice, "Good, you've got the general idea." In actual fact, not one of us aspiring sailors was able to locate a small island, a ship at sea, or anything else.

We returned to Antigonish, all bushy-tailed and enthusiastic. It was soon time to hear about our cruise.

As luck would have it, Sneaky B and I were assigned to the *Haida*, a Tribal Class Destroyer with quite a wartime history. This was the first time Sneaky B or I had ever seen a vessel larger than Billy Mahoney's lobster boat.

The *Haida*, Canada's most beloved wartime ship, then under Commander H.G. "Hard-Over-Harry" DeWolf, had sunk several German ships and submarines. In all, she had accounted for eight individual victories, including the sinking of a German ship, an Elbing Class Destroyer T-29. The German destroyer had just sunk the *Haida*'s sister ship, the *Athabaskan*, when the *Haida* attacked, reducing her to a blazing hulk. Slowly, the *Haida*'s exploits received publicity. She gradually became the darling of the Canadian Navy. Now, years after war's end, Sneaky B and I found out we had been assigned to a ship with a glorious past. The plaques here and there on the *Haida* didn't mean much to us. We had never heard of the Murmansk Run.

We were told we were to go on manoeuvres. The night before sailing from Halifax, Sneaky B kissed his sister Irene goodbye. I kissed my sister Lukey in the same dramatic fashion. We were going off to war. Well, not exactly. We really were going on a cruise that the Navy was going to pay us for taking.

As the only two officer cadets aboard the *Haida*, we were treated as something like mascots by the crew. That first day,

Lieutenant Atkinson gave us our instructions. We were to visit certain locations on the ship and pick up an object at each location.

I studied the instructions, which seemed simple enough. I found the bridge and requested a box of dots and dashes. The officer in charge didn't crack a smile. He directed me below deck to a locker room where I could pick up the dots and dashes. Once there, a seaman steered me to the heads, where I could complete my assignment. I ran around that ship for over an hour. Everyone had a good laugh at my expense. I met Sneaky B on my travels. He hurriedly told me he was having trouble locating his post holes.

After our initiation, we shoved off from Halifax to conduct manoeuvres down the east coast of the continent. That evening we had to put up our hammocks, or as we salts call it, "sling our mick." This took some doing. I won't go into the art of sleeping in a hammock. Once mastered, you sleep like a log.

By our third day at sea, we had made friends of certain crew members. I think many of them had a degree of sympathy for "the college kids," as we came to be known.

I informed my mates that Sneaky B was in the habit of sleepwalking. They made light of the matter, if they heard me at all. The proof of my warning occurred when Sneaky B gingerly got out of his hammock in the middle of the night. We all knew he was asleep because of his loud snoring.

"Newfie" Johnson from Heart's Content, Newfoundland, whispered, "The college kid is walking in his sleep, the silly arse."

"Don't worry," I replied, "he does it all the time."

Newfie said, "He better watch out for the open hatch."

"Sask" Fredericks, who hailed from Floral, Saskatchewan, whispered, "They say that sleepwalkers go around obstacles just as if they were awake."

Newfie volunteered, "Well, the son of a bitch better walk around that open hatch. The kid is mumbling something."

I didn't reveal that I had heard Sneaky B walking in his sleep many times and knew exactly what he was saying. Sneaky B hailed from a farm just a few miles outside of Antigonish. The farm was operated by his older brother, Bobby. Sneaky B, for some reason known only to God, had the strange habit of planting potatoes in his sleep, mumbling to his brother as he planted row after row. Here he was, in the middle of the Atlantic Ocean, planting potatoes in his sleep.

Someone said, "Maybe we should wake him up."

"They say that's the worst thing you can do," Chuck Francis from Sudbury piped up.

It was agreed to let Sneaky continue sleepwalking. He would return to his mick in due course. That's when he stepped into the open hatch and plunged ten feet down. All we could hear was, "Jeetis, Jeetis, Jeetis," which was a familiar expression of Sneaky B's. When we reached him he was bleeding profusely from an open gash down his right leg, extending from his hip to his ankle. Years later, Sneaky B would show the scar to girls on the beach, claiming it was a war wound. This would always elicit a great deal of sympathy. That was Sneaky B all over, playing every angle. We called the ship's doctor that night and had Sneaky stitched up. Newfie summed up the incident rather nicely: "Those college kids are crazy."

Next day we were going ashore in Gloucester, Massachusetts. We were briefed to behave, as the stop was a "goodwill visit" by the Canadian Navy to the citizens of Gloucester. This well-known fishing town holds services every year for men lost at sea while pursuing their occupation.

A limping Sneaky B and I couldn't wait to go ashore. We knew we would have a good time, because the entire town was bedecked with Canadian flags and signs welcoming us sailors. There was to be a dance that night at the community centre in our honour.

As we set foot ashore, Sneaky B told me, "If you don't score at the dance tonight, you might as well take the train back to Antigonish."

Before we left the waterfront we saw a sign, "Main Deck Tavern." Hailing from a town that didn't have public drinking of any kind, we were attracted to the Main Deck like iron shavings to a magnet. Another sign, "Ice Cold Budweiser," didn't discourage us in any way. Neither of us had ever heard of Budweiser, but we guessed it was the U.S. version of Oland's.

Sneaky and I strolled into the Main Deck. We were instant celebrities. "Have one on me," was heard from one patron. Sneaky B and I thought we had died and gone to heaven. "Your money's no good here, Canada!"

A woman named Joannie noticed Sneaky's limp. "Nothing serious," Sneaky B said, "ripped her open rescuing a fellow sailor in the engine room."

"Poor baby," Joannie cooed.

Above the bar was a black-and-white television. It was the first time either of us had ever seen TV. The old Boston Braves were playing the New York Giants. I was totally captivated at actually seeing my baseball heroes rather than imagining how they looked while listening to the game on the radio.

As the hours passed and the copious quantities of Budweiser took their cumulative effect, I couldn't help but notice that Joannie and Sneaky B were becoming close friends. She had his bell bottoms rolled up and was soothing his stitches with the aid of a cool bottle of Budweiser.

It was at this juncture that a blond woman with cleavage that would put Dolly Parton to shame sauntered into the tavern. It was obvious that she was a regular patron because one of the men asked if she had any new stock. With that inquiry, the blond lady with the cleavage opened a flat box and displayed her assortment of prophylactics. These were no regular rubbers slipped to you behind Wong's Café in Antigonish. These were high-fashion prophylactics, some with tiny fingers, others with spidery webs, still others in shades of bright pink and fluorescent green. Every animal in Christendom was represented.

At the rate Sneaky B and Joannie were progressing, I figured it was time for us to leave the Main Deck and take in the dance that was, after all, in our honour. When we staggered out of the tavern, it was dark. We had spent the entire day as guests of the good fishermen of Gloucester. A thick fog had rolled in. I don't mean those city fogs that play havoc with traffic. I'm talking east-coast pea soup, where you can't see three feet straight ahead.

The streets were apparently deserted. It was well past midnight. Not to worry. I could make out the form of two girls across the street who would give us directions to the community hall. "Jeetis, let's pick them up and take them to the dance. I've got those fancy safes," Sneaky suggested.

With notions of lust and sin dancing through my head, I told Sneaky B, "You stay here. I'll go over and pick them up and hustle them across the street. Never fear, Casanova Max is here. I'll deliver." Sneaky B agreed.

As I approached to within a few feet of the pair, I realized that I had made a terrible mistake. There stood a giant of a man, well over six feet tall, broad, muscular, and growling like a bear whose cubs are endangered. Beside him stood his very pregnant wife. I was trying to apologize, at the same time explaining that all I wanted was directions to the dance. Without saying a word, the growling bear-man swung. The blow landed on the side of my face just below the temple. I have seen bulls meet their end at bullfights in Spain. I slumped to my knees, then fell on my face to the concrete sidewalk. My entire head throbbed as if a Mack truck had run amuck inside my skull. As the bear-man stood over me waiting for me to get up, I made up my befuddled mind that if hell froze over, I wouldn't rise from that sidewalk. Simply put, I didn't want to die.

As these desperate thoughts were being processed through my mind, I heard the ever-increasing wail of the familiar words, "Jeetis, Jeetis, Jeetis." Sneaky was coming over to give me a hand at picking up the two "girls."

At the third "Jeetis," the bear-man swung. Sneaky B hit the sidewalk beside my prostrate form. Instead of staying down like any thinking sailor would do, Sneaky B said, "Jeetis, Jeetis," and rose to his feet. The bear-man swung again, with the same results. I don't know how many times Sneaky B rose to be poleaxed, but it was several times. Finally, as much as he tried, he couldn't gain his feet. The growling bear strolled away with his pregnant wife.

I could feel my jaw swelling, but I was in good shape compared to my friend. After three days at sea, his government-paid cruise had left him with twenty-nine stitches down his right leg and a face that resembled that of Arturo Godoy after Joe Louis knocked him out. In addition to a face that looked like stew, Sneaky B had false teeth. Those teeth were now distributed throughout his mouth, including the roof.

Eventually, we both rose from our prone positions and were escorted back to the *Haida* by the Shore Patrol. Sneaky B received emergency treatment to fix him up so that he would be able to attend Sick Bay the following morning.

While we both waited to receive medical attention, we realized we were not unique. Many of the sailors had had adventures leading to injuries. We exchanged details of our goodwill visit. Stuffy Galbraith, whose neck resembled raw hamburger, had an interesting tale to relate. He had managed to pick up a cooperative young lady at the dance. Stuffy escorted her home to discover that both her parents were out for the evening. One thing led to another, until Stuffy and the young lady proceeded to do what men and women have been doing since Eve took a bite out of that apple. Suddenly, the room in which they were coupled was filled with the light of a car being parked. The girl's parents had returned. Stuffy only had time to gather up his uniform and dash out the door naked as a jay-bird. He was running full tilt and felt he had made good his escape when he ran flush into a clothes-line. Stuffy was running so fast that the clothesline dug back and forth into his neck until it catapulted him backwards to the ground. The rubbing of the rope had broken the skin and had torn it to ribbons.

Sneaky B lost two of his false teeth, which were never found. In addition, four had been extracted from various locations in his mouth the night before. He was a mess. As for myself, other than the swelling, the doctor assured me that I would be as good as new in a few days.

For two days, the entire ship's complement talked of little else than our adventures in Gloucester. The rumour went around that damages to the town, particularly the community centre, were so extensive that the town was submitting a bill to the Canadian Navy. So much for our goodwill visit.

Just when shipboard life was becoming routine for Sneaky B and me, we were advised that we were going ashore in Port Mouton, Nova Scotia. This was a place so small that no one aboard ship had ever heard of it. Because there were no facilities to accept a ship the size of the *Haida,* we would be going ashore via liberty boats.

Those of us not on duty were in uniform. We could see our fellow Tribal Class Destroyer, the *Ontario,* and Canada's capital ship, the aircraft carrier *Magnificent,* preparing to launch liberty boats in anticipation of shore leave. We were accustomed to seeing the two ships, since for the past several days we had been on manoeuvres with them.

As we sunned ourselves on deck, it was Sneaky B who nonchalantly piped up, "It seems to me the *Maggie* is mighty close to shore." Stuffy, Newfie, and the boys paid little attention. Someone said, "Stupid college kid."

At that precise moment, Canada's capital ship went aground. Bells that hadn't been used since the war rang out loudly on the *Haida.* Sneaky B and I didn't know what to do, but seasoned crew members took directions over phones and loudspeakers. An officer rushed by me, "Haines, man the phone in the aft canopy!" I made my way to the stern of the ship and heard the phone buzzing. Some officer thought he was speaking to an experienced sailor. He was dead wrong. The officer was talking fast and using nautical terms. I couldn't make out what he was saying. Furthermore, I wouldn't have known what to do even if I could.

Sneaky B shouted to me, "This is serious, I don't want to have anything to do with this. I'm going to hide in the heads." With that proclamation, he limped off, holding his bandaged face in one hand.

Around me there was a beehive of activity. Huge steel cables were being attached to the *Maggie.* Because I was still holding the phone, crew members around me thought I knew what I was doing. No one realized that I didn't understand one command and had no idea what was taking place. An aircraft carrier is appreciably larger than a destroyer. At one point I looked up and could see nothing but the riveted steel side of the *Maggie*. I was gripped with terror. We were dangerously close.

Someone hooked up a radio to a loudspeaker. Our problems were being broadcast on the radio. Normal programming had been interrupted. "Canada's capital ship, the aircraft carrier *Magnificent*, has gone aground off Nova Scotia. Two destroyers, the *Haida* and the *Ontario*, are in the process of attaching cables to the *Maggie* in an attempt to extricate her from the rocky shore. Thus far, there have been no injuries. Next of kin of all three ships are being notified. Stay tuned for further developments."

Back on Court Street in Antigonish my parents were awoken in the middle of the night. They had received a telegram from the Navy that was delivered by phone: "Be advised that your son, Maxwell Haines, serving on the HMCS *Haida*, is taking part in extricating the HMCS *Magnificent* from its precarious position off Port Mouton, Nova Scotia. No casualties have been reported."

My father shook my mother. "Gussie, wake up. Maxie has done something wrong on his cruise. Turn on the radio." My mother turned on the radio and immediately started to cry, which wasn't that unusual. She cried whenever a disaster struck any member of our family or when she was extremely happy.

It took all night to dislodge the *Maggie*. We were advised that all schedules had been revised. Together with the *Ontario*, we were towing the *Maggie* back to Halifax. I was given coffee, toast with jam, and told I had done one hell of a job on the phone. I located Sneaky B in the heads. He could only say, "Jeetis, Jeetis, that was something."

Eleven days after leaving Halifax, we returned with the *Maggie* in tow. My sister Lukey was at the dock. The swelling on the side of my face had subsided. Sneaky B's injuries had not had time to heal. I heard him say to his sister Irene, "I was working the cables all night when something gave way and slashed my leg. At the same time, a piece of metal flew through the air and struck me in the face."

His sister said, "Poor darling," and held him close.

So ended our summer cruise.

HOLY WATER

I suppose it was only natural that when Sneaky B's mother, known far and wide as Aunt Winnie, heard that Sam Brady was about to visit the shrine at Ste. Anne de Beaupré, she would request he bring her back a bottle of holy water.

Don't get me wrong, Sam wasn't going on a religious retreat. Simply put, he had heard that the shrine attracted young French-Canadian girls and Sam thought he would try his luck. Aunt Winnie, a farmer's wife and devout Catholic all her life, never for a moment thought that Sam was travelling to La Belle Province for any other reason than to cleanse his soul.

On the night before Sam's departure he visited Aunt Winnie to say goodbye. Tears flowed down her lined cheeks as she kissed him farewell. She wasn't distraught enough not to turn to Sneaky B and chide him, "You can take a lesson from your friend Sam, travelling to holy places instead of loafing around town at Wong's Café."

"Yes, Mum," was all that Sneaky B could say.

As Sam made his way to the front door of the farmhouse, Aunt Winnie requested of him, "If it isn't too much trouble, dear, don't forget my bottle of holy water."

Sam assured her that upon his return he would make a special trip down the harbour road to give her the bottle. Aunt Winnie's face brightened. She smiled as she stepped outside. Then she told her story, which we had all heard many times before.

"When my late husband and I were married, he told me to pick the most beautiful spot in the entire county and he would build a house on the lot I chose. I picked this very spot and, true to his word, he built me a house right here. Look down at the sun shining on the harbour. What could be more beautiful?"

I had to agree the view from the front of Aunt Winnie's house was postcard perfect. The house itself left a lot to be desired, but the scene was truly breathtaking. The golden hayfields gave way to the sandy shoreline of the bay, where the blue-green water shone in the sunlight.

Sam kissed Aunt Winnie on the cheek, jumped into his father's Pontiac, and sped down the driveway to Harbour Road. In an instant he was out of sight.

That evening, Sneaky B, Sam, and I met for a going-away party for Sam. It was a rather exclusive affair, confined to just the three of us. Refreshments were simple enough—a bottle of Demerara Black Diamond rum with Coke mixers. The location was the interior of my father's cattle truck, parked on the landing road not far from Sneaky's home.

It must be pointed out that there were no legal establishments in Antigonish where alcohol could be consumed. Every bottle sold by the Nova Scotia Liquor Commission was bound by a paper tape that had these ominous words printed on it: Take Directly to Your Place of Residence. This, of course, was an impossibility. At nineteen years of age, we would have been drawn and quartered by our parents if we ever brought liquor into our homes. Instead, we parked, drank, and told stories to each other. All the stories were repeats, but who cared if you were with friends parked down the landing road in a cattle truck. I would be remiss not to remind you that the cattle truck gave off a most unpleasant odour, which seemed to dissipate as the rum was consumed.

The three of us had limited worldly experiences, but we never tired of hearing of how the past winter Sam had picked up a well-endowed girl hitchhiking through town heading for New Glasgow. Sam gave her a lift to Kenzieville. As she got out of his father's Pontiac, she told Sam, "I would have had sex with you if you had taken me all the way to New Glasgow." Sam almost blew a gasket trying to talk that girl back into his car. Just as he was making some headway, a car pulled up. The girl stuck out her thumb. The car door swung open and she disappeared from Sam's life forever.

It had been a close call and never failed to excite and amuse us. The girl had been wearing a green overcoat and was christened the Green Hornet. All we had to say was, "Tell us the Green Hornet story" and away Sam went.

Sneaky B's old adventure involved walking in his sleep. One

night he woke up an entire sleazy hotel in Halifax claiming the building was engulfed in flames. In reality, there was a red neon sign outside his window, which flashed for all the world to see "Rooms for Rent." It was the most exciting night ever experienced by the down-and-out hotel guests. They all thanked Sneaky for the diversion.

I wasn't without my own tale as the rum bottle was passed around. Who can forget my story of being caught up the Copelands' pear tree while still a pre-teen. Mrs. Copeland swung at me with a broom. I temporarily outfoxed her by climbing to a higher branch, until it broke, catapulting me to the ground with a distinct thud. Undaunted by my fall, Mrs. Copeland continued to swing her infernal broom while I scrambled and managed to crawl out of swinging range.

A heavy rain was falling by the time the stories ran out and we decided to call it a night. I was driving Sneaky home down the Harbour Road when he complained of a sore right side. Sam and I didn't pay any attention as we had long since become accustomed to Sneaky's many aches and pains. Sneaky's complaints always became more numerous when he was consuming rum. From head to toe he had pains that always seemed to have disappeared when he woke up the next morning. Tonight was no different from any other night.

Finally we made it in the cattle truck to Sneaky's driveway. Sneaky remarked that the dirt road up to his house was extremely slippery. "Better let me out here, Max, or you might get stuck turning her up by the house."

I agreed and let Sneaky out, despite the now-driving rain-storm. That's when I made my first mistake. After watching Sneaky slip-sliding up his muddy driveway to his door, I attempted to back the truck up just far enough to turn around. The vehicle unceremoniously slipped sideways into the ditch. Try as I might, I couldn't extract that truck. I trudged up to Sneaky's house to use the phone to get Charlie Beaton and his trusty tow truck to get us out of the ditch.

I never knew Aunt Winnie had false teeth until that night. I should say morning because it was 1:30 A.M. when I woke her up. She appeared at the door in her nightie, hair tied in a bun. I thought her entire face had caved in, but found out later that her cadaver-like appearance was due to the lack of her false teeth.

Sneaky, who was only partially undressed, accompanied his mother, complaining all the while about a terrible pain in the area of his right side. All he could say was, "Jeetis, it hurts like hell." The rascal had dipped into his older brother's rum bottle and was now pleasantly intoxicated. That's not exactly true— he was dead drunk and insisted on singing, "What's the matter with Glasgow, dear old Glasgie town, When I get a couple of drinks on a Saturday night, Glasgie goes round and round."

With telephone operator Allison Carruthers's assistance, we put through the call and were able to reach Charlie Beaton, but not before Allison admonished us, "What are you guys doing? Max, if your father ever finds out that his drunken son put his cattle truck in the ditch he'll kill you. Where's Sam? I thought he was on a holy retreat."

I explained sheepishly, "He's leaving tomorrow."

In about fifteen minutes, Charlie was at Aunt Winnie's door. He had thought of everything and had brought his son to drive the cattle truck, noting that we were too intoxicated to drive anywhere. With the responsibility of driving now eliminated, Sneaky came out in the rain with his brother's rum bottle, suggesting that we all take one last swig. After all, Sam was leaving next morning and would be gone a full week.

There we stood in the pouring rain, passing that almost empty rum bottle back and forth, not allowing Charlie's son one drop. He was our designated driver. I thought Sneaky B had a tear in his eye as he embraced Sam for the fourth time that night. Away we went without mishap to Antigonish. As we pulled away I thought I heard Sneaky singing one last rendition of "I Belong to Glasgow."

Next morning, my father glanced out our kitchen window and remarked, "The rain sure cleaned up the cattle truck."

As he spoke, the phone rang. It was Sneaky B. Right away I knew something was wrong. Sneaky was not one who believed in rising before 10 A.M., particularly if he had consumed a third of a bottle of Demerara the night before. We didn't call it Black Death for nothing. "Get over here right away."

"My father needs the truck. I can't drive all the way to your house."

"I'm not home, I'm in St. Martha's."

I rushed to the hospital to find my friend Sneaky B not at death's door, but mad as hell. According to him, just after we left, around 2 A.M., his brother and mother sound asleep, he had a terrible pain in his side. He yelled, waking up his mother, who by now had been awakened so often in the middle of the night that she must have believed that sleep was meant exclusively for other mothers who didn't have a son named Sneaky. Her son insisted that the pain was excruciating. Aunt Winnie and Sneaky's older brother told him that it was no worse than the last time he had had too much to drink. They instructed him to settle down and go to sleep. Sneaky tried his hardest, but finally the pain got so bad he begged his mother to call a doctor. Then he passed out.

Despite the rain and muddy driveway, Dr. Chisholm was at Aunt Winnie's within a half an hour. He quickly examined Sneaky, shouted, "Appendix!" and placed his patient in the car for the drive to St. Martha's. Sneaky fell in and out of consciousness. He told me he heard someone say they couldn't operate on a person who was intoxicated. He thought he heard someone else say, "If we don't, he's a goner."

That's all Sneaky remembered about the night. When he woke up, a cute nurse told him he had had his appendix removed. The first thing he thought of was calling me. There was little I could do for my friend. In fact, I felt sorry for myself. Here I was, with one friend in hospital and the other making a religious pilgrimage to pick up girls. The week passed slowly.

Eventually Sneaky was released from hospital in time to meet Sam arriving home by train. We picked him up at the station in my father's cattle truck. On the way down the Harbour Road, Sam regaled us with his attempts to pick up girls, particularly those cute young things who worked as clerks in the many souvenir shops near the shrine.

As a result of his numerous excursions to these shops, Sam had purchased an impressive array of religious paraphernalia, including undersized bibles, beads, crucifixes, and the like.

It was on the way to Sneaky's home that the day darkened, forewarning us of a storm approaching the area. All of a sudden Sneaky blurted out, "What about my mother's holy water? You promised her, remember?"

Sam did indeed remember. "Stop the truck," he ordered me. I complied. Sam found an empty pint bottle beside the road. He jumped a fence and filled the bottle with water from a nearby pond. We scrubbed the label off that bottle, which incidentally had originally held Bacardi rum, until it shone and sparkled as if it had always been meant to hold holy water rather than the devil's brew. The pint bottle was presentable enough but, we all agreed, lacked a religious theme. It was Sam who thought of draping prayer beads complete with crucifix over the neck of the bottle. Jesus never looked so good. The contents were crystal clear. The entire presentation would have fooled the Pope.

We arrived at Sneaky B's home to be greeted at the door by Aunt Winnie. "Come in, boys, it's going to pour cats and dogs in a minute."

We dashed indoors just as the dark clouds burst forth with a vengeance. As the rain poured down on the old farmhouse, Aunt Winnie felt a nice cup of tea would hit the spot for us all, particularly Sam, who had just arrived all the way from Ste. Anne de Beaupré. As she brewed the tea, she offered us some tea biscuits just out of the oven. Homemade plum jam was soon on the table along with the pot of hot tea. The first flash of lightning lit up the kitchen and scared the bejesus out of us all.

The thunder roared and the lightning flashed as Aunt Winnie brought up the subject of holy water. No sooner were the words out of her mouth than Sam opened his duffle bag and extracted the Bacardi bottle, which looked for all the world as if it had just left Pope Pius's blessed hands.

Aunt Winnie was delighted. When another clap of thunder boomed across the bay and the lightning flashed outside the kitchen windows, she commenced sprinkling the holy water throughout the room, all the while thanking Sam for being so thoughtful as to remember her request. She also mumbled a short prayer to the Almighty just in case the holy water didn't work.

The holy water worked fine. The house wasn't hit by lightning that day or any other day. And, miraculously, neither were we.

MY BOOTLEGGING CAREER

I was lying on Mahoney's Beach along the shore of St. George's Bay luxuriating under the bright rays of the sun with my two friends, Sam Brady and Billy Mahoney. Sam and I were students at St. Francis Xavier University. Billy was a lobster fisherman.

It was summer and the living couldn't have been easier. My father, through his political connections, had again procured a summer job for me, this one surveying on the road. My surveying position consisted of holding a rod and driving a nail into the ground, but it did have certain advantages. The road the provincial government picked to eventually improve was the Harbour Road leading to Mahoney's Beach. Fortunately, the chief surveyor, Bill MacCarthy, was headquartered in New Glasgow, some forty miles away. Bill didn't like the drive, which necessitated him becoming an earlier day weather forecaster. If there was a slight possibility of rain within the next forty-eight hours, or if it was simply overcast, Bill would phone me to let me know that they couldn't survey due to the threat of inclement weather. On those threatening days I headed directly to the beach, where I spent most of my time. For this taxing position, I was paid the princely sum of $27.50 a week.

Sam owned a canteen on the road just as you turned onto the beach. He paid a kid two dollars a day to wait on the precious few customers who stopped on weekdays. On Saturdays and Sundays, he and the lad attended to the rush of business. Sam told me he broke even during the week, but made a hundred dollars on the weekend.

Mahoney's Beach was named after one of Billy's ancestors. He was a lobster fisherman for the two-month-long season of May and June. The rest of the year he didn't do much of anything, if you discount lying on the beach as a full-time job.

There we lay day after day, discussing the fate of the Brooklyn Dodgers and the Boston Red Sox, wondering if Sally MacCallum was really pregnant or if Deanna Durbin was a lesbian. The nights were another kettle of fish altogether. Almost every second night there was a country dance not more than thirty miles from town.

Because Sam and I were too young to purchase liquor, Billy had to travel into town to purchase a bottle of Demerara Black Diamond rum for us to take to the dance. Demerara Black Diamond rum was the cheapest and most popular drink in Antigonish. God, it was terrible, but the legends that grew up around the Demerara company's drink were in general unfounded. Mrs. MacIntosh didn't put half a bottle in the tipsy cake at her husband's wake. The rum cake had nothing to do with Loretta Melanson disrobing right there beside the casket.

Yes, she might have shouted, "Here, MacIntosh, take one last look. Lord knows you did more than look when you were alive." She might have said that, but it had nothing to do with the rum cake. Gilly Mackinnon ran over the Kennedy cat not once, but twice. He did it because the cat peed on the hood of his Chevy. It had nothing to do with rum.

At every country dance, Sam, Billy, and I would chip in for a bottle of rum. In those days it was four dollars a bottle. The dance, which was usually held in a schoolhouse, started at seven o'clock. By nine, everyone was feeling good because everyone and his uncle had brought a bottle of rum to the dance.

Every schoolhouse had a telephone. It was the law. If a child took ill and required medical assistance, a phone was available. Whoever made the rule had no idea that a lineup would form in front of the phone at country dances to call in to town for a taxi. All the taxi drivers were small-time bootleggers. They charged eight dollars for the Demerara rum, plus two dollars for the taxi fare. Within half an hour, a fresh bottle would arrive at a total cost of ten dollars. Usually the taxi driver stayed at the dance. He was more often than not offered a slug or two from his customer's bottle. All in all, it wasn't a bad night's work. He had cleared six dollars, taken in the dance, and had a few slugs of rum for his trouble.

You might ask why, if most people were purchasing a second bottle at 9 P.M., they didn't buy two bottles at the Nova Scotia Liquor Commission store before 6 P.M. at regular prices. I can't answer that question other than to speculate that money was scarce when you were cold sober in the afternoon and was totally devalued at 9 P.M. when you had taken in a gutful of rum.

I have been given credit for the idea, which was simple enough, but had far-reaching effects. We were lying on the beach as usual when I came up with my brainwave. Why don't we buy twenty-five bottles of rum and take them to the dance? When people line up at the phone to order a second bottle, we could let it be known that we heard of a guy who would sell his extra bottle for eight dollars. He had it right there in the trunk of his car. Delivery was instantaneous and the customer would save two dollars in taxi fare.

They say that when Neville Chamberlain, the prewar prime minister of England, came home from a visit with Hitler and uttered the immortal phrase "Peace in our time," everyone was quick to agree. That's the way it was that day on the beach. My two friends saw the sheer genius of the plan immediately. Between the three of us we would have no trouble raising the hundred dollars. Billy even offered to put in the extra dollar.

Potential problems were discussed. Billy couldn't just walk into the liquor store and order twenty-five bottles. However, he had enough friends in town who would help him to accumulate the twenty-five bottles. The rum would be transported in my father's red Fargo cattle truck. The stash would be held under Sam's canteen until the night of the dance. I fancied myself being the wheel man, just like James Cagney in the movies. Billy, who stood well over six feet with a muscular build, would take care of any rowdiness that might occur at the dance.

We scanned the *Casket* for the notification of the next country dance. The following Friday night at the Heatherton School, there was going to be a real live one featuring Henry Snook and his Happy Go Luckies, billed as playing "the sweetest music this side of the Antigonish Creamery."

On Thursday Billy gathered up the twenty-five bottles of Demerara Black Diamond rum. I drove the booze down to Sam's canteen, where it was stashed under the floor. Next night, we picked up the bottles and headed for the dance.

In order to keep the partnership on a strictly business basis, all three of us agreed in advance not to touch a drop of rum while working our bootlegging venture. This was not a huge concession for Sam and me, although, at festive occasions, we were both known to down a wee dram or so. Billy was another story. On occasion he imbibed to excess, but swore that he wouldn't touch a drop at the dance. He would serve as our protector in case of trouble.

I pulled up in my father's red Fargo, which, before being introduced to a life of crime, had served him for many years as a cattle truck and had the smell to prove it. I parked at a distance from other vehicles. Henry Snook and the Happy Go Luckies were playing the Turkey Trot. It was 7:30 P.M. and, as Fats Waller would say, the joint was jumpin'.

Claire MacDonald and I danced. She was quite surprised when I refused her invitation to go out back and take a snort out of her bottle. Claire, who was hot as a Texas salsa, appeared stunned, surprised, and disappointed. Then she mentioned that we could sit in her car, listen to the radio, and drink rum.

When I still refused, she figured that I had a terminal illness. My thoughts were on business. On this occasion romance would have to take a back seat.

Around nine o'clock Charlie Fraser mentioned that he and his buddy Hal Chisholm were going to phone a taxi in Antigonish to pick up a bottle of rum.

"Charlie," I said, "I know a guy who has an extra bottle right here in his car. It'll save you two dollars taxi fare if he still has the rum."

Charlie didn't have to think. "Here's the eight dollars, Max. Go get that rum."

A few minutes later I returned with the bottle. No fuss, no muss. I bumped into Sam. He informed me that he had moved three bottles and was quite disappointed that I had only sold one. I blamed my lack of sales on that sexy Claire MacDonald.

Within an hour we had sold all twenty-five bottles for a clear profit of a hundred dollars. Not bad for a night's work, considering that in those days, in our town, no one was earning that much money in a week.

On the way home we agreed that there was no reason we couldn't play three or four dances a week. That's exactly what happened. We increased our supply to thirty bottles a night. At exceptionally big dances, like the ones at the Dingle or Crystal Cliffs, we would sell forty bottles. Most weeks we cleared two to three hundred dollars, but on good weeks as much as four hundred dollars.

As the weeks went by, there were times when I carried a wad of several hundred dollars in my jeans pocket. I felt a little funny when I received my government cheque of $27.50 for surveying on the road. My parents doled out $2.50 to me for spending money. The balance of twenty-five dollars went toward college tuition. While they extolled the virtues of putting money aside for the future, I sometimes had a roll of nine hundred dollars in my pocket tied securely with an elastic band.

There were a limited number of things I could do with my ill-gotten gains. You might ask why not open a bank account. Well, now, you must remember the entire town consisted of 2500 souls. If I dared walk into the bank with more than five dollars, the manager, Joe McCall, would be on the phone to my father. I could just hear him: "Alex, your son must have stolen money. He just walked in here with a hundred dollars."

There was no way I could go near a bank. One thing I could do for my parents without raising suspicion was fill my father's truck with gas. He often remarked that the old Fargo was the easiest truck on gas that he had ever owned.

That was about it. We three conspirators met on the beach to rest our weary bones under the noonday sun to discuss our mutual dilemma, what to do with our money. In our wisdom, we decided to treat the entire class of student nurses of St. Martha's Hospital to an all-day outing at Pictou Lodge, about fifty miles away.

This required a degree of planning. A fleet of taxis would be our method of transportation. Reservations for a lobster dinner were made at the Lodge. Because there were no credit cards in those days, the Lodge required a healthy deposit. We took exactly thirty seconds to come up with a solution. Sam simply drove to Pictou Lodge and laid down seven hundred dollars in cash as a deposit. That's how thirty student nurses took off one fine summer day in a fleet of taxis for Pictou Lodge. Our personal abstinence rule was lifted for that particular occasion.

Certain events took place that served to make the Pictou Lodge excursion a memorable one. Dot Harris, drinking heavily throughout the trip, brought up before we arrived at the Lodge and couldn't eat a thing. They say that Mary Foley managed to bring a live lobster back to St. Martha's with her. She had read somewhere that lobsters could survive only in salt water. Mary placed her lobster in a bathtub and shook some salt from a salt shaker into the tub. Later, a nun glanced in the tub and fainted. The absence of Rilda Riley was only noticed once we were halfway home, at James River. Sam had to go back for her and found her all alone in the dining room eating the tamale from her fifth lobster. Joan MacCaffrey stubbed her toe, which swelled up like a balloon. She limped so badly that she missed her regular shift next day at the hospital. Despite these minor mishaps, a good time was had by all.

The university semester was soon to begin and the country dances would wind down until the following spring. We still had the entire month of August to continue bootlegging. Then it happened.

Sam's mother was a bit of a wheel in town. She had once run for mayor and had that annoying column in the *Casket*. Sometimes she invited Sergeant Vic Staples and his wife over for dinner. It was at one of those dinners, with Sam present, that Vic said, "It would be a good idea, Sam, if you and your friends stayed away from the country dance at Heatherton tomorrow night." Vic continued, "We didn't mind the occasional taxi taking out a bottle of rum and selling it, but now there's a gang making large quantities of rum available at the dances. It's got to stop. We're going to raid the schoolhouse tomorrow night."

Sam choked on his soup.

Vic wasn't through. "Just as well you don't go there, Sam. Because of the availability of liquor at the country dances, the locals are getting pie-eyed drunk. There are more fights than ever before. Fred Johnson took an axe to another fellow who was holding Fred's wife too close when they danced. Jimmy Casper jumped in his car and tried to run down the entire Lloyd MacDonald clan. Frank Wilson came home from the dance with his wife, Dora, and tried to strangle her with a clothesline for no apparent reason. I could go on, but you get the idea. Enough is enough. We plan to put a stop to the bootlegging operation tomorrow night."

Sam managed to get through the meal before getting Allison Carruthers to reach me on the phone. This called for an emergency meeting. Sam and I drove to Mahoney's Beach to confer with Billy. There seemed little doubt about it. Sergeant Vic knew the identity of the bootleggers. He would have to be deaf, dumb, and blind not to have heard about us selling rum out of a bright red Fargo cattle truck. What's more, he didn't want to catch us. He was giving us advance notice not to show up at the dance the next night.

We took the Mountie's advice and terminated our bootlegging operation. It had been one glorious summer, but we still had a vexing problem. What to do with thirty bottles of Demerara Black Diamond rum? We solved that problem, as we did most problems, in thirty seconds. We would drink the entire thirty bottles during the month of August. The three of us would have quite a job drinking the thirty bottles by ourselves, although Billy said we could try. He was overruled. And so we instituted Rum Day at Sam's canteen. Anyone who bought a Coke received a rum and Coke for the price of the soft drink only. It was so successful we had several Rum Days in the one month.

Our bootlegging career had come to a glorious end.

GHOST SHIPS

Every small town has its secrets. Our town was no exception. An elite group of members of the community knew that on every June 21, just as sure as God made little green apples, you could park your car at Mahoney's Beach facing St. George's Bay and observe the ghost ships sailing by. They not only sailed by, they actually fought battles before those select few who were in on the secret.

There were many theories as to why pirates fought it out off that remote bay in Nova Scotia. Everyone was well aware that Oak Island, with its unyielding treasure, was located 140 miles up the coast. The famous money pit on the island had claimed the lives of several treasure seekers.

From that day in 1795 when Dan McGinnis first stumbled on a depression in the ground, the money pit on Oak Island has been dug, blasted, and excavated to a depth of several hundred feet. Objects such as coconut fibre, certainly not endemic to Nova Scotia, were found at certain levels. An elaborate system of tunnels flooded the pit, making excavation efforts impossible. Whatever is down there must be valuable. Someone went to a lot of trouble to safeguard the treasure over the centuries. A large group of men must have laboured long and hard to construct the pit and the infernal flood tunnels from the pit to the sea.

One of the theories of the ghost ships just outside Antigonish involved the infamous Captain Kidd. Supposedly, the good captain was on his way to Oak Island to bury his treasure when his ship was accosted by other pirates just off St. George's Bay. It was these ships that the select citizens of Antigonish lined up to peer at through the fog rolling in from the bay. Some years the sightings were better than others. It depended on the fog and the moon, but every year at sundown on June 21 you could count on a group of cars and trucks lining up facing the sea with their high beams piercing the brisk night air.

Oak Island, being an authentic mystery that has received worldwide attention, was the focus of many theories. One that appealed to many an Antigonisher was that the treasure was the Holy Grail, somehow buried there by Spaniards who were attacked just off our town.

Maybe the most realistic tale of the ghost ships appearing each year was the story of the ill-fated ship *Nuestra Señora de la Pura y Limpia Concepción*, loosely translated as Our Lady of the Immaculate Conception. The Spanish galleon was loaded with treasure and somehow made it to Oak Island, where the treasure was buried. Later, Our Lady of the Immaculate Conception sank in a hurricane off the Florida coast. Before heading for Florida, the Spanish ship had been attacked off St. George's Bay by the ever-present pirates.

When Europeans plundered the wealth of the Incas in the seventeenth century, it is rumoured that the Incas managed to make it to Oak Island, where they buried their gold. In their race for a safe haven, they often encountered pirates. One such incident took place off Antigonish between the European conquerors and the Incas.

It matters little which of the many theories you adhere to. The battles were seen each year at Mahoney's Beach on June 21 as the sun disappeared in the west. The fog rolled in, obliterating the slight glow of the moon. Cars and trucks lined up to see the sight.

It was Sam Brady who first told me of the phenomenon down at the beach each June 21. He informed me that only certain people in town knew of the strange apparition that took place on that evening. Sam inquired, "You want to chip in on a bottle of Black Death?" I agreed that I would be more than willing to fork over the two dollars for the comfort the liquid refreshment would afford us while we observed the ghost ships.

Finally the day of the sightings arrived. Sam pulled into our driveway in his father's Pontiac. We stopped at Long Lennie's for a few Cokes, which would come in handy as chasers. Off we sped the few miles to Mahoney's Beach. Sam had advised me that it would be a good idea to arrive early so as not to miss the good parking spots where the sand was matted with eel grass. This eliminated the chances of getting stuck in the sand.

When we arrived we observed that the eel grass area was already occupied with about a half-dozen vehicles parked facing the bay. Sam pulled into a sandy spot, muttering, "I hope we don't get stuck."

Other cars and trucks joined us until about fifteen vehicles were lined up in a row. As evening gradually gave way to nightfall, Sam turned on his lights. Others quickly followed. The occupants all peered out into the bay, but there was little to see other than the thickening fog rolling in. Sam said, "She's early yet. I'm going to stretch my legs."

He was just about to open the driver's door of the Pontiac when "Dang" MacDonald stuck his head in the open window. "Do you and Max want a slug of rum? I've got the real good stuff tonight—Captain Morgan."

"Sure thing," Sam said, as he took a gulp of the black liquid directly out of the bottle. He passed it to me.

"Thanks," I said, and let the bittersweet rum flow down my throat.

Dang lingered a few minutes, just long enough for him to have a swig out of our bottle of Black Death. "Dang, that burns like hell," he said. Dang never cursed. Instead he said "Dang" in almost every sentence, until everyone in town called him by this nickname. It's doubtful if anyone knew his real name was Aloysius.

Sam and I walked along the row of vehicles. "Pepsi Pete" MacIsaac offered us a drink of rum, which we gladly accepted. Sam, in his usual generous way, invited Pepsi Pete and his friend Bobby Irons over to the Pontiac so that he and

Bobby could have a swig out of our bottle.

Being a rookie sighter, it occurred to me that there wasn't one car or truck in the entire line that did not have a bottle of rum in the process of being consumed. Donnie "Heatherton" MacGillivray had come prepared with two bottles of Black Death. Donnie was called Heatherton because, at an early age, when asked where he was from, he didn't say Antigonish, as any God-fearing native would have said. Instead, Donnie answered, "Heatherton," which technically was correct, as Heatherton is a small hamlet outside Antigonish and was in fact the birthplace of Donnie "Heatherton" MacGillivray. It was Heatherton who instituted the rather agreeable routine of passing a bottle of rum from one car window to another.

Most observers were in their cars when "Twitch" Fraser said, "I see it!" All eyes stared out into the foggy bay. Twitch shouted, "See the lights in the rigging?" I thought that Twitch was slurring his words, but there was no time to inquire as to his state of intoxication.

Sam piped up, "I see 'er, too—and her lanterns. Cripes, that's a sword flashing!"

Charlie Farnham shouted, "Mary, mother of Jesus, did you see the flash of the cannon?"

Roger MacCarthy got out of his old Ford, bottle in hand, and yelled at the ghosts, "Where did you bury the treasure, you bastards?"

Roger's wife, Mary Lou, one of the few women allowed to take in this almost religious experience, said, "Roger, you get back in the car this very minute."

So startled by this turn of events was Roger that he stumbled in the loose sand. Despite falling awkwardly to the beach, he managed to hold his bottle upright without spilling a drop. This display of athletic dexterity elicited a round of applause from those who witnessed his fall.

Someone said, "One of the ships is limping away. Her forward rigging is dragging in the sea."

Slowly the lantern lights faded in the fog. I thought I saw with my own eyes the fog enveloping the ghost ships and their crews until the last vestiges of the fierce battle disappeared from sight.

The first cars to leave the scene were those parked on the preferred eel grass parking spots. A number of cars required a push by other observers. Dang MacDonald's car was really spinning its wheels, but we managed to push him free. The last words I heard him say were, "Dang, she was almost down to the axle." Sam and I didn't have too much trouble extricating the Pontiac from the loose sand.

Next day, a bright June sun shone high in the sky. I ran into Sam and Dang sitting on the Royal Bank steps passing the time of day. Sam inquired, "How did you like your first time down at the ghost ships?"

"You know, Sam," I replied, "there must be something wrong with me. I have to confess that I really didn't see a damn thing."

As he and Dang walked away, I thought I caught Sam winking at Dang. He shouted over his shoulder, "Hey, Maxie, let's do it again next year."

Sam's companion joined in, "Dang it all, that was some party!"

MARILYN VISITS ANTIGONISH

This would be my wife Marilyn's first visit to Antigonish. I had warned her that this tiny town tucked away in Nova Scotia was like no other place on earth. It was in the late fifties when we arrived from Montreal by train in the middle of the night. We had been married for two whole years and were living in Montreal.

As we stepped off the train, Gregor Myette grabbed our suitcases.

Marilyn inquired, "Who's that man with our suitcases? He seems to know you."

"That's Gregor Myette. Everyone knows Gregor. He drives the station wagon for the Royal George Hotel and picks up passengers who may be staying at the hotel." That seemed to satisfy her for the time being.

As we drove up Main Street, Gregor mused, "Maxie, so that's the missus."

Not another word passed between us. Since I hadn't been home for over two years, Marilyn figured that he should greet me in some way. She whispered, "Isn't he going to say anything more to you?"

We came to an abrupt stop four minutes later. Marilyn clutched my hand. "What's wrong?" she inquired rather apprehensively.

"Nothing's wrong. We're home—on Court Street. This isn't Montreal. Everything's close by."

My parents, who were excited about the homecoming, loved Marilyn with a passion. Pretty well everyone who met her couldn't understand why she would marry a bum like me. The ultimate proof of my parents' affection for my new wife was given expression when they purchased a new bedroom set for the spare room, which was the largest bedroom in the house. The set had been purchased expressly for my bride and me. At $129 it was a steal, direct from Eaton's catalogue.

As a kid, I'd always thought our spare room was huge. I never noticed that if you got up on one side of the bed you would hit your head on the ceiling. I also never noticed the chimney that ran directly through the room. It could be hot as blazes near the chimney and freezing cold on the other side of the room.

Never mind, my parents were out to impress their new daughter-in-law from Montreal. Meanwhile, Gregor had lugged our suitcases into the house. Marilyn whispered, "Aren't you going to pay him?" She simply didn't understand. No one had ever paid Gregor in the twenty-five years he had been driving locals from the station to their homes.

Next morning, I decided to drive up Main Street in my father's Fargo to show Marilyn the town. We had just turned the corner onto Main Street when Billy Mahoney jumped into the middle of the street. I slammed on the brakes to avoid hitting him. "Take me to the liquor store, Maxie." After three years of not seeing each other, there were no hellos, no welcome home, simply, "Take me to the liquor store."

"Sure, Billy," I replied.

Billy pushed Marilyn over as he jumped into the cab of the truck. The gearshift on the floor was now between her legs. In three minutes flat we were in front of the liquor store. "Gimme ten dollars and stay here," Billy demanded. I fished out a ten-dollar bill from my wallet and passed it over. In a flash, Billy was running up the few steps to the liquor store.

At the time, Marilyn and I were saving up for a coffee table. She inquired, "When will he be paying you back?"

I attempted to explain, "Lending money to Billy is as safe as doing business with the Bank of Nova Scotia. I don't know when he'll pay me back. Maybe tomorrow, maybe next year, but I do know he never forgets a debt and he always pays back what he owes."

Marilyn shook her head. "Antigonish is a funny town" was all she could say.

Two minutes after entering the liquor store, Billy returned to the truck. We drove back down Main Street. In front of Goodman's store, Billy said, "Stop." I slammed on the brakes. Billy looked at Marilyn. "Is this the missus? Pleased to meet ya." With that friendly greeting, Billy opened the Fargo door, jumped out, and was gone. I didn't hear from him until three years later when he was passing through Montreal and paid back the ten dollars.

By the afternoon of our second day in Antigonish, I thought it time to introduce Marilyn to Mahoney's Beach. I had to stop her from gathering up towels and beach bags. Using what had become my favourite expression, I said, "This isn't Montreal— just change into your bathing suit and we're off."

We drove down Harbour Road to the beach in my father's cattle truck. Marilyn found the water cold. I chided her for being a city girl who was accustomed to swimming in heated pools. This was Nova Scotia. This was St. George's Bay, hard off the Atlantic Ocean. I even related my much-told tale of swimming in this very spot on May 24 as a kid. I embellished the well-worn saga by adding that there was shell ice along the shoreline when I swam here years before.

Jesus, that water was cold, but eventually we both got dunked and swam far out into the bay. She swam; I alternated between floating and the dog paddle. All the way out to our immediate left was a string of salmon net buoys painted bright red and white. It was while observing the buoys that I had my wonderful idea.

I anticipated some reluctance when I suggested that there was nothing like swimming in salt water in the nude. It was getting dark. The beach was deserted. Why not? I urged her to slip out of her bathing suit. After arguing that she had never swum in the nude in her life and had no intention of starting now, she finally acquiesced and tied her suit to a buoy. Marilyn had to admit that it was a wonderful feeling of freedom as she slithered through the salt water. Modest to a fault, I kept my maroon trunks on throughout Marilyn's "bare buff" swim.

After about twenty minutes of swimming in circles, we both felt it was time to go home. That's when we discovered that the series of buoys stretching out into the bay all looked exactly the same. We swam over and checked one out. No sign of any bathing suit. We spent a good fifteen more minutes searching for Marilyn's bathing suit before I expressed the rather serious thought that we could both drown or freeze to death out there. Marilyn admitted she was getting tired and cold. To alleviate the fatigue she hung on to a buoy. When I voiced the opinion that it would be really something if her frozen nude body was found in the morning, I knew in a flash I shouldn't have brought up the gruesome idea. Marilyn was crying. "There's no way anyone is finding this body in the nude." She burst into tears again. "What will your parents think of me when I show up at your house with nothing on?"

I knew I shouldn't have said it the moment the words left my mouth: "I think my father would rather enjoy it."

We talked, she cried, but finally we felt anything was better than freezing to death. We would go ashore, get into the truck, and somehow sneak into the house without being seen. We drove the few miles back to town, all the while formulating the plan that was to be used to smuggle Marilyn into the house.

I'll never know why Lorraine MacCarthy picked that exact moment to stop me as I pulled into our driveway. It was rather chilly being clad only in my satin maroon trucks, but the heater kept it comfortable enough in the cab of the truck. I must admit it wasn't that comfortable for Marilyn, crunched up on the floor so that Lorraine couldn't see her. Lorraine wanted to know everything about Montreal. Nonchalantly she inquired, "By the way, where's your wife?" I honestly thought about saying, "Crunched up on the floor about two feet away," but I stifled the urge. Instead I replied, "I believe she's in the house with my parents."

"Too bad, I'd love to meet her."

"We'll drop around tomorrow if you like."

"That's swell, Maxie, see you both then."

With that, Lorraine walked away. My wife gave a sigh of relief and said, "I thought she'd never leave."

I came up with one of my more brilliant ideas, which to this day Marilyn claims was my finest. "I'll go in the house and get a bath towel. I'll wrap your spare bathing suit in the towel and bring it out to you. You can change into the suit in the truck. If anyone asks why I need the towel, I'll tell them we dripped water all over the cab and that you insist on wiping it up."

Marilyn swore then and there that my mental faculties compared favourably to those of Archimedes, Galileo, and even Einstein.

I walked into the kitchen. In unison, my parents greeted me with, "Where's Marilyn?"

Once again, I had to suppress the urge to say, "She's sitting nude in the truck."

I don't know how many young women fresh out of Montreal have spent time in a dusty, smelly cattle truck in Nova Scotia. I venture to guess not one.

While I was explaining how water had dripped in the cab of the truck, Marilyn lay on the floor of the truck, convinced that our neighbour, Mrs. T.A. MacLean, would spot her in the altogether if she sat up.

Meanwhile, my mother interjected, "I'll give her a hand. It doesn't matter if a little water dripped in that truck."

"No, no, Mother, it's no trouble. I'll just get a towel from upstairs and we'll clean up the mess in a few minutes."

I managed to extricate myself from my parents, fetch the bathing suit and towel, and get out to my waiting nude wife.

When Marilyn appeared in the kitchen in her bathing suit, Mother inquired, "Did you have a nice swim, dear?"

Marilyn replied, "Yes, delightful."

No one was ever the wiser about Marilyn's ordeal until now. Of course, I am leaving out a few pertinent details.

Exactly nine months after Marilyn's ill-fated swim in the Atlantic Ocean, she gave birth to our first daughter, Susan.

THE GREAT BANK HEIST

Years after I left Antigonish I was flying from Vancouver to
Winnipeg on a book tour of Western Canada when the elderly
gentleman sitting next to me engaged me in conversation. He
was well dressed, sporting a midnight-blue suit and white shirt
complete with designer necktie. I took him to be a seventy- to
seventy-five-year-old retired executive. After we passed a few
pleasantries, he reached up and extracted a carry-on bag from
the overhead luggage compartment.

I couldn't believe my eyes when he took a book from his
bag. It was none other than *Canadian Crimes,* the very book
that I was currently publicizing. I was totally thrilled to observe
someone reading one of my books. It isn't often that an author
enjoys that experience.

My fellow traveller looked up from his book. "You don't
mind if I read; I find it helps pass the time on flights. Besides,
this guy Haines appears in my hometown newspaper, the
Moncton Transcript."

I couldn't hold it in any longer. I informed my new friend,

"I should tell you—I'm the guy. I mean I'm the guy who wrote the book. I'm Haines."

The stranger, whose name turned out to be Zachary Middleton, quickly flipped the pages to the back flyleaf. He looked at my picture, then looked at me. "Well, son of a gun, it's a pleasure to meet you, Max."

We talked pleasantly enough for about half an hour. He was very interested in my occupation and, as a result, the conversation turned to murder, as it so often does when people ask me about my work. Zack, as my companion insisted I call him, remembered hearing about the Bannister case that had taken place near Moncton many years earlier. I had researched the old case and was able to inform Zack of many details about the infamous murder.

"Max," he said, "I see from the book that you were born and raised in Antigonish, Nova Scotia."

"That's right," I replied, "a Bluenoser through and through."

"Well, I have a story to tell you about your hometown. I heard it many years ago when I was employed with the Royal Bank and I have every reason to believe that this story is true. By the way, you wouldn't happen to know an Alice Robinson from Antigonish?"

"You mean Alice the teller at the Royal? Not only do I remember her; she lived on our street. As I recall, she never married. You could set your clock by Alice passing our house on Court Street on her way to the bank. Same thing at the end of the day. She walked down Court Street at the same time every day to her parents' home."

Zack went on, "I never formally met Alice myself. Do you remember what she looked like?"

"Yes, sure, I saw her every day. I picture her in my mind's eye as being about forty years old with bushy hair, not good-looking but not ugly either. She was friendly enough, always said hello when she passed you on the street, although that wasn't unusual in Antigonish. Everyone said hello."

"Well, here's the story that spread right up to the head office of the bank. In the early forties there was a rash of bank robberies that started in northern New Brunswick and spread down into Nova Scotia, culminating in Antigonish, which is why I'm telling you this story. These weren't professional bank robbers, but probably two good old boys from New Brunswick who couldn't find jobs.

"As I recall, it all started one winter's day in Edmunston when these two guys walked into a bank. One stood near the door, while the other went up to the teller. He passed her a note that went something like this: 'Hand over all the money in the drawer. Don't press the alarm button.' The robber then told the teller, 'You see that guy near the door in the overcoat? His hand is in his pocket holding a gun. If you don't give me the money right now, he will shoot you.' The teller passed over all the folding money in the drawer. The bandit had come prepared with a large paper bag. He quickly scooped the money into the bag. In a few seconds he and his accomplice were gone.

"Now, Max, there were only a few hundred dollars in the teller's drawer, no way she was going to risk her life for such a sum."

He continued, "A few days later, the robbers hit the Bank of Nova Scotia in Woodstock with the same results. Across the province they travelled, making withdrawals in Newcastle, Chatham, and Moncton. During the course of each robbery no one was hurt and they never interfered with a customer. Each robbery only netted the bandits a few hundred dollars. Into Nova Scotia they went, robbing the Imperial Bank of Commerce in Amherst before making an unscheduled withdrawal from the Bank of Nova Scotia in Westville.

"It was still winter when the two men walked into the Royal in Antigonish. One loitered near the front door, his hand stuffed into the pocket of his heavy overcoat. The two men were the only customers in the bank. The other robber casually walked over to teller Alice Robinson's cage. She was wearing a blue sweater over a white shirt, open at the collar. She had a distinctive crucifix around her neck, which sparkled when she moved.

"The robber passed her his note. Instead of turning over the contents of her drawer, as so many tellers had done before her, Alice looked her adversary in the eye and said, 'That's the silliest thing I ever heard of. Now you and your friend get out of here just as fast as your legs can carry you.' Startled by this unusual turn of events, the robber stared back in disbelief. Then he spun on his heels, nodded to his companion, and both of them were gone in an instant.

"The rash of robberies came to an abrupt stop. Evidently, the robbers were unnerved at Alice's unexpected response. As quickly as the bank robberies had started, they abruptly ceased."

It was a great story. It had passed the time in a most pleasant manner. As the plane landed, I shook hands with Zack, who refused my offer of sharing a cab to downtown Winnipeg. I thought he dashed away rather quickly as we parted outside the airport.

In my hotel room that night, I got to thinking about Zachary Middleton and the tale he told me five miles in the air. I couldn't help but remember his line about Alice Robinson— "I never formally met Alice myself," with the emphasis on "formally." What a funny way to put it. Wouldn't it be more natural to say "I never met Alice myself"? Then there was her description: "She was wearing a blue sweater over a white shirt, open at the collar. She had a distinctive crucifix around her neck, which sparkled when she moved."

It had been almost fifty years since the day the two robbers had walked into the Royal Bank in Antigonish. Did an elderly gentleman have an irresistible urge to tell someone about a long-ago episode in his life?

My curiosity got the better of me. Through my newspaper contacts I was able to gain access to the names of every passenger on my flight from Vancouver to Winnipeg. There was no one named Zachary Middleton on that flight.